DOROTHY STIMSON BULLITT

An Uncommon Life

DELPHINE HALEY

SASQUATCH BOOKS
SEATTLE

First published in 1995 by Sasquatch Books. Paperback edition published in 2001.

Printed in the United States of America.
Distributed in Canada by Raincoast Books Ltd.
06 05 04 03 02 01   5 4 3 2 1

Cover and interior design: Kate L. Thompson
Composition: Fay L. Bartels

Cover portrait by Margaret Holland Sargent of Los Angeles
used through the courtesy of the Stimson-Green Mansion and the painter.
Back cover portrait by Neil Ordayne.
Unless otherwise noted, all interior photographs are from
the archives of Dorothy Stimson Bullitt.
A number of faded photographs were restored by Mary Randlett.

Library of Congress Cataloging in Publication Data
Haley, Delphine.
      Dorothy Stimson Bullitt : an uncommon life / Delphine Haley.
      p.   cm.
      ISBN 1-57061-327-3
      1. Bullitt, Dorothy Stimson. 2. Broadcasters—United States—
Biography. 3. King Broadcasting Company. I. Title.
PN1990.72.B85H35   1995
384.54'092—dc20   95-20366
[B]

SASQUATCH BOOKS
615 Second Avenue
Seattle, Washington 98104
(206) 467-4300
www@SasquatchBooks.com
books@SasquatchBooks.com

CONTENTS

ACKNOWLEDGMENTS

This book could not have been written without the cooperation of many people. Dorothy Bullitt had a very accessible public image, but much of her personal life was a mystery, as were many of her private opinions. As my primary interest was to understand her essential nature, I deeply treasure the trust she extended over the years and the many things she taught me. I am most grateful to her children, Stimson, Priscilla, and Harriet—the three who knew her best—for giving me complete access to a comprehensive set of records. David Brewster provided invaluable help in early editorial discussions and in shaping a lengthy family biography into a more manageable manuscript. The staff of Sasquatch Books made the manageable tangible: Sasquatch president Chad Haight contributed his vision and friendship all along the way, and editorial director Gary Luke brought his fine judgment, humor, and professionalism to the project. Copy editor Carolyn Smith honed her pen to refine the work, art director Nancy Deahl and designer Kate Thompson brought beauty and balance to the pages, and managing editor Joan Gregory smilingly brought it all together.

Many others kindly furnished research, memories, insights, and perspective. They are not all quoted in this book, but they each added to a rich palette from which to blend information. I am indebted to Michael Haley Bader, J. C. Baillargeon, Sallie Baldus, Douglas Bayley, Frances Stimson Bayley, Frank Bayley III, Thomas Stimson Bayley, Bob Beebe, Nancy Bergquist, Mary Vogt Bevoni, Leslie Denman Boyd, Eric Bremner, William Scott Brewster, Dorothy Churchill Bullitt, Jill Hamilton Bullitt, Katharine Muller Bullitt, Margaret Muller Bullitt, Scott Bullitt/Fred Nemo, Myrna Casad, Mary Ann Champion, Eleanor Clark, Steve Clifford, Charles Stimson Collins, Josiah Collins VI, Josiah Collins VII, William Bullitt Collins, Jack Fearey, Tom Foster, Morris Graves, Andrew Haley, Jr., James Hatfield, Ken Hermanson, Dave Hubanks, Nancy Keith, Kitty Kelley, Lawrence Kreisman, Jinny Kyreacos, Olive Schram Lambuth, Del Loder, Dorothy Malone, Jean McCracken, John Mikesch, Murray Morgan, Ellen Neal, Charles Odegaard, Edward Ohata, Wenda Brewster O'Reilly, Frances Owen, Greg Palmer, Ancil Payne, Guen Carkeek Plestcheeff, Ruth Prins, Douglass Raff, Katherine Raff, Richard Riddell, Albert Rosellini, Victor Rosellini, David Rudo, Ron Saling, Lee Schulman, Ashley Bullitt Schwartzman, Paul Spitzer, Barbara Stenson, Clara Stenstrom, Walter Straley, Susan Vernon, Andrew John Haley Vogt, Steve Wilson, and Anne Pigott Wyckoff. Patrick Chambers helped with computer problems and Dr. Robert Wong resuscitated an ailing hard drive when it crashed, taking a chapter with it. I am also personally grateful to Dunja Lingwood, who, during this book's evolution, stretched both my spine and my spirit. With the help of these people I have tried to render a portrait of a Pacific Northwest original. The interpretations of Dorothy Bullitt's character are my own, as are any errors in fact or judgment.

Life is an end in itself, and the only question
as to whether it is worth living is whether
you have enough of it. —Justice Oliver Wendell Holmes

INTRODUCTION

Dorothy Stimson Bullitt, a charismatic central figure in the story of the Pacific Northwest, always possessed a formidable will to win. Winning was her birthright—a legacy she wore like a mantle throughout her long life. In 1900, pigtailed and pudgy, she was a skillful marble player on the dusty back lots of Seattle's First Hill. There she would meet with the neighborhood boys for a game or two, and she always walked away with a prize. She was usually the only girl in the group—a situation that might have struck her as significant had she not been so caught up in collecting aggies and cat's-eyes from her opponents.

Young Dorothy decided to make the best use of her winnings. She marched down to the soda fountain at the corner of Bellevue Avenue and Pine Street, climbed onto a stool, set her chamois bag on the counter, and announced to the owner that the bag's contents were for sale in return for an account for ice cream sodas. When she left, she had obtained not only her first line of credit, but also the assurance that she could mix those future sodas herself. "It was a very good deal," Dorothy Stimson Bullitt remembered eighty-nine years later, in tones now used for buying an office building or a television station. "I *loved* ice cream sodas and I could *control* how they were made. Believe me, I got *full* value for those marbles."

Childhood incidents like this are intimations of the future. Dorothy Bullitt's early traits of resourcefulness, control, and determination stood her in good stead through nearly a century of change and fortune. As the decades rolled by, she continued to hang out with the boys, preferred their company in fact, and became a master at manipulating them. In the process, she also became one of the wealthiest women in the United States. Although the span of her life accelerated from late Victorian to high tech, the setting moved from back lots to boardrooms, and the challenge shifted from marbles to business and broadcasting, Dorothy Stimson Bullitt always enjoyed the game.

She lived many decades after that early trip to the soda fountain. As she grew, so did the region in which she was born. Dorothy Bullitt was bound to the Pacific Northwest, particularly to the Puget Sound country and the Emerald

v

City set in its center. She embodied its pioneer spirit: the sturdy, spunky quality that characterized its early days was as much a part of her personality as the region's shifting clouds and waters were part of her interior landscape. Since she took her first swim as a child alongside her father's yawl, the salt water of Puget Sound was in her blood. In time, the region enriched her and she returned the favor—during Depression days, the widow Bullitt signed papers to start construction of Grand Coulee Dam, and she followed that with nearly five decades of quality broadcasting in the Pacific Northwest. Dorothy Bullitt never lived anywhere else for long; no other place ever measured up, no other place could hold her.

She inherited more than money from her parents. Her father taught her to succeed, and her mother taught her to do it with taste and high standards. When Dorothy Bullitt died in 1989, she was remembered as "Seattle's last class act" and "the best businesswoman this city has ever known." To these legacies she brought her own native riches—a powerful personality, a fertile imagination to envision possibilities, and a practical nature to carry them out. Time and experience brought her a certain detachment that enabled her to take a dispassionate look at people and their motives, to sift through a mass of facts to truth of her own that many respected as wisdom. Dorothy Bullitt was rich, but her true wealth was not so much in what she accumulated or accomplished. It was in who she was.

I first met the remarkable woman in the 1940s when she became interested in broadcasting. My father, Andrew Haley, was her attorney in Washington, D.C., and "Mrs. Bullitt" was his favorite client. In my young eyes, Dorothy Bullitt was perfectly paced, with an economy of gesture—no fidgeting, flailing gestures, or hilarious laughter—that made her seem unhurried despite her urgent business dealings. Most memorable was her deep, husky voice, which mesmerized me more by its tone than its content. She spoke dramatically at measured speed, emphasizing the occasional word and breaking the cadence with a humorous comment or a low chuckle.

Years later, in the late 1960s, I went to work for Dorothy Bullitt's daughter Harriet, who was then publishing a small natural history journal, *Pacific Search,* which later grew into *Pacific Northwest* magazine. From Harriet I heard more about her mother, stories revealing a complexity that was contrary to the great lady's public reputation. When Dorothy Bullitt's children asked me to write their mother's biography in 1981, I quickly agreed, without realizing exactly what it entailed. I had known many of Dorothy Bullitt's friends and competitors in broadcasting but was pitifully unaware that she had lived at least three other lives before that.

For eight years, we spent time together at dinners and social functions, at her home watching movies (her favorite was Katharine Hepburn in *The Madwoman of Chaillot*), and on trips to Hawaii and the San Juan Islands. Sometimes we worked at filing papers, which triggered anecdotes and personal stories; occasionally we played Monopoly (at which she excelled) or Trivial Pursuit (where her favored tactic was intimidation).

Dorothy Bullitt was as hard to catch on paper as she had been in 1900 when she raced her pony over Seattle's hills. She could change her multifaceted persona at will to be somehow warm and cool at the same time, shy and supremely confident, humble but imperious. She could display such ineffable charm and empathy as to make her appear mutable, yet manifest a will so indomitable as to make her seem fixed. In appearance she was small but somehow grand, radiating self-confidence and wealth. Though her patrician bearing proclaimed perfect taste, she wore suits that were decades old, glasses hinged with a safety pin, a large sapphire ring on one finger and a rubber band on the next. Her features were not outstanding but the force and range behind them were extraordinary. Sparkling with humor one moment, her blue eyes could also quick-freeze into an icicle stare, or glaze over in abject boredom (usually when people talked too long about themselves). Her manicured hands could orchestrate a deeply personal conversation or form a tight fist to pound a table. Telling stories, the imposing voice I remembered from childhood alternately whispered soft as velvet, rasped like sandpaper, sharpened with an edge of sarcasm, or sliced like serrated steel. No matter what her mood or motive, one trait prevailed—her formidable personal power. At core, Dorothy Bullitt had such a clear sense of self that when she fixed her full energy on what she wanted, it was automatically hers. She used this power to overcome deep personal loss and to compete out in the world when few women of her social background did. In her dealings as a well-bred matron in a good old boys' world, she perfected techniques of psychological jujitsu that threw men off balance simply from the sheer weight of their own egos.

Many people thought they knew Dorothy Bullitt, but few did. She had as many facets as friends, and everyone believed that their relationship was special. She had two public reputations: to many, she was a great heart who enriched both community and region; to others, she was a cold fish, ruthless and unfeeling, who stopped at nothing to get what she wanted. Both were true. She was a woman who spent millions but quibbled over the price of paper clips; a "people" person who visited the private worlds of thousands but never stayed. Guided by high ideals, she was still supremely practical. Like a ship trimming sails with the winds of change, she could tack when the going got rough—all in order to keep on keel and reach her various ends. Only a few things anchored her—certain fundamental principles, a loyalty to the Pacific Northwest, and love for her children.

I was alternately charmed, enchanted, terrified, and fascinated by Dorothy Bullitt over the years. As she unfolded before me stories of family and career, sorrows and secrets, and the sort of wisdom that results from reflection on such an accumulation of experience, I came to realize that Dorothy Bullitt's long life was not so much about worldly power and accomplishment as it was about ongoing inquisitiveness, overcoming, courage, and transformation. This was the most important game that she ever won, and in the end, her triumph shone like sunlight on her beloved Puget Sound.

–Delphine Haley

Delphine Haley, a freelance writer and editor, wrote this biography with the cooperation of Dorothy Bullitt and her family and associates. A recipient of the Washington Governor's Writers Award for a book of natural history, Ms. Haley divides her time between Seattle and Guemes Island, Washington.

By far my parents were the best part of me. I loved them so much. I didn't love my brother as much, but my mother and father I adored, and I don't think they ever knew it.

1 PARLOR CAR PIONEERS

1889

IN 1889, THE YEAR WASHINGTON JOINED THE UNION, THE rugged realm of Puget Sound was a vast uncut jewel that sparkled with promise. A pristine place of dense, dark-green forest flanked by mountains and carved by rivers that emptied into a glittering inland sea, it beckoned to the hardy and colorful pioneers who settled along its shores. Seattle, the principal city, had been founded thirty-eight years earlier by families named Denny, Terry, Boren, and Bell, followed by thousands of sturdy souls who, seeking a new life, brought their skills and savvy to the small settlement pitched alongside the deep waters of Elliott Bay.

The first settlers had come for a variety of reasons. A few, like Seattle's founder Arthur Denny, pursued the dream of a community that would one day stand on its own and flourish. Others fled from marriage or money problems; among these was hard-drinking David "Doc" Maynard, who named the new community after his Indian friend, Chief Sealth. Many were motivated by greed, such as tight-fisted Henry Yesler, who established the first sawmill, the first restaurant and meeting hall, and later profited from real estate. Some saw quick opportunities and left: John Pennell, a migrant from the Barbary Coast, built a dance hall and bawdy house on the tide flats; and young Asa Mercer, first teacher and president of the University of Washington, went east twice to recruit single women for the lonely male community to wed. Most, however, were content with less dramatic dreams of peace and prosperity, living on small farms and starting the businesses that fed and served the community as it grew.

The settlers chopped back the forest and cleared a community from the raw wilderness around them. They bartered and fought with native tribes over the years, eventually banishing them to reservations on the Sound. They contoured and constructed a harbor with docks for waterborne commerce, milled logs and mined coal to export down the coast, staked their claims on the surrounding stump-studded hills, and laid out muddy streets that would hold the homes and businesses necessary for survival. Growth was slow for the first thirty years, but by 1889, three years before Dorothy Stimson was born, the territory of Washington was on the brink of statehood and Seattle had burgeoned from a scraggly settlement of twenty-four to an independent port of forty thousand. Although the town would eventually be called the Emerald City, it was then an emerald-in-the-rough—still spattered with sawdust and mud, rugged and ragtag, with unpaved streets and planked sidewalks, poorly lit and plumbed. But the city functioned, supplying itself and settlements nearby with the services of banks, breweries and bakeries, retail stores, foundries and furniture makers, doctors and lawyers, carpenters and artisans, hospitals, churches, a few streetcars, a fledgling university, and, from nearby Tacoma, a railroad—the Northern Pacific—that connected Puget Sound to more civilized counterparts elsewhere.

A second wave of western immigrants began to arrive around 1889, bringing an era of gentrification to the frontier settlement. This new influx was to double Seattle's population to eighty thousand within ten years. Although most were working-class citizens, a number of businessmen and their families were among them, strengthening the city's commercial base. Having heard of the region's vast natural resources and the city's potential for rapid development, these already-moneyed migrants—called "parlor car pioneers" by historian Murray Morgan—boosted the city into a new era of prosperity. They came, not by sailing ship around Cape Horn or by wagon train on the Oregon Trail, but in Pullman railcars from points east. When they arrived, they stayed in hotels rather than leaky log cabins, until their homes were built. They brought money and financial connections, along with higher levels of education and culture than the first plucky pioneers. The men were tough, seasoned, and shrewd, having proven their mettle on business battlefields elsewhere. Confident and financially secure, they set their names on buildings, streets, and landmarks as tributes to their success. The women were hardy, community-minded, and intent on bettering the muddy frontier town that greeted them. They were the pioneers of politeness and refinement, with cultural and charitable work their way of life. It was a time for polishing the rough edges in this hitherto crude part of the world, a time for stiff collars as well as coveralls, for high heels as well as hob nails, and for calling cards as well as quaint Chinook *Klahowyas*.

Among this second wave of migration was the Stimson family, which ventured West from Muskegon, Michigan, in 1889—thirty-two-year-old Charles

Charles Douglas Stimson—known as C. D.—was the one-armed scion of a Michigan lumber family sent to the Pacific Northwest in 1889 to find new forests to log. A shrewd businessman and dealmaker, he built a further fortune in real estate and became one of the state's wealthiest men.

Douglas Stimson, his twenty-seven-year-old wife, Harriet, and their five-year-old son, Thomas, the family into which Dorothy Stimson would be born in 1892.

Charles Douglas Stimson was an ebullient, energetic man with a ready laugh and blue eyes that could twinkle with humor or turn glacial when it came to the tough business of buying timberland and selling lumber. He was a man of action, little given to philosophical musings—a Republican in politics because it befitted his social standing and an agnostic in religion simply because he spent little time contemplating such matters. Although short at five feet six inches, his strong personal presence gave him stature. A trim, sturdy build and a perpetual tan attested to the amount of time he had spent outdoors cruising for timber, shrewdly appraising at a glance the financial prospects of a forest.

"C. D.," as he was called, had succeeded in a field that required considerable brawn—in days when muscle, horses, and steam engines provided the power to turn trees into salable logs—and brains for selling lumber in a highly competitive, ruinously cyclical market. Combining solid business acumen with the instincts of a gambler, he was a tough bargainer with a knack for knowing when to wait and when to forge ahead. He thrived on competition and counted a man's word as sacred. When a price was finally reached during negotiations, C. D. Stimson was known to tolerate no nonsense. Once agreed upon, every penny counted. On one occasion, C. D. sold a timber tract near Wallace Falls in the Cascade Range at an agreed price of $600,118.42. "When it came time to write out the check," an old logger recalled years later, "one of the purchasers said, 'Mr. Stimson, I presume you will throw off the odd dollars?' [C. D.] said the price had been agreed upon and should not be changed. Another purchaser teasingly said, 'Of course, you will throw off the forty-two cents?' and [C. D.] stood up, gathered up his papers and said, 'When you gentlemen are ready to complete this purchase as has been agreed let me know.' Thereupon he would have walked out, but it ended agreeably."

C. D. Stimson was a lumberman of some means by the time he reached the Pacific Northwest. Of English ancestry (by way of ten generations in New England), his father, Thomas Douglas Stimson, had left home as a lad in Pontiac, Michigan, and worked his way up Horatio Alger–style. Over many hard and determined years, beginning as an ox driver and logger, T. D., as he was called, acquired timber holdings in Michigan and surrounding states and a successful mill in Chicago. Four of his five sons assisted him by this time: in birth order, they were Willard Horace (W. H.), Charles Douglas (C. D.), Ezra Thomas (E. T.), and Frederick Spencer (F. S.). Two other children, Olive Jane, second eldest, and Jay (J. D.), the youngest, did not join the family business.

By the late 1880s, although he was rich, T. D. Stimson foresaw the depletion of Michigan forests and began to look for new lands to log. He sent his two oldest sons to scout in northern Michigan and Minnesota, but they returned with the discouraging news that the whole Great Lakes region was either logged over or had poor quality timber. Next he sent his foreman on a nationwide search. The results—from Arkansas, Virginia, and California—proved disappointing, until the foreman, accompanied this time by his boss, reached the Pacific Northwest. There both men found a lumberman's heaven-on-earth in endless stands of Western red cedar, Douglas fir, and Western hemlock that grew to the water's edge. The region, they noted, was enhanced by its proximity to Seattle, which had an excellent market for logs and lumber, and a deep saltwater harbor that was perfect for coastal and foreign trade. T. D. took out his maps and called in his boys. Placing his finger on Puget Sound, he told them that this was the region that held the most promise.

When C. D. Stimson and his family rode the Pullman westward, it was a first step in a strategy devised by his father to make profitable use of his sons. It called for expansion in two directions: two sons, C. D. and F. S. (Fred), would go to Washington State to log and mill lumber, while T. D. and two others, W. H. and E. T., would market that lumber in southern California. It was a clever, integrated plan based on resources in one place and demand in the other. In executing it, the Stimsons, father and sons, would be enriched even more.

Although well-equipped for this challenging future, C. D. Stimson bore one handicap: he had only one arm. While swimming in a river as a ten-year-old, he had skinned his right arm on barbed wire. When the wound became infected, his mother, Achsah Jane Stimson, forbade him to swim and sewed up his shirt so that he wouldn't use his injured arm. Undaunted, the boy swam on the sly, each time persuading his sister Jenny to resew the shirt before he saw his mother. This deception continued until, after a brother-sister spat one day, Jenny angrily stitched C. D.'s shirt with black thread, instead of the white thread their mother used. When Achsah Jane Stimson discovered her son's disobedience, she scolded him roundly, but no amount of motherly concern could heal the sore. Doctors told her that amputation was the only solution. Dreading the inevitable, C. D. questioned his ability to cope with life without an arm, to survive the day-to-day—saddling and riding a horse, driving a team, using tools, splitting kindling for the stove. In despair, he told his mother he'd rather die than have his arm cut off. It was the last resort when his right arm was amputated above the elbow.

The loss of a limb was a terrible setback. But Achsah Jane saw to it, in unyielding fashion, that her son was treated no differently from the others. Her relentless demands were characteristic. When C. D. was seven, she had cured him of stammering by sending him to the back of the barn to practice speaking with stones in his mouth until he could talk without faltering. Achsah Jane now applied her considerable will to strengthening C. D.'s already competitive nature until he became even more determined and self-confident. On one occasion, C. D. obtained a shotgun in a trade. Lacking shells for the gun, he asked his mother if he could work for money to buy them. Pointing to a pile of wood alongside an outbuilding, she replied, "All right, split that pile of wood and stack it in the basement." Although the task would have been easy for his brothers, it posed problems and danger for the one-armed son. He spent the day splitting the wood, then devised a leather sling that he attached to one handle of a wheelbarrow, carried the wood to the house, loaded it into a chute, and stacked it in the basement.

C. D. had to relearn many basics: to tie his shoes, to dress himself, and to manipulate the morning paper with one hand. He had to learn to write with his left hand, a skill he developed so well that years later bank clerks complained his handwriting was so perfect it might be copied. For some tasks, such as tying a fishing fly, he used his teeth. Wearing a wooden right arm attached at the shoulder, he continued to excel at sports in school, playing baseball, football, and track. His left arm became powerful as well as skilled; even the fingers were muscular. Once a strong swimmer, he didn't swim for a number of years, until passing a pond, he heard cries of distress. Without thinking, he dived in and rescued a drowning boy, pulling the youth and himself up onto the beach while shouting the only thing on his mind: "I can swim! I can swim!"

Working alongside his brothers, C. D. more than held his own. He worked without pay during school vacations at his father's mill and learned all phases of the operation. With each challenge that was overcome, C. D. grew more confident. After leaving school—he attended Racine College in Racine, Wisconsin—C. D. worked for his father in Big Rapids for twenty dollars a month but soon quit when T. D. refused to raise his pay. Determined to do better elsewhere, C. D. set off for Grand Rapids, where he found work as a copier in an insurance office. He went on to become a telegraph operator for higher pay. His frustrated father eventually pursued him and offered his son a position as co-manager (with his brother Willard) of the planing mill, along with half of any profits it produced, and a triumphant C. D. returned to Big Rapids.

C. D. Stimson thus developed a character rich in self-worth, tenacity, and resourcefulness. His handicap never hindered him. Throughout life he remained agile and athletic. He hunted duck and pheasant with a shotgun, holding it like a pistol in his powerful left hand, and hitting birds on the wing. He drove an automobile across the country and sailed his seventy-five-foot yawl in every kind of weather throughout Puget Sound. He was an excellent golfer, winning a seniors tournament in Victoria at age seventy-two, the year he died. He liked to fly-fish, and daughter Dorothy—who as a child thought that "all fathers had only one arm"—remembered watching from the bank as he cast the fly across the stream and dropped it, without a ripple, just short of the bushes on the other side. He not only coped, he went through life in style. When C. D. drove his car, he used his one arm to steer, shift, and salute his friends, smoke a cigar, and tip his hat to the ladies on the streets of Seattle.

All of this steely tenacity was tempered by an ability to enjoy life. C. D. Stimson bought the things that brought him pleasure—the first gasoline car in Seattle and a series of yachts to take his family on explorations for weeks at a time. When the first ice-skating rink was built in town, he arrived home late for dinner one night, confessing happily that he had been skating all afternoon. "Father used to always tell me, 'Don't wait until you're old to have fun,'" his daughter Dorothy recalled. "'Go *now*—on trips, go fishing, skating— whatever you like to do, and fit it into your life.'" His family was caught up in this enthusiasm, particularly his daughter, who adored him. Saying that he was balanced in all facets of his life, she called him the "most whole person I have ever known."

IN 1882, AT AGE TWENTY-FIVE, C. D. STIMSON MARRIED Harriet Mary Overton, a young music teacher in Big Rapids, Michigan. (There had been another suitor for her hand, a minister, and it was later a joke between C. D. and Harriet that when the two rivals met and shook hands, C. D. nearly paralyzed the minister with his forceful grip.) She was as tall as he, with red highlights in her hair and serenity that rested in her eyes. She wore no rouge or lipstick but had, as her daughter Dorothy later described it, "the most beautiful mouth in the shape of a cupid's bow," and "the most elegant hands I have ever seen." Harriet's hands, with widely spaced and long, slender fingers, reflected her talent for piano. As a girl in Adams, New York, she played the organ in church. Later she attended Hungerford Collegiate Institute in Adams and acquired more musical education. Her family then moved to Ann Arbor, Michigan, where she taught piano and met C. D. Stimson while he was working at his father's planing mill in nearby Muskegon.

Harriet Overton Stimson was a classic offspring of New England, a descendant of passengers who came on the *Mayflower*. Austerity and self-sacrifice were her way of life, virtues that translated into acts of friendship and kindness and over time earned her a saintly, if sometimes intimidating, reputation. Her family portrait, painted late in life, portrays her as the quintessential grande dame, with erect carriage, a proudly lifted head, and eyebrows that arch over her pince-nez. Her dignified, disciplined, and puritanical outlook on life included a certain amount of intolerance,

Harriet Overton Stimson, wife of C. D. Stimson and a great civilizer, was a founder of the Seattle Symphony Orchestra Society and the Children's Orthopedic Hospital.

and an insistence on strict codes and standards that were sometimes harsh and controlling for those around her. C. D., however, at most only received a soft and smiling, "Oh, Charlie," as a rebuke for his levity.

Harriet Stimson was as self-made as her husband. Although marriage and moving to Seattle interrupted her career as a music teacher, she found time to serve as accompanist to well-known singers who came through on tour. Her daughter recalled years later, "She tried to transplant some of the culture that she had known in the East—into music, hospitals, gardens, and trees." Harriet Stimson was a founder of the Seattle Symphony Orchestra Society and became its first president. She was a founder of the Children's Orthopedic Hospital and president of its board for many years, a board member and financial supporter of the Cornish School, the Visiting Nurse Service, Lighthouse for the Blind, and the League of Women Voters. She was active in the Seattle Art Museum and the Seattle Garden Club, and later a prime mover in the establishment of the University of Washington Arboretum.

Despite their different temperaments, the Stimsons were well-matched and suited to the Seattle of their time. The town was then, as perhaps even today, a mix of the rough and refined—a place where children sloughed through mud en route to music lessons. C. D.'s rough-hewn ebullience was offset by Harriet's refinement, his pioneer energy with her civilized composure. Their marriage was more an affectionate partnership than an intimate union, one driven more by social mores and shared goals than passion. Although to strangers she was as distant as he was approachable, the balance that they brought to social, civic, and cultural occasions made them popular. Dorothy described her parents as a "perfect pair." Harriet tended her husband with devotion. If she disapproved of his rough-cut ways, there was never any outward sign of it. He called her "Hattie," a name that she despised, and blithely went his way, while she followed loyally, swept along by his sheer enthusiasm. C. D. in turn appreciated the principles and refinement that Harriet brought to his life. He contributed large sums to her causes, attended the formal functions she enjoyed, and never complained about household expenses. He showered her with expensive gifts over the years, usually accompanied by an affectionate card that might seem insensitive by today's standards. For her long slender hands, he once gave her a five-carat diamond ring surrounded by seventy-two brilliants and accompanied by a birthday card that read, "To my fair, fat, faithful frau at forty."

The "perfect pair" may have stood well in Seattle society, but C. D. and Harriet's differing temperaments would later cause conflict as their two children sought to define themselves in life. Their son would often defy his father, risking ostracism. Their daughter would struggle to please both parents, combining her father's business shrewdness and life-relishing character with her mother's stern and civilizing attitudes. The parental marriage of fun-loving husband and aloof-but-kindly wife would become her model, and the unspoken hopes they were to invest in her would become a momentous challenge.

Two years after their marriage, a son, Thomas Douglas, named for and by his paternal grandfather, was born in Muskegon, Michigan. Thomas's life ahead, although blessed in many ways, would not be without problems. An only son, he grew up largely as an only child—sister Dorothy was not born for eight more years—and the product of a devoted mother and a high-achieving father. He was not tall, but his features were handsome. Sensitive and introverted by nature, he was the antithesis of his powerful father, and was destined to spend a great amount of his life seeking his father's approval. That paternal endorsement never really came, according to Dorothy, in spite of the fact that Thomas married a fine woman, was a good husband and father, became a prominent member of the community, and gained a reputation as an accomplished aviator in days when flying was a heroic adventure. His efforts at independent action were often ignored by his father or met with impatience and disapproval. Thomas lacked the boldness and judgment necessary for financial success, nor did he have much interest in making money, since he already had more than enough.

Such was the family of Stimsons that rode the Pullman toward the Pacific Northwest to pursue the family's business scheme. From the windows of the Seattle Hotel in Pioneer Square the day after their arrival, the Stimsons beheld a hodgepodge of hastily constructed one- or two-story wooden buildings, divided by muddy streets and surrounded by tide flats and stump-scarred hills. Typical of Western pioneer towns, the rutted streets, bustling with tradesmen and delivery wagons, exuded a rough-edged energy, refined only by a horseman tipping his hat in greeting or a gloved matron riding regally in a carriage. Much of the commerce took place on the streets, at the docks, or in one of the eateries run by Chinese cooks. A few Indians hung around the corners with little to do, as if still dazed by the extraordinary changes that had occurred in their lives.

The family settled in an apartment at the Griffith House at Second Avenue and Pike Street, their home for the next six months while C. D. sought potential sites for a mill. Traveling by horseback and steamer as far south as Olympia and as far north as Bellingham, he became even more convinced that Seattle would become the center of commercial development and was the best place to put down roots. Within a few months, his brother Willard came up the coast from Los Angeles to buy timberland. Willard spent $500,000 on claims in Washington's Snohomish County, along Hood Canal, and in Oregon's Tillamook County. He was buying old-growth forests for as little as $1.25 an acre.

That spring, C. D. heard about an old mill that Captain W. R. Ballard had for sale on Salmon Bay, a small township just north of Seattle's city limits that Ballard had acquired on a bet and which now bore his name. C. D. hired an Indian to take him by canoe from Elliott Bay around Magnolia Bluff to see the mill firsthand. It proved to be in dilapidated condition, but he could envision the plant as the center of the future Stimson lumber operations on the

West Coast. The site was less expensive than property downtown, yet it still had the necessary access to salt water for moving logs on Puget Sound and shipping lumber out to Hawaii, Los Angeles, or Japan. C. D. bought the mill and soon thereafter ventured across the Sound where he acquired a cut-over tract of land. Using Michigan white pine salvage techniques, he gleaned enough timber from the tract to feed the mill for two years, while Willard established lumber camps at Kingston and Marysville, north of Seattle. About the same time, C. D. also purchased a corner of land partway up the south side of Queen Anne Hill and began construction of a home from which he planned to commute daily by horseback over the hill to Ballard.

The summer of 1889 brought catastrophe to Seattle. On the hot afternoon of June 6, near Pioneer Square, a woodworker's glue pot heating on a gasoline stove overturned and set fire to the woodshop. The blaze spread quickly. In spite of the volunteer manpower that came to the rescue, the city's horse-drawn equipment and water pressure were inadequate to combat the inferno. Within twenty minutes, the streets were crowded with citizens fleeing on foot or in carriages piled high with belongings. C. D. Stimson, working in his office on Columbia Street between Second and Third Avenues, was aware that a fire had broken out to the south, but he paid it little attention until Harriet arrived to say that it was moving rapidly north toward his office. The office was spared because of a small stand of trees that diverted the flames, and by the efforts of bucket brigadiers who cooled down buildings nearby, but the inferno razed what had been the heart of the city a few blocks to the west and south. When the smoke cleared hours later, Seattle's dazed and exhausted citizens surveyed what had once been the town's business district—thirty blocks of docks, stores, hotels, offices, and restaurants—all in cinders and ruin.

The Great Fire of 1889 was devastating at first, but within the next few years, a safer, stone-built, and more architecturally coherent phoenix of buildings rose from the downtown ashes. As the laborious business of clean-up and rebuilding began, stores and lunchrooms, even theaters, carried on their business in tents. Those who had lost their offices sought temporary work space, and C. D. shared his suite, reserving a corner for himself. Perhaps it was the cramped quarters both at the office and at the Griffith House, or maybe it was the confusion of living close to the ruins of the fire, but he soon grew restless for more permanent domestic quarters and easier access to his Ballard mill, now beginning to profit from the city's restoration.

Sooner than planned, C. D. moved his family to Queen Anne Hill. Although the house under construction there was not finished, the Stimsons agreed they had been uprooted long enough. Seattle was now their chosen place.

Oh, I was a nasty little piece of goods!

2 EARLY DAYS ON QUEEN ANNE
1892–1900

DOROTHY STIMSON'S FIRST MEMORY WAS AS FRAGILE AS THE recollection itself, yet it remained imprinted on her mind for ninety-seven years. "I remember watching Mother as she went around the living room to light the Wellsbach burners mounted on the walls. The burners were candle-shaped and they had a webbing that gave off a brilliant glow when she touched them with a match. The webbing was frail and I was entranced as, one by one, they lit up the room." For Dorothy that image was a magical ceremony that brought feelings of comfort and security to her earliest days.

Dorothy Frances Stimson was born in what she described as "just a little gray wooden house" perched partway up the south side of Seattle's Queen Anne Hill on February 5, 1892. Her parents gave the infant a first name which, according to their daughter, "they took from the air—they just liked it." The name gave its new owner only one small problem over the years: it was mis-pronounced as "Dor-thy," instead of receiving the three-syllabled treatment it deserved. Her middle name, Frances, was the first name of her maternal grand-mother.

Thinking back, Dorothy Frances expressed doubts about the auspiciousness of her arrival eight years after that of her brother Thomas. "At the very least, I was a *surprise*," she commented years later with a wry smile. "Afterwards, I might have been welcome, but I don't think the whole idea was very *promising* at the time." Such a remark was false, of course; she knew that the opposite was true. In another mood, she admitted, "My parents liked me, I think. Actually they liked me too *much*—I wasn't all that good. From the beginning, they gave

The Stimson family in 1894 at Port Townsend, with baby Dorothy the center of attention.

me a lot of freedom and I repaid them with nothing but mischief."

In fact, her parents adored her. From the start, young Dorothy Stimson enlivened hearts and household with a hell-bent zest that stood in stark contrast to the quieter nature of her brother Thomas. To her father, she was a center of attention; to her mother, she was a daughter well-loved but equally in need of discipline; to her brother, who tolerated her with dutiful affection, she must have been a pest and a usurper of his parents' devotion. From birth she took center stage, claimed the spotlight, and played her part as daddy's darling and mother's naughty sweetheart, while Thomas drifted to a lesser role in the background. A curious snapshot taken in 1895 depicts this family dynamic better than words. It shows brother Thomas and parents C. D. and Harriet standing on the front porch of a building in Port Townsend. Standing apart from them and out on a dirt road is Dorothy, a chubby child with her back to the camera. She wears overalls, a blouse, and a huge white sunbonnet that claims the viewer's attention immediately. Planted on sturdy little legs, she seems to be talking to her parents, yet looks as if she might tear off in any direction momentarily. She has her father's full attention and also that of her mother, who stands, partly hidden, behind him. Brother Thomas, an eleven-year-old dressed in knickers, jacket, and boater hat, stands on the step with his father, but his back is turned to the others as he grasps a support post on the porch. Energy emanates from the small sunbonneted child, while the two parents gaze at her and the brother turns his back. The photo is a telling portrait of the C. D. Stimson family.

Little Dorothy Stimson was the Center of the Universe—not just her child's cosmos of neighborhood and playmates, but her parents' universe as well. She was a small sun, a self-luminous little body around which C. D. and Harriet Stimson circled like Jupiter and Venus, a child whom they worshipped, encouraged, and applauded. Brother Thomas never obscured her glory; as far as Sister Sunshine was concerned, he was merely a distant, uncommunicative satellite, orbiting somewhere out on his own. Dorothy often said years later, "We were years and worlds apart."

As Center of the Universe, she possessed a clear sense of self and took control of her surroundings even from her earliest days. Confidence seemed to be her birthright, and it showed in the determination with which she took on life. She was willful and self-centered, the pivotal point around which everything and everyone else in her life revolved. From tying her shoes at three to securing a broadcasting network at sixty-three—whatever she was doing at the moment was the only thing really happening at the time. So ingrained was this attitude that, later in life, she had no trouble taking an unused appointment calendar from years prior and reorienting the days to suit her current life. And why not? She was the prime mover and time was at her disposal. Throughout her life, she made templates or models from paper, cardboard, and even wood to construct her most current environment—office, garden, or home—and enjoyed moving the various bits and pieces around. It was also her habit to manipulate her children, friends, and employees as though they were movable pieces in her life.

This central position in the universe would have other implications during Dorothy's life. Although it gave her focus and control to achieve her objectives, it would also make her feel responsible, for better or worse, for those in her orbit—for the happiness of her parents; for the illnesses and successes of her children, their marriages and divorces; for the lives of her servants and employees. People so strongly empowered may appear to others as megalomaniacs in their zeal to shine, to realize themselves. To family they can be unremitting controllers from whom escape is difficult; to friends and employees, they can be inspiration; to the public they can be benevolent but unapproachable. It is a component for achievement, as well as for narcissism, one also well-suited to the ambitions and opportunities of Seattle's decades of heady growth.

Dorothy remembered little about the house in which she was born, but photos show that it was not really a "little wooden house." Situated at the corner of Ward Street and First Avenue North, its three stories were large enough to accommodate the Stimson family, a governess, a cook, and eventually Dorothy's maternal grandparents, William and Frances Overton, who would move from Michigan in 1896. Dorothy slept in an anteroom to her parents' bedroom. The house was bordered by a large lot that contained a vegetable garden and a barn for two horses and Thomas's pony, McGinty. A short walk away was the more palatial fourteen-room home of C. D.'s younger brother, Fred, at First and Prospect atop Queen Anne Hill.

The Queen Anne neighborhood was a quiet world without sidewalks, paving, telephones, or electricity. The houses were set well apart—a change of pace from downtown a mile to the south where laborers and artisans hastened to finish rebuilding the burnt-out core of the business district after the Great Fire. Queen Anne Hill did not invite much traffic. Occasionally a truck farmer braved the steep slopes with a wagonload of vegetables to sell, or a Diamond Ice Company driver made the rounds from house to house, bringing twenty-pound blocks of ice and chips for children to suck on during hot summer days. Otherwise life on Queen Anne was uninterrupted stillness. Dorothy later recalled that life went along at a walking, not running, pace, with few demands and even fewer choices. "It was measured by the steady clop, clop of a horse a block away, or the squeak of the cable car wheels as they took the curve at the bottom of the hill. Sometimes I heard the whistle of a steamship as it came into the harbor; but otherwise we were just suspended in silence with what is now Kinnear Park on top of Queen Anne, just a patch of woods behind us, and the Magnolia Hill area to the west pretty much a wilderness. Ballard was far away; there weren't many people there—except those who worked at Father's mill."

The uneventful days rolled by, punctuated by an occasional celebration. Certain days were set aside as "calling days" for residents in various neighborhoods in town. On Queen Anne Hill, this ritual occurred every Tuesday, and Harriet Stimson, or "Mrs. C. D." as she was customarily called ("Never by her first name, no matter how close the friend"), prepared refreshments, received friends, and learned the news from other parts of town. Every morning C. D. dressed in his dark suit and high stiff collar, tied his lunch to his saddle, then rode his horse over the spine of Queen Anne Hill, down to a creek crossed by a small bridge, and onto the road to his mill. When he returned each evening, dusty or rain-soaked, Harriet greeted him at the door and accompanied him to the bathroom, where she helped him wash before dinner. All meals were prepared by a Chinese live-in servant named Chong.

Her parents, the key figures in her life, guided Dorothy's early days. While one spurred her on, the other corrected her passage. Her father indulged her every whim. "I was spoiled *rotten*," Dorothy repeated often with a self-satisfied chuckle. "I was *so* spoiled that I never had to ask for *anything* because Father always knew *ahead* of time what I liked and got it for me before I thought to ask." Many of her early memories were associated with the gifts he showered upon her—bracelets, pins, pets, and all sorts of vehicles—everything from red wagons to horses to cars.

Given such constant pampering, the spoiled little daughter of C. D. Stimson might have remained content simply to collect tribute and coast through life on entitlements, were it not for the intervention of her mother. Harriet Stimson, in contrast to her husband, was a strict disciplinarian with high expectations and standards. "I think she was a school teacher," stated one contemporary of Dorothy's, "at least she had that mentality." Harriet protected her daughter from an undirected life of idle pleasure and instilled in her the self-discipline needed for achievement. She required correct behavior in manners and morality and insisted on restraint in all things, whether drinking, eating, buying, or having too much fun. She taught the willful little Miss Stimson—and no doubt it took years of training—to control her emotions, especially anger. Anger, her mother cautioned, was unseemly and demeaning; it was a loss of control that served no purpose other than self-indulgence, and often it was counterproductive to achieving one's goals. Dorothy learned this lesson well; her life was one without emotional displays. She appeared reserved despite whatever was rumbling beneath her surface, channeling the excess emotion into the competitive nature she had inherited from her father.

Harriet Stimson brought down swift punishment when her well-defined limits were transgressed. Discipline took various forms, although it usually assumed the form of frequent spankings with a hairbrush. "The first time I remember being punished was when I was three and Mother locked me in a closet," Dorothy recalled with humor. "I don't remember exactly *what* I had done—there were *many* possibilities—but as Mother closed the door, I put my hand around the hinge. When I didn't stop screaming, she opened the door finally and took out my hand and my fingers were as thin as paper. Oh, she felt so badly. I think that one saved me a couple of future spankings," she said with a sly grin. "It gave me a little edge on life." She was not a child given to smart remarks or verbal sparring, but she was intent on her goals, however small, and would risk punishment when necessary. "I didn't enjoy it," she added with a smile, "but sometimes it was *worth* it in order to do what I wanted to do."

Neither parental approach was cut-and-dried—C. D. Stimson often challenged his daughter and Harriet Stimson always cherished her—but the combined result was effective. Both were trustworthy parents and their naughty daughter ingested what they said as true, including both compliments and criticism, with the knowledge that she was well-loved and the suspicion that she was probably in need of an occasional comeuppance to keep herself on track.

Chong, the Stimsons' live-in houseman, was the first in a long line of servants involved in Dorothy's life. He became her friend but was reminded from time to time that, no matter how comfortable the relationship, his status was lowly. Chong did everything; he cleaned the floors, cooked on the wood-fired kitchen stove, and washed the family clothes with a scrub board and laundry tub. Dorothy described Chong in warm but somewhat doglike terms as "so good, so faithful, so patient." She regarded him in the stereotypic way of the late 1800s, when racial groups were described in clichéd phrases, and Chinese were considered "honest and hard-working, good gardeners, and cooks." The friendship between the loyal Chong and the spoiled young Dorothy had its upsets, testing the servant's devotion from time to time. When Dorothy was about four, a dog followed Chong home and C. D. said he could keep it if it was well behaved. "One evening I was out in the kitchen—which I often did because Mother and Father had other things to do—and playing with Chong. Sometimes he tried to teach me how to tie knots and sometimes we roughhoused a little. This particular evening, I pushed him and the dog didn't understand this, thinking I was doing harm to his master. Well, the dog jumped, knocked me down, and bit me on the cheek. Father heard the screams and came out and pulled both the dog and me out from under the kitchen table. My cheek was bleeding like crazy, so the doctor came and said he'd have to sew it up." Next morning, Dorothy learned that her Father had taken his gun and shot the dog. "Chong was sitting in the kitchen sobbing, with a towel over his face. He felt so badly—I don't think he could have felt that badly about anything else." She was not always so sympathetic, however. At about age six, Dorothy refused to come to lunch because she was painting a swing given to her by her father. When Chong scolded her, she splattered red paint all over his white uniform and, marching up the steps to the house, sloshed each step with angry blotches of red.

When Dorothy was five years old, the Stimsons hired a French governess to redirect some of their daughter's willfulness onto more cultured paths. Mademoiselle Blanc was a tall, thin woman in her thirties who spoke no English. Teacher and student were an unlikely pair as they took walks on the hill, each speaking a garbled language and trying to understand each other. Until she was about eleven years old, Dorothy had French lessons every day and her love of that language lasted. Decades later, her library reflected an interest in French literature and her accent remained flawless.

From her third-story study room, Dorothy would scan the Seattle skyline. She watched the new docks as they were built and kept track of the schooners and steamships loading or anchored in Elliott Bay. The city and its port below became imprinted in her mind and heart during these years. Seattle had one of the two deepest harbors on the Pacific Coast, she often stated, so it should always be a working port. Even in her nineties, she scolded Seattle Mayor Charles Royer for trying to remodel the waterfront into "boutiques and tourist things" instead of keeping a working waterfront.

When she wasn't with her governess or visiting in the kitchen with Chong, Dorothy was outdoors. She spent time among the hazelnut trees along the path behind her house, removing the burrs and breaking open the nuts. It was a great revelation, she remembered, that there could be something to eat inside and she always carried hazelnuts in her pockets. Pockets, she learned, were important for carrying what she needed, a habit that lasted from the days of pinafores to the French smocks of her later years. Pockets were also a convenient place to house her hands and she tended to dig into them when she was excited about some idea, flapping as she talked and paced the floor. People came to know that one reliable way of judging the intensity of her mood was by the amount of flapping she generated in those pockets.

She developed a great fondness for stationery and other purposeful implements during these early years. She had few toys, and dolls were never her playthings. "Someone once gave me a doll," she remembered with a puzzled look years later, "but it didn't *do* anything, so I never played with it." Instead she had wagons, swings, sticks, and a bicycle to ride on the path that substituted for a sidewalk on Ward Street. Sometimes she visited her cousins Achsah and Harold, Fred Stimson's children (a third child, Fred, came along later) at the top of the hill. Achsah was close to Dorothy's age, but she liked to play dolls and preferred to be in the house most of the time. Otherwise, except for one escapade in which the two girls were spanked for parading around in the fields wearing two of Harriet Stimson's fancier gowns, their friendship had limits.

Animals—strays and pedigrees—were another big part of Dorothy's life. Faithful and affectionate, animals never criticized—they kept the secrets whispered to them. Besides, if she trained them, they would do as they were told, and this early sense of control brought her great satisfaction. There ensued a parade of birds, ducks, rabbits, dogs, cats, horses, and even monkeys and bears into the Stimson household. The first of these was a pet canary that Dorothy, at the age of four, took from its cage and squeezed in a rush of such unrelenting affection that it expired. ("I didn't *mean* for it to die. I just took it out of the cage and *loved* it . . . and it didn't recover.") Thereafter she turned her attentions to Thomas's Shetland pony, McGinty. However, her brother would not let her near the pony, so she had to be content to pat it furtively every now and then.

The Stimson children, Thomas Douglas and Dorothy Frances, in 1895. "We were years and worlds apart," Dorothy remembered.

Another animal, a parrot, became a bird of contention when brother Thomas gave it away to a friend. ("The parrot didn't talk or do anything. He wasn't much good but he was *mine*.") Dorothy was deeply hurt when this happened, recalling the event in chilly tones as the beginning of a long antipathy between the two siblings. "I *never* forgave him for that," she said ninety years later. When questioned about her brother, she lowered her eyes and voice to say, "He was never my favorite person. We didn't fight, but we were never very close. The difference in our ages just followed us from one stage to another."

Dorothy looked forward to weekly shopping forays with her mother to Pioneer Square. Stepping from the cable car, mother and daughter crossed the planked streets to the west side of the square where Stewart & Holmes Drug Company was located. Owner Alexander Bruce Stewart, from whom Stewart Street in downtown Seattle derives its name, was a successful businessman and a friend of the Stimsons. While her mother chatted with Mr. Stewart or shopped for sundries, little Dorothy wandered about the tidy store, stopping to look longingly at the candies, in particular the animal crackers. Mr. Stewart would usually appear at her side and give her a box to take home. As this ritual was concluded, the two would agree that they were "great friends." This became such a reliable occurrence that one day Dorothy's hopes were dashed when Mr. Stewart had to tell her that he was currently out of animal crackers but that he hoped they were still friends. "We are *not* friends," Dorothy declared, stamping her foot and heading for the door. "I was very rude," she recalled. "I told him we were not friends and he said, 'I'm so sorry, I'll have some next time you come,' and I said, 'That won't do me any good *now.*'" Fortunately, this childhood storm passed and Dorothy and Mr. Stewart managed to salvage their friendship, thanks no doubt to a new shipment of animal crackers. Some twenty years later, on her wedding day, she received a handsome silver clock inscribed,

"To D. F. S. from A. B. S.—Still Friends." And when she died in 1989, the little clock still stood on a desk in her sunroom.

From Stewart & Holmes, Dorothy and her mother trudged over to Lausch & Augustine's, a large grocery store where Harriet selected items to carry home and Dorothy wandered the aisles until they departed for Frederick & Nelson, the city's main department store. The store itself, at Second and Madison, did not stand out in her memory, but Donald E. (D. E.) Frederick, a close friend of C. D. Stimson, did. "Mr. Frederick was a very shy man, a Southerner, but without the Southerner's natural gregariousness," Dorothy recalled. "He married late in life and his wife wasn't outgoing either; they never really mixed socially but kept to themselves. Mr. Frederick did like to shoot ducks with Father and he seemed to get over his shyness when they were together. The story went around that his partner, Mr. Nelson, was a Swede who had some money and Mr. Frederick suggested that they go into partnership. Otherwise no one knew anything about him, except that it was rumored that Mr. Nelson would often go into the furniture storeroom and stretch out on a mattress to take a nap." When Nels Nelson died in 1907, D. E. Frederick tactfully found a way to support Nelson's widow. He went to her and, instead of offering her an annuity or a widow's pension, asked if he could buy from her a consent to use her husband's name for the store, thus preserving both her dignity and her financial future.

On one of her earliest trips downtown, Dorothy saw Princess Angeline, Chief Sealth's daughter, sitting cross-legged on the sidewalk in front of Frederick & Nelson, selling baskets. The sight of the wizened old Indian woman reminded Dorothy of a story she had heard from her father—about how, in younger days, Angeline had paddled from Suquamish to Seattle in her canoe to warn settlers of an impending attack by Chief Leschi. But by the 1890s the days of confrontation with the Indians were gone and Angeline was only a frail reminder of their former presence. That early sight of Angeline stayed with Dorothy over the years, a reminder of how recent the settlement and how short Seattle's history were in this corner of the world. Having seen the daughter of Chief Sealth, the daughter of C. D. Stimson seemed to include herself as part of the process, as an integral figure in the unfolding of this part of the world.

———

THE STIMSONS BEGAN TAKING ANNUAL CHRISTMAS TRIPS TO Los Angeles in the 1890s. C. D.'s parents, T. D. and Achsah Jane, had by this time relocated from the snows of Chicago to the sun of California, where T. D. engaged in selling lumber and dealing in real estate. On Figueroa Street, he built a palatial thirty-room home next to the mansion of oil magnate Edward L. Doheny.

Just before her fifth birthday, Dorothy strikes an executive pose.

Known as the Stimson House, it was a four-story fortress fashioned of rough-cut brownish sandstone and embellished by a tower, tall chimneys, a circling veranda, and an orange grove in the back yard. It was considered one of the most elaborate and expensive homes on the West Coast, costing the enormous sum of $130,000 to build in 1893. More recently, a guidebook to well-known Los Angeles buildings described it as "a great architectural atrocity . . . light Queen Anne fantasy congealed into ponderous Richardson Romanesque sandstone, nearly overwhelmed by ivy, shrubs, banana trees, and palms." It stands today as a Catholic convent, surrounded by used-car lots and other bleak modern edifices.

In Los Angeles, the Seattle Stimsons were among the twenty-one children and grandchildren to spend a week at the Stimson House. Dorothy was one of the youngest grandchildren. During one of these visits, her cousins locked her in the tower, where she yelled for half a day before being released. Sometimes she went to town with her grandmother in the brougham, an elegant carriage with a coachman and a Dalmatian coach dog ("one of those blotter-looking dogs") sitting in front. Dorothy was a bit intimidated by her grandmother, Achsah Jane Stimson. "My grandmother never made a fuss over me like Grandfather did," she reflected. "Children were not her thing. She was a disciplinarian, and she ran a good household, but she didn't have much warmth. She treated everyone the same."

Grandfather Stimson was a different matter. The strength seen in his formal family portrait is softened by signs of warmth, joviality, and compassion. Self-made, he was remarkably free of social restraints—a Democrat in politics and spirit, and a free-thinker in his religious beliefs. He didn't care for formal occasions or travel; he preferred the comradeship of work, wit, and good friends, and advised his children and his employees to do the same. He was convinced that the Los Angeles area would grow and prosper, and he played an important part in its downtown development. Selling his holdings in Chicago at a profit, he invested in Los Angeles city lots and a series of building projects in what became, during that time, the commercial heart of the city. At the corner of Third and Spring Streets, he built the Stimson Building, the tallest building (at six stories) in Los Angeles and one of the first buildings in the nation to have steel reinforcements.

T. D. took a shine to granddaughter Dorothy immediately. "My grandfather and I were *good* friends. When we visited at Christmas he'd always latch onto me, put me on his lap and ask me to tell him about the 'Owl and the Pussy Cat.' He made quite a fuss over me, which he didn't do over the others. Grandfather openly had favorites, and I was it. He was a very *human* being." She was fond of recalling one New Year's Day when T. D. loaded the family into an open coach and took them for a picnic to a distant meadow he enjoyed, now known as Hollywood and Vine.

Dorothy enjoyed watching her father and uncles during these reunions. The four Stimson brothers spent hours together, joshing, talking over business deals, and telling stories about each other. Although different in temperament, each son had inherited from his father the ability to indulge in the pleasures that wealth permitted them. This fun included racing in motor cars and sailing yachts, building luxurious homes, gathering at Christmas in Los Angeles, and much good-natured teasing and late-night joking during their meetings together. Dorothy could never understand why the brothers didn't quarrel, given that each was strong and temperamental. Perhaps, she observed later in life, their different personalities brought a certain balance to their relationship.

THE STIMSON FAMILY BUSINESS—WITH C. D. AND FRED LOGGING and milling lumber in Seattle, and Willard and Ezra marketing it in Los Angeles—was clearly thriving. C. D.'s business in the operation, thanks to luck and shrewd planning, was booming. The Stimson Land Company was incorporated early in 1889 under the laws of Washington Territory, with $500,000 in capital stock, most of it controlled by T. D. This sum represented the family's first large investment in the Pacific Northwest and contributed a great amount of clout in the highly competitive lumber business along the West Coast. The Stimson Mill, incorporated a year later, also began to expand, almost from its inception, into Seattle's largest lumber mill. C. D., who was both president and general manager, had secured handsome profits from the rebuilding of Seattle after the fire of 1889, when there was great demand for wooden partitions, framework, shingles, and floors. Stimson scows were towed from Ballard to Elliott Bay piled high with supplies for sale. Although this market dropped off within a few years, the demand for lumber was sustained by new arrivals to the area and increased when the Great Northern Railroad reached Seattle in 1893. At the railroad's opening ceremonies, President James J. Hill acknowledged that one of the principal motives for constructing the new railroad was the need to move the mills' products to eager new markets.

With more outlets for his lumber on the horizon, C. D. launched into a risky business phase. The West Coast lumber market, famous for its ruinous cycles in prices, was at this time dominated by a cartel, the Pacific Pine Lumber Company, which controlled the price and production of lumber, particularly around the Bay Area. C. D., who believed fiercely in free competition, set out to break Pacific Pine by signing an agreement to supply an Oakland lumberyard at rock-bottom prices. He virtually gave lumber away, even paying the freight from Seattle to Oakland. (The Stimson lumberyard in Los Angeles made up for some of the money lost in Oakland.) His motives were not totally based on an excess of self-confidence; C. D. reasoned that the year or more of financial sacrifice it would take to establish himself on the coast was worth it for greater gains in the future. Unlike other mills, the Stimson Mill was well-financed, free of debt, and had a large inventory of timber to deliver on demand.

The gamble succeeded. By 1895, the Stimson Mill had cut so far into the lumber market that prices were fluctuating widely. In response, another cartel sought to consolidate both lumber retailers and wholesalers into a single organization, known as the Central Lumber Company. Every company on the coast joined—except the Stimson Mill Company. When at a meeting for those who might join, C. D. rose from his seat and announced he would not participate, the members were alarmed, knowing by now that the one-armed lumberman was perfectly capable of breaking into any highly controlled market. When they asked what reasons or suggestions he might have, he replied that he had none of either. Finally, after some door-slamming and several hurried conferences, C. D. agreed to join, but with one extortionate proviso: that for one year, every company involved in the trust would promise by written agreement to buy a certain percentage of their lumber from the Stimson Mill Company at five dollars per thousand board feet above the market price. The combine agreed, in effect subsidizing C. D.'s operation for a year, in order to prevent another price war. This produced a banner year for the Stimson Mill. A year later, when C. D. required the same agreement again, the Central Lumber Company was dissolved. It was the end of the lumber consortiums on the Pacific Coast.

The same battle was fought over shingles. The Stimson Mill had a shingle

Dorothy christens the three-masted schooner Stimson *in 1896, the first of many boats in her life.*

manufacturing subsidiary, which at 150 million shingles a year amounted to over half the number of shingles produced yearly in Washington State and was the largest such operation in the world. Refusing to join the Shingle Mill Association, C. D. consistently undercut it in markets that by now extended as far east as Denver and Omaha. This warfare continued until the price of shingles fell from $2.50 per thousand to ninety cents, at which point the shingle trust was also broken. The Stimson Mill and three other shingle producers then formed a combine that elected C. D. president for four consecutive years. At the end of that time there were so many manufacturers involved in the organization, 256 in all, that C. D. felt it was too large to be effective. He resigned, and shortly thereafter the consortium collapsed. Despite his success, C. D. was not devoted to the shingle business, feeling that it was full of labor unrest and not worth the infighting required to market the product. He closed down the shingle mill in 1893 and devoted his time and profits to milling lumber.

C. D. also plunged into real estate. In 1893 came a worldwide financial panic, the greatest economic crisis yet seen in American history. Banks, railroads, and other businesses failed, triggering a stock market collapse and causing four million workers to lose their jobs. For a few months, the Northwest was insulated, but soon circulating cash grew scarce and rail and cargo markets in the region collapsed. Northwest mills, particularly those in outlying areas, began to close or curtail production. Protected by a cash cushion, a reliable market in Los Angeles, and a chance to reduce wages in such a competitive job market, C. D. survived, but not without registering some caution. With a certain amount of pride, he wrote his father in Los Angeles: "We have not failed yet to meet every paym't & every pay day with Cash & are the only mill on the Sound that can say that & we are doing our level best to keep the good start we have, as these times are going to be memorial."

After several years, the Panic of 1893 subsided, but meanwhile C. D. decided to take advantage of the plummeting prices of property downtown. As his father had done in Los Angeles, he carefully appraised the city and the market and finally decided to invest in the north end of the business district. With a grub stake of $35,000 recovered from loans he had made to his brothers, he selected some buildings at Second and Pike, offered $30,000 cash for the $40,000 mortgage remaining on the properties, and was surprised to have it accepted by the lender, Cornell University. For three years, he collected rents from these buildings and then sold the properties for $100,000. This was the first step in a career of buying and building in real estate that made him a fortune. Within twenty-five years of his initial $30,000 purchase, he had made nearly a million dollars, based on a strategy of selling and reinvesting downtown. Once again, timing was on his side, this time the onset of the Alaska gold rush of 1897 and the prosperity it brought to Seattle. Among the city's sawmills, the Stimson Mill was Alaska's leading supplier, shipping nearly four million feet of lumber in December 1897 alone.

To young Dorothy, gazing from her vantage point high up Queen Anne Hill at the busy harbor, the world of gold, real estate, and business was unknown and unimportant. Although her universe of back lots, birthday parties, and occasional forays downtown was enough for the time being, it too was about to expand.

I was just a little girl growing up in a town that was growing up too, and my childhood couldn't have been happier. I had no world view—my world was very small. It was First Hill, and all of it was MINE.

3 THE LITTLE WORLD OF FIRST HILL

1900–1912

BY 1899, THE QUEEN ANNE HOUSE WAS BECOMING TOO SMALL for the Stimsons, so C. D., enjoying the profits from his mill, looked to build a larger home. For a neighborhood, he chose First Hill—a half-mile-square slope just east of downtown that overlooked the city and the Sound. The prominent location, its proximity to downtown, and the thirty or more impressive residences already constructed at the turn of the century secured First Hill as Seattle's most fashionable address. For an architect, C. D. chose Kirtland Cutter, a brilliant young designer from Spokane who also built such classic revivalist Northwest structures as the Rainier Club and the Seattle Golf Club north of the city.

Cutter, assisted by his partner Karl Malmgren, attended to every detail of the ten-thousand-square-foot home he designed for the Stimsons at 1204 Minor Avenue. Tudor in style and generous in size, it stood on a corner and was flanked by a carriage house with coachman's quarters, a hayloft, and a stall for a Jersey cow to satisfy C. D.'s passion for fresh, thick cream. The house was a gracious space that flowed from one room and level to another. Downstairs it gleamed with polished hardwoods, carved panels, and a painted canvas ceiling. The large living room could accommodate numerous guests, and musicians to entertain them; its grand fireplace was guarded by carved oak lions and contained large copper-and-steel dragon andirons that reflected the glow of the fire. The sycamore-paneled dining room, also with fireplace, seated eighteen at a long table. In the basement, a Turkish-style den and a billiard room with mosque lanterns and carved minarets were refuge for the gentlemen drinking

The Stimsons' home on First Hill became a gathering place for Seattle's social and business elite during the early 1900s. Dorothy kept her pet bears outside on the balcony.

brandy and smoking cigars after dinner. A more feminine reception room upstairs, with ornate moldings of palms, garlands, swans, and draped figures, was an elegant parlor for receiving callers and entertaining for tea. The two upper stories, with eight bedrooms (four with fireplaces) and four baths, were made more spacious by walk-in closets outfitted with built-in drawers and shelves—a clever innovation in days when armoires provided the usual storage.

After the Stimsons moved in 1914, the Joshua Green family occupied the house for sixty years. Since Joshua Green's death, it has survived several owners, escaped demolition, and is now listed on the National Register of Historic Places in America. Today the house embodies Seattle's spirit of historic preservation, a pioneer residence, maintained by private means. It is again in the Stimson family, owned by Dorothy Stimson's daughter Priscilla Collins, who operates the home as a catering business for receptions, weddings, and other occasions.

To eight-year-old Dorothy Stimson, however, the mansion was just home—a place from which to set forth at top speed each day, a haven where she could refuel and rest her "fat little legs" as she called them. With her move to this new home, life began to expand; her days were more active and her memories more vivid. Although the neighborhood brought the excitement of new playmates and new territory, the daily pace remained as steady and predictable as the horses' hoof beats along Minor Avenue. Certain people passed the house with regularity, including Mr. Frederick, who drove his twin black horses home just after five o'clock every day.

First Hill's world was safe and one's senses confirmed it. Sounds were comforting—wagon wheels were muffled, and on an evening's walk one could hear soft crunching sounds as horses fed in their stables. Even at a mile's distance from Elliott Bay, Dorothy could smell kelp and clams when the tide was out. Sometimes there was a whistle from a ship in the harbor, but there were no sirens or automobile horns. For Dorothy Stimson, the taste of water in those days was sweeter than it would be for the rest of her life, and blackberries picked on the way home were compensation for time spent indoors at school. Like other little girls, she wore cotton pinafores, solid or checked and subdued in color. Children's shoes were high-topped, either brown or black, and when Dorothy walked to school on board sidewalks, the grass between the planks caught on her shoe buttons. To receive a telephone call—the Stimson's exchange was Main 92—her mother lifted Dorothy up to the speaker while holding onto an earpiece. Ovaltine was her favorite drink, and a really good time was a trip to the soda fountain at the corner of Bellevue and Pine, three blocks away.

Breakfast was at 7:00 A.M. for the seven-member household—C. D., Harriet, the Overton grandparents, Dorothy, and Thomas, as well as cousin Cully, Willard's son, who had come to Seattle from California to learn the lumber business. Dorothy attended the Pacific School, a mile away at Eleventh and James Streets. Every day she ran or walked at least four miles—to school, carrying her books bound by a strap and slung over her shoulder, then home for lunch, and back to school again ("I got a little exercise"). Lunch was served hot and promptly, with all but C. D. present. Dorothy sat next to her mother at the table, "in case a little discipline was needed."

Dorothy's attendance at Pacific School was short-lived. One morning when Dorothy was in third grade, her mother received a kidnap note, demanding that money be put in a post office box or she would never see her daughter again. Frantic with worry, Harriet phoned C. D., who in turn called the police. "The police embarrassed me to death by coming to school and taking me home," Dorothy recalled. "It turned out to be a prank played by a boy at school, Thomas Green, who was not popular because he was mean to animals. He thought it was funny, but I never went to public school again." After the kidnapping incident, Dorothy was tutored at home for a while and later took lessons at the home of another girl in the neighborhood, Carrie Gillespie, who lived on Terry Avenue.

After school there was play with plenty of friends. What her playmates' parents did on the Seattle business and social scene did not interest Dorothy.

There were few toys around; instead she and her friends used "stray things"—a stick or a can—and boys and girls joined together in games of hockey or run-sheep-run. Later, when the streets and sidewalks were paved, roller skating and bicycling became popular.

It was a cozy neighborhood with children in almost every house. Just north and next to the Stimsons lived the Josiah Collins family. Collins, a Southerner who had come west before the Alaska gold rush, had been chief of Seattle's volunteer fire department during the late 1880s, warning the city fathers to no avail that the wooden water mains were inadequate. His two sons, Wetherill and Josiah VI, were not yet born when the Stimsons moved into the neighborhood. Across the street from the Collinses lived the Walkers, whose daughter, Mary, according to Dorothy, "didn't run with the hoi-polloi—she grew up and married a Weyerhaeuser." The Waterhouses were next with four children usually good for a round of marbles or a game of kick-the-can. Then came the Peters family. William A. Peters was C. D.'s attorney and his son, Sid, was Dorothy's playmate. There was also another boyfriend, Harry Hanford, the

Dorothy in costume.

youngest son of federal court judge C. H. Hanford, who lived on the way to school and sometimes carried her books. "But that one wasn't a heavy relationship," Dorothy insisted with mock seriousness at age ninety-five, "Sid Peters was a little heavier." Across Seneca Street to the south lived the Hawkins family with five children and a father who was absent most of the time building the White Pass and Yukon Railroad in Alaska. One of the Hawkins girls, Clarissa, was Dorothy's friend, and the eldest of the three Hawkins boys, Nathan, was an unacknowledged boyfriend. ("He never knew it; I never told him. I just thought I had to be in love and carried his picture around because the other girls carried pictures.")

Beyond Madison Street, only two blocks south, Dorothy had few play-mates, except for Bertie Collins, a witty boy who grew up to write two popular novels, *The Silver Swan* and *Rome Express,* based on life in Seattle. Bertie came from a colorful background. The artist Morris Graves, who knew the Collins family well, described Bertie as "wonderfully honest and amusing." Once he asked a mature Bert Collins what had been the source of his father's money and Bert replied, "whorehouses." Bert's father, John Collins, was an Irish émigré who had begun his checkered career in New England peddling whiskey and later logging; eventually he pursued various activities on Puget Sound, including timber and real estate. An ardent Democrat and fighter for everything from sanitation to education, he was elected Seattle's fourth mayor in 1873; during the same decade, he was also elected to the city council four times. He built the Occidental block downtown, a 200-room structure that included the Occidental Hotel and was said to be the largest building north of San Francisco; it was razed in the great fire of 1889.

One of Dorothy's many playmates on First Hill, Dorothy Terry, would become a friend for life. "Dee" Terry's roots extended more deeply into the Northwest than those of her friend "Stim." Both of Dee Terry's grandfathers were significant to Seattle's early history. Charles Carroll Terry, for whom Seattle's Terry Avenue is named, had been one of the original settlers who landed at Alki Point in November 1851. A bachelor of the Episcopalian faith, Terry married a woman named Mary Russell against the objections of her Catholic parents; the marriage took place on Puget Sound in a canoe furnished by Chief Sealth. Dee Terry's maternal grandfather, Jacob Furth, was the most important influence in the city's financial development at the turn of the century. A Jew born in Bohemia, Furth arrived in Seattle from San Francisco in 1882 with $50,000 and founded the Puget Sound National Bank (later called the Seattle National Bank). An impressive-looking patriarchal figure, he had a long pointed beard and piercing eyes with which he sized up potential borrowers. Using only his own judgment, he loaned money without collateral during Seattle's early days.

Furth courted and married a schoolteacher, Lucy Dunton, herself a pioneer who came west from Indiana by ox cart. The marriage produced three daughters, Anna, Sidonia, and Jane. Jane, the youngest, eventually married Ed Terry, son of Charles Terry. Dorothy described Ed Terry later as "one of those attractive devils who was always just a little bit drunk." Jane Furth married him against her father's objections and they had two daughters, the younger being Dorothy Terry.

The two Dorothys became instant friends when they met. "Dee" was the more socially adept of the duo, while the more thoughtful and solitary "Stim" participated in the fun that resulted. They had much in common; their mothers were friends, having spent hours together hemming diapers in anticipation of their births. Born nineteen days apart, the girls were matched in wit, social class, and interests, sharing a sense of elitism that came from being entitled to the best. Probably most important for Dorothy Stimson was her new friend's easy and accepting nature. Dee's lively and uninhibited disposition lightened and loosened her more serious-minded counterpart—a trait that was welcome amid the rigid social mores at the turn of the century. The two girls devised a string-and-can telephone between houses over which they held long conversations in French. They also shared a love for the sea, taking boat trips together—first as girls aboard C. D.'s yawl, *Olympic,* then in their teens on the *Matsonia* to Hawaii, and later in their seventies aboard Dorothy Bullitt's yacht, *Mike,* when they cruised the inland waters of the United States. Early on the girls' friendship was interrupted when Jane and Ed Terry separated and Jane took her two daughters to live in Europe. The two girls easily renewed their friendship when Dee returned for summer visits. Years later, the two Dorothys were to marry Bullitt brothers and share the same last name.

The regulars of Dorothy's First Hill "gang" consisted of Sid Peters, Bertie Collins, and Nathan Hawkins and his sister, Clarissa. Dorothy loved to reminisce about the hours spent freewheeling around the neighborhood. "With Sid or Bertie or Clarissa I'd jump on ice wagons or lumber wagons and hitch all over the hill. A lumber wagon often had a plank or tailpiece that waved out behind, and you could bounce on it and ride for blocks and then walk home or find another wagon. Ice wagons had a step you could sit on, and we'd ride on it for a few blocks, snagging ice chips on hot days. When we weren't hitching rides, we ran and ran and ran; our legs never gave out. We were all over the hill. I ran loose everywhere with all the freedom in the world and had all the fun that nobody has now. Now children aren't free; they have to be careful all the time." A few years later, Dorothy would switch to hitching rides on streetcars, making sure that she stood on the outer step in order to avoid paying the fare. On one of these forays, she took a streetcar along Capitol Hill to what is now the Cornish School at Roy Street off Broadway—a site that was then dense forest. There she cut two small Christmas trees and brought them home, selling one to Mrs. A. B. Stewart for ten cents.

After-school fun and games continued until Mademoiselle Henault, the stout French governess who doubled as a laundress and chambermaid, came out of the Stimson house and shouted "Dor-tay, Dor-tay," and it was time to wash up and change clothes before dinner. Bedtime was at 8:00 P.M. Dorothy remembered: "My room had a little bed with a partial canopy and an angel sitting on the corner with its legs crossed. Mother would turn out the lights—we had electricity by then—and I'd talk to that angel at night. I needed it there; I was a *hellion.* As a child, I was always afraid of the dark and I still am. I'd tuck the covers around me tight so no one could reach me."

Harriet Stimson, despite her innate composure, was perturbed by the small two-legged tornado who whirled in and out of the house. She scolded her daughter regularly for unladylike behavior and disregard for her appearance. "I always looked like a disaster. My mother, who was always impeccably dressed and groomed, would say, 'It's *summer* now; will you go upstairs and change out of your winter clothes?' I guess I never did go with the styles." These words, uttered with a tinge of remorse even at age ninety-five, reflected Dorothy's life-long regret that she never fully lived up to her mother's expectations. Harriet Stimson was her model, a paragon of proper attire and conduct, and she applied her Victorian standards to her recalcitrant young daughter. In spite of her obvious love for Dorothy, compliments were rare. Punishment was plentiful. "I got *lots* of spankings because I had rung someone's doorbell and run away or because I had lied about something and gotten caught—I was doing a lot of lying in those days—but none of those things really bothered me much."

During the early First Hill years, Dorothy did not distinguish herself as a student. "School was never my forte," she was quick to say. "I got by with somewhat . . . limited capacities." She was more intent on the activities of the neighborhood, her pets, and "reading my own things—not schoolwork." She pored over the tales of James Fenimore Cooper and a set of fairy tales that came in books of various colors.

Dorothy never considered herself to be a tomboy, though others saw her that way. "I was a loner, perfectly happy in my own company," she would reflect on her childhood. Although her social facade was well developed, she was self-contained and sometimes shy—a trait that accompanied her throughout life. Despite a forceful temperament, which by age eight was in full display, she avoided situations in which she might find herself the center of attention. This apparent shyness may have been an outgrowth of Harriet Stimson's insistence on modesty. Or it may have been the discomfort Dorothy felt when under the control of others and having to perform according to certain expectations. More likely, her reserve reflected her anxieties about pleasing two different and demanding parents. As a child, Dorothy never shied from the spotlight when showing horses and winning prize ribbons—as her father had taught her; yet, in the modest style passed on by her mother, she always stated that it was the horse that claimed the attention.

While one parent used the hairbrush, the other softened the blows. C. D. Stimson nurtured his daughter with encouragement at every opportunity. One day, when a boy on horseback galloped down the unpaved street in front of the house, C. D. noticed the look of longing on his daughter's face. He asked if she wanted a pony and when she said yes, he cautioned, "You don't know how to ride."

"But I could learn," she promptly replied. "Father quoted those words to me until the end of his days—whenever something was difficult or I'd hit a snag and complain that things were too difficult, he'd say, 'You told me once you could *learn.*' So he bought me a pony. It had a bridle but no saddle or halter, so I would learn balance. He said, 'Don't just stand there. You have to learn to ride him.' He boosted me up and said, 'Hang onto his mane and grip his sides with your knees.' We started walking and Father shouted, 'Kick him with your heels a little bit.' So I did, and he trotted and I bounced all over the place. Then we went a little faster and he galloped and I fell off. Father picked me up out of the mud and put me on again. The falls weren't bad—it was only a little pony and I fell on soft earth. I don't remember ever getting the least bit hurt. Eventually Father got me a little carved saddle; then he gave me finer and finer horses." He gave her more than horses. Self-reliance and persistence were traits that came naturally to C. D. Stimson, and his daughter inherited them. From his example and counsel, she learned that she could do anything she wanted if she worked hard at it and believed she would succeed. He showered her with presents, but the greatest was the time he spent with her, which gave her confidence, a gift not often received by girls in the 1890s.

Decades after his death, Dorothy Bullitt, never one to indulge in self-congratulation or to accept an easy compliment, would admit, almost shyly, "My father liked me a lot, I think." In fact, her father was probably the one clear and uncomplicated love of her life, and even into her nineties, Dorothy's memories of the times they had shared were still vividly flavored with a puckish sort of delight. Although she voiced obvious love and admiration for her mother, the verbal portraits she painted of her never carried the energy and humor that accompanied stories about her father. She described her mother as "saintly," with few other dimensions, a woman who never did anything for herself alone.

The first pony, Dixie, was soon replaced by a horse that C. D. had seen in a parade. "Doctor" was dark brown with three white-stockinged legs and an "almost human" temperament. He became Dorothy's friend and pride, and her passport to mobility as her childhood world expanded. With pigtails flying, she galloped all over First Hill and Capitol Hill, little more than a faraway forest in those early 1900s. Astride Doctor she watched the workers with rollers as they paved Seattle's streets. Some afternoons she rode across Madison Street to the assay office where she saw men recently arrived from Alaska bringing in gold dust to be weighed. She hitched Doctor to a cart that her father gave her, a trap that seated four. Decorated with carvings, it was quite elegant and, as she drove her mother or her friends around, she felt herself to be the envy of all.

In a stall next to the garage, she groomed Doctor and saw that he was fed.

When a fire gutted the Stimson garage one night, she rushed into the smoke to rescue him. When her nemesis, Thomas Green—the boy who had written the kidnap note at Pacific School—tried to stick pins in her beloved Doctor, Dorothy chased him with her whip and beat the daylights out of him. The boys in the neighborhood, long after they were middle-aged, remembered how she never submitted to their teasing. When piqued, Dorothy brandished her whip and whopped the whole neighborhood. "She buggy-whipped us all," Babe Peters once laughingly told Dorothy's daughter Patsy. When she wasn't taking after the boys, she was teasing the girls. Guen Carkeek Plestcheeff, whose family settled on First Hill years before the Stimsons, remembered one day when Dorothy drove her in the cart "way out to Volunteer Park." Once there, Dorothy threw down her whip and said, "Oh, I've dropped my whip. Get out and get it." When Guen got out to pick it up, Dorothy drove off without her. "She did that kind of thing," Guen Plestcheeff remembered. "Dorothy was a real little tease." And, in her childlike way, a real little powermonger.

Dorothy kept Doctor until she left for finishing school at age sixteen. He was to be the first in a succession of horses that Dorothy rode and showed for awards over the next ten years. Of all her childhood treasures, she always kept the trophy that she and Doctor won at the First Seattle Horse Show in 1906.

She always loved animals, not just horses. "You can talk to them and pour out your troubles and they don't talk back or judge." She even had bears as pets. One day when Dorothy was at home alone, the doorbell rang. It was the foreman of C. D.'s lumber camp, explaining that a tree had fallen on a mother black bear that had just given birth to cubs, and he didn't know what to do with the newborns. Reaching into the pockets of his jacket, he produced the two tiny creatures and held them out to her, one in each hand. "I'm afraid that these two little waifs are going to die. Maybe you can bring them up," he said hopefully. "Here they are." With the approval of her somewhat stunned parents, the bears, named Johnnie and Irish, were kept on the second-floor veranda adjoining Dorothy's room. They had no cage; the porch was enclosed by a railing and cleaned by a brisk hosing. Every day Dorothy fed them and took them downstairs to play or out for a walk. "I'd bring them down into the living room where they'd play around in the fireplace with the andirons," she recalled with a laugh. "Then I'd take them out on the street. They didn't have leashes; they followed me everywhere and when someone came down the street, they'd climb a tree or a pole, and I'd have to wait until they came down." Gradually the sight of Dorothy escorting two bumbling bears around the block became commonplace. As the bears grew larger, however, the play got rougher. When Dorothy returned from school each day, they literally bowled her over with enthusiasm. "When I returned home to feed them, they'd come galloping at me and knock me down," she said laughing. "They licked and pawed at me until my clothes were in ribbons. I was in shreds every day!" The bears were eventually given to the Woodland Park Zoo. Dorothy visited them there a few times, and they would stand on their hind legs when she appeared.

The Stimsons often entertained friends and visiting dignitaries at home. On these occasions, Dorothy liked to sit on the upper stairway in her nightgown, talking to the musicians on the landing or surveying the festive scene below. She watched couples arrive, the ladies in long gowns and the gentlemen in white tie and tails, to greet her parents in the drawing room. The guests were prompt; no cocktails were served. The dinners were long and lavish, after which the men lingered at table or in the den, smoking a cigar and sipping a glass of port, while the women retired to the drawing room for coffee. Harriet planned the menus in detail.

Dorothy paid little attention to the serious conversations of these influential adults, nor did she give much thought to where people's prestige or money came from. "That wasn't of any interest to me when I was little. In fact I wondered why they talked all the time about such *uninteresting* things." Preferring the company of her pals, she remembered swinging on the side porch with Dorothy Terry and Bertie Collins while her parents entertained the Japanese consul. When the cook slipped them some of the champagne ice cream being served for dessert, the trio climbed into the big swing on the porch and lurched about like drunken sailors while Dorothy chanted, "I wonder what the Japanese are up to now." Decades later, whenever she met Bertie Collins at a social function, he greeted her with "Well, I wonder what the Japanese are up to now . . ."

One guest who did make an impression on nine-year-old Dorothy was photographer Edward Curtis, who was in Seattle after completing his monumental photographic work on the Indians of North America. Dorothy remembered him as young, small, and rather handsome. Spellbound, she heard him describe an incident in Alaska when his party was returning on horseback over precipitous terrain. While crossing a narrow footbridge over a gorge, one of the horses stumbled and fell to its death, taking with it all of his photographic plates, which were lost in the water far below. "Father thought his photographs were exceptionally fine and encouraged him to take them East for the backing to publish them. Mr. Curtis said he didn't have money to take them anywhere, so Father gave him money enough to put together a package along with an introduction to J. Pierpont Morgan, the great financier. Mr. Morgan was interested and he backed the enterprise, and Mr. Curtis was always grateful to Father."

Other Stimson friends came for less formal occasions. Nearby, at 1116

Minor Avenue, lived Horace Henry, a construction engineer who surveyed and built the route for the Great Northern Railway through Washington's Cascades to its terminus in Seattle (and who eventually endowed the University of Washington's Henry Gallery). Sporting muttonchop whiskers, Henry had an air of great dignity, leavened occasionally by his wry brand of humor. Confined once for many days to jury duty, which resulted in a hung jury, he was asked why a verdict could not be reached. With a shrug he replied, "They were just eleven of the stubbornest people I ever met in my whole life." His wife, May, also ample in shape and spirit, was an accomplice to some of his pranks. Dorothy remembered one impromptu dinner party at the Henrys' home when Mr. Henry, in process of carving the chicken, pulled a small note out from under one wing. It said, "Go easy on the white meat; there are a lot of people at table." Mrs. Henry was fond of recalling one afternoon when she beckoned from her window to young Dorothy walking home from school. She watched as the youngster, aware that she was wearing a dirty pinafore and would be expected to appear well-groomed for an exchange of cookies and courtesies, quickly removed it and stuffed it in a huge lump into the front of her dress before knocking on the front door.

––––––––

LIFE WAS BRIGHT AND NEW IN A CITY AND A CENTURY THAT were just beginning. With it came a new mode of travel—the automobile. Never one to turn down a challenge, C. D. bought his first car on a Christmas trip to Los Angeles in 1902. He shipped it north—there were no passable roads—and was delighted to own the first gasoline-powered car in Seattle. Called an Autocar, it was bright red with black-and-gold striping and red leather trim. It had no top, seated five passengers, could go twenty-five miles an hour, and cost $1,700. At first there was no one to repair or service the machine, so C. D. proceeded to teach himself how to take apart the engine completely (with one hand) and then reassemble it.

In a short time, the Autocar caused so much commotion and frightened so many horses that the chief of police requested its owner to drive it only after seven in the evening. C. D. complied; he was getting tired of pulling off the road whenever a horse appeared. At night there were fewer people and more open space for exercising the Autocar. With a heavy foot on the brake, he descended First Hill on Pike Street; then drove to Spokane Street—the only "paved" (in reality, well-planked) street in the city—for a short ride, returning home in low gear and at top engine speed. In 1903 C. D. drove to Tacoma and back in one day, an accomplishment that made the newspapers. It was the first of many excursions he undertook, and the famous little red Autocar was the first of many cars he owned, among them, a Packard, a Pierce Arrow, a Simplex, and two Rolls-Royces.

One frequent jaunt was to some land C. D. and his brother Fred had bought on Squak Slough (now known as Sammamish Slough) on the east side of Lake Washington. It consisted mostly of willow trees and low-lying marshland—perfect for hunting ducks. On a dry site, C. D. built a small lodge with bunks for his guests. The Willows, as this lodge was called, was also a destination for informal social events. On Sundays C. D., with family in tow, took the car by ferry from Madison Park to Kirkland, across Lake Washington, and down a rutted road a few miles to the lodge. Usually he found a shady spot en route and stopped the car to clean the spark plugs with a toothbrush and a little gasoline. When Harry Houdini was performing in Seattle, C. D. invited him to The Willows, where the great magician entertained C. D. and his friends for several hours. Houdini received the loudest applause that evening when he asked the group to choose a card from a deck, put it back in, and return the deck to him. After hurried consultation, the businessmen agreed on the ace of spades. When they gave him the cards, Houdini threw the entire deck up to the low, timbered ceiling. All but one of the cards fell to the floor; the ace of spades remained stuck to one of the beams, where it stayed for years.

Fred eventually moved to The Willows and built a substantial year-round home, complete with greenhouses and commercial barns where he raised and bred prize-winning poultry, cows, and swine. In 1919, one of his leghorn hens produced 366 eggs in 365 days, a world record at a time when no other bird in American history had laid more than 300 eggs in a year. Fred also became interested in the quality of milk and, with a physician friend, was instrumental in establishing standards for milk purity statewide. His house, now on the National Register of Historic Homes, is owned today by Chateau Ste. Michelle Vineyards and Winery.

True to form, C. D. gave a car to twelve-year-old Dorothy in 1904. It was a beautiful blue model called a Flanders, with two comfortable seats and a silver interior piped in blue. "Father showed me how to start it with one big yank and warned me that horses had the right of way, so that, in order not to scare them, I'd have to pull over and turn off the engine. I'd take that little Flanders downtown to Frederick & Nelson, and while I was in the store, a crowd would usually gather to admire it."

The Stimsons also took to the Sound. In 1899, C. D. bought a yacht under construction at the foot of Battery Street on Seattle's waterfront. It was a sea-going craft built in the grand style—a seventy-five-foot gaff-rigged yawl that, at

C. D. Stimson and his brother Fred frequently raced their sailboats on Puget Sound. Years later, as chairman of a luxury hotel under construction, C. D. named the hotel after his seventy-five-foot sailboat, the Olympic.

that time, was the largest yacht in the Pacific Northwest. It carried a crew of three—a cook and two sailors—and slept twelve. The mainmast stood over 100 feet tall and carried 1,350 square feet of sail; a main topsail even higher picked up the slightest puff of wind. The boat had two jibs, or foresails, in the bow and a jigger, or small sail, in the stern. Thus equipped, the *Olympic,* as it was called, could handle a variety of conditions. One of C. D.'s favorite Sunday afternoon pastimes was to challenge brother Fred in his seventy-foot ketch *Bonita.* The two large boats became a familiar sight as they heeled over in the wind like giant gulls in tandem, racing side by side on Puget Sound.

Sailing on Puget Sound at the turn of the century was no simple pastime. There were no precise charts, no radio reports to predict weather, no marinas for safe anchorage, no replenishments when food and water supplies got low. If there was no wind and no motor, one could remain becalmed for days at a time. Sailing, like driving, was C. D.'s sort of challenge. "When the boat was finished," Dorothy remembered, "Father invited several friends to go out for a week-long maiden voyage. Mother was getting settled down below and Father was on deck with the sails. The food supply was a jumble below decks and the boat was already rocking vigorously when Mother came to the companionway and said, 'Charlie, we just can't go—the salt is all mixed up with the pepper.' That became a saying in the family whenever things went wrong. When 'the salt was mixed with the pepper,' that meant it was the last straw."

C. D. taught Dorothy to swim during one early voyage. "Father just *dumped* me in," she said proudly, almost a century later. "I had a rope around my waist and he held onto it, leaned over the railing and shouted, 'Now *swim*'—that's how I learned." The fact that she learned in cold deep water was much more exciting than wading out on a sunny beach. As a youngster on board, Dorothy was tethered to the mainmast. Safe, but still mobile, she could move as far as the rails on either side but was usually content to sit still, reading books and occasionally munching on a peach or a cookie brought up by the cook from below. Seated at the base of the mainmast, her child's mind and senses thirsty as a blotter, she absorbed the sea, awash in pleasure as the *Olympic* ventured throughout Puget Sound and north into the San Juan Islands and the inlets of British Columbia.

Best of all were the hours becalmed, when her father whiled away the hours reading from George Vancouver's *Voyage of Discovery* and told her about the early European explorers of the Northwest's inland waters. From him, Dorothy learned the landmarks—where Captain Vancouver had anchored in 1792, the inlets Lieutenant Peter Puget had explored, and all of the places where both had set names on this new and mysterious land. Her favorite story, heard over and over, was about Chief Sealth, a boy about her own age when he saw Vancouver's ship; he had paddled out with his father, Chief Kitsap, to greet it, circling three times to keep evil spirits away.

The *Olympic*'s journeys, which sometimes took several weeks, were made along pristine shorelines with few other humans or boats in sight. If supplies ran low, they looked for smoke from a chimney or listened for the crow of a rooster, signals that people and food were nearby. Then one of the sailors rowed ashore to buy eggs, maybe some chickens, or milk. Sometimes they bought fish or clams from Indians, but usually they caught their own. When the water supply was low, they cleaned up one of the two dinghies, pushed it under a waterfall ("there were more of them then"), filled it with water, and then pumped the fresh water aboard.

Sailing wasn't always smooth. When the wind was high, the huge mainsail had to be lowered quickly. Dorothy remembered more than one stormy crossing of the Strait of Juan de Fuca, with the skipper and sailors struggling on deck to keep the boat from heading out to sea, while she and others below decks fell out of their bunks or stumbled among broken dishes.

The Stimsons invited friends on many of these expeditions. Guests came prepared for any eventuality, weather foul or fair, a day or a week becalmed at sea. They made their own fun, naive and quaint as it now seems. There was little drinking, except for wine at dinner. If the sails were slack, someone brought out cards or checkers; others grabbed a book and retreated to a quiet spot, while the more lively brought out the gramophone for dancing on deck. People paced themselves with no complaint. On one trip, Horace Henry wrote in the *Olympic's* guest book:

> *We've been on the annual cruise,*
> *We've drunk the good commodore's booze,*
> *We've dined at his board*
> *By the grace of The Lord*
> *Better fortune one scarcely could choose.*

The *Olympic's* guest book read like a civic roster of early Seattle. John H. McGraw, Washington's governor from 1893 to 1897, was a guest several times, as was President Theodore Roosevelt during his visit to Seattle in 1903. Families that frequently accompanied the Stimsons were some of Seattle's most influential. They included the James D. Hoges (banking); the E. A. Strouts (insurance), who brought along their son, Win; the Maurice McMickens (law), with their red-headed son, Maurice; and the Charles H. Clarkes (banking), who brought along their son, Caspar. Mr. and Mrs. M. F. Backus (banking) also came along with their son, LeRoy.

One sailing companion who stuck in Dorothy's memory was Marian Engles, a feisty little girl with the self-confidence of an adult. When straight-haired Dorothy beheld Marian's long curly locks, it was hate at first sight. "Whenever I could get my hands on those long curls, I'd pull as hard as I could. Then she'd pull my pigtails and we'd knock each other over. I remember once playing tennis at the country club on Bainbridge Island when Marian took her racket and began to swat butterflies that were fluttering around. I got furious and flew at her and she hit me with her tennis racket and then we drew blood."

In 1909, C. D. sold the boat to a Californian. It was wrecked on a trip down the coast. The *Olympic* did not disappear without leaving a legacy, however. Years later, a hotel was under construction in Seattle, one that promised to be the most luxurious in the Pacific Northwest. C. D., as chairman of the board of the new venture, was one of many to suggest a possible name for the hotel. "Everyone had thought of different names—The Cascades, The Vancouver, The Puget—and a lot of them were being considered. And then one night at dinner, Father laughed and said, 'I know what that hotel should be called—it's perfect and it applies—the same name as my boat. That's it! We'll call it The Olympic Hotel.' And that's the name they took." Today it is the Four Seasons Olympic.

Throughout her youth Dorothy entertained friends aboard her father's sailboat, Olympic. LEFT: *At age seventeen, relaxing onboard;* RIGHT: *at age seven, casting a jealous eye toward Marian Engle's curls;* INSET: *rowing an exploration party ashore (Dorothy is at the oars in the dinghy).*

SEATTLE AROUND THE TURN OF THE CENTURY WAS BOOMING and changing in fundamental ways. City engineer Reginald H. Thomson, a tough, undaunted visionary from Indiana, recognized that if certain basics were not secured for the city, it would lose its dominance in the Northwest. During Thomson's tenure, Seattle streets were paved and lighted, the sewer system was rerouted from Lake Washington to West Point on Puget Sound, a new site for city water was established at the Cedar River watershed, and a hydroelectric power plant adequate to absorb future growth was built. The city's landscape was transformed, literally cut, sculpted, shifted, and shaped; tidelands filled, rivers dredged and widened, and manmade Harbor Island created. Parts of Beacon Hill to the south and Denny Hill to the north were regraded and flattened to make way for a burgeoning business district. And to bring Lake Washington shipping traffic to the sea, work began around 1910 to carve a waterway between Lakes Union and Washington, today's Montlake Cut.

The first decade of the century also saw the acquisition of green spaces that secured the vistas and quiet idyllic settings that Seattle has today. Some areas then outside the city proper, such as Woodland Park and Volunteer Park, were also acquired at that time. To integrate these sections of greenery into the urban landscape, the city park board commissioned the Brookline, Massachusetts, firm of Frederick Law Olmsted, father of American landscape architecture and planner of New York's innovative Central Park, to design a comprehensive park system. Lake Washington Boulevard's gracious curves joining Seward Park to the south and University of Washington's arboretum to the north are among the Olmsteds' legacy to the city.

During these years, the vacant lots of Dorothy Stimson's world on First Hill were becoming landscaped settings for more homes. The streets, once dirt roadways lined with seedling maples, were now paved and shady. By 1906, the "first" First Hill was gone, replaced by a denser neighborhood, noisy with the mixed traffic of autos and horse-drawn carriages. In the fourteen years since the Stimsons first arrived, Seattle's population had soared from 42,000 to 144,000.

The Stimson Mill Company continued to expand. Having won the wars of competition and secured a leading position in the lumber business on the coast, C. D. turned his attention to downtown Seattle real estate. His natural gregariousness, his interests in golf, sailing, and motoring, and his participation in many of the city's clubs and associations brought him in contact with most of the early "movers and shakers" in town. He served as president of the Rainier Club downtown and was a founder and first Commodore of the Seattle Yacht Club. He was appointed a director of the 1909 Alaska-Yukon-Pacific Exposition—a successful world's fair held on the grounds of the University of Washington.

Shortly after it was organized in 1907, C. D. invested in the Metropolitan Building Company. This company was formed to buy the existing lease and develop ten acres of downtown real estate that had been the first site of the University of Washington—a gift of Arthur Denny, Charles Terry, and Judge Edward Lander in 1861. Although the university was relocated to its present site in 1894, it still owned the original land downtown. Called the Metropolitan Tract, it was prime commercial property, extending on both sides of Fourth and Fifth Avenues between Union and Seneca Streets. Over the next twenty years, the investors' group built at least eight office buildings and annexes, plus a theater—the Metropolitan—tucked into the north side of the Olympic Hotel.

The Metropolitan investors regarded their office buildings as symbols of personal status and success. They named the buildings after themselves—the White Building for lumberman Chester White, the Henry Building for engineer Horace Henry; the Cobb Building for lumberman C. H. Cobb, and the Stuart Building for E. A. Stuart, head of Carnation Farms. The twelve-story Stimson Building, named for C. D., opened in 1924 across Fourth Avenue from the Olympic Hotel. Last to be constructed was the Skinner Building, named for D. E. Skinner, another lumberman who went on to develop additional business interests. The original lease, which expired in 1954, has been changed and renewed, as have the buildings—only the Skinner and Cobb Buildings and the Olympic Hotel remain—but the original ten acres and its present buildings still constitute the business hub of the city.

BUT THAT WAS MEN'S WORK, IN THOSE DAYS. EVEN THOUGH she would play a key role in the shaping of modern Seattle, Dorothy was being trained for more social things. Her rough-and-tumble days of backlots and blackberries were now tempered by more "grown-up" requirements. She swapped her checked pinafore for a middy-bloused dress called a Peter Thompson suit and reluctantly passed up games of kick-the-can for sewing lessons. She enjoyed dancing lessons, though. Carrying a small satin bag for her slippers and wearing a "good dress," Dorothy walked to Mr. Frederic Christensen's dance studio at the corner of Madison and Broadway every week. There, she lined up with other girls and boys to learn the two-step and the waltz. Boys were taught how to approach a young lady and ask her to dance, and the girls in turn learned to appear pleased and follow a partner's lead with a modicum of grace. "What else would you do when you grew up if you didn't know how to dance? There were no movies, there was no television, so they danced, for goodness sakes. And they came to our house—the boys would help push back the rug and someone would play the piano and we danced."

Dorothy also took singing lessons in the same building. Sometimes, as she left, she ran into Miss Nellie Cornish, who also had studios in the building. Miss Cornish, later known as "Miss Aunt Nellie" Cornish by her students, was a short, plump dynamo of a woman who founded The Cornish School in 1914. For its few students, she somehow secured as teachers artists who later became well known, among them Mark Tobey, Martha Graham, and John Cage. Although Nellie Cornish had the soul of an artist, she lacked business sense and Cornish's early days were often touch-and-go. Dorothy's mother, who eventually served as chairman of the board of The Cornish School, often came to Miss Cornish's aid. Many decades later, when Dorothy Stimson Bullitt gave to charitable causes, she bypassed Cornish School, saying, "It was done once for Nellie Cornish. I don't feel I have to do much for the school now. Now they have a lot of support."

Dorothy was being prepared for her mother's world of refinement and charitable causes. Harriet Stimson took part in many endeavors during these years. In 1907 she was a founder of the Children's Orthopedic Hospital, served as president of the board for many years and as a board member for the rest of her life. But her deepest passion was music. Though she had taught piano before marriage, she now lived in a city that still offered few opportunities for more refined cultural entertainment. The Seattle Symphony, founded in 1903, brought some classical music to the city, but it could not compete with popular minstrel shows. By 1907 the orchestra and its future were on the brink of ruin, due to a constantly changing corps of twenty-four musicians and a lack of funding and attendance. Broader financial support was needed, and Harriet became a prime mover in the effort. That year she called a meeting in her home to form the Seattle Symphony Orchestra Society. The civic-minded women who attended agreed that they wanted an orchestra that had "never been equaled on the Pacific Coast." They elected Harriet president of the group; Mrs. Horace Hanford, Mrs. A. B. Stewart, and Mrs. John L. Wilson were vice-presidents, Mrs. Sigmund Waterman, secretary, and Mrs. Edwin C. Hughes, treasurer. The William Howard Tafts were visiting not long thereafter and, while the future president of the United States golfed with C. D. and his group, Mrs. Taft lunched at the Stimson home with the Symphony Society and fired more enthusiasm by telling them about the Cincinnati orchestra.

On the night of November 18, 1907, Harriet saw her dream come true. "Mother called her music teacher in the East, Michael Kegrize, and he came out to conduct the first symphony concert. On opening night, the performers had no dress suits to wear, so the committee women borrowed their husbands' dress suits for the musicians and the husbands went to costume companies for something suitable. I remember sitting in the box at the Grand Opera House and seeing the tears run down Mother's face when they played the overture from *Tannhäuser.* She had worked so hard. Father sat beside her and patted her hand and said, 'That's all right, Hattie, now there's music in Seattle.'" The first Seattle Symphony concert featured forty-five musicians and Louise Van Ogle as soloist. The box office took in $1662.00 that night and, after expenses, realized a profit of $281.75.

ANOTHER IMPORTANT EVENT IN YOUNG DOROTHY'S LIFE WAS the arrival of an invaluable member of the household, a young man new in town and looking for work. Fred Ohata—always known simply as Ohata— was described by Dorothy as "one of the most perfect persons I've ever known." Dorothy was fifteen years old when Ohata came to work for the Stimsons. "In Ohata, Father thought he'd found the answer to everything, and he was right. He could do anything with machinery and tools and was meticulous in all he did. Father loved that. Ohata liked me because I was interested in *everything* he did. I watched him work; watched him handle tools and the perfect way he set them down and where he placed them so that they could be reached without cutting oneself." During his long stay with the Stimsons, Ohata taught Dorothy the value of practical work done well. By his example, she came to respect thoroughness and attention to detail. Throughout her life, she admired anyone who was proficient in craftsmanship, no matter what skill was involved. As her grandson Bill Collins described it years later, "She admired industry and dedication of any kind. A slick executive was never on a par in her book with a decent potter or a herdsman in the hills."

Immediately C. D. taught the quiet young man to take apart an automobile engine and bought him the tools he needed for repairs. With his innate skill as a first-rate mechanic, Ohata soon rearranged the steering and shifting to the left side to accommodate C. D.'s missing arm. If there was no suitable tool, he made one; if there was no part, he made that too. He took apart every automobile that C. D. owned. His skill extended beyond the garage to repairing or remaking anything in the house. He was also an excellent driver and soon was chauffeuring Harriet into town for her shopping.

Dorothy was fascinated by the household's new member. "Ohata was so *balanced*," she remembered many years later. "He had perfect manners, yet he could laugh and have fun if the occasion called for it." Even more impressive than his skills was his impeccable character. Quiet and trustworthy, he served as driver, mechanic, and handyman with the utmost discretion and dignity. Ohata's appearance was equally impeccable; photos of him show a slight, well-groomed man who radiated a kind of self-contained elegance. Twenty-six years after he was hired, after the death of C. D., Harriet Stimson asked if he wanted to leave, perhaps to find a better job. Ohata replied no, he did not want a better job; he just wanted to do his job better.

IN 1904 HARRIET STIMSON'S BIRTHDAY PARTY FOR HER TWELVE-year-old daughter may have been the last of Dorothy's childhood celebrations. Attended only by girls, it featured a dance by Dorothy, her cousin Achsah Jane Stimson, and her friend Olive Kerry, and games of pin-the-tail-on-the-donkey. The prize for the largest bubbles in the soap bubble contest was won by Nellie Cornish who, at age 28, was probably there as a guest of Harriet Stimson. Also present was a vivacious youngster, Emma Baillargeon, who ten years later would marry Dorothy's brother Thomas.

In another year or two, an equal number of boys' names appeared on the guest lists. Dorothy's calendar was filled with social events, from milk-and-cookie get-togethers around the piano to more formal occasions for dinner or dancing. "Everybody went with everybody as teenagers. The boys didn't drink anything, even when they were in college. Nobody kissed anybody under any circumstances. You didn't kiss boys good-bye; you just *didn't kiss*. Usually you had one boy you liked better than the rest, but there was no pairing off. Everybody laughed and had fun though, and if one of the group was depressed because of grades or something, everybody would cheer that person up."

By this time, Dorothy was known for driving "anywhere there was a road." With Win Strout, Clarissa Hawkins, and Jim Haight, she drove to Tacoma and back, the girls wearing long-skirted suits and veils over hats and faces to keep out the dust. It was a slow trip that included three flat tires on the way. On July 4, 1906, the same foursome made an overnight trip to Olympia, a jaunt that included rain, several tire changes, picnics, and a visit with friends at Priest's Point. The new-found mobility was a tonic for Dorothy, who later won the distinction of being the first woman to drive an automobile to Portland.

Dorothy Terry was always good for a fling or two when she was in town. "Dee and I would borrow her Aunt Sidonia's car. It was an electric car that had no top and steered with a rudderlike handle. We'd drive downtown to Stokes Ice Cream Parlor where you could get wonderful homemade vanilla ice cream with little black bits of vanilla beans in it. Down there we'd call a friend—usually Bert Collins—and he'd come running down on his own two feet and join us. We each paid for our own sodas—10 cents—and they were the best ever made. Bert never reached into his pockets; he'd joke about Dee's grandfather Furth owning a bank and my father owning timber and real estate and that 'you'd think that these two girls would be full of funds.' But no such luck—he'd have to pay his own way."

Dorothy took many drives with her father, who loved to propose an automobile ride on sunny mornings. "This started when I was a young girl and continued even after I was married. We'd spend the day driving around the countryside, following new dirt roads. Then we'd find a spot somewhere and have a couple of apples, some cheese, and bread that he had brought along. All the while, we'd talk, or rather Father would talk, about real estate and other business—which went right past me." It did not go past her. On these trips, C. D. Stimson taught his daughter the strategies of earning and keeping every penny and the value of patience in negotiations. Years later, thinking back on her long business career, Dorothy admitted, "Maybe I paid more attention than I knew because so many times years later when I wanted to do something that looked impossible or I had a hard problem, I'd think, 'Well now, how am I going to solve this? What would *Father* do?' He'd always say, 'Well, if you want it, go after it.' So I'd get up off my desk chair and go downtown and talk to someone."

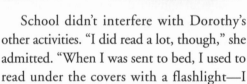

The Stimson family's pilgrimages by auto to California at the turn of the century were an odd blend of hardship and luxury. TOP LEFT: *Lunching at the side of the road;* ABOVE: *digging the car out of knee-deep gumbo;* LOWER LEFT: *departing from the Green Hotel in Pasadena (Dorothy is standing).*

School didn't interfere with Dorothy's other activities. "I did read a lot, though," she admitted. "When I was sent to bed, I used to read under the covers with a flashlight—I could never read enough." At the Washington Preparatory School, conducted by Miss Julia C. Mann from a three-story frame house at 1200 Harvard Avenue, Dorothy received a full complement of college preparatory subjects that leaned heavily to the classics—Latin, German, ancient history, and the major works of world literature. Dorothy didn't find her studies "overly inspiring." School pranks were far more memorable—throwing spitballs or dropping books in unison during study period.

———

DOROTHY GRADUATED FROM WASHINGTON PREPARATORY SCHOOL in 1908. Among the "Class of Naughty-Eight," as they called themselves, Dorothy Stimson was voted Most Popular. Shortly before graduation, she left with her family on an auto trip to California. Auto trips to California were expeditions that included an odd blend of hardship and luxury. The primitive route was almost impassable in places, many times no more than a series of meandering dirt roads that rose and fell from mountain passes. There were few gasoline stations and no roadside restaurants or rest stops; passengers had to be prepared to push, pull, and repair, to put on chains in knee-deep mud and change tires on rutted mountain passes with people few and far between. Yet the stayovers on these adventurous trips were luxurious lodgings, like the Del Monte Lodge in Monterey, the Potter Hotel in Santa Barbara, or the Hotel Del Coronado in San Diego.

During that trip in the winter of 1908, Dorothy's diary reveals a somewhat depressed sixteen-year-old, beset by physical ailments—rheumatism, frequent headaches, and trouble with her eyes—and a difficult relationship with her mother. Dorothy described herself as run down, homesick for her friend Clarissa in Seattle, and anxious about her future after graduation. Unable to communicate with her mother, she found comfort in the company of the Stewarts' daughter Alma. "Had the blues. Awfully lonesome future," she wrote one day. "I got a getting after from Mother," she noted glumly at the Del Monte Lodge. "But Alma heard me, saw me, was dear to me."

Dorothy was concerned about boarding school in the fall. It was custom in those days for the well-bred rich to go East to school. Clarissa Hawkins was bound for Miss Baldwin's school in Bryn Mawr; her brother Mason was already at St. Luke's in Wayne, Pennsylvania, along with Win Strout; Marjorie Kittinger was attending the National Cathedral School in Washington, D.C.; Bertie Collins was at Harvard; Henry Colver, Harry Heilbron, and George Gund at Yale. After much discussion—and in spite of their wish to keep her at home—the Stimsons finally agreed that Dorothy would attend Briarcliff Manor, a finishing school for girls in Westchester County, New York.

Before heading East, Dorothy competed in Seattle's third annual Horse Show. What had begun two years before as a relatively modest event for a few enthusiasts (when Dorothy had won a First Prize on Doctor) had become a festival attended by all of Seattle's elite. Due to the work of flamboyant and wealthy entrepreneur Harry W. Treat, the Horse Show was now the social event of the year. Store windows displayed silver trophies and rosettes and depicted horse-dominated scenes. Horse show hats, horse show wraps, even horse show furs and gowns were sold especially for the occasion. On opening night, the Western Washington Fairgrounds on Madison Street were sumptuously decorated with flags, bunting, and flowers hung from the entrance to boxes and grandstands.

In their boxes, the Treats, Struves, Henrys, Stewarts, the Joshua Greens, the Fred Stimsons, and C. D. and Harriet Stimson entertained while watching relatives and friends perform. Harry Treat opened the ceremonies riding a road coach pulled by four high-stepping thoroughbreds. From the C. D. Stimsons' box, Dorothy Terry watched her friend "Stim" compete on a new copper-colored harness horse, Blaze O'Glory, that her father had bought from Harry Treat.

Another important family event in 1908 was the founding of The Highlands. C. D. had become an avid golfer, playing daily as part of a three-some, well known in Seattle because of their first initials: A. B. Stewart, C. D. Stimson, and E. F. Blaine. This trio and others became dissatisfied with the paltry nine holes at the Seattle Golf Club in Laurelhurst. In 1907 a committee headed by C. D. set out to explore any wild tracts near the Sound between Richmond Beach to the north and Three Tree Point to the south. They sought a location near water so that they might also establish a yacht club. On horse-back and on foot, the men stumbled and thrashed through miles of salal, net-tles, alders, and firs in search of their own promised land. Finally they came across 340 acres of forest overlooking Puget Sound, about three miles north of the Seattle city limits. The parcel was so heavily wooded that the committee members at first could not visualize the ground contours and feared that it was too flat to make an interesting golf course. But C. D., an expert at seeing right through forests, knew otherwise.

The group's goal was to build an eighteen-hole golf course, a clubhouse, and individual residences along the bluff bordering the Sound. The original twelve investors were a congenial mix of prominent businessmen, among them C. D.'s brother Fred, Harry Treat, George Kittinger, Horace Henry, and Frederic K. Struve. All shared a desire for more privacy, safety, good health, and good sport as Seattle's streets became more numerous and crowded. Within the next ten years, more like-minded investors joined: attorney Edwin C. Hughes, department store owner D. E. Frederick, entrepreneur William Boeing, banker M. F. Backus, and additional Stimsons—Cully Stimson, Thomas Stimson, and A. S. Downey, who was related to Emma Baillargeon Stimson, Dorothy's future sister-in-law.

At a meeting at the Stimson house on Minor Avenue in 1908, the group decided to call their new venture The Highlands. Its owners wanted the best that money and planning could provide in skill, craftsmanship, and materials. For the layout of the roads, residence tracts, and park areas, they hired the firm of Frederick Law Olmsted, America's premier landscape architects. The Olmsted brothers worked their magic in The Highlands. They sited each house with privacy, view, and sunlight in mind. Without lessening the rich effect of the forest, they softened its edges with bulbs and native plants. Narrow winding roads lent the overall effect of a scene from some enchanted fairyland.

When it came time to select the house tracts, the members drew numbers out of a hat. Judge Thomas Burke, an influential lawyer who fought tirelessly to establish Seattle as the terminus for both the Northern Pacific and Great North-ern railroads, drew the first choice. "Father got number seven or something,"

Dorothy recalled. "The judge was very fond of Father and Father liked him very much. Anyway, he said, 'Look, you've got a family. You could build here and you would love it. I have no family and I don't play golf. I just like to be with these friends. I'll trade places with you.' Of course, Father agreed and Judge Burke took one of the inside parcels. There was no money exchanged—they were good friends. Judge Burke never did build. The piece he swapped to Father was quite large, about sixteen acres, and it was the *prime* location in The Highlands. When you looked out, there was a sweeping view of the Sound and the Olympics and to the side there was forest. It was very, very beautiful."

The Olmsteds laid out more than a dozen estates over the next few years, one of which was C. D.'s Norcliffe. Today The Highlands is an exclusive, independent, and self-governing entity, with new members accepted only by committee approval. Its own water supply and roads are maintained by a superintendent, its forests monitored by a tree committee, and its gates tended by guards. To the original golf course and clubhouse were added a chapel, school, playground, tennis court, and pool. It remains today an ultimate sanctuary for the privileged and one of the most desirable residence clubs in the United States. Soon the Stimsons, with C. D. as president for the first ten years, would take up residence in The Highlands.

––––––––

THE FIRST LEG OF DOROTHY'S THREE-YEAR SOJOURN EAST TO Briarcliff Manor began as the sixteen-year-old joined other Seattle students on the long train trip to New York. Calling each other "buckaroo," they laughed that they would appear as a bunch of cowboys who had temporarily left the Wild West to experience the refinement of an Eastern school. She was quickly introduced to the customs and rituals of a boarding school that expected proper conduct and hard work from the well-dressed and mannered young ladies whose parents paid $1,100 yearly to send them there. Once past Briarcliff's giant front doors, she entered a world emanating stability and permanence. The school was under the firm command of a Mrs. Mary Dow, who had founded it in 1903. Stiff of spine and ample in form, this middle-aged martinet reigned with strict attention to what she called "customs," not rules. The curriculum offered a full complement of courses in English, French, Latin, history, and science, with heavy emphasis on music and the history of art. There was also a course called "Fancy Dancing and Deportment," in which students learned to curtsy, sit, and stand properly, play hostess, come and go at formal teas, dance the minuet, and manage a long gown with a train. Dorothy avoided that course, exclaiming to her mother, "Wouldn't you give half a farm to see them all!"

The pudgy girl from Seattle with straight dark hair and bands on her teeth was regarded at first as a bit of a barbarian. She relied upon the example her mother had set of propriety and solid good sense to make herself "passable." She arrived properly coiffed, her long hair pinned up in a soft bun and attired in the Gibson girl fashion of the day. After years of French governesses, her French came in handy. Otherwise she appeared artless and unsophisticated—a "naive" from the wilds who mispronounced words and lacked culture. Hearing her accent with its flat As and hard Rs, the Briarcliff girls were amused, most of them coming from a world where one ate "scahlops" and "tomahtos." Once they picked up a waste basket and asked Dorothy what it was. When she replied, "a basket" with a flat A, they lapsed into convulsive giggles. Dorothy concealed her mortification and quickly learned to soften her Rs, add a French accent or an occasional British usage, and tighten up careless nasal sounds. Expert became "expeht," partner was "pahtneh," and vase, of course, "vahse." Salmon ("saumon"), blouse ("bloose"), and baby ("bébé") all received a French accent; room and roof became a more Anglicized "rum" and "ruff." Mrs. Dow carried out this "custom" mercilessly; correct speech was the mark of a lady, as was proper posture, standing, or sitting. For Dorothy, these habits would last a lifetime.

A series of roommates ensued over the three-year stay. A favorite roommate was Marjory Stearns, a petite dark-haired beauty from Chicago, known as "Shrimp." A renowned flirt, Marjory was usually engaged to be married or thinking about it. Another roommate, Caroline Rulon-Miller, was so untidy and determined to keep fresh air out of their stuffy room that the two nearly came to blows. Bertie Collins, her childhood friend from First Hill, encouraged Dorothy to stand her ground on this one. "I bet you could lick her in a good old scrap," he wrote. "One of those upper cuts you used to try on me when we stuck pins in Doctor."

Dorothy did not particularly excel at her studies, although some teachers inspired her, and she remembered them and details from their courses all her life. Nor was she interested in sports, except horseback riding. In one tennis tournament, she wrote home that she was "put out in the first round and literally wiped off the face of the earth." She trained for track, but only to keep her weight down. Among her svelte-figured classmates, she was self-conscious. In one letter home, anticipating a trip to New York, she worried that she was growing so "portly" that it would take a flatbed car to get her there. When she complained to Bert Collins about her weight, he was merciless with wisecracks only an old friend could deliver. Complaining that he hadn't heard from her, Bertie theorized that she had evaporated entirely, "just like Niobe, into salt tears or something, though little 'Stimobe' would make quite a substantial young pond, don't you think?"

Dorothy frequently visited New York City during her Briarcliff years. Accompanied by a chaperone, the girls shopped and attended operas and plays. The love of music that her mother had cultivated began to bloom for Dorothy on these trips, and she not only attended operas but took up voice lessons as well. The New York forays accentuated her anxiety about fashion, however, especially since she was traveling in the company of fashion-conscious young women. Without her mother's advice and taste, she wrote home constantly for suggestions. Prudish and penurious, she refused to buy a mid-calf skirt and accounted for every penny ("lost under the bureau—one cent") in letters home. As for fashion, she eventually stuck to classic suits which, as she grew older, became threadbare and frumpy. Guen Carkeek, later Plestcheeff, a childhood friend from First Hill who had spent many shopping seasons in Paris, once chuckled about Dorothy, exclaiming, "Why, my *dear*, in 1988 she was wearing *jabots*, can you imagine? Why that was the fashion in 1917!"

The years at Briarcliff were crammed with the classics, scoured with decorum, enlivened by parties, proms, football games, and riding, and by summer trips to Seattle and winter jaunts to New York. Three years later, Dorothy returned home poised and polished, having been honored as the student most representative of Briarcliff's principles.

RETURNING HOME IN 1911, DOROTHY FOUND A CITY IN THE throes of a building boom. The Metropolitan Building Company had begun construction of the first of many office buildings, this one topped by an eighteen-story skyscraper being built by financier J. D. Hoge. The retail shopping area had shifted some blocks north of the new commercial district. D. E. Frederick had created a block-wide new department store at Fifth and Pine—a move many had thought was too far from "downtown"—and another store, the Bon Marché, rose a block away. With a population of 250,000, the city now sprawled west to Ballard, north as far as Green Lake and the University of Washington, and south as far as what is now Renton. Apartment buildings rose on the flanks of First Hill, Queen Anne, and Capitol Hill; small tract neighborhoods in Fremont, Ballard, and Wallingford were connected to the city by streetcar. The well-to-do took up residence on shady streets around Volunteer Park, west Queen Anne Hill, and along the ridges above Lake Washington. But Seattle's most exclusive residential area was The Highlands.

Many of the old gang were home from college. Win Strout, Henry Colver, and Harry Heilbron graduated from Yale, and a more sophisticated Bert Collins was home from Harvard, though said to have been spoiled for Seattle. Dorothy, at age nineteen, free from books and schedules and at home among her friends, was relaxed and eager to enjoy life. She was pretty when she dropped the severe, formal look that she sometimes wore. When she smiled, her blue eyes sparkled. She was more confident in her home territory. There was time now to flirt and many young men to practice on. Her flirting became an art—a delicate mixture of light banter, self-deprecating humor, and a blue-eyed gaze that could be either shy or disarmingly direct.

One of the new men that Dorothy met about this time was Conrad Westervelt, a career naval officer destined to play a key role in the development of the Pacific Northwest. An engineer, "Westy" was Superintendent of Construction at the shipyards in Bremerton. He had attended the U.S. Naval Academy at Annapolis and was disciplined, intelligent, high-minded, and patriotic. He was also determined, as evidenced by the firm set of his jaw, the solid stance of his short stocky frame, and by the relentless manner in which he pursued Dorothy Stimson.

They met at an October wedding. ("Weddings are bad places to meet because everybody's in the mood.") Adamant in his attentions, Westervelt tried every weapon in his arsenal to monopolize Dorothy's social life. He lavished her with gifts, prescribed books like medicine, penned love poems, and even composed a complete comic opera entitled *The Festive Fillelooloo*, which he dedicated to her. She enjoyed his talk about every subject, since lively conversation always captivated her, even if she didn't consider herself an able participant. "I was empty in a lot of areas," she remembered many years later. "Oh, I knew horses and a little bit about music and languages, but I only skimmed information off the top."

Her parents were not enthusiastic about this relationship. "Father never said anything," Dorothy remembered, "but I could tell he didn't like him." Of more practical importance was the fact that Dorothy herself didn't like him—at least in the way he wished. "He had everything, but there was only one thing wrong," she once said. "I wasn't in love with him."

If Westervelt failed in his attentions to Dorothy Stimson, he was quite successful in other areas. Soon after his arrival in Seattle, he met wealthy entrepreneur Bill Boeing. As their friendship developed over lunches at the University Club and card games on Boeing's yacht, the two men found they shared many interests. Both were bachelors, impersonal and conservative in nature, intensely patriotic, and avidly interested in the new field of aviation. The marvels of flight had captivated both men—Westervelt as a student at Annapolis and Boeing when he attended the first air show in the United States in Los Angeles. Over cognac and cards, they discussed the possibilities. In its fledgling stages, with the only manufacturing plant of any note run by Glenn Martin in Los Angeles, aviation was then a profession without purpose, pursued only by barnstormers who flitted aimlessly from place to place. With the advent of World War I, however, aviation found its place in history. The two men took flying lessons and founded an aviation club—the Pacific Northwest Aero Club—a sort of yacht club for the skies. Eventually, with Boeing's pocketbook and Westervelt's technical know-how, the two formed a partnership; Boeing was the stickler for quality and detail and Westervelt the creative spring with an expansive conceptual view. In 1915 Boeing purchased a Martin open-cockpit biplane on floats, and Westervelt, applying engineering standards from the Navy not yet used in aviation, improved on the design. That year they built and made the first flights in two of what they called the B & W planes, the forebears of all Boeing aircraft.

Another suitor was George Gund, a tall, handsome Yale man who came to Seattle to visit his wealthy aunt, Mrs. A. H. Anderson. "George was fun, but I really didn't want to marry him. I remember he said, 'You marry me and we'll be *very* rich.' Well, that didn't mean anything to me because as far as I knew I'd always been rich. I didn't really know what money was, except that Papa always paid. If I wanted a horse, I had a horse. Anyway, George did become *quite* rich. He became the man who took the caffeine out of coffee—president of the Sanka Corporation."

———

C. D., CAUGHT UP IN REAL ESTATE, THE MILL, GOLF, HUNTING, and an active social schedule, still found time to pursue his automania in 1912. Shipping two Packard cars by train to Chicago, he took the family on a tour of the East Coast from Washington, D.C., to New England. They returned to New York where Dorothy, her mother, and Thomas boarded the west-bound train, along with the larger Packard, while C. D. and the faithful Ohata drove cross-country in the other. In 1912 this was no small adventure: there was no highway system, only a haphazard maze of washed-out wagon and cattle trails, rutted and dusty or choked with mud. Only a few autos had completed this New York-to-Seattle trip—in a "race" for the Guggenheim Trophy undertaken to publicize the Alaska-Yukon-Pacific Exposition in 1909. The roughest segment of the journey was west of Laramie, Wyoming. For nine days, the travelers sloughed through some of the muddiest terrain imaginable. Hip-deep in "gumbo," they repeatedly had to be pulled out by a team of horses. They ran into snow and they ran out of road. As the landscape grew grander, cities with hotels grew fewer. They drove until they were exhausted and slept in haymows. Unable to cross Snoqualmie Pass because the "road" was unrecognizable, and unsuccessful in finding passage on the north bank of the Columbia River, C. D. was forced to ship the car from The Dalles to Portland. On the afternoon of June 23, the bronzed and weary travelers, looking, in C. D.'s words, as if "they had been going some," reached Seattle. They drove over 3,997 miles in seventeen and a half traveling days with twelve punctured tires along the way. They beat the Guggenheim Trophy record holders by four and a half days.

———

PERHAPS TO ENCOURAGE HIS DAUGHTER TO STAY IN SEATTLE— or just to make her happy—C. D. indulged Dorothy's passion for horses by buying her a new one. Jester stood like a statue and obeyed commands instantly. On Jester, Dorothy learned to exercise the control necessary to perform perfectly in ring competitions, and she practiced hour after hour over the next two years. Now a sophisticated equestrian, she began to enter and win competitions in Portland, Vancouver, and Victoria. She also began to train a team of four dark chestnuts for rig competitions. Prancing in tandem or galloping four abreast, the chestnuts and the girl driving them were a wild sight as they thundered around The Highlands.

But the relaxed life at home, the attentive young men, and the glamorous competitions in horse shows didn't hold. Even though she came quite easily by her father's ability to enjoy life, Dorothy had also inherited her mother's sense of purpose. She needed more direction. Restless, she took a trip to California to visit relatives and friends, but returned to Seattle with no new resolutions, except the awareness that now, due largely to the years at Briarcliff, her tastes were more sophisticated. She was also more lonely. She missed the energy of the East Coast—the bright exchanges with teachers and friends, the stimulation of New York. The West, for all its beauty, was not providing these things. Finishing school had not done its job. She wasn't finished, she wanted more— more culture, more voice training, and above all, more independence. She sought out an old Seattle friend, Florence Williams, a steady ally and confidante since childhood. Tall in stature and practical in nature, Florence had an almost maternal relationship with Dorothy. She shared with her a great love of music and, though socially very popular, also longed for more than Seattle offered. Above all, Florence was a favorite of Harriet Stimson. If Florence was with her, her mother would approve. Dorothy had also been corresponding with her old roommate, the petite and petulant Marjory Stearns, who, bored with life in Grosse Point Farms, no longer engaged, and anxious to escape her domineering mother, wanted to seek a career in ballet. She was eager to join the other two in New York.

And so it was arranged, approved, and activated. The flirtation with New York, begun during Briarcliff days, was to blossom into romance.

Three of us got together and we cooked up our own course of studies. It was a great education, but it wasn't a standard one. In those days, young girls living alone in the city just wasn't done.

4 LOOSE IN THE WILDS
1913–1915

"STIMMIE! JUST THINK. INDEPENDENCE!" WROTE MARJORY STEARNS, in anticipation of the girls' move to New York. Through her theater connections, Marjory had located an apartment at the National Arts Club at 15 Gramercy Park. The location passed parental scrutiny, and permission was given to go. Full of hopes and plans, Dorothy and Florence hurriedly packed their trunks in anticipation of New York in all of its sophisticated glory. "I know I won't ever regret this trip," Dorothy confided to her diary. "It is the best thing for me for a hundred reasons."

The two girls arrived in September 1913. On their first day, they hired a hansom cab and rode up Fifth Avenue and Broadway, taking in the familiar sights and smells of the city. Marjory Stearns joined them a few days later, accompanied by her doting mother. When Marjory showed them the apartment she had found, the two more conservative roommates were relieved to see that their flamboyant counterpart had chosen suitable lodgings. The National Arts Club was a reconstructed mansion on East Nineteenth Street, conveniently located half a block from a Madison Avenue streetcar. Towering twelve stories, it stood on a corner bordering Gramercy Park, an aristocratic old neighborhood, where trees cushioned city sounds and a church across the way tolled on quiet Sunday mornings. The club's membership included persons interested in the "literary, musical, architectural, dramatic, and graphic arts, as well as painting and sculpture," and honorary officers on its board included Theodore Roosevelt, Woodrow Wilson, George Foster Peabody, Louis C. Tiffany, and Henry C. Frick. Western artists—Edward Curtis, Robert Service, and Frederic Remington—stayed there when they were in town, and foreign poets—Masefield, Tagore, Yeats, and Noyes—were entertained at receptions. It was a center for all artistic occasions, the home of the National Society of Craftsmen, and the monthly meeting place for the Poetry Society of America. Two dining rooms provided meals or delivered room service when members in the building did not wish to cook. With its comfortable and cultured ambiance, it was just the sort of "digs" that the girls wanted.

Dorothy pronounced the apartment "a wonder." Located on the third-floor corner, it had two bedrooms and a small sitting room that was immediately consumed by a rented Steinway baby grand. Rent was $85 a month. They planned to eat most of their meals downstairs or at Maillards, a nearby restaurant popular for its lunches and desserts. Years later, Dorothy claimed that during those New York days she had never had so much mulligatawny soup in her life. The early bedazzlement with the surroundings was to tarnish within a few months, however. By the next spring the girls were calling Apartment 31M "Dirty-One M," and Dorothy would comment that "everyone says that New York is famous for its dirt, but our rooms are the worst in all the city, I'm sure."

Harriet Stimson was skeptical about the "artsy" ambiance. "I've noticed one thing," she wrote, having received the club brochure, "that in your list of names of patrons of the club there were no women." She fretted that "the presence of a predominating number of men would make it rather more Bohemian." Dorothy immediately rejected her mother's impression. "To begin with," she explained in a hastily written letter, "there is not a man on our floor. All the apartments are owned by women. There is a nice old lady in the apartment next to us whose daughter is studying music abroad and is about our age, I should imagine. Mrs. Stewart lives just down the hall and her maid or housekeeper, or whatever she is, brings us gingerbread and cakes when she cooks them, and that is as 'Bohemian' as we have gotten."

A daily schedule soon evolved. After a quick breakfast, the girls parted ways, Dorothy and Florence to search for a singing teacher and Marjory to head uptown for ballet classes. At her mother's insistence, Marjory had taken the second bedroom for herself, because she expected to be very tired every night and could rest better if she were *alone*.

Dorothy and Florence soon scheduled a singing instructor named Nicholas Brady. A bespectacled bachelor who lived with his parents, he was only half the size of the young women, but they respected him immediately. "He told us in a minute what was wrong," Dorothy wrote. The girls agreed to take three lessons a week at five dollars each, absorbing more by listening to each other's lessons. "Mr. Brady is awfully strict," Dorothy complained within a few weeks. "He can fill a half an hour the fullest of anyone I've ever seen." Yet within a month she did not mind the sound of her voice.

Next, they found a German teacher, Ludwig Wielich ("very foreign-looking with flowing mustaches"), a descendant of a fine Viennese family, who had formerly been a writer for *The Musical Courier* and was now a teacher of French, Italian, and German. The cultured and well-educated Wielich had numerous contacts in the music world; he published a new monthly review called *The Opera Magazine*.

Florence and Dorothy set up a schedule of daily practice of scales and vocal exercises, German grammar, and conversation. Three times daily for fifteen minutes, they closed all doors and windows and made "the most unholy noises you ever heard singing." At night, accompanied by Marjory at the piano, they "raised the dead" in a "regular debauch" of songs. "We have music morning, noon, and night," Dorothy wrote home. "No one is in the apartment next to us, so we don't worry about disturbing people when we close the windows."

Some evenings the trio went out on the town. They opened an account at a nearby stable and took evening drives around the city, tucked into a little coupe with a horse and a liveried driver. They used this transportation to go to the theater as well, which they did often. Dorothy and Florence attended opera, plays, concerts, and recitals several afternoons and nights a week. Equipped with their librettos and opera glasses, the young women absorbed all of the splendor of grand opera. These were the times of Caruso, Scotti, Amato, and other great Italian singers. "I saw *every* opera that was produced in New York in those seasons, some of them twice," she recalled years later. "I heard Caruso in every role he was in, also Amato and some of the great bassos. I heard Melba who was from Melbourne and Calvé who was a great Carmen. Sembrich was another great one—a concert singer. I went to her farewell concert, and people wouldn't leave when it was over. When she finished, people crowded out of their seats onto the stage and beat the stage with their umbrellas, shouting, 'One More Song! One More Song!' and she came back and back. But it was the Italians who were the greatest—they have something that just doesn't *care*. They just open up and it comes out."

Acquiring tickets was tough, however. For the gala opening night of the opera season at the Met, Enrico Caruso and Geraldine Farrar were scheduled to appear in Massenet's *Manon*, conducted by Toscanini. Dorothy got tickets through Max Smith, a friend and Seattle transplant who was music critic for *The New York Sun*. Eventually, knowing that she could not depend upon the generosity of friends, she devised a better system for procuring tickets. "There was a scalper across the street from the Metropolitan," she reminisced. "He had some awfully good seats at a fairly good price and he said, 'I'll make you a deal. You stand in line at the Metropolitan box office at six o'clock in the morning to buy tickets for me. Get at the very beginning of the line, among the first five people. Then you buy the best seats that have been turned back, bring them back to me, and I'll give you free seats in the Family Circle just under the roof.' It was a cold, chilly business, but I had a pretty good wool coat. We went at least twice a week for two years, usually to Italian and French operas." Once she saw six operas in one week. Sometimes she stood; once she sat on the stage. Usually she and Florence sat in the Family Circle just under the roof, among the "ordinary folk," the first-generation Italians and Germans who, Dorothy contended, were the true aficionados of opera. She enjoyed the unself-conscious warmth and vitality of the Family Circle crowd, and she looked forward to being swept into their worlds as well as into the music itself. "If it was an Italian opera there was the smell of garlic everywhere," she recalled with a low chuckle, "and if it was German there was beer and belching all around us. Being there, in our cheerful little coop under the roof, we felt we were part of it all."

Another device for obtaining free opera tickets was to attend as a critic—her first paid employment. "Herr Wielich, our German teacher, had recently begun publishing *The Opera Magazine,* a very slick publication that appeared monthly for a while. He was lazy enough not to do everything himself but paid me to do it. I'd get free seats to any recital he wanted me to cover—piano or violin—and then I'd write an article. What was I doing writing up somebody's violin concert? Whew! Of course, the magazine eventually failed, but it would with critics like me."

THE CORRESPONDENCE BETWEEN DOROTHY AND HER MOTHER in 1914 and 1915 is full of discussions about music—a mother-daughter duet, critiquing opera, concerts, symphonies, and musicales each had attended. "I never hear anything without thinking of you and wondering what you would think of it," Dorothy wrote. She knew the plots, parts, and performers thoroughly and was not shy about her opinions—at least to her mother. She looked for the perfect operatic combination—a blend of voice and acting, the merging of a glorious vocal passage with the talent to live out the part. About *La Bohème* she wrote: "The production last night was good, I thought, although I don't really like Polacco's conduction. He drowned out the voices several times. The new tenor [Giovanni Martinelli] I liked very much. He has a strong, virile voice with a nice rich quality, but it is not smooth and seems to lack finish. His acting is no better than most of the other Metropolitan singers . . . Scotti, though, was really to me, the star of the whole performance. His voice was in every way more perfect than anyone else's in the cast and his acting was really wonderful . . . I sort of forgot what a consummate artist Scotti was." Caruso, however, remained her lifelong favorite; no one else achieved such a perfect blend of voice and acting style. She stood next to him one Thanksgiving night in the back of the Met during a performance of *Parsifal.* "I was so surprised," she wrote home. "You'd sort of expect to see him in a box or something, but he was with another man and seemed so quiet. He's always acting the clown on the stage, so it's a surprise to see him so serious, almost sad looking off the stage."

Herr Wielich not only entertained the girls with backstage gossip about opera singers, he also showed them around the city. Once he proposed meeting at an Italian restaurant on Mulberry Street, where they enjoyed what Dorothy called "one of the funniest meals I ever poked down in my life!" They began with some "little fishes with Italian olives and sweet peppers." Then came the salami, which looked like sausage but turned out to be donkey meat. The girls had just managed to eat some spaghetti when a friend of Herr Wielich's arrived, the throat specialist at the Metropolitan "who attended every performance backstage with atomizers and throat pastilles." More food followed. "An Italian vegetable, something like our spinach, only a little fresher and done in olive oil—Ugh!" Then they were served an Italian welsh rarebit with dried fish grated on top ("that looked exactly like a caterpillar on the plate. Whew!"). "Oh that awful food!" Dorothy concluded, showing her provincial taste. "I shall gladly welcome a rhubarb pill tonight to get it all out of my system. And all that man talked about during the entire meal was how indigestible American food and cooking was. Well, it may be, but I hope I've had my last *Italian* meal!"

DURING THESE MONTHS, DOROTHY WAS KEPT APPRISED OF developments back home. Her mother reported on her own continual quest for personal betterment, attending lectures several times a week on everything from suffragettes to modern dramatists to German composers. She was interested in the labor unions that were gaining power during 1913, causing financial problems for the Stimson mill. One lecture on the subject prompted this comment: "I am really getting to feel that your father and brother are more nearly right in their attitude toward this question. It is certainly a very serious question and seems to be a very strong factor in ruining business. The logging camp is shut down and the mill only half running. The Laboring Class and the non-property owners have so recklessly voted improvements that the taxes are the highest of any state in the Union and many small property owners have had to lose their land because of this. I do not see what the remedy is to be but hope it will not be too long in coming."

If there were hard times, there were no signs of it in The Highlands. Grand homes were rising among the treed lanes, most of them occupied by C. D.'s close friends—the Fredericks, the Stewarts, and Cully Stimson, the nephew who had lived with the Stimsons early on. In 1913 Thomas wrote Dorothy that Bill Boeing was building in The Highlands and that his home would be a "much more expensive house than ours." Harriet Stimson continued to oversee every stage of construction and landscape design. She relied heavily on a book titled *The House in Good Taste,* saying that the author, Elsie DeWolfe, approached her own idea of what a home should be better than any other decorator. Her letters, full of plans, questions, decisions made, samples of paint, tile, and material, reflect her intensity. "I am so anxious that it should be in good taste," she wrote. "I am sure to make mistakes but hope they will not be irreparable." Harriet rejected anything that hinted at being too popular or overdone. She dismissed Dorothy's choice of material for her own rooms (a bedroom-sitting room suite, complete with fireplace and piano), commenting, "It is sweet but has been too much used here." Harriet monitored the architect's decisions, criticizing him when she "found at Frederick & Nelson many of the same things that he had sent [away] for . . . identically the same in color and design."

Both Stimson children were involved in the project. Thomas predicted that the house would be "attractive but a great deal of trouble." When Harriet decided upon two large rugs for the forty-foot-long living room, Dorothy countered, "I should think that one rug would be so much better. It would bring the whole room together and make a unit of it, and then you wouldn't be stumbling and sliding about between the rugs." True, it would take almost a year to have such a rug made, but "it seems to me that it is worthwhile waiting for everything to get it right, because I think the interior of a house always shows whether or not the furnishings were slowly and carefully selected." Her mother concurred and ordered a carpet from Belgium to be woven in a single piece. The finished product was twenty-four feet wide and thirty-nine feet long and weighed over half a ton; it was at the time the largest rug of its kind ever shipped to the United States. In 1990, after seventy-six years of use, it still graced the living room at Norcliffe in The Highlands.

Tango fever hit Seattle about this time, and Dorothy heard about it in letters from home. A teacher from Chicago arrived to instruct the young and old in techniques of twirls, dips, and glides—the fashionable Treats, the short Judge Burke and his much larger wife, the Josiah Collinses from next door, the Merrills, Struves, and the Joshua Greens all took lessons. "The only real excitement is the tango," Thomas wrote his sister. "Everybody is doing it now, from Mrs. Burke to children five years old." He advised her to take a few lessons before coming home. Harriet wrote Dorothy that at a dinner party at the newly founded and somewhat staid Sunset Club, everyone tangoed from dinner until time to go home. She complained, "There is scarcely a gathering of any sort in which dancing is not introduced in some way, and such a man as Mr. Merrill, who has never danced in any way, is quite crazy about it, will put off business rather than to miss a lesson, and they all get so lame they can hardly walk up and down stairs after lessons." She was particularly critical of a matron named Mrs. Ainsworth. "There is much gossip about Mrs. Ainsworth just now. She seems to have gone mad over the new dances and takes a lesson every day. She goes to every dance and dances the whole evening with such young boys as Henry Weston. Mr. Ainsworth sits and looks on and seems very patient about it. She is quite a schemer and invites a lot of young men to dinner before a ball . . . All the mothers are so indignant that they can hardly speak to her."

As for herself, Harriet added humorlessly, "Someone has started a story that I am taking dancing lessons—but do not believe it, I am not."

––––––––

AT AGE TWENTY-TWO AND LIVING IN NEW YORK, DOROTHY still behaved with her mother's sense of modesty and propriety. "Speaking of 'debauches,' I bought a new suit!" she exclaimed, in a letter home. "Not the customary blue piece of cloth with pockets in the side and buttons to hold it together, but a perfectly respectable wine-colored velvet suit at a perfectly respectable price. Don't know whether you'll like it or not when you see it. Don't know myself whether I'll like it on closer acquaintance, but I got it and it's delivered . . . The next thing will be to find some one that will make a blouse and then to get a hat. Then I'll be all fixed up like a cover of *Vogue,* and you won't know me—perhaps you won't want to." She also ordered a suit in creamy white, which brought to mind her insecurity as marriage material. "Will you tell me why fat people always want to wear white things?" she asked. "I always thought that white satin was so 'bridy' looking, but as long as I'll probably never wear just that kind, I thought I'd have this one that way."

Tensions arose between Dorothy and her roommate, Marjory Stearns, who entertained a constant stream of guests and was, according to Dorothy, a "chatterbox with nothing to say." The young Miss Stimson did not like Marjory's sophisticated mother either, judging her materialistic and social and illiterate. She noticed that Mrs. Stearns often said "darn" and was lax in her standards of behavior. "She certainly lets Marjory do things that I should never think of doing." These "doings" included smoking, drinking, and staying out at cabarets. "I guess I'm getting blasé and 'old maidy,' " Dorothy ruminated primly, "but when I take my exercise I want it in the open air with the horses or at tennis or golf."

The beginning of January 1914 brought Dorothy her first real encouragement from Mr. Brady, the voice teacher. Sore throats often forced her to abstain from lessons and practice. Yet she pursued the singing diligently and, given her powerful will and sense of purpose, must have been discouraged when success was slow in coming. In late spring, Dorothy had another heart-to-heart with her instructor and came away again encouraged. "Mr. Brady feels he has just gotten my voice to the point where he could work with it, that he has just cleared away the underbrush, so to speak," she wrote. "I do hope he hurries up and does something with it before I go home."

Since her arrival in New York, Dorothy had begun to attend church services at an Episcopal church across from Gramercy Park and was even considering baptism and confirmation. Her only interest in religion until this time had been in the music offered, but she found that the minister made things "clearer" than anyone else. She knew that her mother, the most spiritually oriented member of the household, would understand her decision to join the church, but she was fearful that her father and Thomas might think she was getting "overly religious." "Only good can come from it," responded her mother, "and your father feels that it is perfectly all right to follow your own convictions in such a matter, knowing that you have been thoughtful and considerate about it." Thomas grumbled, "I hope you won't look down on your brother who happens to be an atheist." The Reverend Theodore Sedgwick, a prominent Episcopal minister of the day, gave her religious instruction, and Dorothy was baptized and confirmed on March 23, 1914.

In decisions such as this, Dorothy still deferred to her parents' wishes, in spite of the independence she was hoping to find in New York. No cause or interest superseded her love for her parents; no lifestyle as an artist, no career was significant enough to risk displeasing them. Nor did any teacher inspire her otherwise. Unknowingly, Dorothy was held by her parents in the most subtle confinement, a velvet prison walled by love and dependency. Her parents adored her, provided all she needed, and did not encourage her into challenging areas, sensing perhaps that if she developed strong interests outside of the family, they might lose her. In effect they gave her two directives, the first spoken and the second implied: have fun and marry well. When she returned home each year, the familial bonds strengthened; she felt the power of their support and only vaguely sensed the defects of her dependency. She saw in her father's smile the joy of having his "pal" to indulge and cherish, quashing any purposeful goal she might want to set; she noted in her mother's calm voice the implacable social standards and impeccable taste that neutralized any desire she might have to forge a life of her own. The relationship was a closed circle; yet for Dorothy, it was incomplete.

Before Dorothy's departure for Seattle in April 1914, she received her mother's wire that Grandma Overton wanted to give her granddaughter $1,000 for a grand piano to be used in her sitting room at The Highlands. Accompanied by her friend, music critic Max Smith, she went to the Mason & Hamlin showroom, where they decided on a used piano. "It seemed new. I learned that it had been returned by the owner, so I said that I'd like to have it shipped to Seattle. After I had paid the money, the salesman told me that the piano had belonged to Fritz Kreisler," a violinist whose playing she esteemed highly.

On arriving in Seattle, Dorothy was surprised and pleased to learn that Thomas was to be married to Emma Baillargeon in June. It promised to be a happy union between two of the city's most prominent families. The vivacious Emma had been seeing Thomas at social occasions for many years; although he was not an avid devotee of music and art, she liked his quiet manner. Emma was the middle daughter of Joseph A. (J. A.) and Abbie Collins Baillargeon. Emma's mother, Abbie, who died when the children were very small, was from an early Seattle family. (Abbie's father, John Collins, was, by way of his second marriage, the father of Dorothy's childhood chum Bertie Collins.) Emma's father, a merchant, came to Seattle from Quebec by way of Oakland after the gold rush, established a lace store in Pioneer Square, and later built the Baillargeon Building, which still stands at Second Avenue and James Street in the heart of Seattle's business district. "The old man was a strict French Catholic patriarch," Dorothy recollected. "He had a trim pointed white beard like a Prussian general and he had the nerve, or the courage or whatever, to open a lace store. Can you picture a Frenchman who spoke English badly having a lace store in a lumber town at the turn of the century? Handmade French and Italian lace in all of that *mud!* Well, he was very successful—women regarded lace as a sign of gentility in those days. He was also very crusty and scared his children with his strict ways. I sassed him a little in French, and he loved it, and we used to converse together. He was tough with his children. Emma was the only one who could handle him."

Widowed early in marriage, J. A. Baillargeon sent his children to boarding schools back East. Emma attended St. Loretto Abbey in Toronto and later graduated from Trinity College in Washington, D.C. During vacations, she traveled to France, an experience that added to her cultural sophistication. Since 1908, she had lived with her father at 431 Harvard Avenue, where she ran the household and was active in Seattle's social scene. Emma was popular and pretty. At age 28, she had the look of a French gamine, with a charming tilt to her eyes and a gap in her front teeth. From her rich cultural background, she inherited a sophisticated sense of humor and style; from her schooling, she learned the value of discipline and practical solutions to any problem; and from her own birthright, she possessed the eye and the soul of an artist. Although her cultural sense was finely tuned, she also possessed an earthy laugh and a talent for squirting water through the gap in her teeth that one day would send her children into gales of laughter.

Dorothy was enchanted by her future sister-in-law, in spite of their differences. "Emma played the piano beautifully—I did, too, but not as well as she," Dorothy observed. "She was socially a lot better than I was; I never had anything to talk about, but she always had something amusing to say. I remember one evening at The Highlands when Father suggested that we all go for a walk, and Emma said, 'Oh yes, let's—*all* of the bugs will be out!' My friends sailed, played tennis, and did outdoor things, but Emma didn't spend time on that," Dorothy continued. "She was much more artistic in her tastes. We were always very close, despite the fact that her husband and my husband didn't get along too well."

One difficulty with the marriage-to-be was that the Baillargeons were Catholic, and this made the Stimsons, especially C. D., uncomfortable. Thomas's marriage to a French Catholic brought on an animosity that had ignited when C. D.'s sister married a Catholic who took her away from the family. Thomas must surely have loved Emma Baillargeon to defy his father in this manner, and, in time, C. D. became very fond of the charming Emma. The wedding was held in the Baillargeon home on Capitol Hill, with Dorothy in attendance as maid of honor. It was June 24, 1914, four days before the world was shocked to hear of the assassination of the Archduke Franz Joseph at Sarajevo, the incident that set off World War I.

That summer C. D. and Harriet prepared to move to their new home in The Highlands. They swapped the house on Minor Avenue for a prime corner property at Pike and Fifth downtown. C. D. leased this land to the Coliseum Company with an agreement to build and furnish a theater for $265,000; the lease was for twenty-five years, after which the building and furnishings were to revert to him.

At The Highlands, a majestic mission-style home awaited the Stimsons, one resplendent in grandeur as it stood facing northwest, high over Puget Sound. Despite Harriet's reservations, architect Kirtland Cutter had produced what she required—a balance of classic elegance and family livability. Upon her return from New York, Dorothy walked through the rooms with her mother, amazed by the size and style of the place. Norcliffe, as it was called, was entirely graceful,

The Stimsons were among the founding residents of The Highlands, where they built their home, Norcliffe, overlooking Puget Sound.

as feminine with curves and as full of light as the Minor Avenue house had been masculine and Gothic with its dark paneling. Dorothy's daughter Priscilla once described it as "a sexy house." As much as the First Hill house had reflected C. D., Norcliffe personified Harriet Stimson.

Norcliffe was twice as large as the Minor Avenue house: 21,000 square feet with tile, curving roofs, cloister, colonnades, balustrades, arched doors, and windows built around a courtyard. There were a dozen fireplaces and bedrooms, a nursery for the grandchildren-to-be, and a ballroom with stage, dressing rooms, and an adjoining room for supper after dances. Special rooms stored the wine, vegetables, and fruit, and a third floor housed servants and an enormous volume of linens, silver, and clothing. The graceful curves extended to the grounds. From the arched entrance gate, a long drive wound through firs and rhododendrons to a porte cochere and circled in front of a brick courtyard with a formal garden flanked by rows of French doors. Curving paths meandered to the ivy-walled tennis court, to the stables, or, overlaced by madronas, toward the cliff where a small octagonal teahouse surveyed Puget Sound.

The Olmsted brothers' subtle artistry, evident everywhere, respected and enhanced the natural landscape and its vegetation. Great care was taken to preserve the fifty-foot firs and cedars, their towering conical shapes standing in contrast to the red-barked madronas that twisted into dervishlike forms. When Dorothy returned from New York in 1914, the flower garden was beginning to take shape. It filled the courtyard, the center of the circle formed by the entrance drive and the borders of the house. The garden provided color from daffodils in the spring to chrysanthemums in the late fall, with special emphasis on mid-summer flowering of delphiniums, heliotrope, and white lilies reminiscent, according to the plan, "of the most delightful old-world memories of an Old Cottage Garden on some country lane in England."

Norcliffe's stable, which accommodated four horses, a groom, and two carriages, became one of Dorothy's favorite haunts. She took up again the training at competition driving that had begun the previous summer. On sunny afternoons, the quiet of The Highlands' grounds was broken by the heavy thud of hoofbeats as she drove four-in-hand along the fir-lined lanes. Workmen building other homes looked up in surprise to see a young woman in a carriage, riding crop in hand and hair in the wind, drawn by four dark chestnut steeds that thundered along at perfect pace.

During the summer of 1914, war was declared in Europe, but it was months before American lives were affected by it. Social activities still claimed Dorothy's days—tennis with Dee Terry; parties with Harvey Carr and Henry Colver; concerts, theater, and vaudeville with Conrad Westervelt. And another suitor was claiming her time, an older man named Howard Hughes, the son of an eminent lawyer in town and himself an attorney. "One day—it was when the tennis club was on Madison Street—I was called to pass out sandwiches, to assist the ladies. We were all dressed up with parasols and everything, and I was serving nasturtium sandwiches when a call came from Howard. He said, 'I just bought a car, a convertible Model T'—there were very few in town. 'I'm coming by to get you; be out in front and be ready to jump on board, because I don't know how to stop this thing, and if it stops, I don't know how to restart it.' So I left the nasturtium sandwiches and jumped on board when he came by. We drove out north, and as we were crossing the Montlake Bridge, along came the fire department with all the bells going. They were coming up right behind us, and we both jumped out of the car in the middle of the bridge without stopping it and ran to the side and looked the other way until the engines went by. Then we ran after the car, which was still chugging along, and jumped in and went on our way. Whew!"

Like her other suitors, Howard Hughes fell head over heels in love, while Dorothy kept her part of the relationship under control. He wrote her a short note during the summer of 1914:

Hello Dorothy dear, just a line before running to court, to remind you that our date is for tomorrow evening sure. I haven't been able to think of anything but that and I swear that if I don't have that talk with you pretty soon, I might just as well go out of business, because I can't get you out of my head even for a minute.

If you put it off again believe me, the results are on your head. I have been holding it back so long that if I don't get it out pretty soon, I am bound to swell up and bust—"pop" like that. And also I want to call your attention to the fact that I don't carry life insurance yet, so for the love of Mike, have a heart. Yours as always with bushels of you know what,

Howard

The summer went by in a blur of picnics and parties, hours at The Highlands, and evenings with beaux. Before they knew it, Dorothy and Florence boarded the train to New York again for another year of cultural immersion. At the train, admirer Henry Colver gave Dorothy a copy of *Paradise Lost,* which bore the inscription: "As a gentle reminder that you are missing much that we would have tried to give you had you only stayed with us."

This second year in New York, the trio was installed across the street from the Arts Club, at 20 Gramercy Park, where Marjory had reserved a two-bedroom apartment on the second floor of a converted coach house. They admired their quarters, with its brick fireplace and mullioned windows that opened onto a small roof where they could crawl outside on balmy days to dry their long hair in the sun. Dorothy and Florence were wandering through the small rooms when Marjory arrived in style—laden with packages and valises and followed by a maid carrying a Persian kitten. "Three old maids and a cat, isn't the picture complete!" Dorothy wrote to her mother.

New York teemed with sad stories that winter. Dorothy had many encounters with singers, dancers, and artists affected by the war, refugees trying to eke out a living in New York, some teaching foreign languages. "All the artists have come to New York because they thought they could make money here and couldn't in their own countries," she wrote her mother, "and the field was so full here in the first place that it has created a pretty bad state of affairs."

Dorothy stepped up her singing lessons to five a week, reasoning that "if taking a lesson every day won't get *some* results I'm the *darndest blockhead* that ever lived." Practice took place behind closed windows, with levity provided by the Persian cat who sat on the piano strings, pouncing on the black hammers that rose and fell around her. Dorothy soon complained of "dry stupid old vocalizations" and, despite her earlier resolve, wondered if it was worth the trouble.

Conrad Westervelt had sent Dorothy roses each year on the date of their first meeting. In 1914, he enlisted the reluctant help of roommate Florence to provide a surprise matinee party for the three roommates. Seattle's social grapevine soon sent back a story that an engagement was in the offing. When she heard the news, an irate Harriet Stimson wrote her daughter, asking for an explanation about this highly improper situation. In a long letter Dorothy hurried to say that it had all been a complete surprise and that, once she knew about it, she had participated only with great reluctance, planning to tell her mother when she saw her rather than try to explain it all on paper. "I don't expect to see him again," she wrote, hoping that this would assuage her mother's ire. "He said he would be gone when I got back, that he had been there [in Seattle] quite a while and he would find it very easy to be transferred." Claiming that her relationship with Westervelt was practically all over, she reflected, "I know I never should have been so foolish as to let the party go ahead, but I thought that it was the last, and that refusing would mean all sorts of argument and row."

That Westervelt would not take no for an answer was old history. Dorothy once asked him point blank if he thought that the things he did for her would in any way change her mind toward him, and Westy replied that it made no difference. His gifts to her gave him pleasure and that was the only favor he asked. As proof he composed a poem to her:

I'm giving thanks—because her eyes
Not only rhyme but match with skies;
Because her voice is sweet and low,
And Nature's roses come and go
Where other color never lies.

She does not smile on me, I know
And yet she seldom frowns, and so
The less my cause for joy than sighs,
I'm giving thanks.

But most of all that, here below,
To take my meed of wrae and woe,
The Fates have placed me in such wise
And so much kindred made our ties
That her true worth I've come to know,
I'm giving thanks.

The "engagement" episode sparked tension between mother and daughter. Dorothy wrote letters of apology that showed more than a little fear of her mother's disapproval. "There must be something wrong with my reasoner," was one explanation. "I guess if I didn't take the trouble to reason at all, I'd get along better. All of this gossip and these mountains out of molehills, are detestable . . . No one ever talks about my being engaged to Harvey [Carr]," she pouted. "Yet I like him much better than Conrad. He hasn't the mind and isn't as interesting to talk to. If I knew a man with Conrad's intellect, Harvey's disposition, some of Mac Burney's [another beau] nature . . . I might love him—but I don't know anyone that comes anywhere near that description and what's more I don't believe they grow like that. But I never have cared for a man in my life—nor thought I *might* care." She signed off with more apologies and the hope that "perhaps sometime I'll learn to behave so you won't be ashamed of me."

The subsequent lonely holiday season away from family and friends caused Dorothy to question the value of staying in the East. Was all of this work worth missing her family? "If I only *knew* that I *was* gaining something it would make me happier, but I just don't know," she wrote her parents. "When you pay very dearly for a thing it makes such a tremendous difference whether that thing turns out to be good or bad—and I feel that I have paid very dearly for something that is more than likely to turn out badly. I have worked and am working just as hard and as well as I know how and Mr. Brady is doing the same thing, but whether in the end there will be anything to show for it I very much doubt." Her heartsickness was cured when Harriet and Emma arrived to celebrate her birthday on February 5, 1915. The two visitors stayed for two weeks, during which time Harriet met Mr. Brady and heard her daughter sing. She felt confident that "with perseverance and good health" Dorothy could have a beautiful voice. Next, Dee Terry and her mother breezed into New York after a year in Europe and a couple of months in Kentucky. Dorothy had received lively accounts of their European tour from Paris, Geneva, and Florence, as the nomadic Terrys wandered the continent. Dee Terry, slim and sexy at age twenty-three, was surrounded by male admirers wherever she went, keeping her mother busy monitoring her romances. With each new city and each new face, the Terrys' social network grew, woven with charm, connections, and enthusiasm. After Europe, the active life in Louisville was no problem for a professional partygoer like Dee Terry, but she conceded in a letter to Dorothy that her "Stimmy Darling" would be bored to death. "People here are delightful to strangers and visiting . . . has kept me busy." She enjoyed Southern hospitality and Southern men. "Just between you and me and the lamppost," she confided, "I'm having a rush from a very clever young lawyer! My brain is kept active trying to parry his home thrusts but of course I seldom succeed . . . Considering most of the men deal in nothing but dance steps and bon mots, he is a welcome relief."

The suitor was Keith Bullitt. "He is a young lawyer, in the early thirties, with a mind like a whip and a face like cast iron," Dee wrote her friend. "Yesterday

I motored with him to the county court thirty miles away and heard him put a motion to get a case deferred till next session. Believe me, after seeing him work that judge and get what he wanted without being entitled to it, I decided to be careful! Why, I'm almost afraid I'll be married without knowing it, his arguments are so irrefutable."

Dorothy continued her hectic schedule of lessons, practice, and performances, although by this time she had decided to return to Seattle. As a result of their classes in woodcarving and painting, Dorothy and Florence had developed such an interest in crafts that they made plans to open a shop in Seattle the next fall where they would sell handcarved crafts and other novelties that could be procured in New York.

In early April, Dorothy and Florence boarded the westbound train, accompanied by the paraphernalia from living two years in New York. But their finest mementos were the experiences of cultural life to be found nowhere else and lessons learned but not included in letters home. Wandering New York's crowded streets, Dorothy had developed a larger sense of the world and its workings. Running for taxis, bargaining for tickets, or climbing up to her crowded coop at the opera, she had sampled cultural fare far richer than that which the Sunset Club or The Highlands could offer back home. New York had been a palatable experience, one she ingested thoroughly. It developed her taste for music and language; it seasoned her eye for humanity in its myriad forms. But the independence she had originally sought was only briefly tasted and not yet assimilated before the security and comfort of home called again. She returned, as she always knew she would, to the world of her parents.

There were plenty of boyfriends—I was never short. I liked them each for different reasons. But they didn't all like me just because of my blue eyes.

5 IN LOVE AND WAR
1916–1918

AFTER THE RUSH OF NEW YORK, SEATTLE WAS A REFUGE, MADE more secure for Dorothy by the serenity of home at The Highlands. Riding into town, she saw that the canal connecting Lake Washington to Lake Union and Puget Sound was finally finished. After years clogged by mud and machinery, the landscape had yielded to stable water levels regulated by two locks that now controlled boat traffic to and from the sea. Downtown a pyramid-capped skyscraper built by typewriter tycoon L. C. Smith rose 522 feet above the city, at the time the tallest building west of the Mississippi and remaining so for another half century. Seattle, of course, lacked the glamor and sophistication of New York. Prohibition had been voted in four years before the rest of the country, and the plain ankle-length dresses that women wore indicated more austere times. The city increasingly reflected the workingman's spirit. Around Pioneer Square, Dorothy noticed organizers for the Industrial Workers of the World—the "Wobblies"—handing out leaflets in support of their union and against timber barons like her father. Unions and labor problems were on the rise; and in 1919 Seattle was to be the site of the first general strike in the United States.

Dorothy Stimson was neither of the working class nor interested in liquor or lavish dressing. She was intent upon returning home to her family, visiting old friends, and having a good time. Plans to open a crafts shop with Florence were soon swept away by the current of their social lives.

At twenty-four, Dorothy recognized that she was not driven toward a career. Although equipped with a formidable arsenal of willpower, directed toward various pet projects—painting swings as a child, showing horses, securing opera seats, and generally getting her way with her parents as an adult—she was scarcely focused on meaningful work. She regarded a profession as a teacher or nurse as too dull and anything more menial, such as a stenographer's job, out of the question. A career in the arts might do eventually, but for now, these were her courting years, made bittersweet by the war raging in Europe.

Were she to have written her own autobiography, Dorothy Stimson probably would have omitted much mention of romance. In fact she "edited" her life several times, culling her diaries (only a few pages remain) and letters, removing sections that revealed frailties or excess emotion. She was always reticent about acknowledging her deep personal feelings, as if expressing them made her too vulnerable. Guarded about her correspondence with men, she cut out personal sections from the reams of letters she received. Time and experience—and her mother—were teaching her discretion. Harriet Stimson had done her work. Slowly but surely, she had sculpted her daughter, molding her character and smoothing her rough edges. Mrs. Dow and Briarcliff had refined her speech and comportment, and had introduced her to people from all parts of the country; New York had safely expanded her world. Dorothy was now a finely polished product of post-Victorian womanhood. The spontaneity that had enlivened her childhood was now replaced by reserve. There were no more emotional scenes, of either anger or joy; instead a cool restraint distilled any impulses toward excess of any kind. The original vitality was still there, but it was now more subtle and refined. Like the trained horses in which she took such pride, Dorothy Stimson was under control.

Full-bosomed, with a low earthy voice, sparkling blue eyes, and a soft mouth that brightened into a disarming smile, Dorothy was in fact a sensual young woman. Only her mother's Victorian teachings and a certain tough self-respect joined with the customs and attitudes of her time to keep her appetites in line. Like her father, she had a great capacity to relish life's smallest pleasures: sunsets and moonlight, the sound of winds and rain, the curve of islands, and the gentle gray-green slopings of winter trees. The poetry of the Northwest landscape surpassed any that she ever remembered. She loved the land and enjoyed its fruits, savoring a fresh tomato as if it were a taste of the sun and an oyster as the essence of the sea. She took her morning coffee in slow sips, methodically mixed with cream and sugar from heavy silver into fine bone china. She harbored such a discriminating passion for "real" sodas that she almost bought Seattle's last soda parlor later in life. She mucked about on boats and beaches; the squish of sand at low tide was as soul-satisfying for her as any opera. She swam frequently in the frigid waters of Puget Sound, so it was no surprise to her father and his friends one afternoon when she swam out a quarter of a mile to intercept them as they cruised past The Highlands in his yacht. She preferred a fast game of tennis to a slow game of golf. As ever, animals were her antidote

Dorothy Stimson at twenty-five.

to the rigors of propriety. Horses had a nearly aphrodisiacal effect on her; she viewed the struggle for control that arose between a spirited steed and a spirited mistress in terms of her relations with men. "A horse has got to know and be told in no uncertain terms that he's *not the boss*," she said often. "It's like a man—you can love him, but you have to keep control."

Maintaining control was much of what this sensual young woman was about. Surrounded by suitors, she sought a balance between keeping her popularity and keeping admirers at arm's length. In matters of love, Dorothy Stimson was tough in her appraisal of prospects, wary of flattery, and sensitive to motivations. Seattle was still a small town, and the offspring of its first families intermarried with regularity. Because the wealthy Stimsons were high on the social list, their eligible daughter was aware that her popularity was not based entirely on her charms. She knew that her choice of a husband was crucial to her future social standing, and that it must coincide with her parents' wishes. Most of her girlfriends had already married, yet she was determined to marry for no other reason but love.

To most of the young men she knew, Dorothy was a delightful enigma—a cool and distant star that also radiated warmth. Ladylike and proper, but capable of having a high old time, she propelled herself through life with one foot on the accelerator and the other on the brake. She was a conflicted product of her parents' attitudes, having internalized her mother's habit of guarding against too much fun, yet spurred on by her father's sense of camaraderie and play. Part of her charm was her ability to encourage people to talk about themselves, which endeared her to men in particular. Men flocked around her, wondering whether she wanted flirtation or friendship. With shrewdness equal to her great personal charm, she kept them interested in her while avoiding a serious relationship.

The simple fact was that few people deeply held Dorothy Stimson's heart thus far—her parents, her friend Dee Terry, and members of the families she had known all her life. Although she liked men and usually preferred their company, she didn't need them unless they complied with her terms. Marriage was not at all out of the question—it was still her dream—but, unless she met the right man, she was resigned to go it alone.

Young men looked on her as an ideal—a perfect product of the genteel times they shared, made more desirable by the thousands of poems and earnest literary works they read and recited in school. For some, Dorothy grew into a romantic figure, an unattainable princess who lived in wealthy splendor. They dared not reveal their deepest feelings since they idealized her and sensed correctly that she did not want to hear them. With quiet devotion, they placed her high atop an emotional pedestal and crossed their fingers, hoping that one day she would smile upon them.

None was more given to this fantasy than Henry Colver, the hard-working son of a widow, who had known Dorothy since they were both ten years old. The two were fast friends, bonded by afternoons of roughhousing on First Hill, and they kept in touch when they both went East—she to Briarcliff and he to Andover and Yale. His mother was a friend of Harriet Stimson, which gave him, though he was almost penniless, some currency for Dorothy's affections. He called her "Pokey," short for Pocahontas—a result of the "Wild West" mystique they all had brought to the East—and the two commiserated by mail about missing the "dear old town and the Sound." He confided to her about dreading the staid parties of his New England friends, when he longed instead for a chance to see someone like her, "to whom I wouldn't need to be so darned formal." From his school he wrote her every few weeks, signing his letters "Yours" or "Always the same." At the end of one, he went so far as to send his love but added, "Don't you get mad, Pokey, because I mean it on the level I do."

Dorothy didn't mind; she'd had a crush on him in the early days at Briarcliff. They exchanged gifts and photographs and, chaperoned by Henry's mother who had also moved East, attended football games and dances. After one occasion, Henry wrote her, "Don't bother getting a carriage for that elopement. I'll bring my airship—say, could you imagine anything funnier than me in one of those dark hallways of that big school at midnight trying to find out where your room was, and can you imagine what would happen if I found it?" At the Yale junior prom he gave her his pin, which she readily accepted, perhaps more for the enjoyment of its status than for its meaning. But the unclouded heights reached on the night of the prom were never attained again.

While Dorothy returned to Seattle for the summers, Henry stayed in New York to work for a real estate company, living with his mother in rented rooms in Brooklyn Heights. He had little money. "Believe me, Pokey," he wrote, "when I submit to a lashing by landlord, grocer, butcher, fuel man, gas, etc., the end of each month finds me gasping for breath and feeling deep down into my pockets for the price of a haircut." Henry Colver was a devoted son and diligent student. Voted "Hardest Worker" in his graduating class at Yale in 1912, he returned to Seattle with confidence about a future career.

Henry worked as a broker for the real estate firm of Henry Broderick. He and Dorothy saw each other at parties or for evenings at the Orpheum Theatre. He daydreamed about confessing his feelings to her but guessed that she did not want to hear them. Only an occasional letter hinted at his dreams.

When Dorothy returned from New York in 1915, Henry was more entranced than ever. He wrote notes that began, "Dorothy dear," and took her to lunch and concerts, sometimes accompanied by his mother. He spent evenings at Norcliffe sitting by the fire with her. Afterward, walking to the interurban with the cool night breeze and the tall firs silhouetted by a harvest moon, he waxed semi-poetic, once writing that "the lunar effects were very strong on a man's heart strings," reminding him of the "love of a man for a maid, as it was in the days of yore." For three years he had asked her to attend the Junior Masquerade—the young set's social event of the year—but circumstances always interfered.

In 1916 they were both living in Seattle, but other men interfered with Henry's courtship. Harvey Carr, a devoted admirer of Dorothy's since his arrival in Seattle from Minneapolis in 1910, was one. Accepting and easygoing by nature, he called Dorothy "Bright Eyes." There was a sweetness about him that she found very attractive. They shared a fondness for the outdoors and together spent hours skating, riding horses, or hiking in the mountains. When Dorothy departed for her last year in New York in 1914, Harvey was bereft. Anticipating that their parting might be difficult, she invited him for a weekend at Norcliffe but avoided any discussion of their relationship. To Dorothy, Harvey was primarily a friend.

There were others, but Dorothy's most aggressive suitor remained Conrad Westervelt, who had pursued her relentlessly since their first meeting in 1911 and by 1916 was a regular in Dorothy's crowd. Short and feisty, military in

Conrad Westervelt, Dorothy's most
determined suitor, waged his courtship
like a military campaign.

background and bearing, he was
nicknamed "Scrappy" because he
loved opposition. "I am so fond of a
good argument," he once wrote her,
"that it is with great reluctance I
have decided to have, if possible, no
more of them." Westervelt, an
admirer of Napoleon, waged his
campaign for Dorothy with force
and skill, neither of which ultimately did him any good. Using
every weapon in his arsenal, he
mowed down his enemies in long
wordy letters: Harvey Carr and his
male friends, he wrote her, "are a
hot little household of 'anti's' when it comes to women's suffrage." Win Strout's
effort to look more masculine with a new mustache made him look even more
effeminate. When Henry Colver stole Dorothy's attention by singing at a party,
Westy wrote her that he "found his high, middle, and low notes so little attuned
to my ear."

From his headquarters at the Bremerton Naval Shipyard, Westervelt fired off
daily missives, bombarded her with invitations, sent salvos of flowers and other
gifts, complete with patronizing orders not only to enjoy them but *how* to enjoy
them. He enlisted young architect Carl Gould (who later designed several
University of Washington buildings and the home in which Dorothy and her
husband lived) to design a bookplate, which depicted Dorothy standing majes-
tically, wearing a broad-brimmed veiled hat and long, fitted coat, parasol in
hand and a dog at her side. He gave her a gun as a token of his affection—a .32-
caliber automatic pistol that she kept all her life—and showed her how to
handle it so that she "might disturb someone if they tried to interrupt her." In
his zeal he interfered at every level of her life: advised her to be kinder to her
friends; planned careers for her and courses to take to secure them; had his
friends contact her when she was out of town; had a fellow passenger track her
down on a boat when she was returning home from a trip to San Francisco; gave
her books and told her what to think about them or, if she did not like them,
told her *not* to like them.

Even so, Dorothy could not help but be amused and invigorated when she saw him. Westervelt upset her innate sense of privacy and decorum, yet she enjoyed his agile mind despite his attempts to dominate her. When he became too demanding, she resorted to the tactics she used with all of her admirers—she avoided him with excuses of sickness, travel, or otherwise being unavailable. When enough time had lapsed to rekindle her interest, she contacted him again.

Dorothy kept busy in other ways. She double-dated with Dee Terry, and the two took time out in ladies' rooms to gossip and giggle between dances or acts in a play. On stage herself, Dorothy danced in a gavotte at the annual Children's Orthopedic Kirmess at the Moore Theater. She and sister-in-law Emma joined the Fortnightly Study Club—a group of women who discussed philosophical and historical topics at bimonthly meetings. She became chairman of the Fine Arts Club, which staged theatrical productions throughout the year. With her father, she enjoyed day-long rides in his latest automobile; with her mother, she traveled to Victoria for horse shows and shopping.

However, an entry in Dorothy's diary from 1917, one of a few that survived her purges, reveals, as it did when she was 16, a somewhat depressed young woman, anxious to please others, particularly her mother, but determined to remain true to herself. At a crossroads and without specific goals or direction, she was low on energy, worried about her weight, and full of health complaints about her eyes, teeth, and back. At twenty-five, she was unmarried and with few clear prospects for the future. Although she wanted to marry, she was unwilling to take the step unless that certain man came along. No one she knew fitted the bill.

At home, the social whirl began to lose momentum. Perhaps it was the sense of impending war that stirred thoughts of mortality, but it seemed to Dorothy as if all her suitors were growing too serious. Even her old reliables were becoming tiring: Cebert Baillargeon, Emma's brother, and Win Strout could talk of nothing but war, Bertie Collins was becoming "an awful old gossip," and Henry Colver had taken her rejection hard.

It was no use. Although she was fond of him, Dorothy never seriously considered Henry Colver as a husband. He had no money, no family, and no status. For all of his idealism, there was no power or real inspiration in his vision of life. She scanned her mental list of other eligibles: Win Strout was the most handsome and Cebert Baillargeon the most socially acceptable. But Win had never made a strong bid for her, and Cebert, although there had been some recurrent romance between them, was too willful for her equally strong personality (and he was Catholic—a definite disadvantage in the Stimson household). Howard Hughes, the attorney who had taken her on joy rides in his

Model T convertible, was still attractive and attentive, although the difference in their ages might cause her parents to object. Among all of them, Harvey Carr had always been a most devoted suitor and friend. For the time being, she held out some hope for Harvey.

Another disappointment came when her reliable pal, Dee Terry, in spite of protests to the contrary, weakened in the direction of the attorney from Louisville, Keith Bullitt. Dee announced by mail on January 23, 1917, that she had decided to let herself "be shaken from this dear old lemon tree." She had known in Honolulu that marriage was inevitable, she explained, but it was such a momentous decision that she put the thought aside. Later, when Keith met her in Chicago, she knew within minutes that there could no longer be any question.

Dee's engagement to Keith Bullitt represented a great loss. Dorothy had depended heavily on her since girlhood—on Dee's larger-than-life energy that drew others, Dorothy included, to forget their troubles, and on the whole-hearted acceptance that her friend always reserved for her "Stimmy darling." Dorothy was aware of this dependence and fought against it. "I'm such a darned fool," she confided to her journal when she learned that Dee and her mother would go East again. "Thought I had learned something in the last four years, but I guess I'll never change. Dee means such a lot to me. I can't bear to think of her going away again. I have known my failing for her so well and guarded against it, but it is no use."

Intuiting her daughter's low spirits, Harriet suggested a restorative trip to New York. Dorothy immediately perceived it as a chance to see Harvey Carr, who had moved back to Minneapolis and was to meet them en route. The two women were reading and knitting when he walked into their Pullman car at Glencoe, Illinois. "He looks very well," she wrote happily in her diary that night. "His cheeks are pinker than they were—he looked so weary when he left Seattle. He had on a soft hat, a dark suit with a faint stripe, a dark flowered tie, and a soft collar. We exchanged all the home news and gossip, he sat next to me opposite Mother." Promising to meet them on their return, Harvey bade them cheerful adieu in Chicago, but Dorothy noted that "Mother didn't seem very enthusiastic."

In New York that winter, Harriet and Dorothy spent their days shopping and being fitted for clothes, sending gifts and flowers for anniversaries and birthdays, and enjoying evenings with friends at the opera and theater. Often Dorothy preferred to stay in the hotel room, resting or writing letters. Worried about her weight, she went to a Turkish bath, which "was packed with the fattest women I've ever seen and made me so disgusted." She went on a diet of milk and potatoes on and off for the remainder of the trip.

There were many long talks between Harriet and Dorothy, not all of them friendly. Harriet was constantly after her daughter to spruce up her appearance, and Dorothy bought the clothes that her mother suggested. "Mother said I looked like such a tramp," a discouraged Dorothy wrote after she had bought a gray hat and bag for herself; Harriet embellished the accessories with a set of silver fox which Dorothy dubbed "a wonder." Harriet also took issue with Dorothy's reluctance to go to dances. "She accused me of not making an effort and I know that I do—I've always dreaded meeting people and probably always will."

On their return to Seattle, they stopped in Boston to visit with Dee Terry and her mother. Jane Terry seemed to sense intuitively what Dorothy was experiencing. In a long discussion about Dorothy's future, her "second mother" strongly advised Dorothy to make her own decisions about her life and have the strength to stand by them. Meanwhile, Harriet Stimson consulted a psychic in Boston and returned, deeply moved, saying only that she would reveal what the psychic had predicted after she and Dorothy left Chicago.

Dorothy's much anticipated return visit with Harvey Carr gave her time for a private chat in Chicago. "He said he had kept away from me the last year in Seattle because it was hard for him," she wrote in her diary. "I didn't know that and was awfully glad I hadn't done anything to hurt him. Said he felt just the same and that he was coming to see me in September. Glad of that," was her reaction. In the cold light of the next day, however, she concluded, "I'm afraid I can never make up my mind to marry him even if I do love him in a way." This realization plunged her into momentary despair. "I wonder what will ever become of me," she fretted. "I can't bear to think of being single all my life but there never can be but one man and if he doesn't find me . . ."

During their hours on the train, Dorothy told her mother about her disappointment with Harvey. Then her mother recounted what the psychic had predicted. The woman had described Dorothy clearly, her mother said, and saw that there were a good many men around her, that she liked them each for different qualities, and predicted that she would not marry any of them, but would marry "another and finer one." Relieved and elated, Dorothy confided to her diary that night, "Heaven grant it may be true and soon, or I shall be such a crabby old maid no one will want me." Two days later, as their train began its westward climb toward the Rockies, Harvey was already a person of the past. "I don't understand why I don't feel more keenly my disappointment over Harve," she ruminated, "but I've hardly given him a thought. I'm fond of him, of course, just as much as ever, but I guess it doesn't go very deep. I most sincerely hope that his life will turn out happily for him—but it wouldn't matter to me if I never saw him again." And she never did.

By this time, the United States' involvement in the war was imminent. In New York Dorothy had sensed a wild sort of patriotism in the air: at the Met the programs concluded with the national anthem, while the packed houses stood and sang, cheered and whistled. Dorothy warned her mother that if it came about, she would go into active Red Cross service.

Dorothy was in Seattle when Congress declared war on Germany on April 6, 1917. "There is a great deal of excitement in the streets," she observed. "Congress has agreed to back Wilson in the war against Germany. There are flags everywhere and a company of marines marched by. They are such youngsters that it gives me a lump in my throat. I can't believe that they will really see action, but nobody knows. It is too horrible to think of." As a full moon rose over Fourth Avenue a couple of evenings later, she watched a parade marching in support of the President. "The streets were terribly crowded and men in uniform were hurrying everywhere," she recorded in her diary. "There was speech making at the Arena later, and the crowd was impassable."

The mobilization for war did not affect Dorothy at first. She continued her work with the Fine Arts Club, met friends for lunch, ran errands in town, played golf and tennis at The Highlands, and took her evening walks with her dog Boy. For a few months, she continued an active social life, but it was not long before Dorothy's male friends were packing for training camps around the country, setting Seattle's gracious social balance askew.

DOROTHY, TOO, WAS SOON CAUGHT UP IN THE WAR EFFORT, volunteering at the first aid desk of the Red Cross. Inspired by a lecture on the Red Cross Women's Volunteer Motor Corps, she told her parents that she wanted to work for the motor corps more than any other local work. "How I wish I could go to France," she wrote in her diary, "not to nurse but to do clerical work or something of the sort. There must be loads of things a girl of average intelligence can do, particularly knowing the language. I don't imagine for a minute that either F[ather] or M[other] would hear of it. I wanted to go at the start but I want to so much more now that America is in it."

Dorothy adapted to the sudden departure of many of her escorts. She canceled a lavish performance scheduled for the Performing Arts Club because many of the actors were now recruits. She secured for herself a small office in the Natatorium, a building at Second and Lenora downtown, owned by C. D. and managed by Thomas, and traded in her old typewriter for a new Smith Corona, the first step in starting up a Red Cross Motor Corps for Seattle.

As the war progressed, Dorothy participated vicariously through a steady stream of correspondence from the men still in training and those already in Europe. Each letter gave her a hint of the grim reality that was unfolding. Cebert Baillargeon and Bert Collins wrote from a Cunard liner "somewhere in the Atlantic," that the officers were nervous and the watches doubled in anticipation of a U-boat attack. One warm night with a full moon—considered the finest U-boat weather—Cebert wrote her that he had wandered the decks in his pajamas and climbed to the crow's nest on the forward mast. As if looking to the future, he predicted a two-year fight that would require "all we are worth . . . Everyone will have to do their share in one way or another." Bert Collins, bound for duty in France as an ambulance driver, cautioned Dorothy against any idea of coming to Europe, saying he wouldn't entertain it for a moment unless she went in some particular capacity, but never as a nurse or a driver. Conrad Westervelt, on a military mission for the Navy, echoed Bert's warning. In a letter from Paris, he wrote, "The atmosphere here is of a stark, savage quality, and, as long as possible, men only should do it." He found the City of Light somber with "a sadness and a depression one cannot escape— buildings closed, women and children in black, no lights at night, no young men anywhere." During a trip to San Francisco, Dorothy spent a disturbing evening with Howard Hughes, who was in officer's training at the Presidio and assigned to an artillery "suicide squad." Hughes met her for dinner at the Palace Hotel. "We danced to 'Poor Butterfly,'" Dorothy recalled, "and it was quite romantic. That evening he gave me his watch and asked me to take it home to his sister because he wouldn't be coming home. When I said, 'Don't talk that way, it's dreadful,' his reply was 'I'll be pushing up daisies.'"

Meanwhile, Dee Terry had arrived in Seattle to make preparations for her marriage to Keith Bullitt. The ceremony was to be held at the Highlands Chapel and the reception at the home of Dee's aunt, Anna Struve, in the house from which the girls had strung their tin-can telephones in the early days on First Hill. On their walks together, Dee described the apartment she had chosen in Louisville and discussed with Dorothy her plans for the wedding. "Golly, it made me feel queer—can't say I like it much," Dorothy complained to her diary. During that summer the two women regained a closeness they had not enjoyed for years, and Dorothy accepted the changes to come.

Dorothy continued to work at Red Cross headquarters while helping Dee with her wedding preparations. "One day," Dorothy recalled, "Dee called and said, 'For goodness sakes, help me out. Keith's sister-in-law, Nora, is in town with her husband and I'd like to drive her around and show her the town a little bit. If you'll drive your car, I'll take us to lunch.' I said I would, and while we were having lunch Dee inquired about other members of the family.

Dorothy (LEFT) and her lifelong friend Dee Terry. Born in the same month and year, given the same first name, they would eventually marry brothers named Bullitt.

'How is Scott?' she asked. I didn't know who this was—it was the first I had ever heard of Keith's brother. Nora laughed and said, 'He's fine, although he was in the newspapers recently for creating an incident with the fire department when he climbed up on the roof of the Old Ladies Home.' I thought, 'I don't know who Keith is, but he certainly has a funny brother. Bizarre kind of man, this.' Anyway, Nora went on to explain that Scott had been visiting one of his mother's friends—he always took trouble to do those things—and before leaving he had gone up to the roof to see the clouds—he'd been reading a book on clouds. He was up there watching the different kinds of clouds, completely unconscious of a crowd gathering below. When he moved to another side of the building, they followed him, and when he took off his jacket because it was hot, they thought he was going to jump and called the fire department. He was on his way downstairs when he met his friend, the fire chief, running upstairs. Scott asked if he was looking for a fire, and the man said no, that there was a crazy man on the roof. Scott laughed and told him that he was the crazy man—and that was the first I knew about this man named Scott Bullitt."

At the same luncheon, Dee asked what had brought Nora and Keith's brother, Marshall, to Seattle. A prominent attorney and oldest of the four Bullitt brothers, Marshall had been commissioned by the Red Cross to find a district director for the Red Cross in the Pacific Northwest. "At dinner that evening at Norcliffe," Dorothy remembered, "Father said, 'Well, I've just taken another job. I was just about to leave to go on a hunting trip when this man called for an appointment. I said I could see him next week, but he said he wouldn't be here next week, so I met him.' It was Marshall Bullitt! He said he had talked to people locally and in Washington, D.C., and had been told that C. D. Stimson was the man to do the best job, but that he wasn't too easy to get. Mother said,

'You didn't take, it did you?' Father said he really didn't want to say yes, but he couldn't figure out how to say no."

C. D. took on his assignment in customary style. From his Seattle head-quarters, he supervised 113 chapters of the Red Cross with 85,000 members throughout Alaska, Washington, Oregon, and Idaho. By the time he resigned two years later, the region had oversubscribed every request for funds and over-produced every quota of garments and surgical dressings, while maintaining the lowest administrative expenses of any of the regional divisions. He created a Red Cross Motor Corps and put Dorothy in charge of it, much to her delight. From her space at the Natatorium, Dorothy put together a staff of twenty volunteers, including six drivers.

Red Cross activity helped put out of her mind the news of more and more friends engaged to be married. One day she received "an awful blow" in the morning's mail. Carolyn Rulon-Miller and Anna Potter, two Briarcliff school-mates, and Mildred Gibson, a friend from The Highlands, wrote to say that they were altar-bound. Marjory Stearns, the diminutive ballerina from New York days, also announced she would be pirouetting down the aisle. "Prepare for tulle," Marjory chirped by telegram, "I am going to marry Lieutenant Edward Hubbard." "Oh Lordy," Dorothy groaned to her diary, "I'll be the 'Last Leaf.' " And then a series of events occurred with such swiftness and intensity that it still surprised her seventy years later.

Dorothy was working at her Red Cross desk in September 1917 when Dee phoned to say that Keith's brother Marshall was too busy to attend their upcom-ing wedding as best man. Another brother, Scott, would come in his place, she said, and then she asked if Dorothy would include him in the dinner for the wedding party. Dorothy agreed to "put another place at the table"—an under-statement for what was to be an elegant occasion—and promised to drive into town and pick them up.

Marshall was too busy to be best man, but Scott was no less occupied—as a candidate for re-election as county attorney in Kentucky—and in the middle of the campaign. "I thought, 'This brother Scott sounds like a man with feelings. He doesn't let his brother take this important step in a strange land unsup-ported by any member of his family.' That was the sum of my knowledge of Scott when I drove up in my Marmon four-seater convertible to the Struve house to carry them all out to the rehearsal in the Highlands Chapel and dinner at Norcliffe."

When Dorothy arrived, Dee and Keith came out to the car to say that they were unable to find Scott. They ran back inside to search the house while she waited in the car. Finally they found him in a corner reading a book. As he followed them out the front door—a slender blue-eyed man of about forty—he paused to smile at the young woman behind the wheel. "The sight of Scott standing on the porch, smiling a little, has never dimmed in my memory," Dorothy said decades later. "I looked and thought—this is a man the likes of which I have never seen before. He was the finest-looking piece of man I had ever seen." In that instant Dorothy Stimson began a new life.

*It was love at first sight—mutual and permanent. I
wasn't in love with any of the others, but with Scott it
just exploded. I'd never met anybody like him—his
manners, his knowledge, courtesy, and procedures.
I just fell hook, line, and sinker. I didn't analyze it. I
just knew how I felt about this man, and I was right.*

6 THE ANSWERING EYE

1918-1920

SHE NOTICED FIRST HIS EYES, CLEAR BLUE AND WITH A GAZE
as direct as her own. Then a broad smile so disarming that it eliminated any
reserve she may have had toward a stranger. He was slim, of medium height—
about 5 feet 10 inches—with a high forehead, a chiseled chin that suggested
intellect and will, and a voice and manner that brought to life the grace and
gentility of the Old South. The attraction between the two was immediate,
intense, and reciprocal. As they drove toward The Highlands, Dorothy tried
talking about the scenery. "I pointed out the Olympic Mountains on the left,"
she remembered, "and as I pointed toward the Cascades on Scott's side of the
car, I saw that he was looking at me—he wasn't looking at the mountains at all!
Every time I looked at him, he was looking at me." And how did she respond to
the unexpected intensity of their connection? "I wasn't flustered or nervous," she
replied with a throaty laugh. "No, I had an electricity of my own."

Dorothy Stimson and Scott Bullitt were a matched pair—twin suns from
different universes. Both were charismatic and had many admirers, yet each
had decided to remain single unless the "right person" came along. They were
astounded to have found each other on the same path. Decades later, a penciled
quotation from a book titled *Marching On* was found among Scott Bullitt's
effects. It read, "two deep gray, quiet eyes, warm, kind, yet humorously pene-
trating, that looked up into his." At the bottom of this slip of paper, Scott had
written, "History repeated itself Sept 11, 1917." Dorothy Stimson had, as he
later termed it, "the answering eye."

Surrounded by the gaiety of the wedding celebration, maid of honor and
best man had eyes only for each other. Their meeting had a trancelike quality
that neither could understand, and both would use the word "dream" in the

letters they exchanged over the next months. Scott called it a "fantastic dream of the far future." Dorothy echoed the sentiment in a letter to him: "Oh Scott dear, I am almost afraid to think. I can't quite believe it is all true. I am afraid I shall wake up and realize it was all only a dream. I don't want to wake up, I just want to keep on dreaming."

For amusement at the rehearsal dinner, each guest was presented with a "character reading" from his or her handwriting. One paragraph in Dorothy's summed up her behavior that evening: "She has tact and that finer tact, intuition; and a discretion of manner which increases greatly the comfort of those about her. She is reserved, yet not cold, and has much personal magnetism." Magnetism was radiating on a grand scale that evening and the next day. From his seat at the dinner, Scott watched Dorothy at the head of the table, captivated by the curiously opposing qualities she seemed to possess. "I was subconsciously fascinated by you from the beginning," he told her on their second wedding anniversary, "held by your winsome expression combined with the latent potential power reflected in your voice and manner. I was in love with you before I knew it."

At the reception and dance that followed the wedding, amid the several hundred well-wishers of Seattle's social elite, the two found each other and danced in the large ballroom. "Jack Ballinger told me afterward," Dorothy later recalled, "that he said to his wife Alma, 'Dorothy is stuck with that man from out of town. I guess he doesn't know any other girls—I'll break in—she doesn't know how to get rid of him.' While I danced with Jack, Scott assailed the wedding cake. In those days they used to put souvenirs in the cake—a penny for someone who would be rich or a button for a bachelor. He took that cake apart until he found the little tin ring, which stood for the next one to be married, and he gave it to me when he broke in on Jack. Later that evening he came to Norcliffe, and we spent a long evening by ourselves. We talked about everything—horses, boats, and life. He asked me to marry him, and I guess in some bewilderment I approved of the general idea." Unable to say a word when he asked her, she winked. Remembering that evening years later, she waved a hand in front of her face, rolled her eyes and said, "Whew!" It was a passionate encounter for these two vital people, and a baffling one. Scott confided to his son Stim years later that he had expected never to marry—probably from having observed his own parents' unhappy union. For Dorothy, it was equally confusing. Proper to the point of hardly holding hands, much less kissing a man, and accustomed to evaluating her suitors with a jaundiced eye, she found herself overwhelmed with emotions that bypassed her brain entirely. They were both dazed by the suddenness of events.

Scott decided to stay another day, though he had to return to Kentucky to continue his campaign for county attorney. They spent their last day together driving around the city, getting to know each other. On a ferry ride across Lake Washington, they tried to tell each other all they could. From the heights of the Smith Tower, Dorothy pointed out her Red Cross office on Second Avenue to the north, and the two gazed silently at the distant mountains and the Sound, puzzled by the present and excited by what the future might hold. They said good-bye at the train station and Scott promised to return in two months.

During those few days, Harriet and C. D. Stimson were out of town. Dorothy, once she got her feet on the ground, greeted them on their return with the news, "Well, I've met a *man.*" When C. D. was finally convinced this was serious, he called S. P. Davidson, a man he knew in Washington, D.C., who knew everyone. As luck would have it, Davidson was one of Scott's good friends. By wire, C. D. received the following "report":

> Following is first report from excellent source for which have great respect. Begins he is from a very good family and is himself good man about thirty-eight to forty years, lawyer by profession, educated at University of Kentucky and Princeton, went in for athletics at college and always has taken care of himself physically, is well bred and quite above average intelligence. Have known him and his brothers since their boyhood and regard him as ablest of group. Regard him quite favorably and have confidence in his character and capacity. Will advise you of further information as received.

Indeed, Alexander Scott Bullitt was first class; his bloodlines were as fine as those of any registered thoroughbred to come out of his native state. His father, Thomas Walker Bullitt, was a distinguished Louisville lawyer until his death from a stroke in 1910, and his mother, Annie Priscilla Logan Bullitt, was the daughter of Louisville Judge Caleb Logan. Both sides of the family were steeped in American history, having crossed the Appalachians from Virginia during the 1700s to settle in north-central Kentucky, where they became moderately prosperous farmers and professionals who doubled as civic leaders. Scott's forebears rode and fought with George Washington, were related to Patrick Henry and Chief Justice John Marshall, were friends with Thomas Jefferson, Benjamin Franklin, and James Madison.

As surveyors and Indian fighters, Scott's great-great-grandfathers ventured into eastern Kentucky twenty years before Daniel Boone—one, Thomas Walker, led the first exploration party into eastern Kentucky in 1750, discovering, and naming, Cumberland Gap on the way; another, William Christian (before he was killed by Indians), explored the area with Boone a generation later. The

Kentucky they explored was an area known by Indians as "the dark and bloody ground"—a vast, foreboding forest filled with marauding Indians, bears, and wolves. Armed with ax, adze, rifle, and scalping knife, the settlers hacked out a place in the wilderness. Scott's great-great-grandfather, Benjamin Logan, led the first movement for Kentucky's statehood. His great-grandfather, William Logan, was judge of the Kentucky Court of Appeals, and a U.S. senator. The great-grandfather for whom he was named, Colonel Alexander Scott Bullitt, surveyed the area which became the city of Louisville, co-drafted the state's first constitution, and served as speaker of the state senate and Kentucky's first lieutenant governor. Five Kentucky counties—Bullitt, Christian, Henry, Logan, and Marshall—are named for Scott's ancestors.

The short "report" submitted to C. D. Stimson contained some errors. Scott Bullitt attended the University of Virginia for two years, and then Princeton, where he was president of the Ivy Club and from which he received a Bachelor of Arts degree *cum laude* in 1898. He had also attended Harvard for a couple of years before receiving his law degree from Louisville Law School. He was an avid athlete. An amateur boxer, he was lightweight champion at the University of Virginia and at the Louisville Athletic Club. At Virginia and Princeton he played on the football squad and, later in Louisville, coached football at his old high school. He was also a good swimmer, once winning a race across the Ohio River.

Ancestors, honors, and trophies aside, Scott Bullitt's greatest asset—and one that could never be captured in a telegram—was his considerable charm. "He was always very popular and made loads of friends," Dorothy observed. "Why he didn't get married earlier, I don't know. The ladies all liked him. He had all the courtesies that go with Southern polish." His pleasant, soothing drawl conjured images of warm Southern evenings orchestrated by cicadas and lit by fireflies. His vocabulary evoked the comfort of a country where a young man was "right clever," the weather "mighty fine," and a grateful person "much obliged." His was a reassuring world where there was time, courtesy, and a place for everyone. He was a popular figure in Louisville society. Announcing Scott's engagement the following year, the Louisville *Courier Journal* described him with the obvious affection reserved for a hometown boy:

Do you remember that delightful little incident that Scott Bullitt's friends like to recount as being indicative of just the sort of chap he is? How when Scott was a little chap of three years old the family was spending the summer at a certain watering place and Scott was observed coming across the lawn with his pinafore filled with hot cookies. When his mother inquired, in some dismay, just how

Alexander Scott Bullitt, a lawyer who hailed from one of Kentucky's oldest families. "He was the finest-looking piece of man I had ever seen," said Dorothy.

and where he had obtained these same cookies, he smiled in his ingenuous way and, with his ingratiating voice, replied, "Oh, I'm friends with the cook!" He has been friends with everybody almost ever since.

Like many Southerners, Scott Bullitt was a vivid raconteur. Leaning back in his chair, he could spin out a story that held his audience spellbound. At Princeton, he was known for his lively speeches sometimes delivered while standing on a billiard table, speeches recalled by alumni a half century later. He had a wide range of stories in his repertoire, from the Bible and history to jokes and tales from the South spiked with dialect and wit. He was also a born visitor, often stopping to chat on the street (it took some time to reach his office), tipping his hat to the ladies, and making courtesy calls on older relatives or family friends. As a Southerner accustomed to knowing bloodlines, he was quick to place people, to remember their names and families, and to understand the roles they played in the community. All of these qualities combined to make Scott Bullitt an excellent lawyer and a natural politician. He was fond of telling about a politician who, when asked how he stood on a certain issue, replied, "I don't know, I haven't yet decided—but whatever it is, I'm going to be very, very serious about it." His gentle, self-deprecating humor came in handy during tension-filled trials, enabling him to disarm the most rigid juror; yet he was capable of fiery oratory in attacking an opponent's argument. He was self-confident enough that he didn't take himself too seriously. One of his favorite incidents occurred on a steamy August evening, late in a long political meeting. Choosing to speak second for advantage, he had awaited his turn while his opponent made a lengthy boring speech that ended with, "And now, ladies and gentlemen, beer will be served in the basement!" "He loved to tell that story on himself," his daughter Patsy remembered. "Those words became a family joke. Whenever anyone wanted to have the last word, we would say, 'And now, ladies and gentlemen, beer will be served in the basement.' "

Scott first practiced law with his father and older brother Marshall, but later moved out on his own because he could not work with his overbearing brother. He preferred trial work, particularly personal injury cases. "He was a jury lawyer," recalled Dorothy. "A people person. He could appraise the jury expertly, and he could usually sway them and *win*." Defending an ice cream company that had used a substitute for one of its ingredients to save money, Scott arranged to give his summation on a summer day when the courtroom was stiflingly hot. As the jury fanned themselves, he had ice cream brought in and served to them, saying, "Taste this and tell me if this is good ice cream." They ruled in his favor.

Scott was not afraid to question the law or to come down hard on those who disobeyed it. He once encountered a man being threatened with nightsticks by the police, and was taken to jail for remonstrating with the officers. Another time he righted wrongs at the Louisville racetrack. As recalled by Dorothy: "There was great corruption out at Churchill Downs with the betting pro-cedures. The sheriff called Scott and asked him his opinion about the track betting that was going on. Scott said he didn't like it and the mayor said, 'I want you to do something about it. I'm going to appoint you a deputy to go out and break this up. Gather your friends together—your young guys who don't care what happens—and I don't care how you do it.' They went out with axes and hammers and smashed the works, and that was the beginning of betting machines at Churchill Downs, instead of picking pockets right and left. That was what put him into politics, more or less." The governor of Kentucky appointed him Jefferson County Sheriff for a partial term. Between 1910 and 1918, he also served two terms as Jefferson County attorney. He was running for a third term (and was defeated) when he met Dorothy Stimson.

Letters between Scott and Dorothy flew back and forth, cheerfully cautious at first, then gaining in intensity. He called her "Stim," sometimes "Flora McFlimsey," and after a while, "Sweetheart." She called him "Scott dear" or "Antonio Scotti" and signed her letters "Yours," or "As Ever." The romance was further fueled by Dee Terry Bullitt, now settled in Louisville, who assumed the role of Cupid. At every family visit, she managed to take Scott aside and ply him with questions that made him blush. In December, Dee was thrilled to learn that Scott was to travel west again. "Of course, according to the natural sequence of events," Scott wrote Dorothy, "she and I soon drifted to one side and proceeded to spend the whole time she was there talking about the person who was first in my mind and certainly a safe second in hers."

Scott arrived in Seattle and soon declared that he should talk with C. D. about marrying his daughter. "Of course, Father had done his research," Dorothy recollected. "So they had a talk and I guess it was a pretty good one. Father was very pleased with him—he was a lawyer with his own office and clients and he had been to school. He expected to take me back to Louisville where his practice and home were, but said that we could come out from time to time. So he wasn't just someone passing through. Father liked his independence and ability to take care of me. It wound up a very, very close friendship. Scott just loved my father and my father loved him."

In January of 1918, C. D., Harriet, and Dorothy stopped in Louisville for three days en route to the East Coast. "Mother was kind of—well, they both were kind of embarrassed at not having met Scott at the beginning. They had expected me to marry the wrong one [Westervelt]—and they were a bit floored at first. They were also a bit puzzled by Scott's mother. She had more wrinkles on her face than anyone I've ever seen. She was a little woman, very strict, and her deportment was perfect. She lived in a nice house, not an elaborate plantation or any of that nonsense, just a good house on a main street. The parents probably spent a couple of hours together and then we all left. Scott went to New York, we went with Father to Washington for Red Cross business, and then Mother and I went on to New York."

All hell broke loose in New York when Conrad Westervelt appeared. Somehow he had gotten wind of the romance and was determined to stop it. "In Louisville there will be few messengers knocking at your heart to ask admittance for me," he wrote Dorothy in Washington, D.C., "and I shall never have needed them more." He pled with her to defer her decision and bring "this man of Louisville" to New York where the two suitors could meet eye to eye. With uncharacteristic passion, he asked further that she pin his letter to her bosom where her heart might hear it.

When Dorothy and her mother entered the lobby of the Chatham Hotel, "There they were—Scott and Westy—sitting in the lobby! Somehow I avoided introducing them, but Westy got me aside to say, 'You can't deny me an hour or so. I want you to take a taxi with me to the park, and I'll tell you what a mistake you're making.' On our ride, he told me I was making a *great* blunder—the war was on and Scott had no part in it. What kind of an American was he? And, if I married him, I'd be raising a crop of *wrong* Americans—my children would have no sense of their country—and on and on. Well, I lived through that, but it was very difficult."

Conrad was not to be dismissed with a ride through Central Park. Whether by accident or design, he ran into Dorothy and Scott the next night at the opera. During the performance, Scott, who wasn't musical, fell asleep, but was jolted into alertness at intermission. "Who should appear but Conrad!" said Dorothy. "The two of them shook hands—and I lived through that one too." Conrad's reaction? A brief note, saying, "He is very nice, but if you wait six months, you'll never take the name of Bullitt."

The New York stay was a mix of pleasure and confusion. "One night, Scott took Mother and me to dinner, and during dinner I could hear some rustling of paper under the table. Suddenly out came a case, and Scott passed it across to Mother and asked, 'May I give this to your daughter?' and there was a beautiful diamond ring! Golly, I'd give my eye teeth to get that ring back!" [Dorothy gave it to her son Stimson when he was to be married, explaining that "he didn't have any money for a proper ring and he was the only son I had, so I gave it to him."] "It was a large diamond in a Tiffany setting with two or three other diamonds tapering off. Mother was speechless, but she knew the value of gems. I can't remember, but she must have said something like, 'This is a beautiful ring,' and, 'I guess if you've both made up your minds . . .' She didn't have any speech ready; this was a courtesy and a procedure she'd never been through before, and she had never pictured it this way. So I put it on and wore it."

A few days later Dorothy began to get cold feet. "We went to Maillards for lunch, and I said, 'I can't marry you. Take the ring back.' And he said, 'Throw it in the river, I don't want it.' We talked things over, but he wouldn't take no for an answer."

She needed more time. Scott accompanied the Stimsons to the railway station for their return trip home, and, as the train pulled away from him, Dorothy felt her heart constrict, not so much from sorrow as from fear. It was the momentum, the gathering speed of a commitment that might propel her headlong along a course she couldn't control. She kept the ring but didn't wear it, and their separation was tinged with sadness and uncertainty.

Scott's emotions plunged into despair. He sent letters ahead to Seattle, expressing his dread that she would decide that the sacrifice of leaving family was too great, that she would say, "I must remain always like Queen Elizabeth, a virgin queen to the end." With uncharacteristic self-pity, he continued, "I have suffered more than you would want me to during the past forty-eight hours, I believe; as the realization began to come over me what a complete change had come over you last week. If you have a doubt in your heart, it would be wrong for you to marry or me to ask you to. I have had only tragedy in my life—the loss of my father—who died in my arms. Now I am face to face with a tragedy in life that means even more to my heart and soul."

Then he received a small envelope containing a clipping of pussy willows—a shrub he had told Dorothy he was unfamiliar with—and a card that said, "I'm surprised that your education has suffered such neglect." A few days later, from her room at The Highlands, Dorothy wrote an eloquently simple acceptance to marry him. "Scott dear," it began, "the five days since I left Chicago have made me just five times as sure as I was then. Instead of any doubts creeping in (as I feared might happen when I was away from you) the opposite occurred and I am now firmly convinced that everything is alright and as it should be. Please let me know if you have changed your mind. I am up in my room now with the door locked and am wearing my wonderful ring—it is such a beauty that I can hardly take my eyes off it to look at the paper. I shouldn't blame you a bit if you had changed your mind; in fact I never will understand how you ever felt as you did in the first place—that will always remain one of the unexplained mysteries to me."

The two were in a trance. Visiting a friend one evening, Scott was so befuddled that he walked home, leaving his car parked in front of his friend's house. He didn't remember the car until the next morning when he was shaving. Dorothy, while discussing Red Cross matters with a superior, suddenly burst out laughing when she realized that she hadn't heard a word that was being said. She called a meeting of the Red Cross Motor Detachment but had to find a substitute to preside over it and went out into the street to walk around and work off some of her excitement.

At home in Seattle, Harriet Stimson suggested that Dorothy should not wear her ring until the betrothal had been officially announced, all according to proper protocol. First, the family letters had to be exchanged. Dorothy received an official welcome from Annie L. Bullitt, who assured her that she was not a meddlesome mother. Scott received his official welcome from the "Chiefs of the Western Forces," although C. D. and Harriet were still finding it difficult to give up their daughter. In her letter to Scott, Harriet tried to explain, "You know, she is the only daughter we have and we have been living the past few years in a sort of fool's paradise—thinking and almost hoping she might not care to marry and if she should, never dreaming of a possibility which would take her way across the country to live. I am much slower of readjustment than my husband—possibly more selfish about it—but it is all in the past now as I am at last convinced that you care enough for each other to eliminate all else and the only consideration is the thing that is best for you both for, of course, her happiness is our greatest joy." About Dorothy, she wrote, "She has many faults as well as many virtues which have made her a good daughter and I am sure will make her a good wife."

C. D.'s welcome to Scott was a bit more direct, if not a little contrite. "Dorothy seems perfectly satisfied in her conclusions & I am most happy with all environments that please her," he wrote in his large, slanted hand. "Of course, one can only know by actual experience what it means to parents to have an only daughter (of an already small family) take this step, besides the prospect of going so far away to live, & if Mrs. S. or I have ever shown you any signs of disapproval, please believe me there was nothing personal intended, & any young man would have gotten the same or worse. She is entirely the dearest girl in the whole world, only one ever lived to compare & I was the lucky young man to marry her."

The engagement was to be announced in the papers on March 3, 1918. Meanwhile, the family agreed to keep it a secret. Dorothy didn't mind this; her head and heart were elsewhere anyway. She removed the star sapphire that she always wore from her finger, a gift from her father, and had it reset for Scott as an engagement present. She had fittings for a wedding gown, a trousseau, even sewed lace on lingerie, and planned a wedding, a honeymoon, and a new life.

When the Stimson-Bullitt engagement was made public, both hometown newspapers announced it with uncharacteristic delight and affection. Scott and Dorothy were each recognized as the best catches their respective cities could offer. Louisville, which prided itself in a friendly interest in all local gossip about love affairs and weddings, was dumbfounded. No one expected that Scott Bullitt, that most eligible of bachelors, would ever marry. The *Seattle Times* announced that the wedding would "take from this city one who has grown from childhood into the loveliest and finest type of young woman." The society page ran several columns, calling Dorothy "one of Seattle's most beloved maidens," who was to be married "quite in the modest, unassuming manner characteristic of everything about the life of Miss Dorothy Stimson, with little show or ostentation, yet surrounded by a large number of friends, who have been identified with her life ever since coming to this city and representing Seattle's Four Hundred."

Dorothy was busy writing personal notes to many friends and relatives. Her eccentric Aunt Anne Stimson, (now divorced from C.D.'s brother Ezra in Los Angeles) a poet and advocate of "new thought" in religion, received the news with great joy—particularly because Conrad Westervelt was not the chosen

*Scott Bullitt and Dorothy Stimson were married on May 16, 1918. The wedding party
included (LEFT TO RIGHT) Charles W. ("Cully") Stimson, Dorothy Terry Bullitt,
Keith Bullitt, Jane Somerville, Scott and Dorothy, Thomas Stimson, Emma Stimson,
Frederic Struve, and Florence Williams.*

one. Such a marriage, she wrote her beloved niece, would have lacked the
"wonderful thrills and heavenly joy that this will have . . . I did so want you to
wait for just such a thing as this—when your kind get it they usually get it
pretty bad and it is well worthwhile waiting for . . . I always . . . wanted you to
get out, to see the world, to have a chance to meet other than Seattle men so
that 'old Propriety' did not have the entire arrangement of your future . . . This
[man], however, is different, new material, different locality, different breed."
Carried forward with enthusiasm and largesse of spirit, she advised her favorite
niece: "Dorothy dear—live, live every minute not recklessly nor carelessly but
consciously joyously each day for its self. Never mind the 'bank roll'—that will
later take care of its self . . . and money is not the real thing any way. We of the
family have thought and worked too much for money . . ."

Conrad Westervelt reacted to her engagement with a flag of truce and an
apology of sorts: "For a year I have been so wrapped up in the subject of
National Defence, so close to its woefully imperfect machinery and so impatient
of all men who seemingly hinder or do not openly help, that I have doubtless
become a poor judge of some of my fellows . . . I do not mind on account of the

Aboard the yacht Lydia, *Scott and Dorothy on their honeymoon.*

man. If he deserves any of it, he is welcome to it; if he does not, it will do him no harm." In the end, he was his same indomitable and stalwart self: "I feel confident of your happiness. I hope it will be as great and as complete as my unfailing wishes would have it."

The wedding was scheduled for May 18, 1918. Scott's mother, Annie Priscilla Logan Bullitt, still in mourning for her husband, sent the Stimsons formal black-edged regrets that she could not be present. She did concede, however, that her new daughter-in-law, Dorothy "Dee" Terry Bullitt was "a joy" and that she looked forward with pleasure to having another Dorothy in Louisville. Dee's grandmother, Lucy Furth, wrote to say that she was intensely amused that the engagement surprised both of their native cities, referring to the couple and their union as, "Two diplomats well met and a well planned campaign!"

The wedding took place at noon in the gray stone chapel in The Highlands, followed by a reception at Norcliffe. *Town and Country* magazine praised it as the leading social event of the year. The ceremony was reserved for a select few. The altar was massed with white peonies and delicate yellow snapdragons ("like bunches of sunshine"); chandeliers were entwined with lavender wisteria and yellow laburnum; pews were decorated with clusters of forget-me-nots, lilies of the valley, and orchids. An archway of ferns and yellow Marguerite daisies crowned the bride and groom. Dorothy, according to the newspaper, wore an exquisite gown of white satin, decorated with pearls at the waist and on the bodice. A tulle veil, fastened to her hair with a wreath of orange blossoms, completely enveloped her and fell the length of the gown. "We were married at high noon," Dorothy recalled. "Emma was my matron of honor, and Dorothy Terry and Florence Williams, my bridesmaids. Scott had his brother Keith as best man. The ushers were my brother Thomas, my cousin Cully Stimson, and Frederic Struve."

At Norcliffe, under a display of white lilacs and white wisteria, Harriet and C. D. received their guests. "It was a stand-up feast. There was champagne, dancing, and two wedding cakes—one freshly baked and the other a fruitcake. I cut the white baked cake, and Scott cut the dark fruitcake, and we each had a piece and danced quite a lot. We wanted to leave as soon as we could, changed our clothes and were ready to go, when we got a telephone call from the minister, a young cadet I liked quite a lot who was in service with the Navy. He phoned to say that we had forgotten to sign the wedding certificate and would we please stop on our way to town and sign it.

"After signing the wedding documents we went into town, and it was still quite early, so we went to the White Building at Fourth and Union, which was where Father's office was. There was a lunch counter there that I liked quite a lot, and we sat and had an ice cream soda because we had hardly eaten anything at the reception. We were sitting up at the soda fountain when Father came in. He'd had enough reception, and he didn't like the wedding very much—I think he thought he was losing me, and it was hard for him.

"The Eddys—nice family and friends—had offered their boat, *Lydia,* for our honeymoon. I don't recommend it for a wedding trip, though—the bunks were little narrow things. They weren't big enough for two, but it didn't matter much. We had a skipper and a cook and headed down to southern Puget Sound—we didn't care where we went. On board, we sat in steamer chairs on deck with big coats and lap rugs. We'd go ashore and walk in the woods or on the beach." The honeymoon lasted one week.

———

THE COUPLE RETURNED TO NORCLIFFE FOR A FEW DAYS BEFORE leaving for Louisville, joining C. D. and Harriet on the train. The climate in Louisville—both physical and social—was overwhelming for the new bride. It was summer when they arrived, and the Ohio River Valley's heat, humidity, insects, pollens, and other rich juices enveloped her like a womb. The Bullitt family was equally stifling, as its many members descended upon her. Accustomed to a small family and selected friendships that were never particularly demonstrative, Dorothy was bewildered to find herself engulfed by a host of brothers, aunts, uncles, cousins, and in-laws who inundated her with honey-coated hospitality. "Scott's mother was interested in heritage, bloodlines, china and silver and all that—which is not my great interest in life," Dorothy remembered. "She would recite lineages and history, and I was supposed to remember it all. She had known the Civil War and heard the guns and troops moving back and forth, and she told me all about it. In her demands, she was very difficult. To say she was critical was putting it mildly, and Scott was not too fond of her, really. He loved his father, but his father had died, and his mother was all about who's who—General so-and-so married so-and-so, and I would listen but didn't remember any of it. I couldn't have cared less, and she cared a great deal."

About this time—maybe because of Scott's mother—Dorothy learned to drink bourbon. "I had never tasted a cocktail until I was married, and I remember one night when we were visiting some friends, Scott warned me, 'Don't ever ask for anything but bourbon, particularly because we're dining with the people who manufacture it.'"

Scott's oldest brother, Marshall, presided as paterfamilias over his three brothers and two sisters. A prominent Republican, he had served as Solicitor General under President Taft and was immensely successful as a corporate trial lawyer in Louisville. He was also an immensely overbearing brother. "Marshall was very difficult, a terrible man," Dorothy recalled, "and I was very fond of him. He was an insufferable snob, brilliant and arrogant as the devil." Brother Jim was a doctor, head of the Pathology Department at the University of North Carolina at Chapel Hill. "He was a Mr. Chips kind of person, lived modestly, was gentle and quiet, quite a philosopher," according to his new sister-in-law. "Keith was the baby of the family, also in the family firm, but he didn't have the self-confidence to move out on his own. He was a little mousy. He married [my friend Dee], and Scott predicted that their marriage wouldn't last—perhaps because she was too much for him. There were also two sisters. One, Agatha, married a German professor and moved to Germany; that was fatal as far as the family was concerned. She was the one I liked, although we didn't meet for many years. The other sister, Mirah, I didn't care very much for. She married a man named Rush, and they lived in Pittsburgh or some place."

Tiny Annie Priscilla Logan Bullitt reigned firmly as the queen mother of them all. Each Sunday at her modest house on Fourth Street, she summoned whatever family members were available to a dinner that she supervised in minute detail. "After church on Sunday," Dorothy recounted, "all the family would gather there in the middle of the day for dinner. She'd be at the head of the table directing conversation a good deal. But primarily she was a housekeeper. When dinner was over, we'd go into the living room and she would excuse herself, go back into the dining room where her old black servant would bring her two basins of hot water, and she'd wash the dishes herself. It was her best china, and she didn't want it chipped—it was only out on Sunday. Her servant's name was Hardy, and she loved him dearly, and vice versa. They were both old and had been together for years. It couldn't have been more different from my house. My mother washed everything when they were first married, but not later. Going into such an old Southern family, I felt as if I were living in a book—they were all like characters in a novel."

Dorothy soon noticed other differences between herself and her new husband. Scott was fifteen years older than Dorothy, and his friends were older, too. His friends were everywhere, and worse for Dorothy, they were everybody. The discriminating and reserved new wife quickly saw that her husband's natural geniality was greater than her own. He seemed to love everyone, regardless of their station, and it made her uncomfortable. "Everywhere we went, Scott wanted to *introduce* me. If we drove through Louisville, we'd stop at every crosswalk and I'd be introduced to the policeman. Traffic would stop and Scott would say, 'Hey Joe, this is my *wife!* I'm not easy with those sorts of things, and Scott was easy with everybody. I wasn't used to it, and it was very embarrassing. I didn't have any bon mots. I couldn't come up to it."

Her husband was also a bit of a daydreamer, given to flights of speculation about ancient history or the positions of the planets. One time in Washington, D.C., he was so lost in a book that he was locked in the law library after everyone else had gone home; months later in Louisville, he let the bathtub run over for an hour while he blithely penned a letter to Dorothy. He did not match her practicality, her ability to research every major purchase in meticulous detail, to balance checkbooks, to keep track of interest rates and endless lists of everything from furnishings to family birthdays. Scott left these things to his new wife, calling her the "business member of the firm." He could never have been the businessman that C. D. Stimson was. His currency was neither dollars nor power; it was charm, and he spent it liberally. Apart from his family, two other interests—politics and the law—brought him to earth, and to life. Both were based on people; and people he enjoyed in all of their varied complexity, visiting with them and learning from them in courtroom or ballroom, on street corners and on county roads.

Dorothy had underestimated Scott's interest in politics, and was surprised when people asked when her husband might run for office. The Stimson family had always held only the mildest interest in politics, but in Kentucky, politics were discussed everywhere, at the dinner table and on the streets, introducing the new Mrs. Bullitt to a more serious world of ideas. In Seattle, the upper-class voters were Republicans; in the South, Democrats. When Scott asked her which political party she belonged to, Dorothy said Republican. "Very well, then," he replied, "I'll show you the Republican polls." He drove her to the heart of Louisville's black district, introducing Dorothy to a wretched world of poverty, where the votes were cast upstairs over the morgue. "I was just agog," she remembered. "I didn't know anything about those people. Most of the blacks had no shoes." Years later, she explained, "I had never known the difference. My father wasn't political, and I never heard politics discussed around the table. But Scott was from Kentucky, which had a long Democratic tradition, and he showed me the difference between the Democratic and Republican points of view. It made sense to me—the people for the good of the country were Democrats and the Republicans were on the upper crust." From then on, Dorothy was a Democrat.

Dorothy had had little contact with African Americans, and she was conventional enough to accept the white Southerner's attitude that segregation was a way of life as incontrovertible as the law of gravity. Although Scott treated blacks with courtesy, he was also of the mindset that "white folks were born to lead and black folks were born to serve." He would not go to the theater if there was a mixed cast, and any hint of miscegenation was taboo. The rest of his family reacted the same way: Brother Jim taught medicine to blacks, but he also believed that they should be educated separately from whites. And with Scott, Dorothy often visited Oxmoor, the family farm founded in 1787, owned by brother Marshall, where slavery had been an accepted part of life.

ON THE HOME FRONT, DOMESTIC DUTIES WERE DIFFICULT FOR the new bride. Accustomed to servants providing for her needs, she was ill-prepared for establishing a home, planning meals, and taking care of a husband. To add to the adjustments, the newlyweds had no sooner moved into an apartment in the St. James section of town when the Stimsons began to arrive. Emma came to town on the day they moved in and stayed for two weeks. "No furniture, no cook, words fail," Dorothy's calendar noted. Next, Thomas passed through on his way from Pensacola, where he was stationed as a pilot in the Navy Air Corps. Within the next few months, however, she managed to decorate the two-bedroom apartment, thanks to furnishings provided by the Stimsons and the constant advice that Dorothy sought and received from her mother. To bring order from the chaos, she resorted to the tactics she had always known: she hired experts—painters, plasterers, upholsterers, carpenters, and cooks.

The culinary arts were a great mystery that Dorothy had no wish to solve. Roasting (even basting) a chicken or whipping meringue had never been her forte, and she avoided such practices throughout her life, assuming a comically helpless look whenever the prospect of preparing food loomed in a conversation. At ninety-five she no longer pretended to have much interest in food. "No one ever lets me into the kitchen," she would say with a shrug, delighted to be so rejected. "I make too much—I make too little—I don't know how to measure.

I can make a little breakfast, that's easy, but I wouldn't cook myself a dinner. I'm not that hungry. Besides it takes a long time to prepare and is eaten up in half an hour, and then what do you do with the leftovers?" However, as a bride at twenty-five, she went through the motions. "My mother suggested that I learn to cook by watching the cook in the kitchen; but, I don't know, I found I'd just rather *eat*. When I married, suddenly I had to do something about it. I read some books, went to the store and bought things, and I managed—but the meals weren't very good. Scott wasn't awfully particular—we had soup out of a can and things from a delicatessen. If we had special company, I got a little black girl to come in to cook the meat and I'd buy a cake."

Probably at no other time in her life did Dorothy pay such careful attention to her living conditions, limited as they were at the time. It was her consuming wish to fashion the most beautiful and comfortable home for their marriage, and she claimed that the little flat had "reached such an exalted state of dignity and grandeur that we can scarcely call it 'an apartment.' " When everything was finally painted, plastered, and furnished down to the last fern, she lit some of her mother's incense and dressed for a romantic dinner with Scott. Afterward they sat "just admiring everything and letting the sensation that it was *all ours* sink in thoroughly."

In spite of the comfortable surroundings, Dorothy was homesick for Seattle. Amid the rolling hills of Kentucky, she found herself searching for a western edge, an open stretch of water, distant peaks reaching to the sky, or the winter green of trees. Fortunately, she had her friend Dee Terry Bullitt to share the new surroundings and the initiation into Kentucky and Bullitt family life. By that winter, Dee was pregnant. She had difficulty adjusting to Marshall's abrasive ways and was pushing Keith to move to Seattle and practice law there. Both brides lived in the same building; and Dorothy, well aware of Dee's natural bent for gossip, was careful not to become her confidante in Bullitt family intrigues.

Only a few months into their marriage, Scott enlisted in the Army and was stationed at Camp Zachary Taylor outside of Louisville. He signed up as a private at a salary of forty-eight dollars a month, but soon he was promoted to sergeant and assigned to teach the men about proper codes of conduct when they were shipped to France. "I was living in town and would go out at five o'clock to meet him at the camp fence, and we'd talk. On weekends, he could get away. I was pregnant, and before he returned to camp on Monday mornings he'd bring some fruit and shredded wheat for me."

Then suddenly, in November 1918, the war was over. Scott became one of twenty attorneys assigned to the Judge Advocate General's Office to review the accumulated backlog of court-martial cases. This new assignment meant a promotion to major, a salary of three thousand dollars a year, and a move to Washington, D.C., which was no doubt welcomed by both Dorothy and Scott, though perhaps for different reasons.

Dorothy's pregnancy proceeded without serious complication, although she experienced many weeks of morning sickness, and spent hours bedridden. As she gained weight, she observed that it was a good thing she never had much of a figure because there was nothing to regret when it disappeared, describing herself in one outfit as "Grant's tomb dressed in a green suit."

In April 1919, seven months pregnant, Dorothy decided to return to Seattle for the birth of the baby before joining Scott in Washington, D.C. She was accompanied by Dee Terry Bullitt and her newborn son, Logan.

Although her life had been little changed by the war, she soon learned how deeply her circle of friends in Seattle had been affected. Captain Howard Hughes, true to his premonition, had been killed in Belgium only ten days before the armistice. Win Strout was unwilling to talk about his experience as captain in the artillery. When one of the neighbor boys asked to see his "souvenirs," Win told him that the only souvenirs he had were both arms and legs. "When he smiles he is the same old Win," Dorothy observed, "but in repose his face has grown quite sad." She also received a poignant letter from childhood chum, Bert Collins, who reflected the confusion and broadened perspective of returning home after the wreckage of war:

> Will we ever go back to things as they were again? You married—Dee married— every man one knew uprooted and flung about the world . . . You sometimes feel that Cairo or Tibet would be easier afterwards, to go into distant fields and begin again than to return to live among the broken limbs . . . It's the people one grew up with, through the rock fight phase and the "first dance" stage that count . . . when all the happy wraiths of the past come laughing by to make you feel there are still those to make you welcome back!

But Dorothy's days were filled with happy expectations rather than grim memories. Her room was bedecked with flowers; she was bedded, coddled, and surrounded by those who cared. Even Ohata, who had planned go into business on his own, changed his mind. His wife Alice revealed to Emma the real story: "We didn't know about Miss Dorothy's pregnancy before, but of course we wouldn't think of leaving now when she will need a careful driver and one she can trust." Seated by her window at Norcliffe, Dorothy sewed as she watched her mother entertain visiting dignitaries in the garden below. On warm spring days, she sat on her balcony to dry her hair in the sun, relishing the blue of sky and water, the mountains mantled in snow, the soft breeze, and the muffled buzz of bees buried in the cherry blossoms.

On one of her few outings, she heard President Wilson speak during his brief stop in Seattle. She was surprised at the President's lack of oratory and more interested in Mrs. Wilson, whom Dorothy found to be "just about the most unattractive human I have ever seen. She may have been beautiful once, but she has gotten bravely over it. She is very stout and coarse-looking, and she sat up there and looked out over the audience as if she wanted to decapitate everybody in the place."

Dorothy wrote to Scott every day. Her letters revealed a sincerity and sweetness kindled by love. For their first anniversary, May 16, she sent him gifts and a card: "Just one year from the day a famished bride and groom sat up to a counter and had a malted milk for their wedding feast. And later, pushed off in a little boat to start life together. Just a year by the calendar—it doesn't seem possible that all that time could have gone by. And oh, my dear, what a year of happiness it has been! I wonder how many women can look back on their first year of married life without one regret as I do. I don't believe one in a thousand. God bless you, dear." On that anniversary morning, her room at Norcliffe was filled with flowers and cards, the most prized being a letter from her husband for "love, confidence, faith in each other at all times, freedom from petty jealousy, liking the same people and the same things, happy together and with other people, and still happier alone, trying to help each other even with little things of life, and feeling all the while that the other was anxious to do the same, have made a pretty good foundation for us, Stimmie, and sitting here alone after everybody has gone for the day, I can feel the tears coming in my eyes, as I think how wonderful and lovable and perfect you have been to me."

Dorothy's days-in-waiting rolled by without event. There were no obstetricians to visit, no tests, no special diets to follow. When the time came, her mother called the family doctor, Caspar Sharples, a Seattle surgeon, beloved by all. Down-to-earth and full of humor, the short and stout physician was a country doctor, counselor, and veterinarian. He was also a friend and hunting companion of C. D.

Harriet Stimson had developed a "birthing" procedure that had begun with the arrival of Emma's first child, Frances Ann. After summoning Dr. Sharples by phone, she settled in at Dorothy's bedside, equipped with an ether drip to be used if pains became severe. On June 16, 1919, at about 4 a.m., Dorothy gave birth to a son. C. D. wired the news to Scott, who was en route by train. At home Dorothy opened an envelope Scott had given her, suggesting that if the baby was a girl, it be named either for herself or for Harriet; if a boy, it be named for C. D., and called either "C. D." or "Stim." The suggestions resolved a family tension that had festered for some time. According to Dorothy, her brother, Thomas, had signed a paper promising to rear his children in the Catholic religion. This commitment caused bitterness for C. D., and he refused to have his name attached to any such child. Thus, when Dorothy (probably the favored of his two children) produced a son, it was appropriate that he carry the family name. The baby boy was named Charles Stimson Bullitt.

HER SON BECAME DOROTHY'S ALL-CONSUMING JOY, AN attachment that for Charles Stimson would be both blessing and burden. "There is such pride in producing a man," she said in her deep voice decades later. "Genetically—for some reason—mother and son are more close than they ought to be."

In letters to Scott, she recorded every ounce the baby gained and monitored his every move. "I watch him and watch him," she wrote, still trying to realize that such a miracle had happened. "I looked at him so hard, for a half an hour at a time, seven times a day, that it gave me headaches." She worried and hovered until her health gave out and a nurse was hired to take over the less desirable duties. Freed then to simply enjoy her prize, she took him out in the fresh air, with his carriage draped in white netting "so some stray bee won't think he is a flower and act accordingly." Her letters were filled with affectionate descriptions: he was her "perky little tea kettle," her "little robin," fat, round, and rosy. "The Robin is lying in here on the couch," she wrote Scott, "staring at the fire and kicking and squealing with glee—as if some angel had just whispered some good joke into his ear." On his forays outside, he became a "merry little sunbeam," as "lively as a cricket," with "cheeks like a couple of Spitzenbergs."

"You'll have to do all the disciplining in our family because I just can't," she warned her husband. "I try to be firm, but if I see a tear or if his lip begins to quiver I just have to take him up and love him. It's all he wants, and it's just stronger than I am, I can't help it." These first months of motherhood brought Dorothy deep joy. In one letter, she wrote Scott, "I don't believe anybody was ever really happier in all the world ever. I am happy way down deep inside, right through any loneliness for you, and when I think of that little child of love sleeping so quietly and think that that belongs to us too, I just get a lump in my throat and can't realize it even yet. When we three are under the same roof again, no matter where it is, my happiness will be absolutely complete."

By November 1919, young Stimson was old enough to travel. Accompanied by a nurse, Dorothy and child crossed the country to join Scott in Washington, D.C., where they took up quarters at the Lafayette Hotel, not far from the White House. They had two bedrooms, one for the nurse and baby, and took their meals in the hotel dining room along with senators, foreign service officers, and the ambassadors and embassy staffs from Russia and Czechoslovakia.

Scott, meanwhile, was enjoying old friends and new contacts in the capital, which he described as a "big moving picture, a continuous panorama of passing figures, glimpsed and heard about from the president on down." Dorothy spent her days with the baby, taking him in his carriage to Lafayette Park to see the pigeons. She began to take more care with her appearance; she had her hair done twice a week. "Living in a hotel this way," she wrote her mother, "you *have* to be careful. People call at the weirdest hours of the morning and afternoon, and it seems to be having quite a reforming effect on me. Then, too, going into a public dining room with a good-looking officer twice every day is quite a strain. It all has a tendency to make me look at my hair in the back and see that my dress is brushed."

By spring of 1920, Scott's term in the service was coming to an end and Dorothy was pregnant again. In announcing the event to her parents, she explained that Stimson was "so outrageously spoiled we thought he shouldn't grow up an only child. Besides," she added, "I was afraid too, that Ohata might threaten to leave again unless I supplied him with another excuse for staying. We've got to do *something* to keep servants. But seriously, isn't it great!"

En route to Seattle in early summer, she and Scott stopped for a few days at the apartment in Louisville, showing off their son to the Bullitt clan. Dorothy also spent several days at the Red Cross, preparing meals for returning soldiers at the train station. This activity proved to be nearly fatal, for she was exposed then to the Spanish flu, a deadly pandemic that between 1918 and 1920 took half a million lives in the United States and twenty million around the world.

With three months remaining in her pregnancy, Dorothy was en route with Stim to Seattle when she began to feel ill. "I got as far as the Blackstone Hotel in Chicago, where I had a room and a little square cage [playpen] for Stim. Scott called me at the hotel, and while we were talking asked about the funny clicking noise he was hearing on the phone. I said I guessed it was my teeth chattering, that I might be catching a cold. 'What!' he said. 'Take that little flask'—he had given me a silver flask of good Kentucky bourbon, which he had great belief in—'and drink that whiskey and call a doctor.' I called the hotel doctor, drank the full flask, and laid out on the bed, thinking I was more drunk than sick. But I was very ill. That was the last I knew for several days. Pregnant women didn't survive in those days—if you were pregnant and caught

the flu, that was the end. They sent for Scott, and Scott sent for Father and Mother. I wasn't about to survive. I do remember hearing the doctor say at one point, 'I can save the woman, but I can't save the child. If the mother gets a cough, that child will never survive.' So I just didn't cough."

Scott, desperately worried, stayed with her until her mother arrived from Seattle, and then returned to Washington. When Dorothy had a sudden relapse, Harriet Stimson telegraphed C. D. instead of informing Scott. For Scott, this incident set up an intense state of anxiety about Dorothy's health. Worried that he would not be told of any more setbacks, he tried to explain: "Unless I hear from you, if only a line every day, I imagine that maybe you are too ill to write, or maybe you have had an automobile accident and are waiting till you get better to let me know . . . You have married a very cranky man," he wrote, "one who swings like a pendulum from one extreme to the other and whose feelings can't run along a quiet channel where you are concerned."

In Chicago, not only Dorothy's health, but that of the unborn baby was at stake. For a long while, she could keep little food down and took hypodermics of strychnine twice a day. Dorothy won the fight but it was not an easy victory. Back in Seattle, Dr. Sharples was unable to find a heartbeat for the unborn baby and prepared her for the possibility that her child might be stillborn. Scott, now decommissioned from the service, arrived in early September to be present for the delivery. He spent the long hours of Dorothy's labor at Norcliffe pacing the second floor. At one point he sat at her piano to pick out the few tunes, hymns that he knew, but when he struck the chords of "Nearer My

God To Thee," the mother-in-waiting sent a strong suggestion that he stop . . . immediately.

A little girl, pale and feeble, was born on September 24, 1920. To encourage her to breathe, Dr. Sharples slipped a spoonful of brandy down her throat and she coughed and took her first breath. The joyous parents named her Dorothy Priscilla, the latter name for Scott's mother, Annie Priscilla Logan Bullitt. In time she was nicknamed "Peach" by her parents—from a Valentine she received from her father at age four that read, "You are a peach and together we are a pear"—and was called Patsy by everyone else. She was a delicate child, the subject of constant concern. She was Harriet Stimson's particular darling, causing Dorothy to write, "She is such an adorable little thing and Mother is just so crazy about her. She is pretty fond of all of her grandchildren, but they none of them seem to hold quite the place in her heart or ever did—that Priscilla does."

Little Priscilla's delicate health was a key factor in Dorothy's relationship to this child. "Priscilla doesn't seem to gain and I just don't know what we will do . . . each day I think, now, tomorrow she will surely gain," she wrote when the baby was two months old. "Fate has funny ways of making you feel this or that way," she later reflected. "I feel *responsible* for Patsy's ill health—I always have. In the first place, being pregnant, I shouldn't have gone to the train station in Louisville to work, because that is where I got the flu. I don't doubt that it has affected her whole life." What would affect Patsy even more was her mother's assumption that she could have determined her daughter's future. For Patsy, that was a psychological burden that took years to overcome.

Another child, Harriet Overton Bullitt, would complete the Bullitt family in 1924. Named for her grandmother, she was always called Harriet, never "Hattie," a name despised by her namesake. This pregnancy was without the high expectation of the first or the fearful suspense of the second; the mother-to-be was ready to deliver by late August, writing to Scott, "You will come back from New York and look perfectly stunning, while I will look more like a covered wagon than ever." Harriet was born in Seattle General Hospital instead of The Highlands, and there was less fanfare over her arrival. From her earliest days, little Harriet showed a certain amount of autonomy, along with a robust appetite and an equally healthy temper. Her mother always admired and empathized with Harriet's independence of spirit, finding in her a soul companion for adventures both vicarious and real. "We *breathe* together," she often said about her last born with a smile.

The birth of the two older children signaled an end to living in the East. Dorothy had had enough of the weather, the constant traveling across country, and the intricate relationships of the Bullitt family, in which her role as an in-law was only a minor one. Seattle was her home. Once there, she was determined to stay, and she received all the encouragement she needed from her parents. In conversations with Scott, she wove an intricate rationale for her plan. As with all of her justifications, they made good sense, even if they might be devices for simply doing what she wanted to do. Basically she informed Scott that she was not returning, but would remain in Seattle, leaving her husband with a hard choice. If he remained in Kentucky, it would mean not only living without his two small children, to whom he was attached, but also living without his wife, with whom he was in love. It would also mean living married but alone in Kentucky, because marriage in those days was a permanent condition. However, Dorothy's later explanation of this situation did not include her harsh ultimatum. "Scott had closed his office in Louisville and had finished his work in Washington," she recollected. "We had no home there anymore, and I didn't think Patsy would survive the Louisville summers. By this time, Scott and Father had become such good friends that Father wanted him to move out—the business had grown and he needed a lawyer at the office—and by that time Scott was so in love with Father that there was really no need for him to go back to Louisville. His friends were gone, and his mother was pretty old and didn't know very much, and she would die very soon. There was nothing holding us there."

Scott agreed, although he did not dismiss his mother so summarily as Dorothy. His letters from Louisville, where he returned to close up the apartment, were filled with concern about telling Annie Bullitt their plans. He put it off by telling his mother that he would move west only for a few months. But the thought of his leaving, however temporarily, was a blow to Annie Bullitt. "She is so softened in spirit that it is almost tragical," he observed. Scott's brother Marshall did not take well to the news either, arguing against it from every angle, as if he were pleading a case.

There is no suggestion that Scott regretted the move, but undoubtedly it was a difficult choice. He was making a profound life change for someone so steeped in generations of Kentucky life and history. He was giving up his identity—both past and future—as a member of a prestigious Southern family with a professional future that was virtually guaranteed a success. He was taking on a whole new social environment where no one knew his name.

*Those were the days when people's homes were broad
and beautiful. It was a life that just doesn't exist
anymore, in a time and a place gone by.*

7 SHANGRI-LA
1920–1929

THE HIGHLANDS IN THE 1920S WAS A WORLD APART. THE
names given to its imposing homes—Glenkerrie, Firbrae, Aldarra, Laurelhedge,
Braeburn—evoked a romantic landscape and a lineage far removed from the
noise and clutter of the world outside. Those who lived behind its entrance
gates heard no din of traffic from Seattle's now-burgeoning streets, only the
whisper of wind through majestic trees, the twitterings of songbirds, a raven's
raucous call, or the occasional passage of a delivery truck on its rounds. There
were no nasty odors of sewage or exhaust, only pure air, sharpened by firs and
salt. No streetcar wires or billboards offended the eye; no grime or poverty.
One saw only the graceful curves of winding lanes and arched stone bridges, the
impeccable shapes of stately homes, and the splendor of the natural setting.

The Highlands was home to the "Right People," families of wealth and
standing. Its membership was carefully screened to provide a compatible citizenry with privacy, protection, and pleasure. The heads of these families were
mostly self-made men, lords of their own creation. They were entrepreneurs
who built their own fortunes—men like businessman D. E. Frederick, owner
of Frederick & Nelson Department Store; wealthy entrepreneur Bill Boeing,
who in the 1920s was coaxing a fledgling aircraft company off the ground;
attorneys Elmer Todd and Lawrence Bogle, founders of the most prestigious law
firms in town; and, of course, C. D. Stimson, who initiated many an enterprise,
including The Highlands itself. Given such company, more decisions may have
been made in this serene setting than in any boardroom in Seattle, in business conducted on the golf course, or in the drawing room after an elegant
dinner. These decisions filtered back and affected the very city from which,
paradoxically, The Highlands was so well isolated. Life in The Highlands

appeared as exquisite and flawless as a well-cut diamond. But for all its superficial perfection, there existed flaws and fissures that its well-bred citizens were either oblivious to or preferred to ignore. The elders of this generation in The Highlands were not interested in self-examination. "These people weren't interested in baring their souls or 'finding' themselves," Dorothy's daughter Priscilla later observed, "they just woke up each morning, pulled back the sheets, and there they were." These were people of action, doers, focused on building a world outside of themselves. They laughed with each other but they cried by themselves. They didn't seek psychiatrists, there were none; they relied as best they could on social structures for coping and support. The elders of this era were the last holdouts of Victorian times—citizens of a controlled reality in which appearances prevailed.

The grubby businesses of hatred, anger, or jealousy took place in the sanctuary of home, if there. Families did not fight or argue, and there was no such thing as depression, mental illness, or suicide. In 1924, a prominent Highlands matron, Virginia Clarke, was found dead of a gunshot wound in her chest. Although the gun and the bullet wound showed clearly that it was suicide, the Clarke family and neighbors were so loathe to put that name to it that it was determined that it might have been an accident, or even possibly a murder. Scott wrote the details to Dorothy in California, telling her that others had noticed privately that Mrs. Clarke had been melancholy, but of course this had never been openly discussed. "She must have been laboring under some suppressed emotion or else had physical suffering that others didn't know about, and she smiled through it all," he surmised. Within hours, a prominent criminologist was hired by the Clarke family. "I think their hope is to show that it was probably an accident," Scott wrote, "as it would be better for everybody—not only for the feelings of the Clarkes, but for her memory and the children growing up; and then for us all, it would not be so depressing as the thought of suicide." Later the newspapers reported the death as an accident, and Scott expressed relief and hope that "everything will be on a normal basis when you get back."

The cult of perfection could be suffocating for The Highlands children. When C. D. Stimson came upon his grandson Stim and young Edward Ohata fashioning a clubhouse from scraps of boards and boxes, he determined that the two eight-year-olds should have a "real house." Before the boys could grasp what was happening, an architect appeared with plans, a concrete foundation was laid, and construction began apace. While parents took home movies, the two boys stood aside and watched their clubhouse materialize into an adult model of perfection. From time to time, the boys were given a hammer and told where to pound a nail or two. The house remained there for many years, but the boys rarely played in it.

Upper-class children were expected to behave like courteous, truthful, brave small adults during the special times spent with their parents; on the other hand, they were left to work out the day-to-day realities—the runny noses, the tattletales, the cranky times—with governesses and nurses. As they grew, they saw that the magical kingdom they inhabited ended at the entrance gates. Between the ideal and the real worlds there was a gap, a psychic no-man's-land that caused some with more fragile egos to lose their way as they matured. Highlands children were hothouse flowers, living under rarified conditions, and some suffered when they met with the harsh realities of life outside. According to the Bullitt children, about half of the first generation born there suffered later in life from nervous breakdowns, alcoholism, and other mental and emotional problems.

———————

NORCLIFFE SERVED AS THE FOCAL POINT FOR THE STIMSON clan during the 1920s. Dorothy and Scott lived there with their first two children, as did Thomas and Emma and their first three. The main house was filled with the best that a great deal of money could buy. Heavy furniture, mostly Queen Anne–style, brought comfort to the huge living room; a long dining table provided ample eating space for the growing extended family. The nursery and four guest bedrooms accommodated a constant flow of grandchildren spending the night and other relatives and friends visiting for a few days. In addition to the cottage that had been a home for Thomas and Emma in the early years of their marriage, there was now a duplex to house the families of Fred Ohata, the chauffeur and mechanic, and Paul Stenneberg, the grounds keeper. Beneath the duplex, five automobiles, ranging from a station wagon to a Rolls-Royce, filled a large garage that also included a workshop and a pit for Ohata's mechanical work. There was a barn, a tennis court, and an elaborate playhouse for the seven grandchildren. Surrounded by a picket fence with hollyhocks growing next to the leaded glass windows, the playhouse was a one-room Hansel-and-Gretel cottage, finely detailed right down to the cupboards and painted woodwork that lined the walls, the stone fireplace ringed by handmade tiles of rabbits, cats, and dogs, and the painting of a witch over the door.

A large staff was required to run the Stimson ménage. A cook, maid, and butler, part-time laundress, and up to five other servants kept the large household running smoothly. Ohata had an assistant; Stenneberg had three to five helpers during the garden's high season. The surrounding gardens, now mature in their plantings, exploded with color and fragrance each year. In photos taken at the time, wisteria and clematis showered purple and white from trellises, while dogwood and cherry trees littered pink-and-white blossoms on the well-groomed lawns. Orange trees grew in tubs in the courtyard entrance. Spires of foxglove, gladiola, phlox, and delphinium shot up in season like so many color-ful rockets, amid bursts of daffodils and narcissus, lilies, peonies, and peach bells that punctuated the surrounding green in well-placed profusion. Hun-dreds of flowering shrubs—azaleas and rhododendrons and kalmia—provided colorful background, while glossy-leafed laurel and boxwood brought definition to the borders.

The C. D. Stimsons entertained lavishly. On formal occasions, Packards, Cadillacs, Buicks, and Rolls-Royces would glide around the oval drive to deposit their elegant passengers, groomed and gowned for dinners where silver, crystal, damask, and gold-rimmed china gleamed in the candlelight. "Father and Mother did a great deal of entertaining, but it was nothing like it is today," recalled Dorothy many years later. "And it was certainly not *my* form of enter-tainment—it was of their era. For a formal dinner for twelve at seven o'clock, everyone was there on time. The women usually wore long dresses with trains. You went straight in to dinner. At dinner you sat next to so-and-so and visited with that person, knowing that you would talk with the others afterward. And then after dinner, the women would leave and go into the living room while the men stayed behind with their cigars.

"The men probably discussed the unions that looked like a tremendous threat because they would cost business a lot of money. There was also violence of a sort among them—you could get a good beating if you didn't belong to the club. But the unions were needed in those days—unless the workers got together for improvements, management wouldn't listen.

"The women didn't talk about the things women discuss today. They were somewhat interested in the front page of the paper and politics but there wasn't a lot of finesse in the conversation. They weren't too well informed politically— whatever their husbands were for, they were for. Mostly they talked about their families, about trips they took, and about volunteer work with the symphony or Children's Orthopedic Hospital. Servants became a big topic—where to find them and what kind were good. After a little while, standing around the fire-place and chatting, they were joined by the men and there was coffee, liqueurs, and conversation for the rest of the evening."

At less formal summer parties, guests were greeted by Japanese lanterns lining the roadway for six hundred feet from the entrance gate to the house. Coupes and convertibles deposited smart couples dressed in crepe and tweed to

In 1922, C. D. Stimson bought Greenway, the house next to Norcliffe, and gave it to Dorothy and Scott.

mix in the garden and dine under tents set up for the occasion. The painter Morris Graves, noted many years later for his paintings of flowers, remembered these sumptuous days, when as a sixteen-year-old, he worked for two summers as a gardener's assistant under Stenneberg. "The quality of people who came through Norcliffe's great gate, with its look of privilege and security, were mostly ambitious people who were keeping the industrial part of the city together," he recalled. "The sort of people any frontier environment has—all the way from the Alaskan with his pocket full of gold to the tycoons who had managed to accumulate enormous wealth."

The young artist was often around when Harriet Stimson entertained in the garden. At these functions, the grounds were awash in a sea of chiffons and cloches, elegant linen suits, and wide-brimmed hats garnished with ribbons and flowers. "When Mrs. Stimson entertained the Garden Club, I managed to position myself at work near the edge of the rhododendrons so I could see the fashionable ladies in the garden," he remembered with obvious humor. "I can remember one time—and it was a kind of not too attractive streak of my young nature—that a flotilla of fifteen or so seagulls drifted over the ladies in their wide-brimmed cartwheel summer hats and I reveled to see one of the seagulls release a great slosh of whitewash and hit madame's hat."

In 1922, C. D. bought for Dorothy and Scott the house next to Norcliffe, a large home surrounded by six acres of lawn and trees. "It had been one of the first houses in The Highlands," Dorothy recounted. "It was designed by Carl Gould and built by Chester White of the Metropolitan Building Company.

During the days when I was out riding my horse everywhere, I watched it being built and I liked it from the start. Especially since it was next door to Father's place. When the Whites moved out, Father thought it would be nice to have me nearby, so he bought the house and gave it to me. It was a colonial, quite simple, and we loved it."

Greenway, as it was called, was a homey, gracious, white clapboard with green shutters and striped awnings, in contrast to the more formal houses around. A giant elm tree welcomed the guests who drove into the oval driveway, and a generous-sized entry hall introduced them to the house. Dorothy liked the low ceilings and the rambling effect of large and cozy spaces. With twenty-three rooms full of practical and charming touches, it was a house built for use rather than display, designed more for family than formality. There was a small wood-paneled den for Scott; a wrapping closet where Dorothy could indulge her passion for ribbon, tape, shears, and rolls of paper; snug and gabled bedrooms and a balcony for the children; an inviting master bedroom with fireplace and dressing room; a generous kitchen; a sun porch with space for Ping-Pong or pool; and a long book-lined library with a tile-fronted fireplace. In time, Dorothy added a more formal living room for entertaining, furnished with velvet drapes, brocade couch and chairs, a piano, and a marble fireplace. This room, high-ceilinged and lined on three sides with windows and French doors, stood out from the house like a graceful ship's bow and faced a large lawn with maples and madronas guarding the edge over the Sound. It was a favorite pastime of the Bullitt children to climb these trees, spending hours out of sight and reach, to watch the sunset over the Olympic Mountains.

South of Greenway, the Stimson compound continued on to the grounds of Archibald and Emma Downey, aunt to Emma Baillargeon Stimson, and further south to the residence of Clara and Cully Stimson, the nephew who had lived on Minor Avenue with the older Stimsons. Beyond Cully's property was the palatial gray chateau of Thomas and Emma, built in 1923. Surrounded by sixteen acres of lawn and plantings, its high chimneys and peaked roofs rose through the trees at the end of a long drive.

The whole enclave, known as "Stimson Row," stretched at least half a mile along the banks above Puget Sound. If Bill Boeing's remark to Highlands' newcomers was heeded—"Never own more yard than you can afford to pay someone else to take care of"—the Stimsons of Stimson Row were prosperous indeed: their lawns stretched for tens of acres all around. The seven grandchildren ran barefoot from house to house in the summer. Before there was a swimming pool, they ran down to the beach to play and swim in the Sound and then back up to Norcliffe where, under an archway of madronas, they left small handprints on the new paving stones to the teahouse, and then tore off to the playhouse to play "store" or hide-and-seek. It was their free-ranging territory, a kingdom within a kingdom, with shady paths from one castle to another.

Establishment of this enclave at The Highlands realized a life's dream for C. D. Stimson, to create a place of grace and refuge for his children and grandchildren. During these years he also achieved other goals. Thanks to shrewd investments and cooperative ventures with his many business friends, he amassed a fortune in property, stocks, and bonds. His Stimson Mill Company was thriving after the war years, shipping lumber to world markets. He held positions of power and respect outside the family businesses, as organizer and director of the General Insurance Company of America (Safeco), as trustee of the Olympic Hotel Corporation (in which he was the largest stockholder) and, during the 1920s, as vice-president, president, and chairman of the board of the Metropolitan Building Company. Everything C. D. touched had turned to gold, and much of the gold went to various private and civic causes.

The Stimson patriarch, now in his mid-sixties, was keenly aware of time's passage; age and accident were taking their toll on family and friends. His brother, Fred, the good-natured younger sibling who had borne C. D.'s jokes in good humor, died in 1921. A year later, Harry Treat, C. D.'s old golfing companion, was killed in British Columbia. "Oh, the shock we received to hear of dear old Kimmie's death," wrote the other member of the golfing trio, singer Chauncey Olcott, who himself suffered from poor health. A. B. Stewart, another early Seattle chum and Dorothy's old friend from his drugstore days, also died. In 1925, C. D.'s own vigor was impaired by abdominal problems that called for surgery. During this time, he lost more than thirty pounds and had to spend eight weeks in bed. The unaccustomed inactivity made him miserable. "I have been so ill that the thought has many times occurred to me that I did not see how a man could possibly feel as badly as I did and still live," he wrote Olcott, "but I am beating it out now."

Faced with his mortality, and with management of the day-to-day business activities turned over to Thomas and Scott, C. D. sought to extract as much pleasure as he could from life. He bought a sixty-five-foot powerboat called the *Gloria,* but soon gave it to his nephew Cully and commissioned a more spacious craft to be built. Designed by Ted Geary, the *Wanda* was a classic ninety-three-foot motor yacht with decks of teak and a hull of Port Orford cedar. Its polished wood and brass interior accommodated up to ten passengers and a five-man crew. Three gas engines and a 1,500-gallon tank provided 1,400 miles of cruising before refueling. The Stimsons celebrated Thomas's birthday aboard the *Wanda,* and Dorothy provided her own brand of humor in the form of "horror-scopes" for the family. Hers read: "The child born on Feb. 5th, the day of the lemon, is under the sign of Vulcan and will have the nature of a blacksmith, without the delicate lights and shades usually present in a normal disposition. Her hammer she will have in daily use and never allow it to get rusty, knocking all the people who have qualities of which she is envious. She will have a liking for the occult without the brains to grasp it, a love of the beautiful without the power to express it. She will have better luck than she deserves, will get much more out of life than she puts into it, will never do any more work than she has to. She has a penchant for Scottology and a weakness for its branches and a disposition like what Hamlet said was in the state of Denmark."

During winters, the elder Stimsons began to seek the sun in Southern California. Thus began a yearly migration to the gracious Huntington Hotel in Pasadena. Leaving home shortly after Christmas, they took the train south, followed by Ohata with the car. For four months each year, they enjoyed sunshine, visited relatives, and made friends with others fleeing midwestern snows or northern rains. They built a duplex cottage on the Huntington grounds in partnership with a Dr. and Mrs. Baer, naming the units Clovelly East and West.

IN THE HIGHLANDS, THE BULLITT FAMILY—NOW JOINED BY baby Harriet—settled into their new home. As ardent Democrats, Scott and Dorothy were aliens in Republican territory, but, because their relatives comprised a quarter of the population, they were tolerated as political eccentrics. Dorothy, now in her early thirties, was earning status as a young matron. Having married successfully and borne three children, she lived in that highest bastion of society—The Highlands—although she never regarded this last fact as an achievement but simply as the way life was. She continued to work with charitable causes, following in her mother's footsteps as a board member of the Children's Orthopedic Hospital, and she established for the hospital's benefit a crafts store called The Corner Cupboard that was much like one she and Florence Williams had wanted to open when they returned from New York in 1915. She presented historical research papers at The Fortnightly Club, was on the board of The Florence Henry Memorial Chapel, and, as a member of the Music Practice Club, played the guitar during benefit performances at Norcliffe.

At home, she managed the household with smooth authority. Unlike her mother, who planned every menu in minute detail, Dorothy supervised on a macrolevel, focusing on general guidelines—meals on time, house clean and orderly, grounds neat and well-kept—and hired the people to do it. She managed the servants with bemused tolerance. About a new gardener named Richard Wagner, she wrote, "Shades of Lohengrin! He doesn't understand me and I don't understand him, but he's a clean, decent-looking fellow, and if he doesn't plant the carrots around the pool and the larkspur by the kitchen I shan't mind." She doled out praise for chocolate sauces, starched shirts, and cut flowers, but the details of how and when they appeared were left to cook, laundress, and gardener. The staff, grateful to be left to their own initiative, returned her compliments with intense loyalty and a well-run household, even during the many hours when she was absent. "Nothing goes to waste" was a household mantra that included everything from daily meals in which everything was consumed, to keeping a supply of tissue paper wrappings handy in case toilet paper was in short supply. "As youngsters we thought nothing about it," Patsy recalled. "It was a way of life and to do otherwise was irresponsible and uncivilized. You ate everything on your plate, and on cook's day off you had leftovers. You had to take care of things. You didn't lose clothes or leave them somewhere—if I left my jacket at the movies I'd never go to the movies again! You didn't just replace things in those days; everything from toys to household items was repaired and used again and again."

The servants understood that Dorothy, not Scott, was supreme ruler in the home. At one breakfast when Scott was entertaining the children with tricks, Stim remembered that his father was interrupted by the governess who said, "Eat your cereal, Harriet, Father is just being funny." Dorothy, also at the table, heard the comment but let it pass, and later Stim overheard his father telling the woman politely that he would appreciate it if she did not speak about him in that way.

In her personal life, Dorothy found herself given over completely to the roles of wife, mother, and daughter, all of which drained her emotions. As the demands of these functions grew, a private part within her seemed to disappear. There were few hours now for riding horseback or walking the beach, few minutes for quiet time in the bath or bedroom. She never examined what was missing—she wasn't analytical or introspective by nature—she only knew that there were times when she felt dragged down by fatigue, migraines, and nightmares that she could not remember. During waking hours, if she was not going to a social engagement with Scott, she was conferring with her mother, attending a committee meeting, or less often, reading to the children. She acted out of love and duty, but in the process the Center of the Universe found herself eclipsed by others and their needs. The roles required of her conflicted from time to time, leaving her exhausted from trying to please and satisfy everyone. In determining her priorities, she regarded herself as more wife than mother, that much was clear. What was not so obvious was that in her heart of hearts, in her values, her allegiances, and fundamental way of life she was more daughter than wife. It was fortunate indeed that there was no conflict between her parents and her husband. Dorothy had enough to do keeping them all happy.

———

SCOTT, NOW ABSORBED INTO THE CLAN, BECAME A FAMILIAR presence in Seattle during the 1920s. He enlivened social functions in The Highlands with humorous anecdotes and historical perspectives, earning a reputation as the liberal "renegade" among his conservative neighbors. If others looked askance at his politics, he shrugged it off, considering everyone a friend. There were no strangers in his world; he knew and remembered by name everyone from the newspaper boy to the editor-in-chief. On his way to the White Building where he worked as attorney for the C. D. Stimson Company, Scott stopped on the street to greet passersby or chat with colleagues; as he entered the offices upstairs, he was surrounded by employees who wanted, as his son Stim later described, "just to bask in the radiance of his smile." When the editor of *The Town Crier* compiled a list of admirable qualities among Seattle's civic leaders he included "the smile and manner of Scott Bullitt."

Within the family, Scott was more cautious. As a male outsider, he was aware that he had joined an elite and powerful clique and that his success as a member depended on harmony and good will. He found such a relationship with his father-in-law. The two were natural friends. "We talked over everything, business, family, politics, all phases of life—except religions," Scott wrote Dorothy after spending an evening with C. D. "I have felt since my own father's death that there could never be his like again. I understand full well how you feel the same way about your father. With my own father gone, I don't believe your father has his equal in the world today." Toward his mother-in-law, Scott was civil and—after she gave him a copy of Harriet Beecher Stowe's *Uncle Tom's Cabin* for his birthday—a bit careful. He realized that his southern charm did little to influence her New England reserve, but he regarded her with enough sincerity and respect that in time she came to accept him and love him dearly.

Scott was most concerned about his brother-in-law. From the outset, Scott was aware that Thomas resented his relationship with C. D. and considered him an intruder in family affairs. Dorothy tied Thomas's feelings to old sibling patterns. "Thomas never liked me very well. There were eight years between us and I was always a pest as far as he was concerned. We had separate friends and he saw to it that I stayed in my own field. But when we were both married he became jealous—of Scott in particular and his relationship with Father.

There was a great *bond* there between Scott and Father—they laughed at the same things, told each other stories and agreed on everything. I don't know if they argued about the Democratic party, but whatever Scott thought, Father also thought it. The only problem was that Scott didn't play golf; otherwise there was complete love between those two. Scott made up for Thomas—a son who wouldn't do anything Father wanted him to do." These words were easily said sixty years later; at the time they were never spoken.

To maintain harmony in the family, Scott became deferential. When Dorothy visited her parents in California, he warned her not to relay any of his business news because Thomas would want to be the one to inform his parents. At the office, he collected the mail and left it on Thomas's desk to be inspected first by him. But these small efforts became useless when C. D. insisted on equal rights for both families in the company business. Dorothy recalled that after years of smoldering resentment, Thomas accused Scott of competing with him to undermine his influence in the family business. Scott, in a long memo, tried to assure his brother-in-law that he recognized his authority "as superior to mine in all matters pertaining to the office . . . I have tried to assist in the office in any way that I could . . . thereby leaving you free to handle the larger problems of financial policy which you were dealing with. But the idea of ever wanting to supplant you, or to take over work which you preferred to do yourself, or to assert any supposed theoretical equality in the office, was totally foreign to my thoughts."

The internal squabblings of the clan never surfaced in public. To everyone else, the Stimsons were a harmonious dynasty, united in their role as prime movers on the cultural, civic, and social scenes. In the 1920s, Scott and Dorothy fell into the social whirl. The Bullitts were handsome and popular guests at dinners, parties, and concerts at people's homes; at the theater and the opera; and at fundraisers—he, with his affable charm and she with her quiet smile and reserve. They went out every evening, and it was customary for the children to wave good-bye to them from the window seat on the second-story landing.

Dorothy continued to be uncomfortable at high-powered "ultra social" gatherings, and preferred less formal gatherings of close friends. At a surprise dinner Dorothy gave for Scott's birthday in 1924, the neighbors dressed up as children and were ready to act accordingly. "They arrived in one bunch and such a sight you've never seen!" she wrote her mother. "The girls with wash dresses on about to their knees and their hair either in pigtails or hanging loose down their backs, with white stockings and little black Mary Jane shoes. The men wore their golf knickers with white shirts and Eton collars and flowing bow ties . . . Brother was awfully funny—he had a little tight Eton suit with a bright red wig—they called him 'Flaming Youth.' Bill Boeing had on a sailor suit that was about four sizes too small and made him look about seven feet tall . . . Bertha Boeing arrived carrying a toy bunny that had a compartment into which she had inserted a flask, saying she was a 'child with debutante tendencies' . . . Genevieve [Henry] was a scream . . . They each had a toy for 'little Scotty' as they called him—a collection of sling shots and mechanical toys, a cow bell on a ribbon for his neck so he wouldn't go astray . . . It was crazy from the start."

Family life also provided its pleasures. Dorothy was always intensely proud of her children. With a smile and a roll of the eyes, she would often say of them, "My Three—with My Three you never know what will happen." Into her old age, she carried mental pictures of them during those early years in the 1920s—a solemn-faced Stimmy, with the curl of brown hair that fell onto his forehead, studying every project with seriousness; Patsy, with her Dutch-boy bob and eager smile, chattering about her imaginary friends; "angel" Harriet, her ringlets a golden halo, presenting two tiny front teeth in a tentative smile. They were ideal children born into an idyllic setting, and their mother sought to maintain this image. As if to preserve their pristine childhood, she took moving pictures of Patsy and Stimmy, looking like small sprites as they sat in a cart pulled by a large dog in harness across a meadow. Later, she had all three photographed by Dorothea Lange, the famous photographer. "Stim wasn't cooperative enough to smile but he did what he was told; Patsy was fine. Harriet wouldn't do *anything* she was told. She wouldn't stand still or turn around to face the camera and she climbed a tree and said she wouldn't come down. So the poor lame photographer had to lug the camera all over the place and finally took a picture of Harriet in the tree."

She enjoyed introducing her children to rituals. On Christmas morning, the Stimson family gathered at Norcliffe for breakfast which, for the children, seemed to take forever. Afterward, the seven grandchildren, with hands clean and hair combed, lined up according to height and marched downstairs to the highly polished ballroom where a giant tree emblazoned with lights and surrounded by presents awaited them. Enchanted, the children received their gifts from a jolly Santa Claus (who bore only the slightest resemblance to Scott), went to their chairs to open them and then write down the names of those who would receive thank-you letters. A more private ritual took place earlier on Christmas morning, when Stimmy, Patsy, and Harriet piled into their parents' bedroom to open the stockings that hung in front of the marble fireplace. Shrieking with joy, they shredded wrappings right and left, while their parents watched from the safety of their twin beds. When asked by a curious grown-up neighbor, "Did Santa come to your house? And did you see him? And what did he do?" Harriet replied matter-of-factly, "Yes, he filled the stockings and then got back in bed with Mother."

———

As they grew, the differences between each of her children became more obvious but only confirmed the early images Dorothy had of them. "There never was such a boy!" she wrote Scott when Stimmy was eight years old. "He is such a manly baby—so little but so serious." Given his role as the eldest, Stimmy had direct influence on his sisters and taught them what he could. Under his tutelage, Harriet learned several oft-repeated phrases, among them "Atta Boy" and "Well, what d'you know about that?" On the occasion of seeing their first moving picture in a theater, *Moby Dick*, Patsy asked him the meaning of the word "asbestos" printed on the stage curtain, and he quickly replied, "It's Greek for welcome." Patsy believed it for a long time. He showed an early interest in earning his way. When his father recounted how he had made money as a boy by polishing his father's shoes, Stimmy went directly to work. He was busy putting tan polish on black shoes and vice-versa when Dorothy found him in the bathroom. Looking up from his work, he announced he had decided to make a little money by polishing shoes and, as Scott described it, "his mother encouraged him in the noble pursuit."

At about age eight, Stimmy began to be interested in everything from knives to natural history and Dorothy was hard-pressed to answer his endless questions. From Palm Springs, she wrote Scott that she was considering hiring a Scout Master who might be able to teach the young inquisitor "where the rattlesnakes live in winter and why—what spiders and lizards are poisonous and how to look out for them—the different kinds of cactus, rock formations, prevailing winds, etc." This intellectual curiosity, coupled with Stimmy's developing athletic ability, nearly wore Dorothy out on their daily horseback rides. During these rigorous rides, sixteen miles or so "and part of it good and fast," her young son kept up a stream of talk. "His mind is on what he is talking about, or how far it is to the river, or which range of mountains is closest—just like his father," she wrote proudly.

If Stimmy was full of questions, Patsy was full of fantasy. Kept out of school most of the time because of poor health, she wished more than anything for friends her own age. Instead, she made do with her grandmother, her nurse, her animals, and her rich natural imagination, which was fired by all the books she could read. Patsy also played with her imaginary friends, the most important being Dickie Tin, a superboy who could do anything, and perhaps an alter-ego for a child who was frail and often confined to bed. She also had imaginary

Dorothea Lange photographed the Bullitt children in 1927.
LEFT TO RIGHT: Harriet, Stimson, and Priscilla.

children, which caused Dorothy concern one day when she found Patsy "absolutely inconsolable" because one of them had died. Earnest, eager to please, a Little Miss In-Between, and a peacemaker—she was also clever and competitive. Once caught playing after lights-out, Patsy claimed the wind had blown her out of bed. "Did you ever see a tiny kitten, one that didn't even have its eyes open?" her mother asked her one day while rocking her. "No, did you?" was the reply. When Dorothy said "Yes," Patsy thought a minute and said, "But I *have* seen them without any fur." "If you tell one better than Patsy," Dorothy wrote her mother, "you'll have to get up early in the morning."

Patsy was also a loving child. She sent postcards and poems that are touching efforts to attract her parents' attention and affection, addressed "To The Nicest Mummy in the World" and signed from "Your Dearest Girl." Her parents' love took the form of concern for her health. It was as if they didn't know what to do for this thin, intense little girl. Fortunately, Harriet Stimson did, and she was Patsy's comfort and refuge throughout childhood. Grandmother took the time to listen; she understood, and she was *there* physically and emotionally.

Harriet added her own distinct imprint to the trio. Four years younger than Patsy, she had a difficult time keeping up with her siblings, which only increased her determination and self-reliance. In time, she polished her skills and became capable at chasing brother or sister with a baseball bat when the need arose. Her mother adored her. "She is merry and full of smiles and wriggles in the bosom of her family but very dignified with strangers," Dorothy wrote about her youngest. "Of course, I can't be just sure, but I *think* she is the best of all." As the youngest, there were fewer expectations and fewer worries attached to

Harriet. She was healthy and undemanding and Dorothy usually found her presence relaxing. "She is so responsive and happy and there seems to be no limit to her good nature—she doesn't get *that* from her mama," Dorothy commented to her mother.

Harriet was as active "as a fly on a griddle" from the start. With great energy, and wearing as few clothes as possible, she decorated her tricycle with flags and tore around, dragging toys behind her. Early on she demonstrated her singular vision of the world and a certain fixity of purpose in dealing with it. She drew colorful pictures of fantasy landscapes that reflected a rich inner life; she spent time in a magical world in which her inventive mind described sand as "warm snow" or a bat in flight that she saw in a children's book as a "little kitten in an aeroplane." One Christmas she received a musical chair that played every time she sat on it. "The problem is that she feels that all furniture should have music in it," Dorothy wrote her mother, "and we have laughed till our sides ached watching her go about the room from one chair to another, trying to sit on each one."

Harriet had well-defined boundaries, and interruption of any of her activities could produce a storm of temper. When she was about four, Scott found her examining some old English brandy glasses that Dorothy had given him as an anniversary present. Seeing her clasp them in her chubby hands, Scott said "Oh, Harriet, don't break them," whereupon she turned on him in one of "her incipient rages," stamped her foot and said with great emphasis, "I'm not breaking them! I've just got my hands on them!" When Scott and Dorothy rode horseback, Harriet went along too, sitting in front on her mother's saddle and refusing to get off. "I tried to lift her down," her father wrote to Harriet Stimson, "but she clung tightly with one hand to the pommel and the other hand to the mane. Every time I put my arms out and took hold of Harriet she shook her head determinedly and said, 'No thank you, Father, no *thank* you!'" Scott described his youngest daughter best: "She doesn't shine in any reflected glory but has a genuine personality all her own."

To all appearances, the Bullitts were blessed with good family, friends, and fortune. Their children were beautiful, bright, and well-mannered. Their home life bespoke a couple devoted to each other and to the ideals of marriage and family. But it was more complicated than that. Psychiatrist Thomas Szasz has described marriage as "a gift a man gives to a woman for which she never forgives him." In Dorothy's case, the demands of maintaining a marriage pressed strongly during the years at The Highlands. The early differences that she had realized between herself and Scott grew more acute as romance faded into regularity. She sought anonymity as much as her husband preferred an audience; she continued to be more discriminating about people and less tolerant of their foibles than he; she remained as reserved in temperament as Scott was demonstrative.

Her cool eye soon began to detect cracks in her husband's smooth Southern veneer: promises that did not result in action, his easy charm with women, the schedules not kept, and excuses that were empty. There were rumors that he was a ladies' man—and certainly he flirted when women flocked around him—but there was never any evidence of scandal. In one of his earliest Kentucky political campaigns, a columnist had predicted, "When women get the right to vote, Scott Bullitt will be President of the United States." Dorothy approached the matter with lightly mocking humor. "Don't forget me when you look upon the charms of Milnora, will you?" she wrote about a famous Washington beauty when he was traveling to the capital. "She is bewitching, I know, but for the sake of the children, don't leave us for her." She noticed that he received letters from women from time to time. Forwarding one to him on a trip, she commented, "I wish you would write as many letters to me as you do to Miss Whitaker—or think of me as often."

She worried that his frequent trips were an excuse to stay away. In 1921, while Scott was visiting in Louisville, she urged him to hurry home. He wrote, "That is what I want to do, and all it needs is a word from you and all other feelings give way. Duty here gives way to love and worship at Norcliffe or wherever you are." But he stayed in Louisville, went to see the Dempsey-Carpenter fight in New Jersey, and then went to Pittsburgh to visit his sister. Some of his jaunts across country seemed purposeless. In 1923, after visiting his mother in Louisville, he went to Washington, D.C., where he spent days at the Income Tax Department and the Geodetic Survey, toured museums, and attended the inauguration of President Coolidge ("more like a funeral than an inauguration"). Dorothy lost her patience this time. There had been a fire at Greenway and she had wired him, asking what to do about insurance. He answered by requesting that she forward his mail to Baltimore, to which she fired off a curt telegram: "When your message came yesterday I saw red. It was only the distance between us that saved you. Had to wait till morning to cool off. Am not interested in your Baltimore mail but have been waiting since June 23 for an answer to my question about fire insurance. What company has it and what shall I do. Dorothy." Scott sidled past her anger. "I don't blame you a bit," he wrote appeasingly, "as it is most exasperating to ask important questions that are ignored, while trivial questions are answered in detail. But really, I thought I had telegraphed last Monday about the insurance company, but I must have failed to do it and simply imagined it."

There were few out-and-out fights over these differences because Dorothy didn't like the histrionics of quarreling and Scott either took what he called her "kindly criticism" in stride or managed to sidestep it with his charm. Sometimes, though, confrontation was inevitable. In low-voiced discussions behind closed doors, she chided him for being "mushy," exhorted him to have more "character," and scoffed when he gave away his time or paid too much attention to inappropriate people.

The children never witnessed a fight between their parents but remembered the voices rising behind the closed bedroom door as a subject became more heated. From the hallway outside, Patsy and Stimmy could not detect the words, but the tone, particularly the cold, harsh sounds of their mother's voice, struck fear in small hearts. As Patsy explained it years later, "I don't think they argued badly—probably only about why they had to dine with someone they didn't like or who was traveling off to where—but they did have their differences in temperament and ideas. Father liked the life of politics—dashing around having chicken in Puyallup—and Mother hated it. She enjoyed the symphony, but he slept through it. She liked to go out on a yacht on the Sound and he preferred to make a speech in Yakima. They always hid their differences behind closed bedroom doors and pretended the conflicts weren't there. That made it spooky for our young imaginations."

Scott adjusted to his wife's remonstrances with equanimity. He was tolerant by nature and eager to smooth things over. In 1924, while visiting his quarreling brothers and sister after the death of his mother in Louisville, he wrote Dorothy, "You have simply spoiled me completely! You have such poise, as well as charm and beauty, and your good breeding shows so at all times, in vexing cases, that I find myself saying things I ought not to when others can't come up to your standard. Even when you are mad, downright angry, with red spots high up on your cheeks and your pretty teeth hidden, the smile gone and the twinkles about your eyes (which first impressed me September 11, eight years ago) vanished, even then you are never loud. But, like Cordelia, your 'voice is sweet and low, a most excellent thing in a woman.' "

Dorothy was more honest about her shortcomings. "There isn't one man in a thousand who would have the patience to get along with me," she wrote him after one outburst; "you are actually sweet to me right in the midst of all my badness." She was as adept at soothing blows with her humor as she was in delivering them with a certain under-the-thumb sort of style. One gift of books to Scott was autographed "To the dearest man that ever married trouble" and signed "With my dearest love, Scott dear, and hoping you won't feel impelled to throw these at me. Stimmie." Mutual admiration also helped the Bullitts' marriage. They were both charming, attractive, and popular, and each appreciated those assets in the other. Daughter Patsy described their strongest bond: "They were proud of each other—which was better than being in the same room all the time."

One way to maintain the marriage was to spend time apart. Their first two anniversaries, celebrated at opposite ends of the country, served as a hint of things to come. Something interfered every year to separate them, in spite of all protests to the contrary about loneliness and love. Between January and April, Dorothy usually took the children to California; in summer or fall, Scott went East to manage family matters, to attend various meetings or political conventions. "Duty" became the watchword that sanctioned separation. "Duty" could summon one or the other east or west or south for months on end, until after a while it became a kind of transparent joke between the two that they could only take a trip when "duty" called. A hint of sarcasm was present. When Dorothy was away on one her jaunts, he informed her that her friends would still be in Seattle when she returned but added, "that is, unless you decided that it is your duty to stay until summer." Sensing that he was thoroughly enjoying the Democratic National Convention in 1928, she wrote that she could not help but hope that he would find it his duty to come home as soon as the convention was over.

Frequent separation seemed to enhance the marriage. In each other's absence, released from the tensions of everyday differences, they were able to find breathing space, and yet nourish the marriage and their own roles in it. They kept close contact through the long letters Scott wrote at least once a day and Dorothy less often. In letters, they said the cherished things, kept up the intensity of sentiment, and expressed the ideals of marriage. Scott's letters, more than Dorothy's, were colored with romance. "When I saw your Italian gray cloak disappear at the station," Scott wrote in 1924, "I felt like jumping off the train and running back . . . The last few months and weeks and even days, seem to have made me love you and cherish the very thought of you more than ever before. We seem closer together and in a more perfect union . . . Each period in our lives has seemed to me more perfect than the last—always moving onward and upward and becoming more beautiful from the days on the *Lydia* to the last night when I went to sleep on your arm. You will be in my thoughts always until am home once more." Dorothy replied in kind: "Where you are now, the whole world is—last week Greenway seemed the most Heavenly spot on earth—and this week it is just a blank. My mind runs back over the time we have had together—nothing else interests me enough to hold my mind—and I have a previous hoard of golden moments that I live over again. It is such a priceless treasure that I don't want one of them to slip into dimness."

When his wife was gone and he at home, Scott didn't fare so well. He refused social invitations and spent lonely hours reading at night or writing letters to Dorothy. His letters had a listless, sometimes insecure quality, particularly during the early 1920s when he was more dependent upon her and not yet well established in Seattle. In her absence, he paid her bills, put her jewels and furs in the vault, forwarded her bank statements, maintained the house, and even had Brooks, the gardener, deliver weekly reports about the grounds at Greenway. "Please let me know anything you can think of that I can possibly do," he wrote. "I just want to be nice to you so you will surely come back, instead of sending for the children, ordering the house to be closed, and suggesting to the Henrys and other family friends that really I have no place to stay."

This pattern—he here, she there—laced with letters, occurred several times a year and lasted throughout their marriage. Central to it was the winter migration south to Pasadena or Palm Springs. Because Patsy's frail health was believed to require bed rest, sun baths, and breathing exercises, it seemed a natural migration during the gray winter months in Seattle that Dorothy dreaded. It also was refuge for her in 1925 when she suffered a depression that, in spite of her great inner strength, turned into a nervous breakdown. "After I had Harriet, for whatever unknown reason, I had a great depression come over me. I wouldn't eat. I had this beautiful bébé and the bébé's papa was very pleased and everything was going well, except that I was in the dumps for no reason at all."

The demands of nursing a newborn, raising two other children, and pleasing husband and parents while keeping a rigorous social schedule combined to shatter her nerves. She lost energy ("I have all the energy of an oyster") and began to experience headaches and nightmares. In September 1925 Dorothy went to La Jolla where, in the company of a nurse, she took a cottage and spent several weeks on a strict rest and exercise schedule. Her condition was extreme enough that she didn't write to Scott or her parents, a habit that she usually followed several times a week. Alarmed, Scott wrote her from Louisville where he was attending his mother's funeral. "Have you been ill?" he asked in confusion. "I just can't make out why I don't get any letters." Finally she answered, explaining that if she had not gone away as she did and taken such a restful change, she "should have been in real trouble." "So please dear, forgive me for not writing," she begged him. "I did go awfully to pieces for a while but have come back stronger than I have been for a long time . . . Don't ever say anything to the family about my not having written for a while—of course I didn't write them either, but they couldn't understand it and they are still cross about it."

In December, after a tonsillectomy in Seattle, Dorothy boarded the train for California once again, this time with a nurse and all three children in tow. The trip itself was an ordeal. Harriet, "the worst little wiggle and squirm that ever drew breath," learned to walk in the aisles, telling passengers she was en route to "Telephonia," while Patsy, who was always carsick, threw up her meals regularly and toward the end couldn't even keep down a swallow of water.

For Dorothy, the unremitting strain was too much. In January, she entered a San Francisco sanatorium: "I can't seem to get rested, and a bed in a sanatorium in San Francisco sounds like Heaven to me." She stayed for a few days under a doctor's regimen for mental and physical rest that excluded any phone calls from family or friends. C. D. and Harriet traveled from Pasadena to San Francisco to be near her, but were limited to very short visits. From the sanatorium, Dorothy went to a small lodge in Carmel where, confined to bed rest, she burst into tears upon hearing Scott's voice on the telephone. His heart went out to her, but his mind didn't seem to comprehend the strain she was under. His attitude was typical of the times—a simplistic belief that good physical health could overcome any adversity, including depression. After a couple of listless months during which not even a horseback ride would cheer her, Dorothy regained her balance. Refusing her parents' invitations to join them each evening at the Huntington, she stuck to her regimen and gradually began to find some pleasure in life again. "It has taken me a long while to learn how to take care of myself," she wrote Scott—this time in a firmer tone.

Motherhood was taking its toll. Although the children's antics were amusing, their constant activity, questions, cries, fights, complaints and demands, their need for continuous attention and discipline, the ongoing earaches, colds, splinters, fevers, and illnesses of childhood all wore Dorothy down. "I don't know how to bring up children," she wrote her mother in exasperation. "I am spending most of my time going from one sneezing, coughing child to another." When they were well, it was all she could do to keep up with their energy. "They are feeling so good that they just run wild and are into mischief *continually*," she wrote Scott from Palm Springs. "I am really glad to see it in a way because I know it's the result of good health and excess energy—and only natural if something better to do doesn't offer. But the climax came Sunday afternoon when Stimmy lassoed some little girls and made their lives miserable, then Patsy and a little boyfriend of hers took all the clothes off somebody's clothesline and hid them all under somebody else's house. And to cap it all, Stimmy and two other little boys set fire to a wooden barrel of waste paper, then put it out with the hose." Dorothy had apparently forgotten her own early years as a prankster on First Hill.

To cope, Dorothy hired experts—governesses, maids, drivers, nurses, and instructors for tennis, swimming, and riding. The team filled the gap day to day;

they baked the cookies, nursed cut fingers, listened to the long stories, structured the time, gave encouragement, and dried the tears. They required proper manners at table, good posture on daily walks; they supervised homework and kept their charges clean and healthy. The experts were on call, day and night, and they traveled with Dorothy and the children to California in the winter.

Dorothy retained the role of overseer, focusing on areas she enjoyed and believed important. As chief critic and purveyor of decorum, she encouraged the children to talk to her, coaxing their speech into the precise ("syrop" not "surrup") and softened ("pehple" not "peepul") diction that she had learned at Briarcliff. She passed on the lessons of Harriet Stimson—the importance of proper nutrition, cleanliness, and daily bowel function. "Mummee," as they called her early on, provided dogs, kittens, ponies, and birds. She emphasized the importance of physical exercise and fresh air. She taught them the value of money and earning their way. Among the effects found after her death was a small envelope containing two tiny teeth. Written on its cover was "Value teeth: 2 at 25 cents, total 50 cents. Value courage: $1.50. Discount for cash—$1.00, net value: $1.00." She taught them to drive a hard bargain—even with the tooth fairy.

The children absorbed her presence like little blotters. They remembered her personal rituals. In her dressing room in the morning, they watched as she unbraided her coal-black waist-length hair, brushed it one hundred strokes, then coiled it into a bun and anchored it with hairpins.

They were closest to her when she read to them during bouts of illness. Enchanted by the magic in her voice, they lay in bed as their mother read *The Three Musketeers, Toilers of the Sea,* and Edgar Allen Poe's *Fall of the House of Usher.* "One of the finest things she did was to read aloud to us," Stim recalled in later years. "It wasn't that she dramatized her reading, but more it was the sound of her wonderful deep voice and the selection of stories that kept us spellbound. When she read 'Horatius at the Bridge,' we were right there fighting the Etruscans at the Tiber." These times were the most intimate moments the Bullitt children ever shared with their mother.

Dorothy's love for her three was oblique. Undemonstrative, she rarely complimented them, told them they were important to her, or spontaneously embraced them. "She would kiss us hello and good-bye and good night," Stim remembered, "but I don't have any recollection of casual affection like patting us on the head, rumpling the hair, or maybe turning us upside down." Rarely did she comfort them in their small (and later large) sorrows, as if her innate reserve were a barrier she could not or did not know how to cross. Only when they were absolutely distraught did she take them in her arms. Nonetheless, they sought her love and when she withheld it—never in loud harsh anger but with cold distant silence—they feared the loss. As adults they remembered that she was "never there," emotionally.

They fared better with their father, although he too seemed to be more warm than openly affectionate. "Father was a great entertainer," Patsy recalled with a smile. "When he'd put me on the train to go to California, he'd say, 'Now watch me out the window because I'm going to feel so terrible at missing you.' I'd look out the window and Father would go up to a post in the station and collapse against it in mock agony." Scott knew the words to many hymns and he delighted in teaching his children the old songs. He also read the Bible to them, dramatizing the story of Jacob and Esau or recounting the tale of Joseph and his coat of many colors. At breakfast, he regaled them with stories about "Uncle Henry," a mythical relative from the South who the children suspected was really their mother. When he told about Uncle Henry's habit of rolling around in bed and taking all of the blankets, Dorothy interrupted, "Oh Scott, not in front of the children."

In this unique setting, the Bullitt children inhabited two worlds: sometimes "upstairs" in the realm of their parents but more often "downstairs" in a domain of nurses, governesses, gardeners, and chauffeurs and their offspring—a world that their parents did not know at all. Although many servants came and went, there were special individuals who acted as surrogate parents, aunts, uncles, and cousins. "They were a close part of our lives," Harriet remembered. "They were there all the time and we lived like a tribe when no one saw Mother or Father very much. We learned a lot from them. They taught us on the swings and how to ride bikes, picked us up when we fell out of plum trees, and helped us when the dogs raided the henhouse and ate the chickens."

Chief Guardian Angel at Greenway was Pearl Pearce, known as Percy, a nurse who, though tiny in stature, was a great dispenser of care and love. Her antithesis was Miss O'Neal. Hawk-nosed and angular, with straight bobbed hair, Daisy O'Neal was a British governess, wholly without humor and dedicated to order and cleanliness. "Tidy" was her favorite word and discipline was her goal.

Another regular was the dignified Ohata, Harriet Stimson's driver and mechanic, who took the children everywhere, from doctor's appointments in Seattle to polo games in Pasadena. The children spent hours watching the diminutive chauffeur repair cars and furniture, admiring the tools (some of which he made) that gleamed in their racks, immaculately in place. (If one wanted something done perfectly, it was known in the family as "an Ohata job.") They played hopscotch and Monopoly with the Ohata children—

Edward, nicknamed "Skooky," and his younger sister Dorothy, nicknamed "Toetoe." During winter, the youngsters congregated over games of Monopoly. In the summer, Alice, Ohata's wife, often made cantaloupe ice cream or blackberry pie to take on picnics to the beach. And mercurial grounds keeper Stenneberg might scold them for trampling his precious rhododendrons, but he was willing to take them on hikes and identify plants along the way.

––––––––––

ONE GROWNUP THE CHILDREN CONSIDERED AFFECTIONATELY was Uncle Thomas. Thomas Stimson was withdrawn, often ill at ease in social situations, and handicapped by a family situation in which he sought his father's recognition but was upstaged by his sister and outcharmed by his brother-in-law. Even so, he found his own particular way to shine and, with wife Emma's indulgence, developed a lifestyle that seemed playful when compared to that of the more serious-minded Bullitts. Thomas had an innate understanding and affection for children and animals. "He was so much fun with children," Patsy remembered. "When none of the other grownups were around, Uncle Thomas was. He played with us when everyone else was playing with the art museum, the opera, the Democratic Party or what have you. When the movie *Ben Hur* came out in 1926, he had two heavy Roman chariots built and hitched to Shetland ponies and we'd have races across the huge lawn. He taught me to ride a bike and always insisted that I wasn't sick when everyone else said I was. 'She's fine,' he'd say. 'There's nothing wrong with her.' He was my champion among the grownups." Like the children, Thomas loved animals. He surrounded himself and his family with a menagerie that included dogs, cats, sheep, goats, ponies, and chickens, and more exotic species—a monkey that rode "dogback," peacocks that spent hours in front of a mirror on the lawns, two sets of orphaned twin baby bears, and two parrots that, from their cage alongside the tennis court, confused the players by shouting "Out! Out!"

Thomas was an outdoorsman when few people spent hours in nature simply for pleasure. An avid hiker, he founded a group called SOYPS (Socks Outside Your Pants Society) with a few friends, and enjoyed hiking and skiing on Mount Rainier. He took long camping expeditions into the High Cascades accompanied by his family, the pet monkey (which rode one of the dogs), and a cow for milk. As many as twenty-five packhorses carried children, parents, nannies, friends, and guides deep into the wilderness on adventures that lasted several weeks.

His great love was aviation. As a pilot, he was both cautious and cavalier—a blend of traits not unusual for aviators in those barnstorming days. He kept a biplane at Boeing Field and flew it often to the Cascades or across the mountains to Spokane or Boise. Sometimes he landed on the beach at The Highlands to take children up for a spin. However, the Bullitt children were never passengers— Dorothy would not permit it. He kept a glider at The Highlands, and the children vividly remembered Sunday flights when Thomas, his nose already broken from one aviation mishap, prepared to take another chance on the wind. "The Stimsons had a lawn that must have been a quarter of a mile long,"

Thomas Stimson (RIGHT) is greeted by William Boeing after Thomas concludes the first flight by a private plane from Seattle to San Diego in 1928.

Edward Ohata recalled with a smile. "We'd all pull to get him airborne—kids, mother, the nurse, everyone, pulling this long cable. He'd get up about fifty feet and then it would come crashing down." Other days, they might use a truck and a long rope for the launch. "There was just enough room on the lawn to get him over the tops of the trees," his eldest daughter Frances Ann remembered.

His most famous flight was not by glider but by airplane from Seattle to San Diego in 1928, the first flight of a private plane down the Pacific Coast. The log from this flight, written by friend and fellow traveler Albert McCown, reflects a seat-of-the-pants journey into the unexpected, one that included missing spark plugs, foul weather, hedgehopping after colts and chickens, lost bearings (of both types), a bout of mal de l'air, one three-point landing (wheel, wing, and tail) in high winds on an airstrip, and another landing with a burnt-out magneto in a pasture. Two weeks later, the aviators returned to Seattle in triumph where they were met by family, the mayors of Vancouver, Victoria, and Seattle, and the maker of the plane, Bill Boeing.

On more earthly levels, Thomas continued to have problems with his brother-in-law. They began when Scott joined the family business, for the two men were unlike in temperament and opposed in interests. Scott was involved in state politics, his time outside the office consumed by meetings, speeches, and Democratic get-togethers, while Thomas was interested in a more aggressive role for the C. D. Stimson company, a direction that his father did not support. For instance, Thomas wanted to build a hotel in Bellingham. His father did not agree, arguing that the city already had a good hotel, the Leopold. But Thomas went ahead and built his hotel. C. D. did not attend the opening and the hotel was never a success.

"Thomas and Scott were not getting along," Dorothy recalled. "Thomas felt that Scott was taking over and he resented his outgoing nature. Scott couldn't help it; he was just naturally outgoing. A jealousy developed on Thomas's part that was unfortunate but there it was, and Father could see that it was bitter and getting worse. I suppose it was a very difficult position for Thomas, and Scott too, and particularly for Father who recognized it, and didn't know what to do because he came to love Scott dearly. Thomas would talk to me about diverting Scott's interests. He'd say, 'You know, Scott doesn't belong in real estate. He should get into the newspaper business—buy the *Seattle Times* or the *Post-Intelligencer* or something.' Scott wasn't interested in the newspaper business—he didn't want to own anything that had anything to say about politics. If he had anything to say, he'd say it himself.

"Then Thomas wanted him to go into the title business—he thought that would be good for Scott. Thomas told this to me and I said, 'Well, he'll do what he wants to do and what he feels he can do.' I didn't have any good answers for anything except to say that Scott was his own man."

Scott Bullitt came into his own during these years, not through newspapers or title companies but through politics. In the early 1920s, he had made several trips back to Louisville to finish work he had started on local precinct disputes, vowing to Dorothy that he was "really done with politics. Honestly, for all times." But, in spite of the privileged comforts of The Highlands, he could not give up his love of politics. To the man from Kentucky, a chance to speak his views, shake hands with strangers, or participate in a political convention was preferable to cruising for timber or dictating contracts at the office.

He joined everything, probably to Dorothy's dismay—Eagles, Elks, Moose, Shriners, Kiwanis, the Chamber of Commerce, and the local Democratic Club. It was the latter association, however, that proved most significant, and it wasn't long before he began to speak for the Democrats in a state where the Republican party had long been in control. He became a major organizer for the state Democratic party, defining the party and its issues and representing it on various levels, including the post of national committeeman for the state. During the 1920s, he made speeches at the King County Democratic Club, was keynote speaker at the Democratic state conventions, and delegate and committee member at national conventions. Whether speaking, debating, or campaigning for the issues or on behalf of his fellow Democrats, Scott's charisma came into play, and with each handshake, each smile and speech, his connections and influence grew. Colleagues, including his opponents, had to admit that Scott Bullitt was bringing a great surge of vitality to a hitherto flagging political party in Washington state.

In the process all else fell away for Scott—quiet evenings at home, social and family obligations, trips to the East—in favor of political occasions, however small or seemingly unimportant. "Scott had what they call charisma," Dorothy remembered. "He was handsome, felt at home on the platform, and had good issues to discuss. He was a fine speaker. He could inspire people. He knew his history, literature, and the Bible, and he had charm and humor. In the Pacific Northwest, the Democratic party wasn't worth talking about until Scott came along. At that time I was still politically blank. When he first talked about politics, I said, 'But everybody here is Republican.' And he said, 'That's precisely why, because *everyone* is Republican. Don't you think there should be two parties?' So he began to build up the party when there was no organization at all. He'd travel around the state and talk to people and get them to declare themselves. There were a lot who wanted to be Democrats but felt there really wasn't any party. Odd to know that there was a state in the United States that had no Democratic headquarters. So he set one up. He taught me what Republican and Democrat stood for when I'd never given it any thought. He taught me to be for the people and I thought that was just fine."

In 1924, Scott went to the Democratic National Convention at Madison Square Garden where he was a Washington state delegate instructed to vote for William McAdoo in his race against Al Smith. It was his first time "on the inside," and he spent exhausting hours at all-day convention sessions and caucus meetings, followed by late-night receptions. At a night caucus over how the Washington delegation would vote on a proposition involving the Ku Klux Klan, Scott proposed a vote to condemn the Klan by name; a few others backed him but most voted to defer the question. Scott summed the session up in a letter to Dorothy as "a religious war mixed with a temperance crusade. Just imagine five hundred Baillargeons and five hundred Stimsons all packed together on a convention floor discussing Catholicism and Ku Kluxism before an audience of twenty times that many Catholics and Protestants in the galleries. Do you think they would ever agree on a candidate for anything?"

Scott relied on Dorothy's advice throughout his political career. He valued her cool sense of strategy and her scorn of the petty political disputes that sometimes involved him. "You are the one person in the world on whose judgment I can depend and in whose mind and heart I have implicit faith," he wrote her from the convention. She in turn enjoyed the drama of the convention, but refused to attend the large unruly gatherings herself, telling him diplomatically,

"Much as I should love to be there with you, Scott dear, I know it would spoil your good time if I were. You would not be so free and independent as you are now if you had me to look after." Nonetheless, she followed each convention closely in the newspapers, "just bursting to talk it over" with him. "With all my Republicanism," she confessed in one letter, "you would laugh to see me devouring the Democratic political news. And discussing the possibilities as though I really knew something. It is tremendously exciting, and I can almost follow your movements from day to day by watching the program that is published every morning."

Scott Bullitt running for U.S. Senator from Washington in 1926. He is credited with mobilizing the state's Democratic party.

IN 1926, SCOTT ANNOUNCED HIS CANDIDACY FOR THE U.S. Senate against Republican incumbent Wesley Jones. His fellow Democrats had a strong candidate at last and urged voters to join the party that emphasized "the man rather than the dollar, human rights before property rights, equal opportunity for all, special privilege to none." The *Willapa Harbor Pilot* forecast that Scott Bullitt would do more to unite the party in Washington than anything that had happened in the Democratic ranks for years. The candidate was touted as "just a plain, everyday American citizen who loves his fellow man." The article concluded, "Personal contact with him discloses a keen grasp of public affairs and an aptness in stating his views which is phenomenal. He is an accomplished orator, a dignified though aggressive fighter."

Scott proved to be a vigorous campaigner, delivering speeches from podiums throughout the state. From Sequim to Spokane, he spent hours shaking hands and distributing campaign flyers. At teas and grange meetings, in labor halls, and at construction sites, he attacked the opposition and steered his party toward more populist goals. At The Highlands, the Bullitt family posed for movies and photographs, and Scott dramatized his fighting prowess in a film sequence with a punching bag. In announcing his vision for the future and denouncing the ills of the past, he pulled no punches. He favored the McNary-Haugen Bill for relief of the farmers, progressive income taxes, and reclamation of the Columbia River Basin; he opposed passage of the law for censorship of theaters and movies, "any further extension of federal bureaus over the morals and personal conduct of citizens," and the federal Sunday Closing Law. "I am against these attempts to prohibit innocent recreation on Sunday," he declared. "The wage earners, men and women, who have no time for amusement during the week, have the same right to go to a movie or ball game on Sunday, or buy candy or tobacco at the corner drugstores, as the rich man has to spend Sunday at his club or playing golf."

Dorothy accompanied her husband during some of the campaign but her heart was not in it. Although she enjoyed discussing the ideals of politics, the realities were disappointing. Scott had taught her "to be for the people" and she claimed that was "just fine," but it was not. She disliked having to "turn on the charm" when she accompanied him on campaign appearances. Alone afterward, she teased him with a comic imitation of his walk, handshaking, and greeting habits. She detested the seamy atmosphere that accompanied politics and the low-life labor-union types who hung around him. They had dirty fingernails, their manners were terrible, and their English was worse. There was no one more boring than some county commissioner who had too much to say and said it poorly. The conspicuousness of it all was distasteful—the horror of being on display and vulnerable to everyone watching was made worse if she was asked to speak publicly. On these occasions, Dorothy's shyness was almost paralyzing, if not physically sickening, a drawback that she had to cope with throughout public life. "It's a curse, and I suffer because of it. You have to do things that are right out in the open and I have never liked it. I never wanted to be conspicuous because people could find all of my weak spots and I didn't want people to know I was pretty dumb."

Another complication in the campaign was the separation of Dee and Keith Bullitt. Dorothy had known for some time that they were in difficulty, but had stayed away from involvement in a marriage that Scott had predicted early on would not last. Divorce was considered a disgrace, and Scott feared that the headlines would be damaging to his campaign. "Beneath my solicitude for them is, I suppose, my revulsion of seeing the family name bandied around in the columns of the papers," he wrote. When both Seattle newspapers eventually announced "Bullitts Divorcing," Dorothy was beside herself with indignation; it would be many years before she and her dear friend would reunite. Scott set about to see that no one mistook the headlines, but it hurt the campaign. In the end, Scott lost to Wesley Jones by fourteen thousand votes, but in the process gained the largest vote ever polled by any Democrat in the history of the state. Dorothy explained the defeat: "He didn't win because there wasn't that much of a party to make a dent in the political scene and because Wesley Jones had been a senator from Washington forever. There were other things too— Scott was Princeton-educated and lived in The Highlands, which wasn't politically good because it had a gate and a fence around it. I guess there was that much stigma attached to a closed membership kind of thing that it worked against him."

Scott took the defeat in stride. With an eye toward the next political opportunity, he continued to address gatherings over the next couple of years— everything from Kiwanis Club meetings to a gathering of I.W.W.s, Socialists, and other labor activists, where his speech on the subject of fanaticism drew hostile questions and loud disagreement. (His thesis was that history proves that the fanatic always hurts the cause he espouses and that great reforms are achieved by lawful procedure.) About this time, he was approached by a young law school graduate named Warren Magnuson who sought advice about a political career. Scott recognized an astute politician in the making and became Magnuson's adviser and friend, an association that would prove valuable to Dorothy in future years. "Warren Magnuson was a student at the university at that time. He was an orphan, didn't know what he came from. When he was graduated, the first thing he did was to go to Scott and tell him that he wanted to put his life into politics, asked him how to do it. Scott became his mentor, and Magnuson always gave him credit for being the ideal politician. Scott believed that public office was the greatest service you could do for your country, and Magnuson was a very good representative, always honest and very powerful. Over the years, I went to him about different problems and he was always warm, sensible and *very, very* smooth. He was a thoroughly political animal." Although they were never close friends, Dorothy always referred to him as "Brother Magnuson," reflecting an affection born of years belonging to the same fraternity in which political clout got things done.

More political possibilities began to open up for Scott in 1928. Washington Governor Roland W. Hartley, a Republican, was up for re-election, but with shaky support from his party because of in-fighting over expenditures on the Capitol buildings under construction in Olympia. There were other Democratic contenders, notably former Supreme Court Justice Stephen J. Chadwick,

A posed photograph taken for Scott Bullitt's 1928 campaign for governor of Washington depicts an idyllic family moment.

who was held in high esteem, but Scott was not about to let this chance go by. He began his campaign with the disarming courtesy that was a hallmark of his political style. At a meeting to plan the state convention, Scott was nominated as temporary chairman and keynote speaker. He responded with a graceful speech, and at its conclusion proposed that the committee hear from Judge Chadwick. This courtesy aroused so much enthusiasm that, amid applause and cheers, Chadwick ascended the platform and seconded the motion for Scott's overwhelming acceptance. Over the thunderous ovation, he said, "Whatever may come, the Democratic party is under deep obligation to Mr. Bullitt for putting it into a militant spirit which it has had but which has been latent." It was latent no more; the party was united and the newspapers took up the cry. A *New York Times* editorial hailed Scott as a "new and colorful national figure" who was attracting party attention by his "unusual political success." Predicting that he had a more than even chance to be elected governor, the article went so far as to list him as a possible Democratic candidate for president in 1932, for a "Northwestern Democrat who has made so much stir, would, if elected governor of a strongly Republican state, unquestionably attract national party attention in 1932." All of this attention, supplemented by encouraging letters from friends, fueled Scott's ambition. Proudly he sent the clippings to Dorothy in Palm Springs, writing, "I am anxious to hear from my kindly critic as to her reaction as to all this presidential business for the year 1932."

Dorothy was dubious about another political race. Although she would never be overtly against Scott's political career, the tone of her comments was clearly not supportive. A few weeks after he announced for governor, she sent him a mock political schedule that included days beginning at 1 A.M. ("shave—

put on a new suit"); a luncheon with the Boy Scouts ("all under twenty-one years—canceled"); speeches at the Business Women's Club on "Why I Am for Woman's Suffrage" and at the Old Men's Home on "The Secret of My Health and Youth—Orange Juice," each followed by two hours of shaking hands; American Legion and Elks meetings ("wear button"); time out to "make deposit to cover DSB overdraught;" and a speech at the Knights of Columbus on "How I Fought the School Bill and Why Meat is Bad for One Anyway." It ended with "8:30—fall asleep. Book falls on floor, end of a perfect week." She concluded the letter with a plea for him to join her in Palm Springs.

At the height of the contest for governor, Hartley delivered a solid punch below the belt, one which Dorothy vehemently labeled as a dirty tactic and the major cause for Scott's eventual defeat. "They tied the Metropolitan Building Company around his neck," she said remembering the incident many years later. This related to C. D. Stimson's role as president of the Metropolitan Building Company, which held the leases on University of Washington properties downtown. Hartley supporters began to circulate rumors that if Scott were elected governor he might further his family interests by appointing a Board of Regents at the university to extend these leases. It was a powerful ploy, alarming Dorothy to such an extent that in a speech to supporters on the closing night of the campaign she took the blame. "As far as I can see from the speeches made against Mr. Bullitt," she said, "I seem to be the chief handicap urged against him. The fact that he married my father's daughter seems to be an unforgivable sin in the eyes of his opponent and the chief objection they find. It would be better for him politically if I could drop out of the picture as a stumbling block to his election, but I prefer to stand by and go down the long, long trail with him."

The public passed judgment against him. Even though a 1923 law had rescinded the regents' right to alter, renew, or extend the Metropolitan leases, the accusations stirred public mistrust. This, coupled with voters marking "straight ticket" Republican ballots in the Hoover sweep of 1928, swung the victory to Hartley, even though Scott ran sixty thousand votes ahead of Al Smith in the state.

———

THE CAMPAIGN ISSUE OVER THE METROPOLITAN BUILDING Company stock served to rekindle the tensions between Scott and Thomas that had smoldered since 1921. Dorothy and Emma, who had always enjoyed each other thoroughly, had become distant, and when Harriet Stimson took them shopping they sat on each side of her in the car, staring out of the windows in silence. The conflict came to a head at a board meeting of the C. D. Stimson Company when Thomas, after unsuccessful efforts to have the company assume a more aggressive posture, insisted on resigning as president.

At this point, C. D. took action. To forestall family rifts that were sure to occur after his death, he came up with a way to divide his estate beforehand. In 1928, he presented his plan to his son and daughter and their spouses. Dorothy remembered it this way: "Father put all of his property on a list—everything—stocks, bonds, and real estate. He put a value taken out of his head on each. Then he told us each to take the list home and choose half of the total value. Whenever we had both checked the same piece of property, he raised the price, and where we didn't choose one—maybe a little place up on Harvard Avenue, a drugstore or something—he dropped the price and we went back to reevaluate what we wanted. There was one piece of property that Thomas had to take because it was his own venture and Father didn't approve of it to start with—the hotel in Bellingham. We both checked the sawmill in Ballard; Scott was interested in it as an industry, but Thomas got it. Scott did most of the figuring for my half and it was pretty trying, going back and forth, but eventually it all divided half-and-half. At the final go-round, Scott discovered a discrepancy of $100,000 in Thomas's favor. We were to meet the next morning to finalize everything. Scott said, 'Wait a minute, there's a mistake here . . .' I said, 'Well, let's not bring it up. Father will probably catch it and we'll see what he does.' So the next morning when we met, Father took me out in the hall and said, 'There's $100,000 left out by mistake. What do you want to do? I said, 'I don't *care*. I've never seen so much money in my life before. If you put it in my column, what would I do with it?' He said, 'Well, I'm glad you feel that way because things being the way they are, let's leave it be.' Eventually Father formed two companies, one for each of us, and he owned most of the stock in both until he died and we inherited them: the C. D. Stimson Company for Thomas and the Stimson Realty Company for me. Father worked with Scott and Thomas on each company from then on. If he had not divided up the property before his death, I don't know what would have happened."

Under the agreement, the C. D. Stimson Company (Thomas) and the Stimson Realty Company (Dorothy) each received over $3 million in stock, bonds, contracts, and properties, appraised at pre-1929 values. Thomas's assets included his development in Bellingham, the old sawmill in Ballard, the Natatorium downtown that he had managed, all of C. D.'s Metropolitan Building stock, and other property and buildings downtown. Dorothy's share included some timberland, several buildings, various stock interests—notably in the

Olympic Hotel and the General Insurance (Safeco) Company—and bonds from the Metropolitan Building Company. The two largest holdings were the Coliseum Theatre and a corner of property at Fourth Avenue and Union Street downtown, on which C. D. planned to erect an office building.

"After I picked the Fourth and Union property, Father said, 'I'm so glad you have that because I want you to build a building on it.' He had bought the land in 1900 from O. O. Denny for $25,000 when it was an empty lot where everyone working on building downtown brought their horses to rest and feed. Its only amenity was a big hollow log with water in it for the horses. By the time it went from Father's company into the Stimson Realty Company [for $489,000] there was a three-story brick building on it, with stores on the ground floor and the Antlers Hotel on the upper two floors."

Soon after division of his properties in 1928, C. D. hired architect R. C. Reamer to design "the best and most substantial building, without extravagance," in the city. The result, at a cost of $1.3 million, was a modified Georgian edifice of steel and concrete that still stands: the 1411 Fourth Avenue Building. Dorothy, out of admiration for her father and her own conviction, always loved the building because of its many solid practical touches. "I don't think there was or is a building in town built as well as 1411. I watched it being built. It's only fifteen stories but it's going to be there for a long, long time. The drainage is good; everything, including the wood in the polished maple floors and the cast bronze elevator doors, is good. The floors were built with springs so that the girls working with file cases wouldn't get so tired. There is no air conditioning and there won't be—you can open the windows and get fresh air. Father supervised every one of the details. When I admired the columns on the telephone company building, he said, 'Every one of those columns is keeping out light. They are handsome but at a cost of daylight, and in Seattle that is important.' So he made sure that the glass windows were not recessed so that the slanting rays of sun could get in." The building, for many years owned and managed by Dorothy's company, is now owned and operated by her son Stim's company, Harbor Properties, Inc. Once, during the 1970s, he considered selling it. "When I told Mother," he said, "she listened with interest and made no objection, but a tear rolled down her cheek." Stim had rarely, if ever, seen his mother cry. "Mother didn't cry any more than a locomotive cries," he remembered. "I canceled the deal."

By the end of the decade, C. D. Stimson was sadly failing. At seventy-two, all of his challenges had been met and bested, and the heart that had always been so unstintingly strong was giving way. On an August night in 1929, he was going upstairs after dinner when he coughed a couple of times and collapsed on the steps. Rushing to help him, Harriet got him into bed and summoned Dr. Sharples. What appeared at first to be acute indigestion developed within days into a serious heart problem. Over the next week, C. D. put up a stubborn fight. One day he gathered enough strength to sit by his bed and visit with his grandchildren. "All of the grandchildren were brought in one by one and each of us climbed up on his lap in turn," Patsy remembered. "We didn't know we were saying good-bye to him, but he was saying good-bye to us."

The brief rally was followed by a relapse so serious that it was obvious that C. D. was dying. The family gathered around to reassure one another and comfort him as best they could. Harriet set the tone with a stalwart lovingness that only she could impart to her husband. Dorothy followed suit but Scott was overwhelmed with grief. "Father and Scott were so close, closer than people ever knew, closer than Father was to his own son. When he died, Scott sat on his bed and the tears rolled down his face. He couldn't help it. He said that next to his own father he loved mine better than anyone, better than he loved his own mother."

On August 29, 1929, the rugged old pioneer departed this world. The dynasty he had founded was bereft, without cornerstone, and the city he had enriched mourned what may have been its favorite son. "To the whole of Seattle, Mr. Stimson stood for what was forward-looking and adventurous," wrote the *Town Crier*. "Whatever the need might happen to be, it was certain that he would be among the foremost to advise and the foremost in action. Seattle cannot better face the future than by thanking God for such gifts as the now finished earthly career of Charles D. Stimson." Flags flew at half-mast from the city's tall buildings, and the funeral service held in the Stimson home, filled with lilies and ferns, drew so many hundreds that special police, state patrolmen, and even Boy Scouts were detailed to direct the traffic. In an affectionate farewell, the *Seattle Times* caught some of the qualities that had endeared C. D. to many:

A kindly man he was—kindly and generous; with a cheery word, and a helpful hand if need be, for everyone with whom he came into contact. And it was because of this that people liked him, and knowing him better learned to like him the more. A man of large affairs, a capable and conscientious business executive, he was most unassuming and, when he chose to be, almost self-effacing.

Mr. Stimson's influence upon the life and progress of Seattle was the influence of a quiet and undemonstrative efficiency. He was a clear thinker, a sound adviser, untainted by arrogance or selfishness. As the years ran on, it was inevitable that he should have collected and held to himself, as he did without palpable effort, the confidence and the love of many, the enduring respect of all.

Dorothy met her grief in resolute style. C. D. Stimson had been the strongest emotional support of her life, and probably because of this she was able to carry on. Since the days of red wagons and first ponies, she had internalized so much of his love and philosophy that it never quite seemed that he was gone. But there were moments when she felt adrift, without anchor. The patriarch was gone. So too was a golden era, and Dorothy knew then what she said many years later about The Highlands in the 1920s—that those times would never come again.

Those days were devastating. But there was nothing
you could do about it. What happened was just
a fact that had to be dealt with and had to be met.
They were rough times and I was in trouble,
real trouble.

8 SETTING THE SOUL
1930–1939

A FLOOD OF TRAGIC EVENTS BEGAN WITH C. D. STIMSON'S passing and engulfed the family over the next ten years. Adversity came in waves, bringing death, violence, and threat of loss, leaving in its stormy wake gusts of grief and long shadows of despair. During this time, Dorothy copied in her notebook of favorite quotations a popular poem of the day by Ella Wheeler Wilcox titled "Ships East and West." The verses must have spoken some deep truth to her, for she copied them on three different occasions:

> One ship drives east, another drives west
> With the self-same winds that blow.
> 'Tis the set of the sail and not the gale
> That bids them where to go.

> Like the winds of the sea are the ways of fate
> As we journey along through life,
> 'Tis the set of the soul that decides the goal
> And not the calm nor the strife.

During the decade of the 1930s, Dorothy Bullitt had to set her soul with all the courage and resourcefulness she could muster in order to pass the most severe tests of her life.

The death of her father was a great, although not surprising, loss. Dorothy realized that his health had been failing and that his life had been as full as any she had known. As she had been taught, she carried grief with discipline and dignity, and concentrated on managing the household, receiving callers, and answering condolences. She gave constant but unspoken comfort to her mother.

Gradually sorrow lost its keen edge as routines resumed on Stimson Row.

Thanks to the provident work of C. D., the family fortunes were already divided and stewarded separately by Thomas and Scott. But the old patriarch could not have predicted the great stock market crash that followed his death by two months. Seattle and the Stimson-Bullitt families, geographically far from the centers of financial power, were not immediately affected by this catastrophic event. The families held little negotiable stock and suffered few losses until a year later when the repercussions of the crash and the Great Depression began to spread to the West.

After the loss of its leader the Stimson clan regrouped for a couple of years. Thomas's Bellingham Hotel suffered from lack of occupants, but this handicap represented only a small part of his holdings. He was now trustee, vice-president, and largest stockholder of the Metropolitan Building Company downtown. He and Emma were active in civic and social affairs and followed a rigorous social schedule. Emma, known for her support of cultural projects, launched into a conservation battle during these years. With her friend, attorney Irving Clark, she spearheaded a campaign to designate tens of thousands of wilderness acres on the Olympic Peninsula as a national park. This was no easy fight in a state and from a family dedicated to taking timber. She took on the governor, her friends in high places, and the powerful logging interests of the state to secure the lands that were established in 1938 as Olympic National Park.

Thomas's activities also had a significant impact on the city. His true interest was flying; he led a successful campaign to establish an airport south of the city, called Boeing Field, and raised $25,000 for a proposed first nonstop flight between Seattle and Tokyo. As a pilot, his own flights were much shorter, usually over the Cascades to Spokane or Boise.

On April 26, 1931, Thomas took off from the new Boeing Field in his open-cockpit Stearman biplane for a pleasure flight to Spokane. He took along a friend, R. C. Brinkley, a machinery manufacturer who, upon arrival in Spokane, was detained on business. Hoping to return early to spend time with his family, Thomas took off at noon the next day, alone. Waving to Brinkley from the open cockpit, he banked and headed his plane low over the rolling sage-covered hills north of the city. He landed at Hellgate, near Nespelem, Washington, and walked a half-mile to a sheep ranch, thinking to bring a lamb home to the children. With the lamb under his arm, Thomas rode with the rancher on horseback back to the plane and invited the rancher to fly on with him to Wenatchee. Declining Thomas's invitation, the rancher waved as the pilot flew off over the Okanogan hills in the direction of the Columbia River.

The causes for what happened next were a mystery for several weeks.

Eyewitnesses reported that, as the plane passed over Stevenson's Ferry at an altitude of about 150 feet, the right wing was wobbling. Farther on, the biplane began to circle. "The circles kept getting smaller and smaller in a dizzy way, and I thought he was going to land," one observer said. "He was a pretty good distance away and across the Columbia River when I saw the circling stop and the plane headed for the ground." As the Stearman faltered a hundred feet in the air, the pilot could be seen standing in the rear, reaching toward the front cockpit. Then the plane plunged. A father and son out hunting came upon the wreckage—a twisted hunk of steel, its nose buried some two feet in the ground, the smashed right wing torn from the fuselage. In the cockpit, they found the crumpled body of Thomas Stimson, his neck broken from the impact. He was forty-seven years old.

Dorothy, Scott, Harriet Stimson, and a friend were dining at Norcliffe when the telephone rang. Scott took the call and found the courage and the words to break the news, weeping as he did so. Incredulous, everyone sat stunned, occasionally breaking the silence to ask an answerless question. That night Harriet Stimson recorded the tragedy in her diary with characteristic stoicism and simplicity. It read: "April 26. Sunshine . . . At home afternoon—Kerrys called—Dorothy, Scott, Lora, and self at supper. Terrible news of Thomas came soon after."

Speculation as to why his plane crashed began. There were rumors that Thomas had been ill, even that he had committed suicide. Emma, accompanying her husband's body home on the train, reviewed the days preceding the crash, searching her mind for possible causes. Thomas was an excellent pilot; the plane was well-maintained, and the weather had been good. Knowing of his occasional bouts with depression, she wondered whether he could have committed suicide. She remembered his sweetness, good temper, and creativity; and his courage to stand by her in the face of his family's disapproval of her Catholicism and her wish to build a home of their own. She went over the days prior to his flight and wondered if she had brought on bad luck, as some friends had suggested, by her constant fear that one day he might crash. The several insurance companies that covered his life for large amounts were also asking questions; it was rumored that a few would go broke paying off the policies.

Investigators determined that the cause of the accident was the little lamb. Evidence from the wreckage showed that Thomas had tied the animal to the controls of the front cockpit. The lamb had thrust its head into a hole in the floor to get fresh air, thereby jamming the controls. The dual control system was not disconnected, and Thomas, unable to overcome the interference from the forward cockpit, had tried to release the animal by reaching forward. In doing so, he cut the speed of his motor, throwing the plane into a spin he could not stop. In his report, aeronautical inspector Captain C. V. Pettis recorded, "The Stearman plane was in good shape, the pilot had been properly licensed, and if the lamb had been more securely tied, the accident would not have happened." The position of the wreckage, according to Pettis, indicated that the plane had turned over twice and, because of its proximity to the ground, Thomas's parachute, which was still strapped to his back, would have been ineffective. Instead of leaping from the aircraft, the inspector continued, Thomas must have rebuckled his belt, which had evidently snapped open when he reached forward, resumed his seat in the rear cockpit, braced himself—and, as the newspapers reported, "courageously [went] to his doom."

Stricken family members stumbled through the motions of their daily routines. Thomas's premature and violent death was far more disturbing than his father's peaceful passing. It was a month before Emma was able to join her mother-in-law for dinner at Norcliffe, and then her grief was so paralyzing that it was difficult for her to stay through the meal. Harriet went into deep mourning for her son. Her daily diary entries ceased for several weeks, and when she finally wrote, she noted that her thoughts "have been too sad." Her health was failing; periodic bouts with the asthma that had tormented her for years were taking their toll. Dorothy was saddened but detached about her brother's death, regarding it as an almost inevitable result of the risks of flying. The bond between the Stimson siblings had never been strong, and it had been further weakened with the recent tensions between Thomas and Scott. To console her mother, Dorothy joined her as often as she could, although the younger woman's duties and interests were expanding. Her father's death had given her more responsibility at the Stimson Realty Company, a role that was strangely familiar after years of listening to her father discuss real estate and the strategies of acquisition. With Scott's help, she was beginning to learn about the intricacies of leases, maintenance, and building management. She now became genuinely interested in politics, joined the newly formed League of Women Voters, and worked with Seattle Mayor Bertha Landes to increase league membership at lectures and teas. (The League of Women Voters in Seattle was initiated with the sponsorship of Harriet Stimson in 1930.) Her years of marriage to a staunch Democrat took deeper root; she was more liberal in her politics— at least on a philosophical level—although she always remained a privileged member of the upper class, with the attitudes and the sense of entitlement that accompanied that social rank.

Scott continued to practice law at the offices of Bullitt, Kennedy & Schramm in the 1411 Fourth Avenue Building, but the limelight that he had glimpsed in two political campaigns still beckoned. His experience as a delegate to the 1928 Democratic National Convention and his election in 1929 as Democratic National Committeeman for the state expanded his national political contacts. One of these was James Farley, later Postmaster General during the Roosevelt administration, who was then forming alliances and strategies to nominate the governor of New York for the presidency in 1932. Farley was immediately attracted to Scott's combination of charm and political know-how and saw him as a forceful ally in his efforts. He introduced Scott to Roosevelt, who recognized in the Southerner a kindred spirit, with a shared background of Ivy League education and a vaulting belief in the future of the Democratic Party. Although they never knew each other well, their association was strong enough that Scott began to plan for Washington State's participation in the upcoming election. "Jim Farley kept track of every Democrat in the country, and he was drawn to Scott," Dorothy observed. "They teamed up together, along with a wealthy financier [John J. Raskob] from New York, to put Roosevelt in nomination . . . Those three became a working crew and agreed that FDR's name should be first presented in a small place—not New York or Chicago. Eventually, they decided to hold the first state convention at Olympia where Scott would propose Roosevelt's name and Washington would be the first state to be committed."

Scott could see his political aspirations finally being realized. Philosophically, he considered Roosevelt the perfect candidate—a patrician of noble purpose, yet entirely sympathetic to the needs of working people. On a practical level, Scott could also see that an affiliation with Roosevelt, if he won the election, might bring him an appointment to the cabinet or eventual election to the Senate. At home the Bullitts spent hours discussing the future of the state and the country, and what the future might hold for them. In January 1932, Scott and Dorothy took the train to New York City, where Dorothy remained for a few days while Scott went on to Hyde Park to work on strategy for Roosevelt's nomination. A few days later at a dinner of prominent Democrats, Governor Roosevelt made what Dorothy termed a "fine speech" but in which there was no mention of his candidacy. While they stayed in New York, Scott had a complete medical checkup. Pronounced in good health, he continued on to Washington, D.C., where he tried a case, then traveled to Kentucky for family matters while Dorothy returned to Seattle.

BUT THE GOOD HEALTH DIDN'T HOLD. "AFTER HE ARRIVED home," Dorothy remembered, "Scott caught what seemed like a bad cold. He ran a temperature and within a few weeks began to look jaundiced. When he started becoming nauseated, his weight dropped rapidly—from about 165 to 138 pounds—and the doctor said, 'He's not throwing this off and I don't like his color,' and ordered him in for tests. Scott objected because he had so much work to do for the state convention, which was coming up soon. I remember he said, 'I've got to get to that convention.' When I said, 'You can't possibly go,' he replied, 'I can't help it . . . I *have* to be there!' Finally Doctor Sharples stepped in and insisted, 'You can't go. We don't know what this is, but we have to find out.' So that beat him down pretty badly.

"So Scott went into Providence Hospital, and the tests showed only a possible liver infection, but he got no relief from any treatment. When Dr. Sharples began to talk about an exploratory operation, Scott said, 'Get me out of this hospital! I don't want an operation here. These nuns and nurses are very nice, but they think it would be lovely to go to heaven. I'm not ready to go and I have no assurance about actually getting there. I want to go to a hospital where they don't like heaven so much.' So we moved to Seattle General, and I stayed with him there in the next room—until the Lindbergh baby was kidnapped, and then Scott said, 'You'd better go home and take care of those kids because they might get kidnapped.' A few days later, Dr. Sharples operated and found advanced cancer of the liver."

When the doctor told her that Scott's condition was terminal, Dorothy did what was for her unthinkable—she lost control. She flew at him, pounding his chest with her fists and shouting, "It isn't true, it isn't true!" Recalling these events in her ninety-seventh year was like reopening a wound that had never healed. Her usually keen eyes became clouded with pain as she repeated in a low, halting voice, "I just didn't think it could happen and I didn't, I didn't want to believe it." Urgently she sought out any advanced treatment that might possibly save him, phoning and sending telegrams for advice. But there was none. In shock, she fought desperately against the inevitable. "My heart aches for her so that I can scarcely breathe," Harriet Stimson, herself now seasoned by sorrow, wrote in her diary.

They brought him home. No one mentioned the disease. No one told him he was going to die. Scott and Dorothy had agreed early in their marriage that she would not tell him if she knew. "Early in our marriage, Scott and I discussed what we would do if one of us was to die. I said that I would want to know and be told about it. Scott said, 'I don't want to hear about it. Promise not to tell me if you know I am to die.' I kept my end of the bargain. Scott and I never discussed it at all—which was too bad, really—that was the way it went." If she did have moments of doubt about keeping this promise, she was encouraged by her mother to keep quiet, thus giving Scott at least the semblance of hope in the days to come. Throughout his last weeks, she sat by his bed, chatting about everything but his condition, scarcely letting on that he was even ill. It was some comfort: by denying his fate, she could ignore the terrible pain in her heart.

She didn't tell the children, fearing that if she did they would run to him in tears. "They all resented the fact that they didn't know," she said regretfully years later. "Everything was shot . . . I didn't know what I was doing." Thinking their father was recovering from an operation, the children continued about their lives, shepherded by nurses and governesses, spending their nights with Grandmother Stimson at Norcliffe. Visits with their father were kept at a minimum at Scott's insistence, for he did not want them to see and remember him in such a wasted condition. Scott never spoke of death—except to the youngest, Harriet, who he feared, at seven years of age, might not remember him. "I was holding his hand and looking up at his big high bed," Harriet recalled of the visit to her father in his last days. "There was an odd odor in the room, and his eyes were so yellow. I remember I was kind of wordless. Then he said, 'After I'm gone, you won't forget Father, will you?' I asked where he was going and he said, 'To heaven.' "

One by one, his brothers, Marshall, Keith, and Jim, crossed the country on the train to say good-bye, bringing with them what comfort they could share— old Kentucky bourbon and wine from the family farm at Oxmoor, books, small family treasures, and aimless, gentle talk infused with grief and love. Propped up on his pillows, jaundiced and debilitated by the disease, Scott was no longer the vigorous, intellectually keen brother they had always known. Only rarely did a slight smile light up his drawn face with the old familiar magic they had enjoyed since boyhood. On April 9, 1932, Scott sank into a coma and died the next morning. He was fifty-five years old.

The morning of his death, Harriet Stimson told Stim and Patsy, temporarily staying with her, that their mother wanted to see them. Stim walked over from Norcliffe and found his mother sitting alone in the bedroom. Quietly Dorothy told her son what he dreaded had happened. When Patsy burst in a short time later, she was surprised to find her mother visiting with family friend Joseph Black. Instantly the girl knew, and at the same moment her mother looked up and said, "Your father has died." Running across the room, Patsy clung to her, sobbing. "Oh Mother," she cried, "what will we do without Father?" Calmly, Dorothy replied in her low voice, "I don't know. We'll just have to get along the best we can." She asked if they would like to see their father, and both children said no. That was the last that was said about their father's death.

"Dorothy is very calm," her mother observed about the next few days, "and holding up wonderfully." Dorothy made arrangements for the funeral to be held at home and for the memorial service later at The Highlands Chapel. Flowers, letters, and telegrams poured in, and a memorial service was broadcast on the radio. The newspapers acknowledged the loss of "the gallant and charming Kentuckian," state- and nationwide. In an article covering the presidential candidates of 1932, the *New York Times* described Scott as one who had "fired the starter's gun" in Roosevelt's campaign for presidency and a leader "to whom many Democrats had looked for the rehabilitation of their party in the West, who was expected to come to the Senate soon and perhaps be national chairman."

It was an unfinished life, politically and personally. Alexander Scott Bullitt had lived two lives, neither of them complete. The first in Kentucky—anchored by history, family, and personal identity—he had abandoned to move west; the second he had not yet realized in any solid personal way before his death. Caught up in the powerful Stimson family, one that allowed for little deviation from its social and commercial priorities, he played out his role as husband, father, and son-in-law at the expense of his personal evolution. He did this by difficult choice, as a result of Dorothy's refusal to return to Kentucky three years after their marriage. With grace and gallantry, he acted out his part: he responded, he smiled, he served. If he fell short of expectations, his own and others, it may have been because he was miscast in a role that ignored many of his essential talents. As a result, he never fully came to grips with his own life, though he seemed to be in the process of changing this shortly before his death. No doubt he suffered remorse in his last days, knowing that it was now too late to make up for promises unkept to his family—that he would spend more time with them and support them with his own money—and to himself—that he would become the quintessential politician that he really was.

Scott left Dorothy little of material value. Shortly before he died, he gave her a sealed envelope to open "only when it is certain that I cannot get better." It contained instructions to deposit to her account $10,000 that he had saved "out of the law practice, out of income from my mother's estate, and out of salary which I was quietly accumulating so that I might be able to help pay back to you what you have lost by my campaign expenses, coming really out of your estate." It was a small percentage of the debt of well over $100,000 that had been growing over the years, but it was his last effort to repay her. Dorothy never complained about the inequity of their finances during their marriage. She never mentioned it, even in moments of frustration or anger. Her complaints were only two: "I hated that when he was dying, he thought he'd never achieved what he had wanted to, and that he was so young—at fifty-three there was a lot ahead," she said decades later. "But those are the things life does to you and you can't argue with it."

In his handwritten will (unwitnessed and therefore invalid in Washington State), Scott left her all he had—a small accumulation of books, jewelry, and furniture. His real legacy, apart from his love for her and the family, soon saw fruition. Just months after Scott's death, Democrats were elected to all major state offices, including a majority in both houses of the legislature, and occupied all of the state's seats in Congress. As principal orchestrator of this Democratic landslide, after a decade of promoting his party in the state, Scott Bullitt would have been "mighty proud."

Dorothy was unable to discuss Scott's death with the children, to console them, or even to acknowledge that he was gone, and this strange reticence was to affect them deeply. For Dorothy, coming from a family whose strong New England tradition required strength in adversity, grief and its processes were not a matter for discussion. The children suffered, but they knew not to cry or ask questions. Well-dressed and well-mannered, they joined the rest of the family for the private funeral service at Greenway. At The Highlands Chapel a few days later, as the organ played the old hymns dear to their father, "Lead Kindly Light," "Rock of Ages," "Abide With Me," and "Jesus Lover of My Soul," they stood like minor spectators, solemn and silent, watching the outpouring of people who called their father "most lovable."

For all three Bullitt children, it was as though their father had vanished. A few months after the funeral, Stim heard his father's name on the radio when Franklin Roosevelt, by this time the Democratic nominee for president, arrived in Seattle and in his distinctive clipped voice expressed regrets that his friend Scott Bullitt was not present for the happy occasion. For three years, his name was scarcely mentioned until one evening when the girls asked to go to the movies. Their mother said no in spite of their pleading. When they continued to complain, she suddenly turned on them, her face distorted with pain, shouting, "Don't you know that today is April 10? It's the anniversary of your father's death!"

DOROTHY TURNED TO STONE. AT FORTY, HER INTERIOR LIFE, her spontaneity, humor, hopes, and dreams, froze into a rigid matrix penetrable by no one. She carried on, her stricken spirit discernible only fleetingly in the fatigue of her glance and lines of resignation around her mouth. In less than three years, she had lost father, brother, and husband. On an emotional level, there was no one to trust, particularly any man who might again desert her. She consulted a palmist who told her that though she had a very strong hand, her struggle would be very "close," and she could not guarantee that Dorothy would get through it. She had no one to turn to, nor could she share the turmoil of tears, anger, and despair that threatened to tear her apart. Instead she shut down, keeping to herself and seeing very few others.

She buried her husband and she buried herself in work. "Mother had her own way of grieving," Patsy remembered. "She went to her room and stayed there. She had breakfast in her room, dinner in her room, and spent all day at the office. She wore black and was driven there by a chauffeur. She had nobody over to visit—only Joe and Jane Black, Aunt Em, and Grandmother were allowed to come to the house. That went on for three or four years. She had nothing to comfort her but going to the office. We were no comfort, and she didn't relate much to us during those times—we were kind of on our own."

Each morning Dorothy descended from The Highlands into the world of downtown Seattle, silently passing the giant Aurora Avenue Bridge under construction, one of only a few city projects that buffered workers against the deepening Depression. From her office in the 1411 Building, she watched the lines below—bank lines of depositors hoping to recoup their savings, and bread lines of those who were hoping for a meal. Along the railroad tracks south of downtown, the unemployed built tarpaper and scrapboard shacks and christened their community Hooverville in derision of the president who had told them, "Prosperity is just around the corner." Business failures were on the way to becoming higher in the Northwest than in any part of the country. Taking stock of her own situation, Dorothy saw clearly that more than her own emotional resources was at stake. She had a business to oversee and salaries and a mortgage to pay. On one occasion she joined a bank line herself, needing cash to pay the elevator girls and janitresses in her building.

She focused on her finances and her new role as head of a family and a company. The 1411 Building was only partially tenanted, and the Depression was putting in jeopardy what reliable investments she did have. Scott had made no provision for the guardianship of the children. She needed someone to sign a bond attesting to her ability to serve as guardian, and she also needed someone reliable to manage her affairs. She thought of her nearest male relative, Cully—C. W. Stimson—her cousin who had learned the lumber business while living with the Stimsons on First Hill many years before. Cousin Cully was family, a successful businessman with real estate interests and his own lumber mill, and he had moved into Thomas Stimson's office the year before to manage the affairs of Emma and her children.

"Mother and I walked up the road in The Highlands to Cully's house to ask him to manage our affairs. Instead he said, 'No, sorry about that, but I have my hands full and my own worries. I guess you're just going to have to go to *work*. It never entered my *mind* that he'd refuse, but it was fair enough. He could have put it a little differently though, but he wasn't very good at that. 'Go to work.' I didn't know from *nothing!* I could have told you about horses or boats, but I didn't know word one about business, I never had to. I had spent my entire life being protected by somebody, always. It never occurred to me until Cully said it that I'd have to 'go to work.' " Then she asked him to sign the $10,000 bond that would attest that she, as a woman alone, would be a responsible guardian of her three children. "It was a court requirement in those days to have a bond guaranteeing my reliability as guardian of three children, assuring the court that I wouldn't sell everything and leave town with all of the money and leaving them helpless. I asked him to sign it, and he said, 'No, I won't. Your father advised me never to sign anyone's bond.' That was the *last* thing my father would have said, particularly in *my* case! Cully wouldn't sign a $10,000 bond for me—he wouldn't risk that money on me."

That did it. Being overburdened with other family affairs was understandable, but to refuse to sign a bond attesting to her character? The humiliation was a blow that put an end to Dorothy's relationship with her cousin. Dorothy was furious. She never forgave Cousin Cully, referring to him as "a tough character—the one who refused to back me up, the one who turned me out."

In the end, without Cully or any other likely prospect to fill the role of caretaker, Dorothy did what her cousin had suggested—she went to work. As her son Stim put it, "She pulled her socks up and said, 'OK, this is what I have to do,' and she took it as very sober, serious, hard work." He added with a smile, "At the same time, she enjoyed it—she must have because she spent all of her time at it for forty or fifty years thereafter." Unknowingly, Cully Stimson had done Dorothy a great favor. With his curt refusal to help, he had incited her anger, sparking a fire that was the setting of her soul. A major turning point, it was the start of Dorothy Stimson Bullitt as a person in her own right.

A NEW DOROTHY BEGAN TO EMERGE. "AFTER SCOTT'S DEATH and when I was going to an office every day, people began to write me off socially. Besides, I was too tired to go anywhere and those invitations I did receive I refused because I was either too tired or bored to attend. I found men so much more fun to talk to than women . . . Golly! Women in those days wanted to talk about their *gardeners*. I'll never forget going through

Mrs. Frederick's house during the Depression, and she apologized for the garden because she'd lost her *second* gardener . . . when people were hungry. I couldn't care *less* how many gardeners she had or didn't have—that wasn't my interest at all. That's not where I wanted to put my time, so I wasn't interesting to them either. Eventually the invitations stopped coming—that was all right. Even good friends you can lose if you don't have time for them. But what did bother me was when I'd meet someone I'd known and they had no conception of what I was doing."

First, she needed an attorney. She looked through the Buyers Guide under "Attorneys" to see if she might find the name of a friend. "Luckily, I found the best one there was—Raymond Wright." Charming, kind, and sensible, with a gentle disposition and eyes that crinkled when he smiled, Ray Wright was a transplant from the East who remembered Scott Bullitt from days when they both attended Princeton. He listened to Dorothy's story and without a moment's hesitation told her that his wife Betty would sign the bond. This single act of trust Dorothy never forgot, and it marked the beginning of a long association that brought her solid advice and support whenever she needed it. "In 1932 he took me on with all of my problems. He thought I was the most amusing person because I always did the unexpected. It was difficult being a woman in the financial world during those days. I didn't know what I was doing, but he guided me and always steered me right."

Cousin Cully's rejection had made her realize clearly that she was on her own. It also signaled that from now on she would have to be tough. Dorothy could see that the passive role of a society matron would never work for the challenges before her. She knew that her privileged upbringing would have to be supplemented with a firm stance, strategic thinking, and straight talk. She would have to combine a soft voice with hard decisions and an ingratiating smile with a will of iron. It seemed an unfamiliar role, but she had been well trained. Her father's practicality, her mother's sense of detail, and the ability of both parents to take charge and work tirelessly were invaluable examples to prepare her for what lay ahead. She was determined to succeed and believed she could. Had she not grown up believing herself to be the Center of the Universe?

To cope with business life, she took her common sense, indomitable will, intuition, and charm and pushed them to the limit. She used everything to her advantage, including her femininity, which was never false or forced, although she was aware that it was certainly appealing to the businessmen she needed to deal with. At forty, she was attractive, though not as slim as she had been, but with the same winning smile and direct gaze she had possessed since youth. She cut her long, dark hair (Scott had always opposed her cutting her hair) into a short, curly style and, after a year, discarded her black mourning garments. Shunning the latest in fashion, she dressed conservatively in subdued classic suits, with a blouse in contrasting color topped by a jabot or floppy bow at the collar. Her mid-calf skirts revealed a glimpse of shapely legs that were planted firmly on the ground by a pair of no-nonsense pumps. She was never without a hat and gloves—the mark of a lady—and a little jewelry, usually only a simple (but elegant) pin or a string of pearls and the star sapphire ring that had passed from her father to Scott and now to her. She did not wear earrings, since her ears were large and she didn't want to call attention to them. She gave the impression of a modest—if not slightly frumpy—middle-aged widow whose dress and demeanor were completely nonthreatening. This style of dress never changed. Ever thrifty, she kept her clothes for decades: in 1989, she was still wearing shoes and jackets from the thirties. Because of her demure appearance, some of the businessmen she met over the years may have misjudged her. Those who were more astute noted that her voice and gaze held all the power of a freight train at full speed. Those who didn't notice the eyes when they flashed, or listen to the voice when it dropped an octave, were bound to regret it.

She developed a style based on what appeared to the brotherhood as weakness, playing upon her femininity and her lack of experience. She was a master of indirection, not only because of her innate dignity but also because it was the most effective way to deal with men. She preferred to ask questions rather than state opinions, to wile and beguile rather than wheel and deal. She was never an outright flirt, but her smile and her enthusiasm, tempered by her gentility, kept her business associates both charmed and off balance. There was no way they could swear or argue in rough fashion in her presence, let alone make a pass at her. Men dealt with her in different ways, she recalled years later. "Sometimes I was treated like a strange kind of animal," she said in a speech to career women during the 1980s. "Other times I was ignored, imposed upon, and disbelieved, but I also had some men friends who counseled me and gave me support that I would never have had if I'd been a man. They taught me that most things were solved with common sense and told me, 'If you're puzzled about anything, we're as close as the telephone.' Women were always after me to know what a hard job it was being a woman alone with men grabbing everything for themselves, and that wasn't what happened at all. Men gave me every help I ever asked for." Then she added, "*And* they still picked me up for lunch, picked up the tab afterwards, paid the taxi fares—which kept my expenses down—and I hope it stays that way."

Dorothy's rules of conduct worked very well. At all meetings, she arrived promptly in order to counter the expectation that, as a woman, she would be late. She remained seated the whole time, refusing to go to the ladies room because it would be a sign of weakness to flutter off and "powder her nose." She didn't smoke, and she didn't talk. "One thing I learned fairly early was to keep very, very quiet. That, I found, fooled everybody. As a result, I got credit for a lot of things I wasn't equal to." When she did speak up, it was always in a very tentative way. "Mother never wanted to look dominant," Harriet once remarked. "She would plant ideas into men's minds but would always have a way of letting them think it was their idea. She'd start off with, 'Wouldn't it be possible . . . ,' but she'd never butt in. She always maintained her femininity and wanted to be soft-spoken. Nothing upset her more than someone who thought she was aggressive. She got along with the boardmen because she learned how to handle them. She won their respect because she did her homework; she was quiet and not strident and never did frivolous things. She understood their male power signals and didn't cross into their territories. And they didn't understand hers. She kept them off balance with her gloves and her quiet manner. She learned how to let them keep their male pride by letting them think that they had all the ideas and take credit." Quiet and unobtrusive, Dorothy was nonetheless a shrewd judge of character. When she saw someone with the abilities she needed, it wasn't long before they were volunteering to help her.

She entered the business world with little specific knowledge. "The responsibility was probably the best thing that ever happened to me. I didn't have time to sit around and mourn." She was soon aided by Hazel Earle, a public stenographer in the 1411 Building, whom Scott had hired for temporary help and who became Dorothy's full-time bookkeeper. The two were both widows and neophytes in the business world. "We just sat across the desk from each other and cried," Dorothy said with a helpless smile years later.

————

DOROTHY HAD THREE BASIC SOURCES OF INCOME. ONE WAS the Coliseum Theater in downtown Seattle—on land for which her father had traded the Minor Avenue house. The Stimson Realty Company leased the property to the Fox Theater Company, which owned the building. This rental provided a steady monthly income until Fox went bankrupt during the Depression, and she found herself with an ornate but empty theater on her hands. "Those were frightening times. Things that had always been secure just melted away, and it was as if we were all in the bottom of a pit together and no one could get out—for a while anyway. Fox just gave me the Coliseum building when they went bankrupt, and what did I know about running a theater? Nothing! Not long after, another company sent a man up from Hollywood to talk about re-opening [the theater]. His name was Frank Newman. He was pretty scared but when he came to see me, after about ten minutes, he said, 'How long have you been in business anyway?' I said, 'Oh, a few weeks,' and he said, 'Oh, for goodness sakes!' From then on we became very good friends, and he coached me on how to talk to his company.

"Frank had all of the theater characteristics. His fingernails were always polished, and whenever he came to the office he brought jokes—some were pretty good, some were not so good—but he was always lovely to me. We'd talk about the affairs of the world and what to do with the new lease, and he'd tell me what the company'd go for, and I'd say, 'Well, OK, if you say so . . . ' and that was the way we did business. One day I met him on the Fourth Avenue sidewalk—at noon you'd see a lot of your friends on that corner. We passed the time of day, and he said he needed new carpet and seats—they were ragged—in the theater, and in order to live out the expense he wanted to extend the lease. I asked, 'On the same terms?' He said yes, and I agreed to that. A few months later, we met on the sidewalk again, and I said, 'I thought you were coming up to talk about new seats and carpets for the theater.' 'Oh,' he said, 'You told me you'd extend the lease, so I ordered them. They're all in.' He trusted me on my *word* on the sidewalk! That's one of the nicest things that ever happened to me. My friends don't trust me like that."

Income also came from logging off the timber on a large piece of forest land near Stevens Pass in the Cascade Range. Dorothy's grandfather, T. D. Stimson, had obtained the deed to this land from a man seeking a stake to go to Alaska for gold. "In those days when the rush was on," as Dorothy remembered the tale, "people all wanted gold, and they'd sell and buy things sight unseen. The man told Grandfather, 'If you can advance me the money, I'll pay you back and then some. But if I don't ever come back, I'll give you a deed to a patch of woods up in the Cascades that I won in a crap game. It's no good to me, I've never seen it and it's not making me any money. And I need money *now*.' Grandfather took the deed as security. The man bought a shovel, a dog, and a pan, and never came back. It was quite a big piece of land. Father inherited it and then sold it to a local lumberman who logged off the acreage square by square, paying in advance for each square. I had that money from the Wallace Falls Timber Company."

The 1411 Building provided the third source of monthly revenue, but it was also her biggest liability. "The New England Mutual Life Insurance Company held the mortgage," Dorothy recounted. "But before the first payment was even made, the stock crash occurred. That alarmed the local agent, Charlie Frisbie, who became even more disturbed when he heard that the building was being run by a forty-year-old woman who didn't know about anything but horses. He sent back east for the higher-ups to come out and look things over. They asked me what was going to happen, and I said, 'I don't know,' or words to that effect. Finally, they said they'd change some dates and terms that they had agreed to. They gave me an extension I would have never had if I hadn't been an ignorant woman. The dollars were the same, but the timing of the payments was changed to my advantage.

"I was just as ignorant as could be, I really was! All I knew to do was to instruct the building manager to keep the tenants happy, no matter what. The building was still unfinished and only barely one-third full, and those rooms emptied pretty fast. One whole floor went out all at once—they were wiped out—a Minneapolis–St. Paul finance company. They said they were sorry and that we could keep the furniture, but that they were packing up and going home. We stored it for a while and then gave it to the Children's Orthopedic Hospital for their boardroom. Then another floor went—a government housing agency of some kind—and I went back to Washington, D.C., a four-day train ride each way, got mad, wrung my hands and everything, but it didn't work. They had an escape clause, and they just said, 'Read your lease.' There was another tenant, an old man who sold stock, and his son came to me and said, 'I don't know what's going to become of him—he's going to have to give up his office.' I said, 'He's going to *keep* his office.' You had to do that here and there . . . when there was a sad case, particularly not affiliated with a large, out-of-state company. People weren't just moving out, they were jumping out of windows and committing suicide all over town, and that was one thing I didn't want—suicide in that building. It would have been bad publicity. So, we dropped everyone's rent except for the four railroads and the Alaska Steamship Company because they had ten-year leases that secured the mortgage. I went to Mr. Frederick, who had a small office in the building apart from the store downtown, and told him we were dropping everyone's rent and it would be unfair to him not to drop his also. He said, 'You'll never drop mine. I knew what I was doing when I signed the lease, and I still know and am staying right where I am.' That was nice. I knew he could, because Frederick & Nelson wasn't going broke. Mr. Bloedel was also in the building—Bloedel Timber had a corner office with the walls carved into trees—and he also stayed. Merrill Lynch never failed in their rent either, but a lot of other Eastern companies closed up shop."

The four large companies whose ten-year leases secured the 1411 Building's mortgage tested the new owner's mettle with constant pressure to reduce their rents. Dorothy refused. The Alaska Steamship Company was the worst.

Once, Dorothy reminisced, "they sent for me to lower the rent. Their lawyers called and asked me to *get down there,* 'which I thought was very rude on their part. I was a woman, for one thing, and they knew me well enough to know that I was inexperienced. They should have come to *my* office if they wanted to talk to me. They very rudely demanded my presence, and I practically thumbed my nose at them and never went. I wasn't about to go trucking down the street to talk to them about canceling their lease! If they wanted to see me, they could come and see me. The building manager, Walter Douglas, advised me against it. He said, 'To hold those great companies, you're going to have to accede to their demands.' I didn't need to hear that—he doubtless would have taken a cut himself. He also said, 'I'll tell you one thing, if you don't reduce the lease for Alaska Steamship, they'll move out when their lease expires.' And they did."

Walter Douglas tested her further until he went too far. Although Dorothy owned the building, Douglas was an employee of the Metropolitan Building Company, which managed (and owned) most of the large buildings downtown. A highly prosperous company, Metropolitan had been founded by Dorothy's father and others, but now a large amount of the company's stock was owned by Thomas Stimson's estate and managed by Cousin Cully—a situation that no doubt made Dorothy doubly suspicious in her dealings with Douglas. As building manager, Douglas was in constant contact with the tenants, and tenants were an important commodity during the economically shaky 1930s. Dorothy did not trust Douglas from the start, and when some of her tenants began to leave and then reappear in Metropolitan-owned buildings, she began to suspect that he was instigating the moves. "Walter Douglas was a stinker of the first order. When Father had been president of the Metropolitan Building Company, there had been no funny business; but with Father gone, Douglas began taking tenants out of our building into his. We would lose a tenant like Western Union—they were good renters—and then I'd find them across the street in one of the Metropolitan Building Company buildings. Then—and this took the cake—one morning I went into the 1411 Building, and there were no doors on the elevators, which had always had nice, bronze doors. The building was not finished between floors—the plaster was rough and it looked horrid! I called Walter Douglas and asked, 'Where are the doors?' He replied that he thought the elevators would move a little faster without them. That was nonsense because they were the fastest elevators in town and the newest. I was very angry and I . . . think he understood what I felt . . . so the doors were back by noon.

"I could see that we were getting very bad treatment [from the Metropolitan Building Company], particularly with the tenants disappearing. When I told other business people I was thinking of canceling my arrangement with them [to manage the building], they'd say, 'You're going to fight the Metropolitan Building Company? Golly! You might as well jump off the docks as cancel them— they're the biggest building managers in town. They have all the equipment and personnel.' 'But,' I said, 'we're coming out the wrong end of the horn.' When I mentioned this to my friends, they said, 'Oh, don't do that, they'll murder you.' And I said, 'No worse than they're doing now.' I went to Bill Boeing, who was in my building, and he said, 'Don't you be afraid of them. Fire them—they don't play a straight game. You've got a great building and you can get someone else to run it for you.' So, I did . . . I finally screwed up my courage and told them I didn't like the way they were doing things and that we were quitting at the end of the month. They didn't like that at all. Then Walter Douglas went back to his office and called me, saying that . . . they were not going to put *anyone* in the building for the rest of the month. 'After today,' he said, 'you're on your own.' So I hired one of *their* men. We made a deal and he cleared out his desk that afternoon and moved over. His name was Burke Taylor, he stayed for twenty years, and he was excellent."

Aided by Taylor's congeniality and easy-going business tactics, Dorothy set the building management's tone with concern and charm. She was at her office every day, visible to all occupants and accessible if there were complaints. On weekends, she inspected the halls and restrooms to verify that they were properly cleaned. She supervised the smallest details and Taylor took care of them. The two spent long hours discussing the finishing of the floors, moving templates of the offices around like pieces in a board game. She was particular about the kind of tenants she leased to, declining space to fortunetellers or palmists. She was secretly pleased when she learned that a stenographer was selling the building's letterhead because that meant that her building was highly regarded. Above all, she monitored the monthly rents. It wasn't unusual for her to appear at an office to collect those that were overdue with little Harriet in tow, as if to remind the tenant that she was a widow on her own. She instructed Taylor to make friends with the tenants and give them anything they wanted— anything that would encourage them to stay on.

ALTHOUGH BESET BY A MULTITUDE OF NEW RESPONSIBILITIES, Dorothy retained an interest in politics. She had never enjoyed the hail-fellow trappings of politics, but her years with Scott had made her a staunch advocate of Democratic principles. After his death, she continued her association with Franklin and Eleanor Roosevelt, whom she had met in earlier days in New York. She also knew their daughter, Anna Roosevelt Boettiger, who had moved with her husband to Seattle during the 1930s. "I was very fond of Anna Roosevelt. Her husband, John Boettiger, was sent out here to settle a newspaper strike at the *Seattle Post-Intelligencer*—some thought that hiring the son-in-law of the instigator of the New Deal would help make peace with the union—and they stayed here. Anna was awfully open-minded and energetic. She was snubbed and insulted by everyone in Seattle because she was the daughter of That Man, but I didn't regard that as a handicap at all. Eventually she, too, worked down at the *P-I* and sent her two small children to the public school, where they earned the reputation of lying like everything when they told their classmates that their grandfather was president."

Only three months after Scott's death, Dorothy was asked to take her husband's place as delegate-at-large from Washington State to the Democratic National Convention in Chicago. There she proposed a platform plank for child labor protection. "During the convention I was seated on the floor and Stim was in the balcony, but when Roosevelt sent word that he would appear for the nomination—something that had never happened at a convention before—I got Stim down to the floor on the last evening. I had a ticket and a badge, and I put on the badge, and he put on the ticket and sat on my lap. We were there until morning. Daylight was streaming through the windows way up on high when Roosevelt arrived and made his acceptance speech for a New Deal."

She contacted Roosevelt four months later. "Mr. Roosevelt was always very nice to me," she said. "When as a candidate he was coming to Seattle, I wrote, asking him to put on his schedule a trip to the Children's Orthopedic Hospital, and he said he'd be glad to do that. One of his party brought me up to his room in the hotel, and we chatted. He said, 'I'll go if you go with me.' In the car on the way, I'll never forget, I said, 'I wish Scott could be here for this,' and Franklin Roosevelt patted my knee and said, 'Scott knows all about this.' It was a wonderful visit at the hospital. Franklin Roosevelt was a cripple who didn't let his condition stop his goals, and I thought he'd be a perfect example for the children."

Another encounter with the Roosevelts in 1933 provided a lasting memory for both Dorothy and fourteen-year-old Stim. Stim and his cousin, David Stimson, had gone to the International Boy Scout Jamboree in Budapest, Hungary, during the summer of 1933. Dorothy went to New York to meet the return boat and took the tired boys back to the hotel, where the phone rang. "It was Eleanor Roosevelt—how she knew where I was I'll never know, but she asked me to come to Hyde Park the next day for lunch. I said, 'Oh dear, I have two young Boy Scouts with me,' and she said, 'By all means, bring them along!' So I washed and ironed suits and bandanas all night long—everything they had was crumpled—and they were spic and span when we drove to Hyde Park the next day. After she welcomed us very graciously, Mrs. Roosevelt farmed the boys out somewhere and then took me for a drive around the park, pointing out the old trees—she knew the name of every one. Then we went to a shop she had started for the young folk around there with nothing to do. She had imagination as well as good thoughts and in this shop they were making copies of old furniture that they had researched. It was beautiful work, all hand-built. I saw a sideboard there and said, 'Oh, I want that,' and she said, 'You shall have it,' and she signed her name on the side of one of the drawers and I signed my name on another.

The luncheon at Hyde Park was memorable for several reasons. Seated with fourteen eminent personages at table, including financier Vincent Astor, young Stim remained respectful but somewhat unimpressed—that is, until Franklin Roosevelt arrived. "When he was wheeled into the room, the president said, 'Hello, boys,' with a friendly wave of his hand," Stim remembered. "His presence was happy, buoyant, and commanding. If you had been in a crowd of strangers and were told that one was the president of the United States, you would have picked him out right away."

Also present at the luncheon was the imposing Sara Roosevelt, mother of the president, and another guest, William Bullitt, Scott's cousin and the first United States ambassador to the Soviet Union. "It was kind of noticeable and depressing that the president sat at one end of the table and his mother sat at the other end, while poor Eleanor sat at the *side*. The mother was overpowering . . . She bossed everyone around her.

"William Bullitt, Scott's first cousin, was also there, and it was the first time I'd met him, although I felt like I knew him well because Scott had been very fond of him. I was seated to the right of the president, which was a great courtesy, and we talked. I said to him, 'That little Scout in his uniform is sitting next to Bill Bullitt, and neither one knows who the other is, and they are related.' With that, the president called half way down the table, 'Bill! Do you know who that is sitting next to you? It's Scott's son!' and Bill Bullitt turned to Stim and put his arms around him.

"After that, people gave me a lot of credit, more than I deserved. When Roosevelt went into office, appointments had to be made. He would call me and say, 'We have requests from so-and-so for this position. What do you know about him?' Somehow people thought I was a national committeewoman. I wasn't, but word got around that if you wanted to get an appointment it would be through me."

Eventually Dorothy, too, received a call from Washington, D.C., offering her a position with the Department of Labor under Frances Perkins, the first woman appointed to a cabinet post. But she refused, explaining years later, "I couldn't pull up stakes and move to Washington—as if I hadn't had anything else to do." She also learned from James Farley that, had Scott Bullitt lived, he would have been appointed Secretary of the Navy in Roosevelt's cabinet.

One appointment she did accept came from Washington State's newly elected governor, Clarence D. Martin. His first executive act when he took office in 1933 was to establish an Emergency Unemployment Relief Administration, headed by a commission to allocate and oversee funding from federal and state sources for various work-producing projects throughout the state. The governor appointed five (unsalaried) commissioners: Frank S. Baker, a Tacoma newspaper publisher; James A. Taylor, president of the Washington State Federation of Labor, from Seattle; Victor Dessert, a Spokane hotel businessman; and Frank P. Foisie, labor commissioner for the Seattle Waterfront Employers Association, an old friend of C. D. Stimson from the Red Cross. The fifth commissioner was Dorothy Bullitt. She took the position hesitantly and seriously. The local newspapers loved the idea. The *Seattle Times* published a cartoon of Dorothy, dressed in black, posing in two roles—one as a society leader being served dinner by her maid, and another as a "woman of the people," leaning over a plebeian lunch of cafeteria spaghetti at the first commission meeting in Olympia. In the accompanying article, Dorothy was quoted as saying that, although she had no background in welfare work, none of the commissioners had previous training because unemployment of this magnitude had never before been seen. Undismayed, the reporter ventured that "if sincerity, industry, and an intense effort to help others count for success on the commission, then Mrs. Bullitt will be a decided success for she indeed has all three attributes." He added, "And there was one training school that Mrs. Bullitt forgot to mention. In the matter of diplomacy, understanding of people and conditions, and in solving the problems of politics, Mrs. Bullitt had an invaluable teacher in her husband, the late A. Scott Bullitt, most prominent and beloved Democrat in the state of Washington."

Work on the Emergency Unemployment Relief Commission was exhausting. For the next two years, Dorothy went to Olympia every Tuesday for day-long meetings. "There we were, a committee of five, plus a young lawyer just out of school who was supposed to keep us legal—Warren Magnuson. I don't think he knew whether we were doing illegal things or not, but he attended the meetings. We met in the Capitol, next to the governor's office. Our meetings were pretty informal, but they were long and full of pressure from people trying to convince us that their projects should be funded. Maggie and I drove to those meetings together. I remember on one trip he said he had gone to a movie with his wife the night before and that she had enjoyed it and he had been so bored that he left during the show. I imagine that was a cold evening! His first marriage was a college something—I don't think it lasted long—and I don't think they had the same ideals. He had a funny growl of a voice that sounded artificial until you got to know him and knew it was real. He liked to talk things over with me. He opened up and told about his vision of the law and what was wrong with things."

Proposed projects ran the gamut from a rabbit breeding program for feeding the unemployed to a plan for the construction of a huge dam on the Columbia River. The letters she received reflected the desperation and resolve of the times. One county official wrote her: "I have been besieged by Island County men needing work. All day they come asking for jobs and telling me that it is harder right now to get something to do than it has ever been. They are afraid of the winter with no work in prospect and no relief coming in to our county . . . Island County has no canneries, no factories, no mills, no railroads . . . Because I believe in furnishing work where such is possible, I have bent my efforts to make a work project that will be worthy of that name and one that will be a monument in future years to the uplifting of the spirit and morale of our men in their great need. That project is the Deception Pass Bridge." The bridge that connected Whidbey Island to the mainland was funded by the commission and completed a year later.

The long hours as commissioner proved to be, in Dorothy's words, "the most rewarding of anything I've ever done." Landmark funding was awarded for projects that provided long-standing assets for the state of Washington. Much of this was appropriated through a $10 million state bond issue for special projects. "Those I remember most distinctly were the Roza Project—the great irrigation project in the Yakima valley; the Deception Pass Bridge in northwest Washington; the Washington Park Arboretum in Seattle; and Grand Coulee Dam in northeast Washington. They covered four parts of the state, and we chose them partly that way. The bridge, the dam, and the irrigation were necessities. The arboretum wasn't, but we needed some project in the densest population area of the state . . . [so that] a man could take his lunch pail, get on a bus, work with his hands, and then go home to his family for dinner. We chose the arboretum not for growing plants and trees, but to employ untrained men who could live at home and work in the city. It had a beautiful location, but it needed the best design, and there were no funds for a designer. So the garden clubs joined together. They gave women's teas and floral competitions, and they raised the money to hire the best designers in the country—the Olmsted brothers, whom

Mother had contacted earlier on during the design of Norcliffe and The Highlands. Then we put city people to work—there was no machinery—with a spade or a shovel, landscaping, planting, and making paths. That's the one thing I am proudest of doing."

The largest project taken on by the commission was the initial funding of Grand Coulee Dam. "Frank Baker was the chairman and I was the vice-chairman, and he was out of town a good bit of the time so I had the responsibility of putting the final signature on our decisions. One was for Grand Coulee Dam—it was the first money ever spent—and it began as a state project. The federal government was interested, but it wouldn't participate until the state put some money in. After we did that, the federal funding poured in." Initially a publicly owned and financed power project was regarded as a radical (if not socialist) idea, and it was only because the dam was sold to the public as an irrigation project that it was approved at all. Grand Coulee Dam was a natural for Dorothy Bullitt—who loved power in all of its forms—and it was a fitting finale to the project when, substituting for the governor, she turned on the water for the dam at opening ceremonies in 1941. "Mother always liked gadgets, especially the kind that run," her daughter Patsy recalled with a laugh. "Well, Grand Coulee was one giant gadget. What a real turn-on it must have been for her to set it in operation."

Dorothy's participation in curing the ills of the Depression extended beyond her work on the commission. In August 1933, just after the luncheon at Hyde Park, Eleanor Roosevelt asked her to become the Washington chairperson for the National Women's Committee of the 1933 Mobilization for Human Needs—a nongovernmental organization of volunteers called to raise public consciousness about the role of private welfare organizations and to enlist women's support of private welfare as a supplement to the massive federal funding of employment projects. The following month Dorothy took the train to Washington, D.C., for a conference called by the president and attended by hundreds of women. After Franklin Roosevelt's opening address at the White House, Dorothy and the other attendees were received by Eleanor Roosevelt, and plans were launched, according to a press release, "for the largest crusade in the interest of welfare work ever undertaken by women in America." Dorothy returned to Seattle and dutifully did her part. In spite of her shyness, she was a fine speaker, setting forth her message with a simple eloquence. In a speech broadcast on Seattle radio station KJR, she exhorted listeners to contribute to private charities:

If the Anti-Tuberculosis League cannot carry on its work of prevention and cure—if the Children's Orthopedic Hospital cannot care for a crippled child when it is at the age where its handicap may be permanently corrected—if the boys and girls of 1933 and 1934 are not given the help that under the circumstances they cannot get in any other way, and the help to which they have every claim—we will be faced with a readjustment of human values that will be many times more disastrous than our present readjustment of economic values. We will have a warped and crippled citizenry that will be entirely beyond our help, but who will nevertheless perhaps be directing the destinies of the country. In the shakedown which all of us have had—isn't it possible for you to put your giving on a new level? Give it a more important place in your budget because your own depleted income has given you a broader understanding and a deeper sympathy with the human needs of others.

In spite of the deprivations of the times, Dorothy managed to keep intact her own lifestyle and investments, while at the same time picking up more real estate at bargain prices. She began to look for a place to build a second home in sunny, dry location near Seattle. She went about it in her special way, using a mixture of method and intuition, studying maps and taking time with people until she got what she wanted. In eastern Washington, she found the town of Leavenworth, "one of the prettiest places I've ever seen, surrounded by the Cascade peaks and canyons carved by rushing rivers." No one in those poverty-ridden days recognized the tourist and recreation potential that this sleepy alpine village was later to develop. In the 1930s the local lumber mill, essential to the economy in the past, was closed; the railroad division point was no more. The town was poor and those few citizens who did have money had little confidence in the local bank. (When they finally brought their money back in for deposit, it was ice cold, having been buried during bank closure days.)

Property regularly came up for auction as people either left or could not meet their obligations, and Dorothy watched for an attractive piece of land at an equally attractive low price. After renting a place in Leavenworth for a summer, she set her sights on an area south of town in a pine-sloped canyon cut by Icicle Creek. Over the next few years, she bought up acreage like pieces in a board game. She studied the ads for county sales. "I put as much land together as I could get and tried to make it into a package, but it didn't matter because there was nobody else at the auction anyway." The "little patch" eventually amounted to about 300 acres, much of it bought for little more than a dollar an acre and obtained by varied and devious means. One coveted property had a cabin that she discovered one day, "as I was following bits of white flag through the brush.

There was a fat old woman sitting outside. When I asked her why she was there, she said, 'Watching the sheep.' When I asked where they were, she said, 'In the cabin.' Then I went down to the county seat in Wenatchee and found that the land was being sold for nonpayment of taxes.

"Another man, who sold me the hillside behind the property, obeyed no laws. I was told I'd never find him, that he owed everyone in town and that he'd driven the IRS man from his orchard with a baseball bat. I finally found him one day in a grocery store—very gruff, with baggy trousers—and we began by talking about soup. When I told him I was interested in his property, he said, 'It's *not* for sale.' So I asked, 'What are you going to do with it?' We got into a conversation, and finally he offered to take me for a ride around the area. So I got into his rattletrap with no top and he took me up on a high road over the property, talking all the while about a trip he'd been on with Captain Peary to the North Pole and that he'd never been paid for it. I was sympathetic with that, very. We got to be kind of friends and came back down the hill, in terror of our lives with the drop-off. He took me home, and I invited him in for soup. By this time we were friends, and we hadn't been talking about the land. After a long afternoon talking about Admiral Peary, Alaska, the dogs, and everything else, he started to leave, and he turned and looked up the hill and said, 'It's nothing but *trees*.' And I said, 'It's a beautiful hillside,' and he said, 'If that's all it is, you can have it.' Right then I got him inside, and we agreed on a price and wrote it up. When I said I'd send him a check, he said, 'Oh, no you don't!' Turned out he didn't like checks of any kind. Ultimately our arrangement went as follows—he asked for twenty-five dollars and gave me a deed, and from then on when he wanted a payment toward the total, he'd come over to Seattle and collect. The day of his last payment was his birthday, and he took me to lunch at a pancake place on Westlake Avenue." She used similar tactics to secure the final acreage she wanted. After a long roadside "chat" with the reluctant owner, she suggested that if he didn't want cash, perhaps they could trade. "He looked past me and saw my car—a fancy little Ford convertible I had recently bought. So I traded the car for the land and went home on the train."

On that land, Dorothy commissioned the design and construction of a lodge that was named Coppernotch. It was a rustic statement of simplicity and comfort, with pine walls, leaded windows, a huge stone fireplace with side compartments for warming, a screened sleeping porch, several bedrooms and baths, and a long dormitory room for the children. Warmed by a giant wood-burning stove, the kitchen glowed with family mementoes—copper utensils from Dorothy's travels, stew pots found by Emma in an abandoned cabin, dried fruit and flowers brought by Harriet Stimson from California, a gourd that Achsah

Dorothy acquired land in Leavenworth, east of the Cascades, in the 1930s and built Coppernotch, a retreat for her family.

Jane Stimson brought back from India at the turn of the century. Today, the furnishings are still sturdy and simple. Except for more modern kitchen appliances, the decor is straight out of the thirties—plaid blankets cover the beds, hooked rugs warm the planked floors, old maps of Washington decorate the walls. In one corner of the living room stands the sideboard signed by Eleanor Roosevelt.

————

IN 1933, DOROTHY WAS ASKED TO TAKE OVER HER FATHER'S position on the board of the General Insurance Company of America, later known as Safeco Insurance Company. "It was simply a matter of courtesy at first—Father had a lot of stock." General Insurance had been founded in 1923 by Hawthorne Dent, a flamboyant and shrewd businessman who sought to form a new type of insurance company, one owned by stockholders and operated on a "preferred risk" philosophy of careful underwriting. Dorothy considered Hawthorne Dent "a mischievous so-and-so. Earlier in his life, he had had tuberculosis, so he didn't have the greatest health in the world. After Christmas, he would go to Palm Springs for a couple of months and take his poodle, which he loved dearly, a standard called Madame. Madame went with him everywhere. Once, he was playing golf in Palm Springs, and Madame was there, and the attendant said, 'I'm sorry, Mr. Dent, but there are no dogs allowed on the golf course.' Hawthorne said, 'Well, she never picks up anybody's ball, and I like to have her with me.' The attendant said, 'I'm sorry but she cannot stay.' So Hawthorne dropped his clubs and marched to the clubhouse and bought her a membership! That's the kind of person he was. In business he had very good judgment and was fearless about what he did. He came up with a plan that no other company had done before and policyholders would get a dividend from what the company made. Father thought it was a great idea. Hawthorne, who was a young man then, would come over to the house and discuss his ideas, and I can still picture Father, with his pencil, and Hawthorne bent over a table working it out. Father helped a great deal in the very early stages. He encouraged Hawthorne when no one else would listen, but when Father listened, others began to also.'

Dent liked Dorothy's judgment and would often call to ask her opinion. "Once, after World War II had started and the Japanese had taken Kiska, he called from California to say, 'What do you think if we took out war risk insurance on buildings? Submarines have just been sighted off the Oregon coast.' I said, 'Well, have you figured it out?' He said, 'Yes, we would spread the risk block by block, with a maximum of $500,000 in any one city block. If you think it's a good thing, I'll come up, and then we'll put it to the board.' I thought it sounded pretty good because he had done his research, and the board did approve it. I had my building insured right away. We made a *mint* of money [more than $2 million] until the government began writing war damage insurance and we dropped out. But this is what I mean: he was fearless when no other insurance company was willing to take the risk."

During the next forty years, Dorothy sat on the boards of many major financial and civic institutions in Seattle, among them, the Pacific National Bank (now First Interstate), the Seattle Art Museum, the Seattle Symphony, the University of Washington Board of Regents, the Seattle Repertory Theater, the Seattle Public Library Board, and the board of Century 21—the 1962 World's Fair. Some meetings she did not attend faithfully. "Always more absent than present," she wrote in her notes for the Art Museum Board and for the Municipal League of Seattle and King County. Her notes, jotted on the back of an agenda or on small notepaper, were simplified versions of the proceedings, spiced occasionally by some quirky, enigmatic remark, such as, "Of sixteen people, one doesn't wear glasses in Exec Com PNB."

IN DOROTHY'S BUSY LIFE, THERE WAS LITTLE TIME FOR THE children. She would return home each evening, her mind crowded with schemes and schedules for days to come. Upstairs, she traded her business suit for a hostess gown and collapsed momentarily on the bed until dinner was brought up on a tray. The drudgery of children's meals, the supervision of studies, clothes, and cleanliness were left to the "experts." She spent time with them each evening, but she did not listen closely to what they said or what they were doing in their lives; her ear was cocked toward the telephone and her thoughts turned to an upcoming speech or an upsetting balance sheet.

The growing children roamed further afield in their activities. Stim, the eldest and most daring, joined his companion "Skooky" Ohata on numerous escapades. They horsed around on the beach, built rafts and drifted around on them. In autumn, they toasted sandwiches over bonfires clearing the gully between Norcliffe and the Boeing property. In winter, they skated on the golf course pond and sometimes fell through the ice. "Stimmie was the gutsy one; he had the courage to do any damned thing there was to do," Edward Ohata recalled with a smile many years later. "On Sunday afternoons right after lunch, we'd run down the beach along the railroad tracks and go to the Princess Theatre in Edmonds, watch a movie, and tear all the way back to the house in time for dinner without being caught." One trip to the movies with the Ohata elders did result in trouble when Stim, who was staying with his grandmother at Norcliffe, neglected to ask permission. "When we returned, there were cars and police all over the place, including a famous criminologist—I think there had been kidnapping threats against the children—and Stenneberg grabbed Stimmie and dragged him into the house."

These sorts of incidents caused Dorothy to feel that she was neglecting her children. She never forgave herself for turning her offspring over to the care of others. "With my children I made every mistake that could be made," she reflected. "But I saw that they were taken care of—they were healthy, well, and in school—which was about the best I could do. There was a catastrophe downtown and I couldn't just close the door and say I had to be with the children. I always spent the evenings with them, though. I did read aloud to them at night and they thought that was pretty funny, but I didn't spend enough time with them. Once they quoted to me that I came into Harriet's room and 'almost stayed.' " Dorothy felt lifelong regret for the choices she made as a young mother, but not so keenly that she felt obligated at any point to change her direction. A small souvenir found among her papers summed up the situation. It was a card from Patsy that read "Mother, a Valentine for You. You're just the finest Mother/ And here's a Valentine/ To bring my love and say I'm glad/ So dear a Mother's mine!" On the back in Dorothy's handwriting was written, "$10,000 down, rents going down—$40,000 came to us—$36,000 City ap— Pays 6% on $30,000=$150 per month rent."

Motherhood had always come third on Dorothy's list of priorities, super-seded by her roles as a daughter and a wife. Now, with her father and husband dead, she began gradually to turn her attention to her children. As they entered their teenage years, she saw the importance of trying to shape their lives. She focused on them with far more force than she deployed in the business world. A possessive mother whether she knew it or not, she regarded her children with little sense of boundary. "Her Three" were extensions of herself. She knew what she wanted from them and she projected it so effectively that they were overwhelmed by her often unspoken demands. She dominated their lives in subtle ways: with a disinterested smile, a glance—sharp or sad—or an oblique, guilt-inducing comment; but there were also angry times when her powerful persona burst upon them with such ego-shattering explosiveness that they were left helpless in its wake. Luckily her strong-arm tactics were offset by humor, encouragement, and generosity.

Dorothy taught her children as she had been taught. As they had learned from her to contain their grief, they also learned to control other emotions as well, as if any spontaneous eruption of interest or joy might separate them from her. She quelled outbursts of joy and anger, and gradually they learned not to brag or talk back. As they became more independent, they saw that their ideas and dreams were of no interest to their mother unless they emanated from her. If Stim, for instance, became excited about an accomplishment or an upcoming event, his achievements or plans were met with a calm, "That's nice, dear," and a frozen smile which he interpreted as disdain. If Harriet talked beyond a few short remarks about a book she was reading, her mother's eyes glazed over in boredom. But when Patsy won medals at horse shows, her mother was present and cheering, because "horses" had been her idea. "Anything we thought of ourselves," said Patsy, "was met with a smirk and a 'Well, dear, whatever makes you happy . . . ,' and that was enough to dampen our enthusiasm. It was years before any of us realized that it was because Mother couldn't imagine anything of value originating outside of herself." She was still, and forever, the Center of the Universe.

The Bullitt children also grew up realizing that each served a different pur-pose in their mother's eyes. Stim had the most difficult assignment. He was recipient of his mother's highest expectations and closest scrutiny as the "man of the family." When he was eighteen, Dorothy went so far as to insist that he wear his father's clothes, kept for years in the closet waiting for Stim, a command made more humiliating by the fact that they were too small. At his mother's request, he reluctantly sat at the head of the table and went through the motions, however sullen, of being a perfect gentleman. Dismissing as arrogant and selfish his expressions of pride or accomplishment, she took him down a few pegs at every turn. "Mother confused egoism with egotism," her son remembered. "It decreased my confidence and sometimes increased my ambition." When he resisted or disobeyed her requests—which he did with rebellious regularity—she delivered an avalanche of ice-cold criticism that crushed him flat. "Those withering diatribes made me feel that I was on the railroad tracks with each car of a train running over me." She often expected the worst from him, which was doubly disappointing because he was highly idealistic. One day, after skating with his schoolmates, Stim tried to stop a boy from harassing another and punched him in the stomach, knocking the wind out of him. "That evening, on my telling my mother of this episode," he remembered, thinking that she would approve of his actions, "she asked me if the blow had gone below the belt." Unable to get her approval, he retaliated with venomous remarks. Gradually he learned to stifle his emotions and, in stony silence, to appear almost as controlled as his mother. This tactic proved effective, causing Dorothy hours of distress. When she told him of the pain she suffered out of love for him, her words fell on deaf ears; the remorse she expressed did not increase his love for her.

Stim rebelled further by fulfilling his mother's worst fears, doing things that embarrassed or terrified her. He brought home all sorts of unlikely friends— bohemians, vagabonds of every creed and color. He took up boxing, which his father had always encouraged and his mother had always feared. (In college, he coached black teenagers, won the Yale title, and boxed amateurs in New York and Western Washington. He won one professional bout in Connecticut under an assumed name derived from his father's—Al Scott—with a TKO in the third round.) To no avail, Dorothy urged him to take up team sports like crew, in which there were no stars. She dreaded that he would be injured; she kept in touch with his coach and worried constantly that, while away and out of her direct control, Stim would do something "foolish." This, of course, he did. At the end of his sophomore year at Yale, he headed home on a motorcycle, and when it broke down he jumped the rails to finish the trip. "Mother was worried sick the whole time," said Patsy. "And to some extent she had asked for it by her controlling behavior."

Although she couldn't control her son, Dorothy doted on him as she had from the earliest days. The two were psychically bound together. "Mother and Stim were a case of unrequited love," Patsy remembered of those turbulent years. "She adored him—if it came to a choice of one of us, she would have chosen Stim hands down. He had great love for her too, although he was very resentful. It's quite a sentence to have a lifetime of ambivalence toward a parent—you can never satisfy that person because his or her needs are boundless." In his efforts to extricate himself from his mother's demands, Stim withdrew from others as well. He became detached, uneasy in social situations, and an enigma to those who did not know him well.

Patsy's mission was to be the obedient daughter. Dutiful and submissive well past her teenage years, the middle child tried to gain her mother's good graces by being indispensable. She was eager, available whenever help was needed, and dependent on what approval she received. She found some closeness to her mother by becoming her confidante. Often she mediated for her two siblings, explaining their behavior, comforting her mother when Dorothy was hurt by Stim's barbed remarks. Patsy was lively, pretty, and popular; her grades were excellent, although she rarely received praise for them. Only when she was ill did she receive her mother's undivided attention, and then only for short moments at a time before she was relegated to the care of a doctor or a nurse. When life delivered setbacks, Patsy could not depend upon her mother for emotional support or comfort. One afternoon while being driven home from school, she learned from the chauffeur that her collie, Terry, had been run over by a train. With little sympathy and no further explanation, the driver simply said, "Terry is no more. Terry's dead." Devastated, the fifteen-year-old tried to ask her mother where he was buried, but true to Dorothy's inability to deal with grief, Patsy's distress was met with cool disregard. The dog, a special tri-colored breed, had been purchased from one of the kennels of Albert Payson Terhune, a well-known author of children's classics. It was a great loss; Terry had been her constant and devoted friend. She was never told where her pet was buried, and she didn't know how to express her loss. Only her grandmother understood; when Patsy ran to her, Harriet Stimson simply put her arms around her and agreed that life could be very sad for a girl. "Grandmother was a *there* person," she remembered. "No matter how many symphony and garden club meetings, Grandmother was a solid presence." Seeking somehow to express her sorrow, Patsy also wrote to Albert Payson Terhune:

Dear Mr. Terhune,

You probably don't remember, but I wrote to you in early part of 1935, asking for a collie pup. You referred me to Mrs. Himevich who had three Sunnybank puppies and from whom I got my dog. I want to thank you ever so much, more than you will ever understand for that dog. It is pretty lonely out here in the country, and Terry was with me constantly. The family had had dogs before but Terry was really all mine. He was the only dog our family knew who would obey me absolutely, and not pay any attention to commands from others. He was friendly, he liked anyone who liked him, and tried desperately to make friends with strangers. He was miserable and distraught if somebody did not fuss over him when he had tried to hold their attention. He was like a small boy in this . . .

Of course I can hardly begin to tell you about him because there is so much and because you'd be bored, but he meant so much to me, you see. When he was killed by a train last month, the family didn't understand just what grief it caused me. It is silly for a practically sixteen-year-old girl to miss a dog so much, but I decided that you have missed so many wonderful dog companions that you and Mrs. Terhune would realize what I mean.

I want to thank you again for helping me get Terry, because I guess the piles of fun and good times I had with him in that short time overbalances by a great margin the loneliness and unhappiness since. Terry was always happy too, even when he was being punished; he was that sort. It was terribly kind of you to take an interest that way. Mrs. Himevich said that you have Terry's brother, a blue merle. I hope he has turned out as fine a dog as his brother, and that he will never be hit by a train.

Patsy Bullitt

Patsy left the letter on Dorothy's desk to be mailed, probably hoping that she would read it. Fifty-two years later, she found it among her deceased mother's papers.

Harriet remained the "angel child," the one her mother could simply enjoy. Much of their communication was intuitive and there were few demands on either part. However, Harriet, too, received her share of reprimands. At first she responded with temper tantrums, but in time the criticism passed over her curly head like so many wispy clouds. When scolded or threatened, she cheerfully acquiesced but continued on her own way with a smile and without a backward glance. As the youngest, she received the least discipline; her mother did not try to control her. Like Patsy, Harriet also lost her pet dog, but unlike her older sister, she received a measure of comfort from her mother. Jake, an Irish terrier that endeared himself to everyone by baring his teeth in a "smile," had been her constant companion since she found him under the Christmas tree when she was five. When Floyd, a neighborhood chauffeur, ran over Jake, it was up to Dorothy to tell Harriet that her dog was dead. "True to the tradition of the family, I didn't see Jake's body or know where he was buried," Harriet recalled. "I just went to pieces and didn't know what else to do but find Floyd and kill him. I was looking for a sharp instrument when Mother stopped me and somehow talked me into getting into her bed. She just took me into her arms, and I cried all night long. The next day I still hadn't given up my plans for murder, but Mother decided it was a 'good time to go to Coppernotch' and piled me into the car and we went for a few days." Eventually the avenging angel returned home and dropped her plans.

Dorothy made sure the children were taught certain values. Proper behavior was paramount; it extended beyond mere manners to a near-Confucian concept of correctness and civility that she herself always exemplified. Correct grammar and speech (a legacy of her Briarcliff days) were the marks of an educated person. Form superseded content, and principles took precedence over causes: conversations about the poor or arguments over social justice were of little value unless they were well enunciated and presented with suitably chosen words. Certain words were "not polite": one did not say "pregnant" ("expecting a baby" was acceptable) or "menstruation" (you were "unwell"). Harriet, when she described her pet Belgian hares as "male and female," was told, "Dear, we don't talk that way." Foul language, of course, was absolutely taboo. Even "gosh" and "darn" were forbidden and the children were quick to notice that their mother practiced what she preached. Good posture was basic, as was proper dress. By example, they learned to be kind to strangers and visitors; their mother was always a model of hospitality and graciousness to all who entered her home or office, a trait so natural that even the most cynical left charmed. She also taught her children it was unfair to attack anyone verbally who could not fight back (a habit that she did not always adhere to herself). Scolding a waitress or shouting at a maid or anyone else who could not reply with equal force was wrong, she told them; they were to limit their disputes to persons of their own standing, a classmate or a colleague, who could fight back.

A good education was important, although high grades were not required. For Dorothy, this meant a couple of years at a college preparatory school in the East and then—something she herself always missed—four years of college. According to her plan, all the children would attend school in the East, for different reasons, and be allowed to make the final choice of the school they preferred. Stim, in the absence of a father and other male figures at home, needed the company of boys and men at Kent School in Connecticut and later Yale, where he would prepare for law school. Patsy, the studious and sheltered one, needed an academic education at Ethel Walker School in Connecticut, and would then enroll in Vassar. Harriet, to improve her grades and perhaps avoid the boyfriends that were beginning to gather, should enroll at Chatham Hall in Virginia and later would attend Bennington College in Vermont. Dorothy's scenarios were not entirely successful: Stim, defying her, left Yale just before senior year finals, declaring that grades were meaningless—it was the education that counted, not the piece of paper. He later attended the University of Washington, clerked at the Seattle law firm of Wright, Innis,

Simon & Todd (predecessor of Davis, Wright, Tremaine), and passed the bar in Washington. Harriet, after a year at the University of Washington, transferred to Bennington College in Vermont, married, and, many years later, took up studies again at the University of Washington. Only Patsy completed her assignment, the first woman in her family to graduate from college. Oddly enough, although Vassar had been Dorothy's wish, she did not attend the graduation ceremonies.

Above all, Dorothy required moral integrity from her children, especially as it related to loyalty, truthfulness, and keeping one's word. When these principles were transgressed, her anger was harsh and direct. In a cold and controlled low voice, she unleashed a stream of accusatory charges that included "contemptible," "duplicitous," "incompetent," and "deceitful." Chastity was another virtue of supreme importance. As members of the Bullitt household came of age, Dorothy could not avoid paying attention to the biological and social dramas taking place. She delivered no direct sermons on the birds-and-bees but did make pithy comments about the perils of kissing and the ideals of virginity. Stim was under heavy scrutiny. For the facts of life, he received a book of some sort from his mother but relied more on the things he heard from older boys at school. However, Dorothy did instruct her son that no nice girl was ever kissed or touched before she was engaged to be married. "This led deplorably to my thinking that if a girl allowed me to kiss her, she wasn't a nice girl," Stim remembered. "It was an attitude typical of the times and also part of those extra-austere New England values that Mother had inherited from her mother, but nonetheless it led to heartless treatment."

The girls received slightly less harsh supervision, although Dorothy was strict about the boys they dated. Her fears about certain young men were described so obliquely that the girls could not remember exactly what had been said, only that a vague aura of foreboding and danger lurked around them.

All of the children were required to be at home at hours they did not always honor. When they argued against the curfews, Dorothy explained with exaggerated patience that she had to wait up for them alone at night and that, were their father alive, she could share the responsibility with him. Once, after a date, Stim was speeding home, anxious at the prospect of a scolding, when he lost his way. This caused him to drive even faster and lose control of the car, which plunged into the brush. He hitchhiked home, dreading his mother's anger, but was surprised at her response when she opened the door. Seeing her son's bloody face, Dorothy reacted with a swift mix of nerve and grit. "First she patched the cuts that the doctor would sew shut the next day," Stim remembered. "Then she reached into my mouth, took hold of my lower front teeth, which were on their sides pointed toward my throat, pried them upright, and pushed them back to where they belonged—and where they stayed."

In terms of marriage, however, no one was good enough for her children, at least not anyone they knew, or were likely to meet. For the girls, Dorothy envisioned a British stereotype—handsome, well-groomed, with impeccable manners and the diction of a prime minister. Her tactics against boyfriends and fiancés were subtle but effective. When Harriet wrote home from Chatham Hall that she thought she might indeed marry Ernie, the lifeguard at The Highlands pool, her mother replied with a warm letter that ended, "but you do seem a little young to be settling down to housework and babies right now." For Harriet, who had dreams of a career, that was the end of Ernie.

DOROTHY ENDURED ONE LAST GREAT LOSS DURING THE tumultuous decade of the 1930s. In 1936, shortly before she was to take Patsy to boarding school, Harriet Stimson was stricken with a cold, which worsened because of her chronic asthma. As the day of departure neared, Dorothy began to have doubts about leaving. "Before we got on the train," she recalled, "I called the house, and Dr. Sharples said, 'If you *don't* go, you're going to have to *pretend* to go because your mother is determined that you will.' So we got on the train, and I found that there were some friends in the next compartment. All night long I was agonizing about Mother. The next morning I was about to get off at Missoula when I received a telegram saying that mother was worse and to come home." She left Patsy with the people in the next compartment, got off at Missoula, and took the first plane back. Dorothy arrived home that evening, and a few hours later her mother died in her arms. It was Patsy's sixteenth birthday, and on her arrival in Connecticut, she received her mother's telegram saying, "She loved you very much." No more was ever said.

Harriet Stimson's passing was a major loss. As she had carefully tended her family and surroundings, she had also started, served, and supported the cultural and charitable activities of Seattle from the early days of muddy streets, when a sidewalk tune on a fiddle was all there was for entertainment, to an era when the symphony, the opera, and performances at the Cornish School were commonplace and professional. More than any other woman of those times she had brought grace to her surroundings, converting her ideals and standards into tangible forms that survived long after her death. The *Seattle Daily Times* called her "one of the most active and beloved figures in the civic and artistic life of the city." As Nellie Cornish expressed it, "Seattle has lost her best friend." Dorothy too had lost her best friend. "She was a wonderful woman, full of kindness. I never knew her to do anything for herself. Everything she wanted to do was for somebody else. I've never known anyone like her."

With the death of her mother, Dorothy was left with an enormous legacy of material goods that had accumulated since the turn of the century. Several years before her death, Harriet had given Norcliffe and its contents to her daughter. However, the reality of supporting such a grand estate was not evident until a few weeks after Harriet's death. As Dorothy walked through the enormous house, she saw that every drawer and shelf between attic and wine cellar was packed with valuables—laces and linens, books, jewels, china, and furniture. What was she going to do with it all? She did as her mother would have done; Dorothy made lists and inventories. She saved the most precious items and sold the things that no longer fitted into her way of life.

Norcliffe itself promised to become a liability during the Great Depression. The grand scale of the house and grounds required too much maintenance. Dorothy, by this time skilled at assessing financial situations, knew that she would have to sell it. "When I looked at that huge house, the beautiful gardens, stables, and garages, I thought, 'I'm going to have to keep this property up for *years* until I get the right price. Rather than support three gardeners and a housekeeping staff, I'd just better sell it now while it's in its prime.' So I began to go through the membership lists of the Rainier Club and the Sunset Club for someone who could pay for it, someone with the 'proper status' and probably with a large family. I found someone I didn't know very well—a man named Paul Pigott, who ran Pacific Car & Foundry, and I thought, 'He's my gate!' So I just went to his office and asked, 'Don't you want to buy a house?' Well, that's not exactly the best way to sell, you know. He was tempted, but he said the price was too high and he didn't need all that acreage. I said, 'How much can you pay? I'll sell you a portion.' So I sold the house for something like $40,000, which is pitiful—I think it cost at least a hundred to build—but I had to be inventive and solve this situation fast with no fooling.

"Then I divided the rest of the land into pieces of pie, each with a view of the Sound. I moved the stable off its base and over closer to my place, made it into a little house with a fireplace and a second floor where the hayloft had been, and I sold it. Next there was the garage with its five great big doors and the apartments on top. The doors were a problem—not very appealing to look at. So I had to solve that. There was a portrait painter out here from the East by the name of Neil Ordayne. He had done portraits of Mother and Father and we had become very good friends. He was very eager to do something for me . . . including move in with me! As I didn't agree to that, what could he do? I said, 'OK, paint trees and shrubbery on the garage doors so that they blend in with the landscape.' He sat out there on a stool in the broiling sun with his palette, painting leaves and branches so well that you couldn't tell the difference. Then I sold the garage."

Of her strategy in selling Norcliffe, Dorothy often complained, "I didn't get anywhere near what the whole thing was worth. But I wasn't having to keep it all up either. Some families in The Highlands waited for their price, but it took a long time, and for me it was a great relief not to have to worry about it any longer." By attending to the smallest details, she extracted every penny she could from the sale, just as her father would have done. She took everything she could from the house, including the custom-built cupboards and bookshelves, along with anything portable in the garden, such as the orange trees that stood in tubs in the Norcliffe courtyard. She dug up Harriet Stimson's dove trees, explaining as she gave them away to the arboretum that they had been brought from China on the proviso that they would never be sold. For all of the "extras" used to run the huge household—garden tools and kitchen implements—she charged extra. For specially designed items that could fit nowhere else—the draperies, the dining room furniture, the oak handcarved grand piano, and the huge living room rug—she extracted more money, to the extreme exasperation of the buyers. As the closing of the sale drew near, Dorothy averted her eyes to the furtive work of the faithful servants. Stenneberg quietly dug up his favorite Norcliffe rhododendrons and daphne, which soon appeared on Greenway's grounds, and one of the maids visited the big house at night, returning with the formal china to save for Patsy and the home she might have one day in the future.

Dorothy shed Norcliffe and most of its contents like an old skin. Her spirits finally lifted, freshened after a decade of doubt, despair, and loss. The 1930s had brought the most painful and exacting years of her life, but she had mastered the challenges. She had taken her parents' legacies—spiritual and material—and transformed both them and herself. Now another life was forming.

A lot of new avenues opened up. One was a road I'd never taken and it included a pretty risky investment in a business I knew nothing about. So I gathered a handful of people and we started out with only an idea to see what would happen.

9 NEW TERRAIN
1940-1948

OVER THE NEXT FEW YEARS, THE NEW LIFE THAT PROMISED TO emerge poured into Dorothy Bullitt, filling the great voids left after the turmoil of the 1930s. It brought new friends and interests, drew her into unexpected areas that connected her more deeply with her mission and her power. There were new loves and new directions, one which sustained her to the end of her days. There were losses as the now-grown children began to leave home. There were tragedies experienced by those around her, not the least of which was war.

On Sunday, December 7, 1941, Dorothy sang in the choir at The Highlands Chapel as she had done every Sunday for years. Driving home afterward, she switched on the radio and heard the news that Japan had attacked Pearl Harbor. "I was still trying to digest what was being said when I pulled up at the house and saw Ohata lying on his back, working on one of the cars. Suddenly it struck me: What am I going to do with the Ohata family? There is going to be bitterness! When I told him Pearl Harbor had been invaded by the Japanese, he was completely silent; he couldn't take it in. I said, 'I'm afraid this is terribly bad news, and I don't know what it means at all, but don't leave the place for any purpose. Keep all the family right here until we know more about what's happened.' "

In her office in the 1411 Building the next day, Dorothy listened on the radio as President Roosevelt spoke to the nation. Looking down on Seattle's streets busy with humdrum Monday morning activity, she heard him describe December 7, 1941, as "a date that will live in infamy," and then he called on Congress to declare war on Japan. "I couldn't settle down to work," she remembered of that day. "I just sat at the desk and tried to adjust my mind." She knew only that war would disrupt her family and friends, most critically her son, now twenty-two, and the Ohatas, now considered an extension of the enemy he would be fighting. She knew, far better than the silent Ohata, how deeply it would affect him and his family. "He was a man of such great dignity that I knew it would be terrible for him," she recalled. "He was going to be embarrassed and humiliated and he would lose face—the worst possible thing that could happen. In spite of his ability to laugh if something was funny . . . I'm sure that after Pearl Harbor he never really laughed again."

Within twenty-four hours, suspicion toward any American of Japanese descent spread over Seattle like an ominous cloud. The West Coast, including Seattle and Puget Sound, was vulnerable to invasion. Its ports, shipbuilding, and aviation industries were prime targets for sabotage or informants for an enemy who had already been bold enough to fly halfway across the Pacific and bomb Pearl Harbor. A mob set fire to Pike Place Market, where many stalls belonged to Japanese-American truck farmers. Within days, Japanese-Americans were jailed or placed under curfew, their names registered, their identities recorded on tags, their schools closed, cameras confiscated, their lives turned into nightmares.

The phone began to ring regularly at The Highlands. "You have a Jap working for you, don't you?" an unidentified voice threatened, which turned out to belong to the butcher's wife. "He's well-known around town. Get rid of him because he's probably a spy. Any boat coming into Puget Sound has to go right past your front yard . . . all that man needs is a pair of binoculars and he could inform the enemy." Each time it happened Dorothy hung up in fear for Ohata's life. She went to the local head of the FBI, who was a friend. "I told him, 'I have had a Japanese working for me and my family for many years and I trust him absolutely. You must have records and information. I wish you'd advise me what to do. I don't dare let him come into town.' He said, 'Oh yes, you mean Ohata. Of course he's completely trustworthy, but he will suffer from this.' He said he didn't know what was going to happen, but there was a strong possibility they might be evicted from the coastal areas and then put in camps for a while. Those proven to be safe would be released. I told him about Coppernotch, and he advised me to send them there. They were at the Notch for about two months and then quite suddenly they were sent to a camp with only what they could carry—and it was a pretty bad place."

Alice Ohata wrote Dorothy en route, describing their trip on a special train that took "Japanese descents" from Wenatchee to Portland, Oregon. The train stopped at Wapato, a small town on the Yakima Indian Reservation where, Alice wrote, "the streets were filled for blocks with friends and neighbors who came to see the evacuees leave—not to mention the pets that were being left behind. Even the usually serious-faced Indians were upset." Amid the confusion, the Ohatas—Fred, Alice, and daughter Toetoe—kept their own priorities. "Through all this our only thoughts were for our boys in service," she added at the end of her letter. "We pray peace will come soon so they may be released."

The Ohatas were two of the 112,000 people of Japanese ancestry west of the Rockies (about eight thousand from the area) to be placed in barracks behind barbed wire and under searchlights. They never complained about this "invasion of citizenship rights" but somehow accepted that it had to be done.

The "pretty bad place"—an assembly center in Portland, Oregon—proved to be unhealthy and humiliating. Accustomed to the serenity of The Highlands, the Ohatas found themselves in a living hell. There was no privacy amid the throng of four thousand evacuees, and, except for the mail, which was censored, there was no outside contact—no phone, no visitors. Rumors about the future ran rampant as they stood in long lines processing their papers. Epidemics of flu and measles swept through the halls; many suffered mental breakdowns. A nearby slaughterhouse produced flies so thick that thousands of fly paper ribbons fluttered from the mess hall ceiling like tattered decorations from New Year's Eve.

Alice watched as her husband suffered, more from nervous strain than anything else. The indignities of camp life were unnerving for someone with such a highly developed sense of correctness. His identity, his key faculties, his sense of order, dignity, and purpose were trampled into the mud by the masses about him. Accustomed to a life filled with projects and goals, he found himself wallowing in time and worry, with nothing to do. He lost weight and enthusiasm for life. Dorothy received only one letter from him in Portland. Written in a thin, formal hand, it reflected his concern. "How is everything going on at your home, Mrs. Bullitt, and how are your cars running?" he asked. "I hope all the electrical appliances in your basement for operating the refrigerators, domestic hot water system, and all the laundry equipments are functioning all right. I certainly miss you and the work you entrusted me because it was joy of my life."

Dorothy did what she could, but never forgave herself for not doing enough. She sent money and crates of fruit, kept track of their belongings, and talked to friends with farms and ranches "away from the coast" who might employ them. When she got word that the Ohatas could be released if they had a job on the East Coast, she thought of the Amoss family in Greenwich, Connecticut. "Dr. Amoss and his wife were friends of mine, and their son Harold was a classmate of Stim's. I thought that Ohata could drive the doctor and Alice could cook and they would be near New York City where their daughter Toetoe would be in school." Happy to have made the best out of a potentially bad situation, Dorothy welcomed the Ohatas at The Highlands for a few days before they were to take the train east. She found them happy to be away from the camp but sorely wounded from months of hardship. From the train after their departure, Alice sent Dorothy an apologetic thank you note. "Again, we're sorry if our stay at the cottage caused you any embarrassment," she wrote. "We just seem to be doing the wrong things since war broke out—we just haven't been able to grasp it all yet."

Fred and Alice Ohata, devoted employees of the Stimson-Bullitt clan, on their wedding day in 1916. After Pearl Harbor, Dorothy was unable to keep the Ohatas out of the Japanese-American internment camps.

At home everyone was mobilizing for war. Seattle's hills were topped with enormous barrage balloons that could be raised to obstruct enemy planes. Puget Sound was draped with nets to foil submarines, and the Boeing factory was camouflaged to look like a suburban village. Unfinished St. Mark's Cathedral atop Capitol Hill became an artillery position. The noon hour downtown was marked by the shrill sounds of air raid sirens. Nighttime in Seattle's neighborhoods was dark, with shades drawn for blackouts. Overnight everyday things became cherished—gas, tires, nylons, sugar, coffee, meat, canned goods, shoes, and clothing. Once again, as Dorothy had experienced in 1915, trains at Union Station rolled out with inductees, only this time they were filled with the sons of her friends. As they reached their wartime destinations, fought and fell, more and more Seattle homes displayed the gold star that signified a relative had been killed in battle.

Stim had enlisted the week before Pearl Harbor, and others his age followed suit. Eligible men who used family pull to get draft exemptions (like young Bill Boeing who had a job with the sheriff's office) were scorned. Patsy remembered, "If you weren't in uniform, you had better be in a wheelchair." Homes facing Puget Sound were draped with black curtains and everyone was supplied with buckets of sand to put out a fire if the house was bombed. At home, Dorothy closed off heat into the library, living room, and bedrooms, and bought a Franklin stove for the dining room, which became the gathering place for dressing and eating breakfast each morning.

The Highlands commuters carpooled, each taking a week-long turn. Rather than motor up the long driveways (some of which could consume half a mile's worth of gas), the passengers waited at the road, with flashlight, umbrella, and briefcase in hand, until the ride appeared. Dorothy commuted with George Greenwood, president of the Pacific National Bank; Ham Rolfe, who managed the Hoge Building downtown; and Lew Stedman. "The men didn't give me any quarter at all," she remembered. "I had to drive too, the only woman in a car full of men."

When it was her turn to drive, Dorothy usually took the blue Mercury—she called it "The Mehcury"—her beloved car that became the subject of much family teasing after one trip into town. Dorothy, driving into town alone one day, decided, in the interest of saving gas, to take Stim's Plymouth coupe instead, a sturdy black relic with bright red hubcaps. She parked it at her usual place, the Metropolitan Garage between Union and University, where the attendants knew her well. But when she returned later, they apparently had forgotten which car she had been driving. When a blue Mercury pulled up with the motor running, Dorothy quickly got in and was preparing to leave when an elegant matron, befurred and bewildered, tapped on the window and announced haughtily, "That is *my* car." Dorothy, looking around for her familiar gloves on the seat, discovered that it truly wasn't her Mercury, and replied with equal but smiling hauteur, "Oh, I *beg* your pardon, it looks *exactly* like my car." Just then the attendant pulled up with Stim's old Plymouth and an embarrassed Dorothy got in and drove away.

During World War II, Dorothy, one of the few women in business, carpooled to work with men from The Highlands.

Washington State thrived during the war years. Workers arrived from around the country to weld warships at the Bremerton Naval Shipyard, to work in aluminum-reduction plants in Spokane, to staff the hush-hush plutonium production complex east of the mountains at Hanford, or to rivet war planes at the Boeing factory in Seattle. During the 1940s, the state grew from 1.7 million to 2.8 million people and

Seattle itself grew from 369,000 to 468,000 residents, close to its current population. A new international airport was planned between Seattle and Tacoma to take the pressure off Boeing Field. In 1941, a floating bridge spanned Lake Washington, opening up the hinterlands east of the city. Car after car paid the forty-five-cent toll as the lands east of the lake gradually turned into homesites for thousands who commuted daily into the city. Dorothy crossed the lake occasionally, remembering the days when she and Dee Terry had ferried across, when a journey over to the Terry summer home on the eastern shore of the lake was an expedition to the countryside.

Dorothy could only watch the changes in her children's lives. She followed Stim's service in the Navy as a chief petty officer stationed in San Diego and Norfolk, then became alarmed when he was assigned to an aircraft carrier escort in the Atlantic. Stim was promoted to ensign, then sent to communications school, and in 1944 volunteered for the landing party that established a communications base during the invasion of Leyte in the Pacific. During this massive battle—one of the most formidable naval engagements in history—he was wounded by shrapnel while carrying radio gear ashore and was later awarded the Purple Heart.

On the home front, Patsy had fallen in love with Larry Norman, a tall, blond young man she had met while working at Pacific National Bank during the summer of 1941. They were immediately attracted to each other, and it wasn't long before Larry took her off to Orcas Island in the San Juans to meet his parents. Charles and Ruth Norman, who ran a YMCA children's summer camp called Camp Orkila, absorbed Patsy into their small family with a warmth she had never experienced. At home, Dorothy watched the romance carefully, never entirely approving—after all, Larry Norman had not attended an Ivy League college and was only a bank employee, although he was a graduate of the University of Washington. She much preferred Charlie Ridley, a charming young Southerner, an attorney and FBI agent, who was probably independently wealthy. When Larry volunteered for the Air Force, Dorothy breathed a sigh of relief, thinking that he would be shipped off somewhere and it would all be forgotten. But at Christmas when Patsy announced that she didn't want to return to graduate from Vassar, Dorothy put on the pressure. "Mother wanted me to go back, partly because she didn't want me to get serious about Larry and partly because she had not been to college and wanted to have a child who finished college," Patsy recalled. "Reluctantly I went back because I could see how important it was to her—it never occurred to me to defy her." Patsy graduated the following June.

During 1942, Larry went into flight school training in Arizona, where Patsy visited him. To the tune of Bing Crosby's "White Christmas," he asked her to marry him, and in April 1943, when he had a few days leave, they decided to announce their engagement. Patsy feared her mother's disapproval, so she fled to Emma for advice. "Aunt Em was very understanding and diplomatic," Patsy remembered of their meeting. "At first she said cautiously, 'Well, I don't know if your mother will approve . . . ' Then she asked if I was in love with Larry and I said, 'Oh, yes.' Then she reminded me that I was grown up and didn't need Mother's approval but that I did need to be considerate as a daughter. That gave me courage." Patsy went home and sent her mother a saucy telegram that read, "Not subject to your approval Larry and I are announcing our engagement."

Larry, now a lieutenant, was a bombardier on a B-24, the long-range bomber known as the Liberator. After twenty-five missions, he would be free to come home. Back at her job at the bank, Patsy patiently tracked his movements through the news, knowing that his was the only group of Liberators on the European front. Successively, the Liberators bombed the oil fields of Romania, the railroad stations in Rome, and the bomb factories in Norway, Austria, and Germany. Larry wrote that he would probably fly his last mission before Christmas, and that at the beginning of the new year they could be married. Patsy began to prepare for a wedding.

Christmas Day was particularly happy at The Highlands when Dorothy and the girls gathered around the radio to hear Edward R. Murrow, the great reporter of the war, broadcast his message from England. "Last night, Christmas Eve," his voice crackled over the radio, "I paid a visit to the place where the Americans take off in the Liberators. There I talked to a young man from Seattle and asked him what he missed most about home. He said he missed his girl and his parents and at this time of year, he missed the Christmas decorations on Queen Anne Hill where his family lives." With delight, Patsy, Harriet, and Dorothy realized that the unknown American was Larry! He was the only Liberator crewman from Seattle and his parents lived on Queen Anne Hill. Patsy sighed with relief. Larry had flown his twenty-fifth mission and had safely returned.

The joy lasted only a few days. On New Year's Day, Charles and Ruth Norman arrived at Greenway with a telegram notifying them that Lieutenant Norman was missing in action as of December 22, 1943. Dorothy had to tell Patsy. "It was Larry's last sortie," she recalled. "He was finished, his service done, excused. He had his medals and he was coming home. Everything was ready except the wedding dress. Before I told her, I called George Greenwood, president of the bank, to warn him that Patsy might not be in for work the next day. But she went in; it was her job."

How could it be? Larry had flown his last mission on December 22 and Edward R. Murrow had said that he was alive on Christmas Eve, Patsy told her mother. Dorothy got on the phone and used her pull. Through political connections, perhaps Eleanor Roosevelt or Postmaster General James Farley, someone reached Edward R. Murrow to confirm Larry's presence at that interview. After several calls, word came back from Murrow that the interview had actually taken place on December 21, not Christmas Eve as he had stated in his broadcast. Larry had flown his last sortie the next day and had never come back. The plane and its crew were never found.

Perhaps it was too close a reminder of her own past pain, but her daughter's abject grief paralyzed Dorothy. Typically she blamed herself for not providing the right kind of comfort. "When I told Patsy, she just went silent, went to her room and I think for many weeks she wrote to him, hoping he might have survived and would work his way back to his base where mail would be waiting. I don't know what I should have said, but I never said the right thing. It has always troubled me that I fell short, but I just didn't know what to do. I just couldn't explain it to her. Patsy didn't blame anyone, really, she just went silent. She looked out the window and didn't hear anything. I was afraid she might be losing her mind. She was deeply in love with Larry and he with her and he was very sweet. She has never really recovered from it."

Patsy learned from others in Larry's squadron that his plane had been in lead position and hit during a raid south of Berlin. As the Liberators fled west toward the English Channel, crews saw his plane lag behind and begin to descend in smoke. No one saw it explode or crash. For a long time, Patsy held out hope that perhaps Larry's plane had landed or the crew had bailed out over Holland and been picked up by the Resistance.

Patsy spent two weeks with the Normans, making a scrapbook of Larry's life and shedding tears together. She could not talk to her mother. Every time she attempted to engage her mother, Dorothy either looked away and said nothing or briskly changed the subject. Somehow the middle daughter understood. "Mother did not like situations or subjects that she couldn't manage. She simply could not cope with our feelings, particularly if we were grief-stricken," Patsy explained. "Often she told me that the greatest suffering in the world was to have your child suffer—it hurt the mother even more than the child. I was thus told not to suffer because it would cause her pain that was even greater than mine." Patsy didn't object; by this time she knew and accepted her mother's limitations.

To cheer her daughter, Dorothy bought her a puppy. This gift—which might have comforted Patsy when she was sixteen and had lost her dog— seemed so unempathetic and callous that Patsy decided to leave home. Now graduated from secretarial school, she went to New York to work for the YMCA Prisoner of War Department, hoping to learn if Larry was being held in one of the European camps. Around V-E Day, realizing that she had to get on with life, Patsy joined the Red Cross as a professional and prepared for an assignment overseas with the U.S. Army. While she was gone, her mother removed every trace of Larry Norman from her daughter's room. His letters, photographs, medals, jewelry, and the scrapbook Patsy had made with the Normans were put away in boxes that remained unseen and unopened until after Dorothy's death in 1989. "She couldn't quite throw them away, but she hid them down at the office," Patsy recalled. "It was over, erased. It was as though it never happened. Larry's name was never mentioned again."

<hr>

PATSY WAS GLAD TO BE LEAVING. AFTER THE HUBBUB OF NEW York City, she found The Highlands a silent and lonely place, darkened with the coming of winter by the tall trees and rain clouds that scudded low across the Sound.

Dorothy, too, found The Highlands lonely. Times had changed, the children were away, and such remote elegance was no longer desirable. She toyed with the idea of moving into town but, as she often did, only made her move at the behest of someone else—as if to avoid the responsibility of selling the cherished family home. She found a house on Capitol Hill at 1655 Tenth Avenue North, with a beautiful view to the west over Lake Union, with Queen Anne Hill and the Olympics in the far distance. They called it the Tenth Avenue House. A brick Dutch Colonial with three bedrooms and three baths, it was much smaller quarters than The Highlands, but it was a cheerful and convenient alternative.

Dorothy delayed the move from The Highlands because of another wedding in the offing. After being refused admission to Vassar (to which Dorothy had made application on her daughter's behalf), Harriet attended the University of Washington, hoping to be an engineering student. This was no small task in the 1940s. Harriet had to contend not only with the challenges of physics and mechanical drafting, but also the fact that she was a woman knocking on a man's door. When she was banned from the school library because her presence was "distracting to the male students," she resigned herself to following the courses that convention dictated for women at that time. Reorienting her goals, she joined a sorority, switched to a major in home economics, and began taking a course in stenography. Progress in her new major reached a climax when she "flunked French toast" and the professor held up her soggy results to the class as an example of a technique never to be followed. Discouraged and uninspired,

Harriet flailed about for months until her friend of many years, Leslie Denman, suggested that she enroll with her at Bennington College in Vermont.

Bennington is a progressive college, where courses are taught by "doers" as well as scholars—Erich Fromm lectured on psychology and Martha Graham taught innovative forms of dance. The curriculum was provocative and stimulating, with a minimum of requirements and a maximum of self-motivation. For the first time in years, Harriet's independent thinking was challenged and accepted. She considered a major in pre-med, but soon fell in love with a premed student she met on a blind date who brought along his physiology text. Tall with curly brown hair and intense dark eyes, Bill Brewster was Mr. Personality. With nervous enthusiasm, he tended to overgreet strangers, shaking hands with both of his while talking at great speed.

Realizing that Harriet was capable of acting swiftly if she decided to marry, Dorothy went east to meet her daughter's suitor and visit the Brewster family in Maine. Patsy, then living in New York, joined her mother and a starry-eyed Harriet, who confessed that Bill wanted to marry her and that she had said yes. "Don't you think you should give it a little more *thought?*" Dorothy stated more than asked. She didn't particularly like this intense young man or take him very seriously—he laughed too much, was too concerned about making a good impression. Harriet was deeply hurt, not so much by her mother's resistance, but because Dorothy didn't share her happiness. Had Bill Brewster been a beautiful horse or a handsome boat, mother and daughter could have found much to talk about, but a relationship that threatened to divide them was not acceptable. Harriet spent the night in tears.

When she saw marriage was inevitable, Dorothy orchestrated Harriet's wedding to Bill Brewster as a perfect formal occasion. "It was mother's wedding," Harriet remembered. "She bought everything—sheets, towels, and napkins embroidered HBB. She supervised the ceremony, complete with rings, costumes, bouquets, and decorations. I only knew about a quarter of the guests." Remembering those days years later, Dorothy described a poignant scene that occurred just before the wedding. "One morning before the wedding, Harriet came running down the stairs and flew into my arms, crying, 'What do you think? Patsy has given me her silver tea set.' It was the tea set Patsy had received [from Aunt Emma] before she was to be married."

On September 2, 1945, to the strains of "The Battle Hymn of the Republic" the bride, escorted by her mother and attended by her sister, walked down the aisle of The Highlands Chapel. Afterward, to the accompaniment of music, cake, and champagne, the young couple received the good wishes of family and five hundred friends at a reception at Greenway, which was festooned with flowers for a final family function. As a wedding present, Dorothy gave the couple some of the acreage at Coppernotch in Leavenworth, saying, "Now it will be the Brewster Place and with it goes my heart's love and every confidence in your happiness."

Dorothy continued her work with civic and cultural endeavors. As her confidence and effectiveness grew, she became so sought after by mayors, governors, and other civic leaders that she needed to pick where to spend her energy. She was faithful to her longtime love, the Children's Orthopedic Hospital, which was then rapidly outgrowing space on Queen Anne Hill. Dorothy, in charge of the search for a new hospital site, found what she might term "a patch of land" out near the University Hospital in a suburb called Laurelhurst. Frances Owen, the youngest member of the board in those days, remembered when the rest of the board members were informed of the site. "Dorothy reported that she had had the land appraised and in her quiet way, stated that she thought we had better buy it. Actually she had already called the real estate agent and said, 'Get us that property,' which he did for $25,000. She really didn't have the authority to do it without full approval of the board, but everyone backed her up. Dorothy did it; she masterminded it all the way, and she was responsible really for the hospital being built where it is today."

In 1941, perhaps after prodding from Emma Stimson, Dorothy was appointed to the board of the Seattle Symphony, but she resigned in high dudgeon over an incident involving the hiring of the famous English conductor Sir Thomas Beecham. "In mid-season, the then conductor [Nikolai Sokoloff] called and asked, 'Why have I been fired?' I didn't know anything about it and thought it must be a mistake. 'No,' he said, 'the president [Tom Pelly] just told me I was through.' I found out it happened because they could hire that great man from England [Beecham] who was willing to come here because he was afraid of being bombed in London. He also had a girlfriend in Victoria and found a soft spot in Seattle that he could break into. It was a terrible thing to do, so I resigned and told them what I thought about it on the phone. The whole thing was just about as crooked as it could be." During his two seasons in Seattle, the flamboyant Beecham alienated many with his acid comments, among them one of the most famous put-downs of this city, in which he declared that Seattle was in danger of becoming "an aesthetic dustbin."

The war brought other responsibilities. Governor Martin, who had worked with Dorothy during Depression days, appointed her to the Washington State Defense Council, an agency that coordinated state and national resources in preparation for possible war. She was the only woman in a group that coordinated a council of top producers in every field—manufacturing, raw resources, transportation, fisheries, farming, medicine, education, law, and finance—to solve problems of production and procurement in case of war, along with helping with problems of aliens, sabotage, and virtually any other war-related emergency that might appear.

Mayor William F. Devin also persuaded Dorothy to be a founding member of the Seattle Civic Unity Committee, established in 1944 as Seattle's first public agency organized to deal with race relations. These were days when blacks on leave or migrating instate for work found nothing—no housing, restaurants, or amusements—open to them in Seattle, and Japanese-Americans returning from the camps were still met with suspicion and hostility. Because of reports of race riots in other cities, the mayor sought to forestall violence in Seattle. Dorothy accepted the appointment heartily, expressing her "unqualified admiration for your courage in tackling as difficult a problem as this is bound to be in the midst of your campaign." With eighteen other civic leaders, she met monthly in Scott's former law library in the 1411 Building (where Mayor Devin, in private life, was a tenant). She took copious notes, full of racial facts and figures, spiced with her own quirky comments: "Crime area—from Denny Way down First to Jackson and out Jackson . . . Office worker at Boeing does not like to be crushed by workmen with dirty clothes—when both white, OK, when one is black, it becomes racial . . . White woman: 'How do you like our city?' Indian: 'Fine, how do you like our country?' . . . What is Uncle Sam's last name?"

The Civic Unity Committee was an education in a Seattle that Dorothy had never known. There were specific cases to handle for those unable to get jobs, those denied school admissions, and others refused certain services. The committee went so far as to scold Governor Mon Walgren in the newspapers for his opposition to the return of American-born Japanese to their home state. Dorothy learned about racism within the police department. In White Center, black servicemen were seeking to gain admission to a skating rink, and in other areas throughout the city they were turned away from bowling alleys. In the Rainier district whites objected to blacks moving in. In Ballard, Chinese-Americans were refused rentals, as were, throughout the city, Japanese-Americans returning home from the internment camps. On one occasion, Dave Beck, the impulsive head of the Teamsters Union in Seattle, attended a Civic Unity Committee meeting. When board members asked Beck to restrain his union members from capsizing the trucks of Japanese-American farmers bringing produce into the Pike Place Market, he bellowed, pounded the table, and denounced the farmers in racist terms. Dorothy didn't join in these confrontations. Her interest in race relations was strictly philosophical, and she was at her most effective when speaking out for ideals rather than slumming with the realities. Here are her notes from one speech:

> No one will meet these problems unless we do—you and I in every discussion—less heat and more light—and in every contact with a member of minority group. If you fail in this, yours will be partial responsibility. Hitler and other demagogues are implemented by the difficulties not tackled by good citizens.
>
> We like to think of ourselves as advanced human beings, and as such can carry through reflective thinking—we must make sure we don't think with our prejudices—we were not born with them. If there is to be Peace on Earth to Men of Good Will, let's see that we qualify.

Sometimes her high principles were tempered by caution. She never lost her sense of class, no matter how liberal she became. For instance, when Toetoe Ohata was refused admission into The Highlands swimming pool because of her race and daughter Patsy complained indignantly, her mother's reply was that it was "unfortunate" but that's the way things were. Yet, not long after, she came to the defense of hospitalized veterans, some of them amputees, who had been invited to swim at The Highlands, but were refused admission because their maimed bodies might upset the children. Hearing this, Dorothy Bullitt became indignant. Fiercely she confronted those responsible, shouting, "Who do you think *began* The Highlands anyway? An *amputee!* My *father*—a man with only one arm!" The servicemen swam.

Life was not entirely committee meetings; romance flared for Dorothy from time to time. Fred Wickman, an old beau, came through town on his way to Hawaii, but the trip was too short for anything more than a brief flirtation. The painter Neil Ordayne continued to pursue her, in spite of Dorothy's assigning him to decorate Norcliffe's garage with paintings of bushes and flowers. Although attentive, Ordayne was too unctuous and although ever cordial, Dorothy found him boring. After one evening at dinner and a movie with him she wrote in her diary, "He criticized everything and we disagreed on everything. Was thoroughly bored. Am never going to waste an evening like that again."

———

DOROTHY BULLITT'S MOST GLAMOROUS SUITOR WAS KEITH Spalding. Heir to the sports equipment fortune, Spalding was a widower whom Dorothy had met through her parents in the 1920s while visiting California. The two had established a friendship based on occasional horseback rides over the hills in Pasadena. After his wife's death in the early 1940s, Keith contacted

Dorothy and the relationship shifted into a romance. Spalding was a Prince Philip–type, with an aquiline profile that brought manliness, refinement, and intelligence into perfect balance. Aristocratic and sophisticated, Keith Spalding had everything that might have mattered to Dorothy. He was also sexy and rich, humorous and full of life. They were both passionate about horses, sailing, and music. Dorothy described him as "dashing," and fell very much in love with him. She admired the way he rode seventeen-hand horses over the highest jumps. His beautiful voice had been trained for opera. He built a 157-foot schooner called the *Goodwill.* "The spinnaker was 10,000 square feet and the pole was so big that you had to sit astride it like a log," Dorothy marvelled. "He was fun and he thought that was what life was for."

They took a couple of pack trips into remote areas of the Montana mountains, accompanied by guides, camp cooks, and luxury outdoor equipment. Days blended into dappled summer afternoons fishing in high mountain lakes and star-strewn nights sitting around the campfire gazing into each other's eyes. "Mother was very much in love with him," Patsy remembered. "Harriet and I knew something was up when mother came home from the pack trip just to get a new set of clothes and then go right back. This was very unusual for her—Keith Spalding was the only one she came home and changed clothes for. We thought it was great, hoping she'd marry him so we'd be free to go our own ways."

But that was not to be. Dorothy summed up the relationship in her own quirky way: "Our interests were very much alike. It was perfect, but that was all." He wasn't really a playboy, she explained, but he had never had any children or cares and didn't really pay much attention to the family business. He had an office but it was used more by his secretary than by him. He gave very generously of his money but he didn't want to give his time. He wasn't interested in committees and would never be—he laughed at them. "It would never have worked for me," she concluded. "He'd call and say, 'Let's do this,' and I'd say, 'I can't.' 'Why not?' he'd ask, 'Business?' 'No,' I'd say, 'I have other things.' And he'd say, 'For God's sake, Dorothy, don't go *civic* on me!' Marriage would have meant that I couldn't have lived in Seattle because he was all over the world and that's what he liked. We would have sailed the South Seas with a doctor on board to see that everyone stayed well and the doctor's wife to be a fourth for bridge in the evenings. I didn't like bridge; I liked civic things."

The children provided another excuse. "He wasn't interested in what my children were doing or where they were going to school or what their aims and interests were. I wouldn't have been able to see them; I'd be in the South Seas during their vacations and they'd be on their own. I wouldn't have been part of their lives and I wouldn't have fit into his kind of life. And *I did love my children*—they weren't the easiest batch in the world and they still aren't, but they were my children." The "children," however, were now adults. Stim was in the Navy, Patsy with the Army in Japan, and Harriet a newlywed in California. Although Dorothy's connection with her children was important to her, in this case they were a substitute for the truth: she did not want a nomadic life, even one among the rich and famous. She had already experienced marriage and she was now beginning to experience herself. Although she refused marriage, Dorothy assumed that Keith would remain attentive and available in between her forays into "civicdom." She was stunned when, a few months later, he married the former nurse of his deceased wife. The blow to both her pride and her social life softened with time, but the two never saw each other again.

Dorothy's natural reserve held her back from being completely at ease except with only the most close and long-held friends. Her sister-in-law Emma, on the other hand, lived handsomely and lavishly. Emma had soul and the ability to bare it with warmth and sensitivity, and her wit enlivened any conversation. Dorothy always envied her sense of style. During the 1940s, Emma became the grand patroness of the painters of the "Northwest School." Artists gathered at her home, shared their creative plans, and escorted her to openings and parties. She maintained her close association with Dick Fuller and the Seattle Art Museum; when Fuller took a year's leave of absence for service in World War II, Emma stepped in as the museum's acting director. By this time, their friendship, which was in a sense a partnership, had produced a brilliant collection of Asian painting, ceramics, and sculptures, many of them selected or donated by Emma. "She had very confident taste," Emma's grandson, Frank Bayley, observed. "She knew how to avoid pretentious art and aimed carefully for smaller but perfect pieces." The personal art pieces she gave to the museum, called The Thomas Stimson Memorial Collection, amounted to more than 150 paintings and objects in bronze, ceramic, and jade.

Dorothy met the prominent artists of the time through Emma. She once invited Morris Graves for tea. The artist arrived, hoping to receive a commission for a painting, but instead he received notice that he could stay only a few minutes. "When I arrived, she let me know that she had another appointment and that I'd better be ready to scram within fifteen minutes. So I came for that brief time and she looked me over and we talked about things that were of no interest to either one of us until she stood up and rather snapped her fingers so that a kitchen maid showed up to take the tray and I was gone." Morris Graves left feeling that Dorothy Bullitt was a snob, that he had been "whistled up like a dog and then dropped." Mark Tobey fared better. In her inimitable fashion, Dorothy described him as "a Jew who followed a funny religion [Bahai]." She recalled, "He stopped by one day when I had moved to Galer Street on Capitol Hill. I said I didn't know what to do with a narrow strip of space over the mantle and he said, 'I'll see what I can do.' A few months later he brought me a painting that cost seven hundred dollars and I paid for it in two installments." The painting is a classic example of Tobey's "white writing" style, and Dorothy often referred to its abstract squiggles as her "sins." It hung in the same place until her death, flanked by sconces that she also persuaded Tobey to paint.

When the war ended in 1945, Emma and Dorothy joined together to buy a house for the Ohatas. In this act of noblesse oblige, they failed to consider the potential occupants, for they selected the house without even asking the opinion of those who would live in it. Dorothy also arranged a job for Ohata repairing equipment at Children's Orthopedic Hospital, envisioning that, with his skill with machinery, he would soon be designing prostheses. "I think this would be a very good thing for you to do," she wrote him by way of encouragement. "You would really be working among people who are trying to do a human job, and I believe you would feel that you were doing something that was very badly needed." The board members did not all react with great humanity, however. Prejudice against Japanese-Americans was still pronounced, but Dorothy prevailed. "And Ohata became the greatest thing that ever happened at Children's Orthopedic," she boasted. "He was put in the shop. Using all of Father's tools, he made shoulder braces and false legs for the children, even an elbow that went into three positions. And he stayed working there until he died."

The Ohatas returned from the East a broken family. "Growing up in The Highlands was another world where everyone was kind regardless of your station, your race, or anything else. The war changed everything," Edward Ohata remembered. "A wall descended between my parents, and my sister had a breakdown from which she never really recovered." The parents, separated from friends and work, had been relegated to the status of traitors by their own country. Toetoe, the daughter who, from age five, had promise as a ballerina, who had studied with Mary Ann Wells and Martha Graham, was instead relegated to institutions for the rest of her life. The son, Edward, the dear "Skooky" of childhood, after graduating from the University of Washington, tried to join the service and was repeatedly rejected. Eventually he joined the infantry, serving with the 442d Infantry Combat Team in the Italian campaign. It was supreme irony that this all-Nisei team became the most decorated American unit in the war, with more than 90 percent of its members honored for exemplary conduct under enemy fire.

Dorothy could not forgive herself for the fate of the Ohatas. Perhaps it was her role as Center of the Universe, but she felt responsible for their happiness. The Stimson, Bullitt, and Ohata families had shared ceremonies, births, and deaths. Dorothy and her parents had attended the wedding of Fred and Alice; the couple's daughter had been named for her. Her children were playmates with the Ohata children. She admired Fred Ohata ever since the days when as a girl, she had watched him work on her father's cars, to the afternoon after World War II when she saw him sworn in as an American citizen. In her last years, when little of her time was consumed with work, Dorothy came to realize that she had "made arrangements for them, but that wasn't what they needed most. They were sent away into a place of strangers and must have missed the people they had known. Through all of the tragedy of Toetoe's breakdown, they had no old friends. I could have given them my time, my emotional support—that's what they really needed. It has always haunted me that there was more I could have done."

Patsy and Stim returned from their wartime service in 1946. Stim needed spine surgery after his injury at Leyte. Patsy returned emotionally exhausted from the loss of Larry, the strains and demands of her work with the Occupation Army, and an unhappy love affair in Japan. At twenty-six, she sought the safety of a husband, a home, and a family of her own. She found what she needed in Josiah Collins, a man she had known since childhood, a "boy next door" who had spent his childhood as a neighbor of the Stimson family when they lived on First Hill. When the Stimsons had moved to The Highlands, the "Collins boys"—Joe and Wetherill—were brought out for visits during Patsy's growing-up years, though Joe, thirteen years her senior, had always been part of an older world. When he came to visit her mother at the Tenth Avenue house after Patsy's return from Japan, a relationship began to develop. She liked Joe Collins because he was safe, he was likable, genteel, and socially acceptable. He was now a partner in a small advertising agency and he was interested in marriage. She overlooked his passivity in favor of securing the home and family she wanted—a situation not uncommon for the times. "Everyone approved of him," Patsy remembered, "but it was no burning love affair."

Dorothy, as Patsy might have predicted, resisted the idea at first, although she liked Joe Collins. "Don't you think it would be a good idea if you got to know some other men?" she asked. When Patsy replied flatly, "Mother, I've gotten to know *lots* of other men," her mother was silent. The wedding was scheduled for February 23, 1947, a date that became a point of departure for a mother-daughter power struggle that lasted during Patsy's early married years.

Patsy Bullitt wanted a small, quiet wedding with no social fanfare. She had been through all of that before, already had the towels, china, and other pre-sents. She didn't want people to go through that again. Most particularly, she told her mother that she did not want her photograph in the paper. This request was made out of respect for the parents of Larry Norman who were to be among the guests. "I just wanted to get married quietly and get it over with—I wasn't that excited myself," she remembered. There was no engagement photograph in the papers, but Dorothy did send out seven hundred announcements of the wedding. At the reception at Dorothy's home after the ceremony in St. Mark's Chapel, Patsy noticed a photographer mingling among the guests. Between greetings on the reception line, she asked her mother why a photographer was there. "Oh, it's only for your album, dear, that's all," replied Dorothy. A few days later, as the honeymoon couple returned from Victoria to Seattle, they stopped to buy a paper and Patsy was shocked to open it to a two-page photographic spread of her wedding. "I was livid at having been lied to," Patsy shook her head years later. "When I confronted Mother, she only said, 'Oh, you didn't *really* mind it, did you dear?' 'Yes, I did,' I shouted back. 'You promised me!' Then Mother began to cry, saying 'I didn't mean any harm, I only want your happiness,' dabbing her eyes. It was impossible—she didn't confront me about it, she just went ahead and did what she wanted."

The contest of wills continued over finding a home. Patsy and Joe, before the wedding, had wanted to live in a houseboat on Seattle's Lake Union. When they found one, Dorothy stepped forward with a wedding present—the two-bedroom house next door to hers on Tenth Avenue. Joe quickly accepted. The house was not actually a gift; for tax reasons, it was held in Dorothy's name. Appropriately, Dorothy called it "The Annex." While the newlyweds were honeymooning, she moved in furniture, along with a couple—Frances and Tom—who were servants at her own house, to occupy the second bedroom. Upon their return, the honeymooners were greeted with, "I *knew* you wouldn't mind if Frances and Tom are living here, dear," and "I have some plans for the place." She had made up a template of the house and its furnishings and proceeded to point out her plans for remodeling.

The newlyweds were stunned. For some months, Dorothy walked in and out at will, brought workmen up to the bedroom to discuss repairs, change doors, and paint. Patsy, overwhelmed by the swift intrusion into her privacy, protested, but her objections were swept away with, "I'm only doing this for *you*, dear." When it came to the frequent invitations from next door, Patsy could not refuse, knowing that her mother had only to look out the window to see that she was at home. To further bind the couple to her, Dorothy hired Joe as building man-ager of the 1411 Building when his small advertising business did not succeed.

Patsy found herself trapped by her mother's powerful presence and in a marriage that lacked the support to set limits. She suffered a miscarriage and was depressed about the future. It was obvious that she and Joe were unable to stand up to Dorothy's manipulation of their lives and the dream of having a home and family of her own was fading. As Patsy grew critical and sullen, her mother, oblivious to her ramrodding tactics, was surprised and hurt. The tension reached a climax when Patsy returned home one day to find her front door painted Chinese red. "*Everyone* wants a Chinese red front door," Dorothy replied blithely when questioned. Patsy decided that it was time to move.

In 1949, following an earthquake that erased the back yard, Patsy found a small rambler-style home across Lake Washington in Bellevue, a new community that seemed to be far enough from the city to put some distance between her and her mother. Dorothy knew that her daughter was house-hunting and that a move might be in the wind. She argued against Bellevue, which she termed "a very far neighborhood." Patsy made plans to sell stock to purchase the home and mustered up the courage to do the dirty deed. "I was such a coward," Patsy remembered years later. "I should have said firmly, 'I am moving,' but I didn't want a big scene. So I did it in the dark of night when Mother wasn't looking." When Dorothy returned to Seattle from a trip back East in 1949, she found that Patsy and Joe had moved to Bellevue. "Mother never forgot it," Patsy observed. "She didn't hold a grudge or say mean things, but she also never forgot."

Stim's plans for marriage were less problematic but more precipitous—they came as a surprise. He had returned from the war to take classes at the University of Washington School of Law while living at the Tenth Avenue house with his mother. In Seattle he had met a bright, vibrant young woman—Carolyn Kizer, daughter of prominent Spokane attorney Ben Kizer, then president of the Washington State Bar Association. A graduate of Sarah Lawrence College, Carolyn was at the beginning of a career that in time would place her among the most respected poets in America and bring her numerous honors, among them a Pulitzer Prize in 1985 for her book of poetry entitled *Yin*. When she met Stim Bullitt, she had already been published in *The New Yorker,* which early on recognized her acute use of language and her acerbic wit. She was brilliant and beautiful—tall, blonde, vital, and very dramatic. An intense physical attraction caused Stim to follow Carolyn to New York. When they both returned in early January 1948, he brought her to a dinner party hosted by his mother. The conversation drifted through the arts and public affairs and suddenly halted when Stim announced that he and Carolyn were going to be married.

Dorothy was stunned. "After the guests had gone home, Mother asked why

I hadn't told her beforehand—it was understandable that she would feel slighted about my making such an announcement before family without telling her privately before. I said, 'Well, Mother, if I had, then you would have taken charge, tapped on the glass and said, "Now, Stim has something to announce to you". . . .' " Dorothy, recognizing the truth of that observation, said nothing. She continued to say nothing, attended the wedding in Spokane three weeks later, and appeared to be a model mother-in-law—generous, courteous, and nonintrusive. When she asked Stim where they would live after the wedding, he replied, "here," thinking it would be unfilial to leave his mother alone. Dorothy thought otherwise, promptly moving into a large brick home at 1014 East Galer Street a few blocks away. When a daughter, Ashley, was born to Stim and Carolyn eight months later, Dorothy said nothing. Loyalty to her children was her first commandment.

Both women tried to adapt to each other. At first Dorothy was courteous and thoughtful of Carolyn in family matters, extending her warmth to Carolyn's parents, particularly to Ben Kizer, whose broad interests always enlivened the time they spent together. She entertained them at dinner and kept baby Ashley when the young Bullitts were at parties. "Carolyn is always responsive and out-giving," she commented in her diary in 1949 after a particularly companionable evening. Carolyn, too, tried to maintain good relations with an equal sense of decorum, but the tedium of marriage and motherhood was stifling. The only child of older parents and a free spirit used to wandering at will, she was unprepared for such a rigid lifestyle with, in short time, three demanding youngsters who constantly sapped her creativity. She lashed out at her husband who, as one might predict from his past, simply refused to be engaged by her histrionics. As communication with Stim worsened, she increasingly turned to the friends who understood her artistic nature. She found that her time away from Stim, either at local gatherings or on trips to the East, was more appealing than an unhappy home where the fires were cooling to ashes. She resented Dorothy's influence everywhere in her world. Carolyn, too, was "Mrs. Bullitt," and she was fed up with her dominating counterpart.

The older Mrs. Bullitt was not the good sport she had vowed to be. As the marriage wore down, Dorothy saw that her "outgiving" daughter-in-law was no apron-clad homemaker waiting sweetly with the children for her man to come home. In fact, the main apron involved in this marriage had to do with Dorothy and the strings that tied mother and son. Carolyn, Dorothy learned, had a will equal to her own and a rapier wit that surpassed hers, one which she exercised regularly on Stim. For Dorothy, an attack on her young was the sin of sins and she could scarcely hold her tongue. By her standards, she had plenty of fodder for maternal fury—the neglect of the children and lack of a proper home atmosphere and, above all, Carolyn's vituperations toward Stim. She communicated her ire with innuendoes and surprise inspection visits. Although there were no out-and-out shouting matches between the two women—no one in the Bullitt family indulged in open conflict—Dorothy years later admitted that with Carolyn, "I stopped just short of getting my face slapped."

As long as Stim appeared to be content with the marriage, Dorothy kept her peace. But once he no longer wanted it to continue, his mother felt free to speak her mind. All in all, Carolyn Kizer, a flamboyant, emotional woman, was the antithesis of her mother-in-law. Dorothy said many years later, "Carolyn was brilliant in a very fast way. She wasn't what I would have selected, and I don't think she was what Stim would have selected, but he came back from the war—he lost those years—and he wanted to make up for them. She was a very aggressive woman. They just weren't happy—they didn't have the same ideas about married life and so it fell apart." The stormy marriage resulted in an equally bitter divorce filled with accusations of infidelity and neglect. According to Stim, the union had been based on a momentary physical attraction and had taken place under threat of prosecution from Carolyn when she found herself to be pregnant. He had knuckled under and tried to make the best of it. It lasted five and a half years and produced three children—Ashley Ann, Scott, and Jill Hamilton Bullitt.

Family matters consumed only a small part of Dorothy's energies during the 1940s. Her buildings were filled with satisfied tenants as the post-war economy improved. She continued to search for new properties. In 1947, through the Stimson Realty Company, she bought fifteen acres in Woodway, north of the city, and gradually added adjacent lands (as she had done in Leavenworth) until she owned one hundred acres. Quiet and pastoral, the property had a view of the Sound and the investment potential of a mini-Highlands, although it never achieved such grandeur. She hired architect Paul Thiry to design a small home, where she installed Stenneberg, the old Stimson gardener from Norcliffe, with a business plan to raise exotic species of daphne and rhododendron.

Dorothy relied on Ray Wright for all of her business decisions. He was the attorney who had come to her rescue when she had been bereft after Scott's death; she knew his background, his friends, and she respected his judgment. Ray Wright was always there to advise her, even if she didn't always follow his counsel. With a mixture of caution and amusement he listened to her schemes, became her trusted confidant, and invited Stim to join his law firm. Over the years, Dorothy became deeply attached to this man, confessing to daughter Patsy that he had become the love of her life after the death of Scott Bullitt. The only drawback was his wife. Harriet, wishing to define the relationship more clearly, once asked her mother, "Well, did you ever sleep together?" "We only dreamed about it," was her mother's reply. Once Dorothy got up the courage to confess her feelings after a couple of glasses of wine at a party at the Sunset Club. Finding herself in conversation with him, the words tumbled out, much to her embarrassment. Ray Wright didn't reply. He just looked at her, then turned away and crossed the room.

ONE OTHER LOVE CAPTURED DOROTHY BULLITT DURING these years. It was radio. Lee DeForest, the man who invented and introduced the radio to the world, called it "the grandest medium which has yet been given to man."

Since 1924, when her father brought home the family's first radio (it was much easier for a one-armed man to hear the news than to unfold a newspaper), Dorothy had been fascinated with the magic of the medium. The idea of transmitting the human voice and other sounds, particularly beautiful music, over airwaves was not only intriguing but soul-gratifying to her. That human events, distant or near, could be reported on the spot, as history-in-the making, only made radio more dynamic and compelling. During the 1920s and 1930s, the Stimson-Bullitt households, like many others, came to venerate the huge boxes, called Spartan or Capehart, that stood in the living room or library like altars to the household gods, with their dimly lit dials aglow. Gathering around the radio, families and friends cheered to the roar of the crowd as the referee counted down during the Dempsey-Tunney and Louis-Schmeling fights. They sat with eyes closed, focusing an inner eye on character, costume, and setting as dramas, love stories, and murder mysteries unfolded. Whole orchestras, string quartets, and dance bands entered the living room, without requiring the purchase of a ticket or the need to mix in a crowd. The fact that one could tune into and experience distant events as they were happening fascinated Dorothy. From Seattle, she was moved to tell her mother in Pasadena about a performance of *Aida* broadcast from the Los Angeles Philharmonic Auditorium and heard at The Highlands. "It was really thrilling to sit quietly by the fire and hear the orchestra, the choruses, and the voices all so clearly, for it was a windy, blustering night," she wrote, entranced by the novelty of it all. "We could hear the instruments being tuned, then the applause when the conductor came into the pit. We could hear the buzzing of the audience between acts and the boy calling, 'Opera books! Correct story of the opera—opera books!' Doesn't it sound unbelievable?"

Dorothy's professional involvement with radio grew slowly. She had no long-range plan in mind; she knew only that her children were grown, her real estate business was stable, her role as a civic leader was well established, and that there were no challenges on the horizon. In the early 1940s, radio was a competitive all-male arena in Seattle, with eight stations vying for the listener's attention, most of them run by savvy executives who had broken territory during the 1930s with homemade local programming—live music and drama, election returns, dramatized news, play-by-play sports events.

Two broadcasters, neither men "one of my favorites," as Dorothy put it, dominated the market. KOMO Radio was a National Broadcasting Company (NBC) affiliate owned by wealthy entrepreneur O. D. Fisher, a personal friend of NBC head General David Sarnoff. (Fisher's other interests included timber, banking, insurance, and the prosperous Fisher Flour Mills.) "Old Mr. Fisher was a skinflint and a 'tough' dealer. He was always very mercenary and never very polite. I had been on the Safeco board with him and he ignored me because a woman didn't belong in such places. Once I called him to ask if he might sell a piece of waterfront property, and he said no and hung up the phone in my *face!* I found him to be a cold, bitter person and very greedy. He was never very fond of me and became even less so once we began competing in broadcasting."

The other dominant station was KIRO Radio, a Columbia Broadcasting System (CBS) affiliate owned by Saul Haas, a difficult personality. Tall and bejowled, with hair that sometimes fell over his puffy eyes, he had a reputation for late-night telephone tirades during which he often fired his employees and then rehired them the next day. When they became disgruntled over low salaries, he gave them new titles as compensation. His office reflected a love for politics and a disdain for too much order. Its walls were lined with photos of friends from Roosevelt on down, and its floors were papered with crumpled memos that he never bothered to toss in the wastebasket. He bought KIRO in 1933 and built it from a failing venture into a successful 50-kilowatt station, the most powerful north of San Francisco and west of Minneapolis. He had ambitions to make KIRO the most influential station in the region.

Aside from the stiff competition she faced, Dorothy also knew that broadcasting was uncharted territory for a woman. There were no female role models for her, and few friends would understand her fascination with this new field of interest. If she was to set out into such unknown realms, she knew she had to proceed as a student. Asking and learning were no problem when she was interested in the subject. She had the wealth to take the trips and interview the experts, and she had another great personal asset that never failed her—the charisma to attract creative people. As television performer Ruth Prins described it years later, "Dorothy knew how to attract people who maximized her. She provided them with a medium for their talents, one that gave force to their ideas, and in turn she expected their loyalty." In time she assembled the core team she needed to enter into broadcasting. Eclectic and as varied in personality and approach as possible, their differences worked in constructive ways. None of them cared as much about money as they did about challenge and creativity. Dorothy offered them plenty of both.

The first member of her team was Fred Stimson, Dorothy's younger first cousin. His father was Frederick Spencer Stimson, C. D.'s youngest brother. A youngest child struck down by a tubercular hip, Fred was spoiled and coddled by his parents into adulthood. He walked with a limp and endured constant pain with a cheerful disposition. Trained as an insurance salesman but uninterested in business, he resorted to living his life as a lovable, mild-mannered, spendthrift, who lavished presents on friends and strangers and lived on liquor until nearly all of his inheritance was spent. By the 1940s, cousin Fred was a ne'er-do-well with little purpose in life, an alcoholic on his way to intensive care in some institution that he couldn't afford. It became Dorothy's lot to help him out.

Fred's only sustaining interest was electronics. Electrical gadgets of all kinds filled his workshop and fired his imagination. An amateur engineer, gifted but without focus, he had joined the Coast Guard during the war, patrolling Puget Sound with the auxiliary radio team. His own boat was fitted with the latest radio equipment and he became proficient at handling it. He began to talk with his cousin Dorothy about communications and broadcasting. He encouraged her to get into broadcasting, mainly, Dorothy recalled his saying, " 'because you like people, and in broadcasting people are everything.' Then he'd go on to persuade me that I could broadcast good music, which was something I was complaining about—the rotten music on radio. I told him that I didn't know anything about it and he said he would help where he could. Well, I already listened to the radio when I was alone, so I began to listen a lot more and I did think that there were better ways to do it than what I was hearing. It was a little shoddy and no one seemed to have a purpose or a policy about what they were broadcasting. They'd take in anything that would pay. I thought there was room for more. So, after about a year, Fred Stimson finally softened me up." In return, Dorothy toughened up her cousin. She convinced him to get his engineering papers so that he could work as night engineer for her station, and she delivered the ultimatum that he quit drinking or be fired. He did both and it saved his life.

As with every project that caught her interest—from writing a speech to buying a radio or even a radio station—Dorothy Bullitt did her research. She kept reams of notes written in pencil on tablets large and small as her investigation continued. Methodically and cautiously, she proceeded, aware of the slightest hint of information that would give her further insight. Her interest began with FM, a system of broadcasting that was relatively new in Seattle, which answered a number of her needs. FM, or frequency modulation, was a highly technical electronic innovation that Dorothy never tried to understand, ("I didn't ask; I was afraid someone would *explain* it to me"), but she did know that it produced clearer and finer tones than AM (amplitude modulation) could ever deliver. "FM was my first love," she declared years later. "I began to realize that maybe we could broadcast good music that would be more beautiful than anything anyone could hear on AM, and that it wouldn't be too expensive once we had the right equipment. I thought, 'Three or four people could run this and it would be a good, inexpensive way to get into broadcasting—that's all we want, that's all we need.' Besides, how else would I break into the business? The O. D. Fishers and the Saul Haases were ahead of me with AM. I wanted to get into the stream and FM looked like the way to do it."

There were problems with FM transmission, especially in Seattle. And, in the 1940s, FM was still unfamiliar to the public. Although it could produce clearer sound, the quality of transmission was limited by low antennas, which could not surmount Seattle's many hills. Receiving sets had not yet been designed to withstand the "drift" that often occurred. These technical problems were corrected within a few years, but Dorothy always blamed FM's technical term as the real reason for listeners' caution. "People were put off by the words 'Frequency Modulation,' " she remembered, shaking her head as if the term were still foreign many years later. "It should have been called 'Finer Music' because that would have drawn listeners. Instead nobody knew what it was. I'd ask my friends if they had FM on their radios and they'd say no, but I could see it on their sets. It just sounded too technical and they weren't tuning in to it."

To learn more about FM, she went to the source. She contacted Major Edwin Howard Armstrong, its inventor, in New York City and arranged to visit him at his apartment. "I took a friend with me, and Armstrong—a kind, lanky man with a charming drawl—gave us a cocktail and explained the equipment, which I didn't understand. He turned some buttons and in came the Boston Symphony. It was the purest tone I had ever heard on radio or victrola— pure gilt-edged tone!" Fascinated, she spent the afternoon listening to Armstrong's stories about broadcasting. Dorothy was impressed, especially by his modesty, remembering that his colleague, RCA's David Sarnoff, had described FM as "a revolution, not an invention." It was a sad irony that within a decade,

Armstrong suffered such disappointment and financial setback over a lawsuit against RCA for royalties that he died a broken man, at odds with family and friends. In 1953, he stepped out of a window from the same thirteenth floor apartment in which Dorothy had heard such beautiful music, and committed suicide.

Back home Dorothy and Fred considered the next step: setting up a company. She wanted a businessman who didn't already have a good job, because she was only offering a wild possibility. "One Saturday morning when Fred and I were staring at each other, wondering what we were going to do to run this great thing we'd dreamed up, I remembered that Henry Owen, the husband of Frances Owen whom I knew and admired from our work at Children's Orthopedic, was getting out of the [military] service. He had been vice-president of Frederick & Nelson, hired away from Proctor & Gamble by Mr. Frederick, who had searched the country over for the best personnel man he could find. Mr. Frederick was always very shy, and Henry had run the store for years before he left to manage the Bon Marché and then to go into the service. He had the reputation, the kind of personality that could run anything. Henry was just back in Seattle and so I phoned Frances and asked if he had affiliated himself with anything. She said no, but he had had some offers, and I told her I had been thinking about a project that might or might not work and I'd be interested to see what he thought about it. I hardly knew him at all, but he got on the phone and said, 'I'll be right down.' He came down and Fred and I talked with him and he said, 'Well, I don't know anything about radio, but I'll think about it and I'll give you an answer on Monday.' He went to the library and took home an armful of books about broadcasting and read them all and said, 'I'll go with it. It sounds to me like any other business—you spend money, you make money, and you run it right.' "

Henry Owen was a Southern gentleman from Virginia with all of the traits Dorothy admired. Courteous in manner and meticulous in appearance—his immaculately tailored British suits were a trademark—sophisticated yet possessing a comfortable "down-home" manner, he was made for the all-purpose role of manager. Like fine Southern whiskey, Henry Owen smoothed over every occasion, from day-to-day operations to high-level negotiations, with a coating of charm that belied a shrewd business sense. A staunch Democrat, he had many political connections and a certain pragmatic savvy that enabled him to handle all sorts of personnel and business challenges as they arose—both areas in which Dorothy needed him for what she termed "this new adventure." His voice was deep and gravelly, mellowed by traces of a Virginia accent and used over the years to hire and fire with so much skill that employees exited wondering what had happened. This talent was especially valuable to Dorothy, who abhorred firing personnel; the few times she had to do it had made her physically ill and she was grateful for a field marshall who would take on the task. Owen was also experienced with tough guys and strong-arm tactics. One Christmas when he was managing the Bon Marché during a trucker's strike, he called Teamster's chief Dave Beck to tell him that the strike had to be resolved and his warehouse of packages delivered immediately. If not, a full page newspaper ad had been prepared, saying that Beck was responsible for killing Santa Claus. During another strike, while vice-president of Frederick & Nelson, Owen called on independent operator James Casey for help with deliveries, a move that launched United Parcel Service, the country's biggest delivery service.

Over the years, Henry Owen became the company policymaker, financier, employer, and charming hatchet man. "From then on I never hired or fired anyone—Henry did both sooo nicely. I couldn't do it, honestly. I hated to fire anyone. He set forth the job descriptions and made up agreements upon hiring the prospective employee who found himself thrilled to sign up for a job. It was a pleasure to be fired by him. There were no temper tantrums or scenes. With Henry, people were never treated so well as when they were fired."

Not all employees appreciated Henry Owen's style, but the boss lady held him in high regard. He was the balancer, always fine-tuning and harmonizing operations. If he had faults, they were minor to her. Dorothy learned not to ride in his car, for he had erratic driving habits that didn't conform to his even temperament and that resulted in a series of wrecks over the years. He also had a penchant for pinching the ladies. "Henry *did* like the girls and he did pinch their bottoms, chase them around the desks, and put his fingers down their necks. I went to New York with him several times and he gave me a little trouble—not much—but we would go for dinner to go over our respective appointments during the day, have a couple of drinks, and in the taxi coming home, I'd have to look after myself. Which was no difficulty—everybody's got something." Years later when sexual harassment policies were common in companies, Dorothy wondered with a smile, "Golly, what would we have had to do with Henry here now?"

Early on, Dorothy saw the need to have a lawyer in Washington, D.C., to guide them through the maze of red tape involved in applying for a broadcasting license. After much interviewing, Dorothy chose "the one I liked as soon as I met him—a young lawyer named Haley. My notes read: 'He is a young, aggressive, very knowledgeable young man from Tacoma. I like his personality— he seems to have more spirit than the others. I think he's the one.'" Andrew G. Haley was a tall, dark-haired Irishman whose most noticeable physical traits

Dorothy's brain trust at the founding of King Broadcasting Company. CLOCKWISE FROM TOP LEFT: Fred Stimson, Henry Owen, Gloria Chandler, and Andrew Haley.

were a large head, a hooked nose, and a girth that even in his late thirties suggested a thorough love of food and drink. Most outstanding were his brilliant blue eyes, which could twinkle with wit, warm with sentimentality, or focus into piercing lasers when scanning for the weak spots that he found. As a young attorney at the Federal Communications Commission (FCC), Haley had drafted the Communications Act of 1934. He left the FCC in 1939 for a private practice in which he handled scores of cases and proceedings before the commission. When Dorothy Bullitt interviewed him, Haley was back from the war and once more practicing communications law in Washington, D.C. The six FCC commissioners who made final rulings issuing broadcast licenses were Haley's personal friends. "They regarded Andy as the fairest and wisest and relied on him themselves for counsel," Dorothy once said.

Andrew Haley, at his best, was a larger-than-life Falstaffian character, the sort who could host two dinner parties at a restaurant, with neither group knowing the other existed. Unafraid of action, he took bold steps that were backed by solid thinking; he had a gift for quickly judging character, and a charm spiced by a dramatic flare that got his message across. He also had some very human faults. A complex powerful man, he was both driven and bedeviled by a temperament that he took little time to control or understand. He was a heavy drinker, a habit that precipitated scenes that were alternately hilarious or horrible. At his worst, he was possessed of a temper that once caused his dismissal from court when he threw an inkwell at a man he was cross-examining. Andy Haley knew when he had met equal force, so his excesses were not apparent to Dorothy Bullitt as she interviewed him. She trusted him immediately. ("It was just something that rang a bell. I believed in him.") He encouraged her to step into areas she had never dreamed of and to know that she would succeed. Dorothy's daughter Harriet described Haley as "Mother's launching platform. He empowered her to do things she hadn't thought of before and was probably responsible for her success in broadcasting."

As she came to know Andy Haley over time, Dorothy became alternately furious and forgiving of his excesses in favor of the service he rendered and the friendship that grew between them. The lady and the lawyer recognized and enjoyed each other, sensing the drive they shared. Phone lines crackled with their calls discussing the what ifs and the what nexts in her adventure into broadcasting. When he called to say, "Meet me at the airport at three o'clock," she learned to ask "Which three?" and, if and when he did arrive, his hair was in his eyes and his pockets jingled with small bottles of booze. For years, she flew east and he west to discuss her unfolding career, sitting with him over papers in his office or plotting over drinks in her sunroom before the fire. She tolerated him because she needed him and enjoyed him. He was tough, gave her orders, challenged her. She relished it, responded, and was proud of the results. Time proved how fond she was of this hard-driving, hard-drinking brash man who pushed her patience. "Andy was *very* blunt when he didn't like my ideas. Sometimes he'd look at me and say, 'Are you crazy?' Other times he'd order me around. Once he called to ask if I could come down to San Francisco and talk business. Gloria [Chandler, a friend] and I went down to the Clift Hotel where he was staying. After breakfast with no business discussion, we went to his room where he said, 'While we're waiting'—and I didn't know what we were waiting for—'read over these papers and see if they are correct.' Next thing I knew, Gloria was at one desk, I at another, and there was another client working at a table—all of us busy as can be—working on *someone else's* application for a radio station! Meanwhile Andy was on the phone or pacing the floor, stopping every now and then to say, 'What are you doing *that* for? Do it *this* way—do it right.' We never did talk about my affairs. At the end of the day, he drove us to the airport and put us on the plane—which was nice of him—having had *no* advice for my own problems at all! But somehow we all enjoyed working with him so much that it didn't matter what he asked us to do."

Remembering the years of Haley histrionics, Dorothy smiled and gave a shrug that suggested mixed amusement and annoyance. "There were moments when I couldn't find him or he'd fail to appear or he'd fall asleep in an important meeting," she said, brandishing a fist. "Then I would have *killed* him if I'd had a knife handy, but somehow he always brought his own forgiveness with him." Daughter Harriet recalled, "Mother would come to me, flapping her pockets, saying, 'I'm so mad at Andy! And you know what makes me even madder? *I can't stay mad!*' Mother never could dislike him because she was crazy about him. He had high expectations of her and made equally high demands. You learn to love someone who'll do that for you."

The woman who became her closest friend also appeared in her life about this time. Gloria Chandler first visited Seattle in 1939 as a delegate for the Junior League of America to its annual conference. As a founding member of the local chapter, Dorothy was asked to house some delegates. Dorothy and Ohata drove to the train to meet the four unknown women. "I met one and then another and there was Gloria. As we waited for the car to bring their luggage, here came one of those flatbed carts with boxes and boxes piled up. They were *all* Gloria's hats."

Gloria Chandler was shaped like a pouter pigeon, almost as round as she was tall. At five feet, two inches she weighed over two hundred pounds, much of it earned through a love of sweets and steak so rare that she ordered it "just run over a flashlight." Her tiny size four feet, deformed since birth, could scarcely support the bulk that bulged up to an ample bosom and then tapered to a curly head. She was all middle-aged femininity—puffed, dimpled, and corseted—with small hands and a cherubic face that displayed cupid's bow lips and a merry smile. Andy Haley nicknamed her "Baby Doll." Hats were Gloria's trademark. They topped her matronly outfits in outrageous combinations of silk and flowers strewn on wide brims or stacked in profusion like millinery bouquets run amok. They tilted coquettishly at luncheons or, straight-brimmed, demanded attention at business meetings. Never married, Gloria had spent her entire energy on her career as director of public affairs for the Junior League. A trained actress, she read and produced children's stories on the radio, mimicking various parts with a facile voice that could capture Tinker Bell as well as

Captain Hook. She had won awards and respect nationwide as an expert on literature and drama for young people.

Those early days with the visiting League staff, and particularly with Gloria Chandler, opened new worlds for Dorothy. These women were not the Junior League's "top brass"; they were worldly, educated women actually earning their way and Dorothy was refreshed and validated by their "hands on" approach in their work. At the end of each day, the women returned to Dorothy's house for animated discussions that lasted until late at night. Dorothy read *The Little Prince* aloud in French; Gloria told hilarious stories; while another new friend, Rowena Rathbone, a professional photographer, popped around corners for candid shots.

After everyone had gone to bed, Gloria and Dorothy sat up and talked about broadcasting. "Gloria was on the active staff of the NBC station in Chicago and she knew the mechanics of programming, about which I knew nothing," Dorothy recalled. "A program for me was just something that came on the air." They also talked about children's literature and how to reach children on radio, and Dorothy realized that in this new friend was a valuable resource who saw the potential of broadcasting. Here was a woman who had ideas, creativity, and critical skills—a change from many of Dorothy's other female associations. Gloria also had important contacts in the broadcasting business and was happy to share them. During those few days of the Junior League meeting in Seattle, the two cemented a bond based on humor, high-mindedness, and shared goals. It was an important friendship for Dorothy. In years to come Gloria Chandler was her companion, consultant, and closest friend.

DOROTHY THUS FORMED HER BROADCASTING "BRAIN TRUST." Fred Stimson, Henry Owen, Andy Haley, and Gloria Chandler provided her with expertise and broadened her world, each with a distinctive imprint. Television performer Ruth Prins ("Wunda Wunda" of early TV) explained, "Dorothy was really a very shy person and she didn't have an awful lot of lightness in those days. Those four were outrageous individuals and they provided her with a kind of vicarious vitality she couldn't easily express otherwise." Unlike Dorothy, Gloria gave lots of hugs and she had humor. "I'm the court jester," she often said, knowing that Dorothy needed laughter around her. Henry was a character with whom she could collude, one who relayed gossip from the men's clubs, unafraid to confront the sticky situations for her. And Andy, with his freewheeling sense of life and possibilities, was a constant source of interests and activities that she would never pursue herself. She trusted, enjoyed, and depended on each of them. Her remarkable gift was to attract just such unusual and varied talent into her orbit and to keep their loyalty.

During the spring of 1946, Fred and Henry spent each day at Scott's law library, which adjoined Dorothy's office in the 1411 Building. Unsalaried, they sat at the conference table, reading FCC regulations and throwing out ideas as they played pinochle between phone calls. They conferred with Andy, discussing the procedures of application for a radio license and the decision of whether to apply for a new station or find an existing one, whether to buy AM or FM or both. With Dorothy they sifted through scenarios they might pursue. They also called Gloria who, hats in tow, arrived a few days later to conduct an informal seminar on the basics of running a radio station. As they sat around the big table, she stressed the importance of good programming promoted well ahead of time. As Dorothy described it, "the air was thick with ideas and possibilities."

On June 18, 1946, Dorothy called together those she needed to incorporate the venture. Present with her at this meeting were Stim Bullitt, Fred Stimson, Ray Wright, Henry Owen, attorney Dick Riddell, and Charles Clark, husband of Thomas and Emma's daughter, Nona. They decided to call themselves "Western Waves." With only $10,000 paid in at the first meeting, Western Waves wasn't exactly awash in capital, but the initial contribution was enough to establish the reality of the effort. Next, applications were filed with the FCC to construct both an AM and an FM station. When they were approved, Dorothy exclaimed in her diary, "Whee! Now for building a station!"

Then fate opened an unexpected door. A tenant in the 1411 Building, Arch Talbot, happened to own a radio station. "We knew each other pretty well, but I didn't know much about his station except that it wasn't very good," Dorothy recollected. "He came up to the office and said, 'For heaven's sake, don't apply for another radio station here in Seattle. I have one and it doesn't have an audience. If you bring another in, it will just dilute the audience further. Why don't you buy mine, for goodness sakes!'" It was an AM station, with an FM attached. KEVR did have a reputation—as the worst station in town. Of Seattle's eight radio stations, it had the lowest listener rating and precious few advertisers to support it. At 1090 on the AM dial, KEVR sent out a feeble ten-kilowatt signal that, in Dorothy's words, "could be heard on a good day from Queen Anne to Ballard." At night its paid religious programs were interrupted by mariachi music from Tijuana, Mexico. She introduced herself to the personnel and inspected the studios on the twenty-first floor of the Smith Tower—the same building from which, thirty years before, she and Scott had surveyed an unknown future. She pronounced the station "shoddy"—just what she wanted— a bargain and a challenge to turn a losing station into a worthwhile business.

"I figured I could buy Arch Talbot's AM-FM license and make what money might come out of the AM to develop the FM for beautiful music. It was going to cost me, but I thought there was room for improvement and we could make listeners. I didn't have the best signal in the world, but it was on the air—then we'd be part of the broadcasting brotherhood."

With her enthusiasm hidden behind a mask of only the mildest interest, Dorothy launched into negotiations—an exercise she had enjoyed since childhood, working deals for sodas on First Hill or dickering for opera tickets in New York City or selling homes in The Highlands. After hours of preparation with pencil, paper, and telephone, Dorothy and Ray Wright met with Talbot in her office. Dorothy remembered how she and her attorney "began to dicker with Brother Talbot on his price, while Fred and Henry were in the next room with the door closed playing gin rummy. Finally we made a deal and while it was being written up, I slipped a piece of paper under the door saying, 'We got it!!' So we were in business. The price was $190,000 and I didn't have the money to spare, so I borrowed it from banks. The bankers were very nice—but then those were the days when I knew the bankers personally. They were Father's friends and they knew me a little and knew what the securities were. It was a great gamble, but we didn't know how great. We were just happy to be in business." She dropped her pending application for a license, and, in January 1947, filled out the application for KEVR, and sent it off for filing with the FCC.

The KEVR purchase was delayed when businessman Elroy McCaw (whose sons would eventually found a vast cellular-phone empire) appeared in Dorothy's office announcing that he had an interest in the station. "Elroy McCaw said I couldn't buy the station because he *owned* part of it. I said, 'Well, it was represented to be owned by one man, Arch Talbot, the application has already gone in and your name wasn't on it.' And he said, 'For $10,000, I'll get out of your way.' I said, 'I don't see how you *could* be in my way because there is only *one* owner.' He left my office, saying, 'You'll hear from me again.' Then Andy called to say that the sale was being held up because of the McCaw thing. So I flew back and with Andy went to the FCC and found that they had been told by McCaw that he was part-owner and that they had never looked up the ownership records. With Andy pounding the table they found that Elroy had never had any participation whatsoever. I never liked him—he had come to me originally dressed in a colonel's uniform and I'll never understand how he was able to wear it."

When the new executives took over at KEVR, they found themselves in charge of a small, listless staff running a sloppy operation. Programming consisted of randomly selected music and what Dorothy called "every funny religion there was." Undaunted, the trio settled into the Smith Tower, with Henry at the business manager's desk, Fred in the studio, and Dorothy at a temporary desk out in the hall. On their first day, reality descended with a thud. "We had been told that the station didn't have an audience, but I didn't realize that it was literally . . . *no* audience, until Henry sat down at the manager's desk and opened the mail. A check fell out and we yelled, 'Hooray, we got some money!' But the letter was from Mr. Hooper of the audience measurement surveys, who said, 'We're returning your check because there was no one listening to your station.' NO ONE! He also enclosed a chart of station performances and ours had zero, zero, zero, zero—all the way down. I said, 'Well, we can't do worse than that—it shouldn't take much to do better.' "

Within the next few months, the trio spent long hours trying to reverse the zero rating. They concentrated on AM because it, at least, had some sponsors. Fred sometimes slept at the station, stretched out on an old sofa. Dorothy "tried everything but running the turntables." The programming had to be changed, and Dorothy called the heavy religious format "the worst I have ever heard. The air was full of paid religion—the humpty-hump church of this or that—fundamentalists who advertised figures of Christ to hang in your car for twenty-five cents. I hated that coming in! It was a terrible format that featured religious hucksters begging the listeners to 'put their hands on the radio and be saved' and 'send in a dollar or God will punish you.' That was the station's only source of revenue—they paid to get on the air so they could ask for contributions. So the decision had to be made about how shall we taper this down—get rid of this paid religion a little at a time, or just cut it all out and put on our own records or whatever we can find, which I thought we might just as well do. We also made a policy decision to support and give free time to the three basic faiths—Catholic, Protestant, and Jewish—whose programs would talk about God and not just talk to raise money. Bit by bit we took steps. We improved the personnel, got a better station manager, and bought some programs."

Dorothy realized that a network affiliation, if she could get one, would provide some secure programming for the station. She flew to New York in 1949 to convince the president of ABC, Robert Kintner, and Otto Brandt, vice-president, that her radio station could do a better job than their existing affiliate, KJR. She had no qualms about taking another station's affiliation; cutthroat competition was part of the game. A few months later, Kintner ("crass") and Brandt ("charming") turned her down. The signal was too poor.

To fill the air time, they bought a series of radio plays and borrowed records from friends. Dorothy brought in her own record collection of 78s, catalogued and timed everything, and then started producing a symphony evening. "It was not done the usual way," she said. "We did it the way a symphony orchestra would do it—by having one conductor for the entire evening. And we programmed it the way a symphony concert was programmed—one piece to start with and then an entire symphony with all three or four movements under the same conductor. So, when we had Toscanini, it was a Toscanini evening. I did the timing and produced it every Wednesday evening or so. It really was a lot of work and I did it for almost a year until one of the salesmen came in and said, 'I have a program sold for that time unless you want to continue with your symphony.' I said, 'Heavens no! If it's paid for, we take it.' And that was the end of the symphony—except that letters came in by the heap."

If the cancellation of her symphony evening caused Dorothy regret, it was overruled by the fact that money began to come in and she was determined that the station stand on its own financially. The team worked long hours to improve program quality and to find revenues. "Golly, I worked harder than I ever worked for anything," Dorothy reminisced. "One day they came in to complain that the station signal was being completely blocked out at noon because the ships in the harbor blew their whistles. No one could hear the broadcast. 'Well,' I said, remembering what Gloria had told us about promotion, 'sell it.' So they talked all morning on the radio about setting your watches when the boats whistled at noon." They were also innovative with the news. "When there was a good-sized earthquake in 1949, one of the announcers *raced* to the office window and stuck his microphone outside while he described what was happening down on the streets below."

King's first logo was drawn by Walt Disney.

Of the many changes at KEVR, none was more important to Dorothy than new call letters. In the course of her research into broadcasting, she had heard repeatedly that a company's call letters were its most valuable asset. The letters K-E-V-R were not easily pronounced, promoted, or even remembered. "I called Andy Haley to tell him that we needed to change the call letters and he sent me an application requiring my first three choices for new letters. I wanted the letters K-I-N-G for obvious reasons—it signified the tops and we were in King County. So, I wrote KING, KING, KING for all three choices. It wasn't long before Andy called to ask if I was crazy. I said, 'Probably.' He said, 'Ha! You don't imagine you're the first person to want those call letters, do you? They're the best call letters there are.' I said, 'I'm sure they are; that's *why* I want them.' He said, 'They're probably already taken,' and I said, 'Well, find out who has them because *we* need them.' A few days later he called to say he'd traced the call letters through various departments to a tramp steamer called the *Watertown,* a big old ship going round delivering packages here and there in the world. I said, 'For a ship called the *Watertown,* all they need is dots and dashes—they don't have to advertise or promote a tramp steamer, they don't even have to say it. We *need* those letters!' Andy grumbled, 'Well, you're a determined woman, and then added, 'I'll see what I can do . . . ' I don't know how he did it—whether he went through the Maritime Commission or the Catholic Church or where, I don't know what it cost him—maybe a case of scotch or champagne—I never knew what he did to get those letters, he never billed me for them, but he got them. And was I happy! More people have asked me how much it cost to get those call letters—others who had tried and been turned down. It's one of the best things that ever happened to us. That's how King Broadcasting was born."

With the christening of King Broadcasting Company, Dorothy Bullitt produced her fourth child—one which she would nurture, coddle, and control for the rest of her days with as much if not more attention and energy than she ever paid to her natural progeny. She changed KEVR to KING-AM and planned its future, first to increase its ten kilowatts to the maximum allowable fifty kilowatts, then to build a new transmitter and buy new equipment. She hoped to upgrade the personnel with people like Gloria Chandler, who within a year was adding her recordings to the format, directing new programs, and bringing in the first of many national awards that flowed in a steady stream for as long as Dorothy lived. Over the next four decades, the fledgling "adventure" matured into one of the finest broadcasting companies in the United States, if not the world.

But that was far in the future. For the present, Dorothy celebrated with a new logo created by Walt Disney and obtained for her by her old friend from the Coliseum Theater, Frank Newman. It was a smiling, ermine-clad little "King Mike" figure with the company call letters emblazoned across his crown. As she held the Disney drawing, Dorothy smiled too, in spite of the uncertain road ahead. What did Mr. Hooper and his surveys know, anyway? Maybe she lacked a map, maybe she lacked experience, and maybe the competition was stiff but she had found out long ago that she could learn, compete, and succeed. She was venturing off the beaten path into trackless territory, but this trip was finally hers alone. She was riding on no one's coattails—neither her father's nor his friends'. This time she was in control—her hands were on the wheel, the machinery was in motion, and reckless or not, it was full speed ahead.

*The men were saying, "Oh, isn't it a PITY—she's
going to lose her shirt and wouldn't her father feel bad
about it!" My friends were sorry for me. I was sorry
for me TOO—I was scared to death!*

10 THE GREAT GAMBLE
1949–1952

TELEVISION BROADCASTING BEGAN ON AN EXPERIMENTAL BASIS
during the late 1920s, in Schenectady, New York. The new medium did not
spread quickly; only a dozen television stations were on the air by the late
1940s. The closest stations to Seattle were St. Paul, Minnesota, and Los Angeles. In between was a vast expanse of airwaves waiting to carry images into
people's homes. Unknown to most Americans, the household gods were about
to change: soon radio would be relegated to a corner of the kitchen or the
dashboard of the car, replaced by a large box with a tiny screen that would
dominate living rooms throughout the land.

Dorothy had first been fascinated by television when she saw a demonstration of its potential in 1939. "I was in New York before taking the children to
Europe and became curious to see the makeshift television station at one of the
large department stores. It was in a curtained-off corner on the ground floor, and
when I peeked through the curtains, there was a show going on with live actors,
so I eased myself in quietly and just watched, absolutely fascinated by this gadget
that was picking *pictures* from the air! When the show was over, the director
came over—I was the only one there—and asked if I found it interesting and I
said, 'Oh, very,' and he told me a good deal about it. I remember that while we
were talking, one of his people came over to say that the coffee table on the set
had to be refinished because the lights were so bright that they had blistered the
surface. I asked a lot of questions then and, years later, I went up to General
Electric, in Schenectady, New York, where the sets were made and the first station was broadcasting. They told me what it would cost and what new things
were coming out. Everyone was very enthusiastic—the sets were selling as fast
as they could make them—and they all said that the time to get in was *now*."

The idea of transmitting pictures was bewitching to someone so taken by gadgets. Dorothy went away excited but she heard little more about television during the war years that followed. Because of national priorities, no sets were manufactured and what little programming might have been produced was curtailed. By 1947, Dorothy heard about television again in conversations at the meetings of the National Association of Broadcasters (NAB), where she mixed with "the boys" who were assessing the new medium with an eye to its financial future.

Television's financial future was highly uncertain. It was a product waiting for consumers, with few viewers, fewer sets to receive the pictures, and scarcely any advertisers to assure commercial success. Those who brought television into the broadcasting business were gamblers facing tenuous times on barely adequate budgets, entrepreneurs who were part curious engineer, part caring futurist, and part fool. Such a pioneer was P. K. Lieberman, an ex-Navy commander experienced in electronic communications. In 1948, Lieberman applied to the FCC to build Seattle's first television station, KRSC-TV. It was built on a shoestring. From its one-room studio, a former neighborhood store at the top of Queen Anne Hill, KRSC-TV transmitted ten feeble kilowatts of power via a 150-foot Navy surplus tower across the street to a smattering of citizens scattered between downtown and Ballard. A brave effort, KRSC's flickering and distorted programs were the only ones to appear on about one thousand sets during the first few months of operation. It was the thirteenth television station to broadcast in the United States.

Dorothy Bullitt was thrilled. Among the first to order a set, she installed the cumbersome wooden contraption in her sunroom and ran a wire antenna between the pictures on the walls. On Thanksgiving Day, 1948, she tuned into KRSC's first broadcast—the state championship high school football game. "It was the funniest picture you ever saw," she remembered, squinting as she recalled the tiny distorted image in which the football players had "long beaks and tails sticking out because of the imbalances in the equipment." That evening she invited friends for another viewing, a movie called *Street Scene* that included a cast of hundreds—"an unfortunate selection for a seven-inch screen." One guest remarked, "Do you mind if I close my eyes—I think I could visualize it better."

Dorothy was fascinated by the images and proud that the city now had a station. To her mind, P. K. Lieberman had a lot of courage. That opening day she sent him her congratulations in the form of flowers. Later that evening, she and Gloria, now an employee of King Broadcasting Company, drove by the small studio. "There in the window were our flowers. They were the only acknowledgment he received."

Meanwhile, television was gathering force in the East, where picture boxes were bringing news, sports, and movies into people's homes. Sets were selling so fast that manufacturers could hardly meet the demand. Within a few years, Americans were captured by the heady thrill of instant experience at the turn of a dial. Advertisers caught on to the commercial power of a medium that gave them a mass audience mesmerized by programs and products to buy. Sales of television sets rose from 178,000 in 1947, mostly in the East, to 975,000 in 1948, to more than three million a year later. The rush was on. An unprepared FCC was forced to re-evaluate the assignment of channels in various cities, a process that had been done helter-skelter until this time. To facilitate this review, the commission in 1948 ordered a temporary freeze on all new licenses until its engineering staff could reallocate the spectrum so stations would not, in Dorothy's words, "collide."

KRSC-TV did not operate long before its owner decided to sell. P. K. Lieberman had been offered an attractive job in the East and was looking for someone to take on the station and relieve him of the debts he had incurred. He went first to O. D. Fisher of KOMO and Saul Haas of KIRO who, noting the station's pitiful audience and revenues, decided to pass. He eventually contacted Dorothy Bullitt, who responded with her usual mixture of charm and caution. Told that the price was $500,000, Dorothy replied, "Oh, I'd *love* to have it, but we just don't have any $500,000." But she knew that he was desperate to sell.

During the ensuing months, Dorothy kept her suitor dangling and thought intensely about the financing a television station would require. She was already operating the radio station at a loss, and had put money on the line for a new tower and transmitter. She talked it over with Henry Owen and Hugh Feltis, the station manager, and they urged her to try for it. She discussed it with Andy Haley and Ray Wright, and both attorneys were optimistic in theory but cautious in counsel. Wavering a bit, she considered taking on a partner to bear part of the burden. "I just didn't want to go into it by myself," she explained. "I went to KIRO to see if Saul Haas wouldn't want to go in with me but no-o-o-o, he said they wouldn't take such a gamble. Then to KOMO where I saw Mr. Fisher and his son-in-law to ask if they'd go in with me. They said, 'Oh no, we'll wait until you build up the number of sets—then there'll be someone to watch when we build our *own* stations.' "

Dorothy went home to sort out her thoughts. Fisher and Haas were right to an extent. Television, with its costly equipment, changing technology, and uncertain future was a gamble. It wasn't reliable like the real estate that had provided her with security for many years. On the other hand, neither was it boring. Television was the ultimate gadget. "I didn't know, but I kept thinking about having that little *box* in your house. Surely, the offerings weren't very exciting, but I knew we'd learn how to put programs on and things were happening around the world that people should know about. I felt that if there were pictures to be seen, people couldn't get downtown fast enough to buy sets." As she sorted through her thoughts and dreams, her logic found its own reasons for buying a station. True, there were only six thousand sets in Seattle, which meant very little revenue, but the FCC freeze on new stations just might work in her favor. While the freeze lasted, she would have a monopoly free from competition. "The FCC had to reassign the twelve VHF channels in every major city across the United States," she recalled. "And no one knew how long it would take. Some thought it would take only a few weeks, but I thought I knew how slowly engineers think and plan with their drawings and figures, and that it would take a very long time—longer than a few months—for them to work it out." Besides, she was impatient. She had been late getting into radio and she didn't want to miss an early opportunity for television. "I was just afraid that if we were going to get into television, maybe we'd have to move fast and buy a station that was for sale now. If we waited until everyone was buying television, which I was convinced would happen, we'd be just left at the stake. We wouldn't win a thing."

Lieberman phoned to tell her that someone else was interested in the station. "Hope to goodness it's not already sold," she wrote in her diary a day later, "as I think we *must* have it." A few weeks later he phoned again, this time to tell her that he was heading west to talk with representatives from the broadcasting division of Marshall Field and with her if she was interested. "Of course I am," she replied cautiously, "but I don't know how I would get the money for it." "Well, I'm coming to Seattle and on this trip I'm going to sell," he countered, "and I'd like your best offer." Dorothy agreed to see him the next afternoon after he had spent the morning with representatives from Marshall Field.

Dorothy hung up apprehensive and excited. Immediately she dialed Andy Haley in Washington, D.C., but eventually found him at his sister's home in Pasadena, California, where she got him out of the shower to tell him the news. "Andy came to the phone and said, 'What's happening *now?*' I said, 'Well, I want to buy a television station.' There was a silence and then he said, 'Did you get me out of the shower to tell me this? Think about what you're doing! You're running in the red with radio, are you going to run twice as red with a television station? There aren't any sets, you can't sell anything, etc. etc., why do you want it?' I said, 'I . . . want . . . it . . .'—I didn't have very good reasons—'and I need you to get it for me.' He said, 'I'll be there.'"

The next morning Andy Haley called to say he had missed his plane and could not arrive until six o'clock that evening. Rather than call off the afternoon appointment, Dorothy decided to keep it and stall the seller until help arrived. That evening Andy Haley, Henry Owen, and Stim Bullitt joined her at her home on Galer Street, anticipating "the great battle." P. K. Lieberman, accompanied by his lawyer and broker, arrived promptly for the drama of negotiations that went on until the wee hours of the next morning. Dorothy relished the story. "It was a comedy—our negotiations were conducted back and forth on the first floor between two battle camps guarded by French doors. Andy and I shuttled between the French doors in the living room where we conferred with P. K. and his men, and the French doors in the sunroom where we hashed over our next strategy with Henry and Stim. P. K. was asking $500,000 and we weren't about to pay that, so we decided on a very low offer. Andy did all of the talking, pacing back and forth, telling them that they didn't have this and didn't have that. Finally, he offered them something like $200,000 and the broker exploded with, 'That's an insulting offer!' Andy—who didn't like brokers at all—whirled around and shouted, 'Shut up, you Armenian rug merchant!' Well, when the smoke cleared from that, we left the room and Andy slammed the French doors, saying, 'See how close you can come to it.' Back behind our closed doors, I laughed and asked Andy where under the sun he had come up with that name for the broker and he said, 'That was the only thing I could think of to call him in front of you!' That was so typical. After a while they came back to us with quite a drop from $500,000 and then we went into a huddle in the den and back and forth until we made a deal. It was one of the funniest evenings I ever spent in my life."

Dorothy was now in possession of an expensive new "gadget"—the first television station to be sold in the United States. She realized that for the purchase price of $375,000, there was precious little to show for it—a couple of cameras, a transmitter with a weak signal, and a decrepit tower to broadcast it—but she planned to boost the ten kilowatts power to 100 kilowatts and build a new tower. As for radio, she planned to use the FM frequency that came with KRSC, actually the first FM station in Seattle, and relinquish the one she had purchased originally with KEVR radio.

Dorothy was confident, but others were not. Her boardroom "buddies" and old family friends who thought she had lost her "feeble mind" whispered behind her back and shook their heads at her folly. However, she had done her homework and thought it all through from concept to completion. Her contract required payments over time, paid at 4 percent interest. To buy KRSC-TV she had to sell real estate piece by piece—the Westlake Square building, the Firestone Building on Westlake Avenue near Lake Union, and two more properties in the University district. Meanwhile, she was happy to learn that her competitor in the bidding, the Marshall Field representative, had come to Seattle with authority to pay up to the full price of $500,000, but that he had bargained too closely and lost the deal.

With the purchase of KRSC-TV, Dorothy Bullitt's life was turned upside down, around, and sideways. She was now one of those pioneering "fools" about to take a glorious bucking-bronco ride that would tear her loose from old restraints. These new people she was meeting were more lively than the staid board members and residents of The Highlands she had always known. They were communicators—quick-witted businessmen, news, theater, and advertising types—interested in the fast-moving present. At regular NAB meetings held in Chicago or Washington, D.C., they came together for a free-for-all of buying equipment and previewing syndicated shows by day, and mixing with FCC commissioners, affiliate executives, and each other in hospitality suites at night. The atmosphere buzzed with excitement. For Dorothy, the energy was contagious; it fueled her imagination, brought out her humor, and validated parts of her personality she had not realized before. Broadcasting also fostered her keen competitive spirit. She found herself fascinated by the "game" of business itself—the intrigue and gossip, the sheer pleasure of outmaneuvering, outwitting, and outcharming any opponent just for its own sake.

———————

DURING THE 1950S, DOROTHY GAVE UP THE PAST AND JOINED the present, gave up grieving and took up smoking. She commented with a shrug thirty years later, "My children were gone and the house was empty, so one day I had a cigarette to think things over and I've been doing it ever since." Her smoking became an art form. Usually she smoked Roosevelt-style, gripping a filter between her teeth as she took slow thoughtful drags. In conversation, smoke seemed to appear from her nostrils and mouth like punctuation, timed for just the right moment. Sometimes she absently knocked the cigarette against the ashtray, more to emphasize an idea than to get rid of ashes. Her smoking served purposes beyond pleasure. If she suspected that an employee was nipping from the bottle, she could test him with a cigarette, according to her grandson Bill Collins. "When one salesman under suspicion reached forward to light her cigarette, I saw her palm his hand as if steadying it for herself—but she was actually checking to see if he was trembling," he recalled. "Then, looking him in the eyes—to see if they were dilated—she lit the cigarette, exhaled to the side and finally let go." Smoking was also a way to deal with men's hostilities. Granddaughter Wenda Brewster O'Reilly remembered hearing from Dorothy that she had three tactics for coping with potential ill will during all-male business meetings: First, plant ideas and let someone else think he had thought of them; second, praise and credit him for the ideas; and third, when the going got tough, smoke. "If she felt backed into a corner by some question," Wenda remembered, "she'd slowly take her cigarettes from one pocket, open the box, and take one out. Then she'd reach into the other pocket and take out her filter. Then she'd put the filter on the cigarette. *Then* she'd start looking for a match and, sooner or later, someone would offer her a light. By that time, she'd had time to think and by that time she had her answer."

Dorothy's children noticed a change in her and were relieved to see that she was happy and that her focus was off of them. She kept track of them, however, at family functions and noted their achievements with pride. Harriet, living with husband Bill and two children in Boston, surprised her mother when she won the New England Women's Fencing Championship. "I didn't even *know* she was fencing," Dorothy said with a smile. Patsy gave birth to her first child, Josiah VII, prompting Dorothy to write, "Am so proud of my children sometimes I can hardly contain myself." Stim ran unsuccessfully for Congress in 1952 and again in 1954, causing Dorothy to exert as much anger as support for her son. When Republican leader George Kinnear wrote a letter to the *Seattle Times* in which he accused Stim of being a rich boy and Dorothy of using her station's power to promote her son's political aspirations, she was beside herself with fury. Kinnear further asserted that Dorothy was profiting from the FCC freeze due to her political connections. "Mother consulted her lawyer Ray Wright about suing," Patsy remembered, "but he told her that, although the charges were indeed libelous, it wasn't worth it. She was furious at Kinnear. He had attacked her young and she never forgave him." Stim's political leanings turned more philosophical in 1959 when he wrote a book entitled *To Be a Politician.* "He has achieved a fine thing in this book," his mother wrote proudly in her diary. "The sociological philosophy makes me burst with pride—his well-read background gives him fine frames of reference, dealt with taste and wit."

Dorothy was particularly pleased when Stim married Katharine Muller in 1954. Kay was a woman after her own heart, as patrician in bearing and manner as Dorothy, community-minded, with a New England background as a teacher, and a dedication to children's education. "Stim's guardian angel really made up for past neglect when he brought these two together," Dorothy noted in her diary. A tall brunette with a soft voice and a sympathetic heart, Kay had met Stim through mutual friends at a meeting of Americans for Democratic Action, a liberal group that attracted Stim's interests during the 1950s. With many ideals in common, the couple was soon engaged and married in Boston on Thanksgiving Day. Dorothy welcomed this new daughter-in-law into the family. "She was very accepting of me from the start, very," Kay remembered of those early years, describing Dorothy as "the antithesis of the stereotypic mother-in-law . . . When I think that we lived with her while our house was being built and had Stim's three older children visiting on weekends," she said, "I realize how patient she was." Stim and Kay were to have three children of their own. When a girl was born a year later and named after her, Dorothy was thrilled. "Stim told me at dinner they will name her Dorothy Churchill," she noted in her diary. "I was so overcome I nearly burst into loud tears—never was so touched and surprised." A boy, Benjamin Logan, and another girl, Margaret Muller, completed their family.

There was little personal socializing during these days. Dorothy made one attempt to entertain old friends, causing Emma to comment in a letter, "Went to Dorothy's party, the first she has given since 1930. Same guest list. Same dress. Everyone's wondering if there will be more, or if they have to wait another twenty-five years." Broadcasting consumed all of her time. "Mother was totally preoccupied with networks and networking during the 1950s," Harriet recalled. "When she came to visit, she'd enter the house and go right to the phone to call Henry or Andy. When she hung up, she was full of the things she was learning about the business and its challenges. Then the next day, after a few more phone calls, she'd be gone." Patsy noticed the same thing. "Mother had been so morose for years," she recalled. "Now she had something exciting to do with Henry, Fred, Andy, and Gloria. Instead of dragging around in dark clothes, she lightened up a lot, and we were relieved that it took the focus off of us."

DOROTHY'S ADVENTURE IN TELEVISION STARTED OUT SIMPLY enough, with an inspection of the station facilities and a visit with her new employees. "The studio was what was left in a tiny shop that also had to hold the transmitter and the transformer and the trans-everything," she reminisced years later. "In one small corner, there was barely room for two cameras and a couple of people to sit. There was also a 'vehicle' parked outside for remote broadcasting—a bread truck that had more room in it than the studio! The station began broadcasting every day around noon for a few hours and again for a while in the evening. At first we showed films in between our meager efforts at live broadcasting. For the news, we'd just read the paper and call it news; for live entertainment, we'd pull people in off the street for a game of charades, or we had Stan Boreson playing the accordion. We never knew what

Stan was going to do on his show and he didn't know either. He'd just bring his accordion, sing a song, and tell a story. And that was how it started."

At their first meeting with Dorothy Bullitt, the staff of about a dozen—mostly engineers trying to correct the constant bars and blips that appeared on the few sets that received them—listened with near-deaf ears. They had become so intensely dedicated to the fledgling station that they regarded it as their personal creation, almost a living thing. Now they found themselves employed by a wealthy matron who looked like she'd be more at ease with a tea set than a television set. Apprehensive about the future, they were thinking of walking out. In fact, unknown to Dorothy, four or five key people had already decided to flee to KTLA in Los Angeles. Among them was the director of programming, Lee Schulman, a young New Yorker trained in filmmaking at UCLA who made up in creative moxie for the lack of television experience that everyone shared in 1949. Schulman remembered that meeting vividly as an early turning point in the company. "The staff was actually giving birth to television," he remembered, "and they had a natural predisposed loyalty to the man [P. K. Lieberman] who had made it possible for them. But when Dorothy began to share with them her early research and observations, they began to listen. She wanted everybody to know that her interest in broadcasting, although she knew it had money-making potential—God knows at that time it didn't—came also from a commitment that went beyond mere entertainment to contributing to the betterment of the community in which the license was held. She said she saw no conflict between making money and public service. She talked about the importance of education and children's programs. She shared her thoughts with us as if we were family. Then she asked questions [of the employees]—personal questions about their backgrounds—did they have families, children, what were their desires and goals? Everyone there was deeply affected by that meeting, so much so that afterwards we advised KTLA that we felt it was inappropriate to deplete the station's technical and programming staff, and we stayed in Seattle."

With this first talk, Dorothy set her management style. She focused on her prime interest—people—knowing that a business is never any better than those who staff it. When a sales executive once said to her that she cherished programs, Dorothy aimed her keen blue eyes at him and croaked in that husky voice, "No. I cherish people." Barbara Stenson, a grand niece of Bertha Boeing and for years a reporter for KING-TV, remembered her family's attitude about Dorothy's success with her staff. "Dorothy Bullitt succeeded, according to my family, because she was able to manage servants well," said Stenson. "There were those who could keep their help and those who couldn't. She could keep her help." She did it by treating them like extended family. With Henry Owen

Dorothy and Henry Owen with KING personnel in 1958.
LEFT TO RIGHT: Stan Carlson, Bob Ferguson, Al Hunter, Dorothy, Paul Sawin, Henry Owen, Lee Mudgett, Lee Schulman, and Jack Shawcroft.

to do the dirty work of firing and reprimanding, Dorothy assumed the role of benign matriarch who dispensed encouragement and empathy to all. In 1952, after the company was consolidated into one building at 320 Aurora Avenue North, her office door was open to the ideas, complaints, and problems of everyone from the mailroom to the boardroom. She mixed with employees in the coffee shop and in the halls. At Christmas she invited them into her office or to her home for Tom and Jerrys so strong that they staggered home in blissful stupor. "When Mrs. Bullitt gave you a drink," Del Loder, one of her first employees recalled, "it wasn't some watered-down thing—it was spiked. I've never tasted such a potent drink in my life." She entered into their lives—knew their names and families, put them up at her home and visited theirs, shared their secrets and their ceremonies, was godmother to their children. Judiciously, and using her instinctive judgment of character, she gave advice and money when it was deemed appropriate. Quietly she dealt with nervous breakdowns, alcoholism, and abusive home situations, with no one being the wiser. "Mrs. B," as they came to call her, gave each employee one of her most special gifts—the feeling that he or she not only counted but was a key member of her corporate family.

She received their loyalty in return. Like a feudal lord, she rewarded them with encouragement, attention, and the unspoken assurance that if they served her well, she would take care of them forever. "Mother did that with honor," daughter Patsy said. "If you were loyal and honest, then you were safe." Key personnel were safeguarded in Dorothy's inimitable way. When popular performer Ruth Prins had to move to Montana with her family, Dorothy saw to it that she came back weekly by train, put her up at her home, and hired a babysitter for her child. When this routine became too tiring, she quietly had her general manager offer Bob Prins a job at KING as Director of Public Affairs. "She never said, 'I want you to do this and I want an answer right now,'" Ruth Prins remembered. "She went all around the edges, with 'Well, wait now' or 'Let's just think this over,' until she got her way one way or another."

Dorothy's protection was not universal, however. Employees sometimes experienced no small amount of terror in the way she ran the company, never knowing when they would suddenly be in trouble with no one to appeal to. Those who fell short of her expectations by lying, creating trouble, or being "crass," soon heard the soothing voice of Henry Owen bid them good-bye. Keeping one's word was paramount. When one contest had more winners than expected claiming rewards, the station manager suggested retracting the offer made on air to the audience. Dorothy was beside herself with rage. "What were they *told?*" she demanded in a loud voice. "What were they *promised?*" When the quivering manager quoted a dollar amount in prizes that represented thousands more than expected she replied, "Well, they're going to get it—that's what we said we would do." Any employee rude to listeners or viewers was sent packing. When a student wrote asking for information about a broadcasting-related school assignment and the radio promotion manager replied in tones that Dorothy felt were "fresh as paint," he was axed so quickly that he left head-less and hatless. "Actually, Mother could have fitted in very well with the de'Medicis," Patsy remarked with a smile. "She would have loved that—creating hopes and destroying a tyrant or two. It was really her element."

The "freeze years" proved to be a precious window of opportunity. The staff responded by unleashing all the creativity they could bring to the medium. Over the next few years, they literally invented television. They were pioneers making their own rules, improvising with whatever they could find, and so caught up in the moment that they took little time to bask in self-congratulation. This was television's stone age—there were no such tools as videotape, cable, booms, zoom lenses, or satellites. Cameras were cumbersome, careening 100-pound monsters called "portable" only because they had handles; lighting was flat and unsophisticated. Program content consisted mostly of films and kinescopes ("kinnies" were recordings of television shows on film), and every-thing produced live was performed with little or no rehearsal and plenty of mistakes.

The driving force behind KING-TV's early programming was Lee Schulman, a flamboyant character (some suspected that he had himself paged wherever he went) who alternately inspired, challenged, charmed, and infuriated those around him. "Lee Schulman was the genius who really ran the operation, a pioneer in early television," Dorothy said of him. "Fortunately for us, he had come with the station. I had heard that the night before KRSC first went on the air, Lee and his wife spent hours wrapping wires around buttons at the transmitter so that it would work as it should the next morning. He was responsible, really, for a lot of good things we did, things that people said couldn't be done. Nothing stopped him; if he wanted something, that's what he got. He was full of ideas—found talent, made up programs, put them together and on the air—and he pulled off the impossible with great imagination."

Like some messianic dervish, Lee Schulman was everywhere, giving orders not only to the employees, but to whomever and whatever was being televised, including the very elements themselves. He directed the Goodyear blimp with as much aplomb as he directed a Christmas Eve service at St. Mark's Cathedral. With unrelenting energy, he stirred the staff with commands and demands in the studio or by monitoring them with a critical eye from afar. From his office, he listened in to the directors at master control through an intercom, interrupting their communications with a constant flood of suggestions. From his car and boat, he supervised via an FM radio receiver tuned to KING-TV's frequency and wrote out copious suggestions and criticisms to be delivered on desks the next day. No one escaped his radar and everyone received his report cards. Schulman was a firm believer in the value of live broadcasting, so much so that cue cards were banned because they detracted from eye contact and the immediacy of the broadcast. Fiercely competitive, he refused (in years after the freeze was lifted) to air any program that had already been covered by another station. He thrived on the challenge that live broadcasting presented and he was forever grateful to Dorothy Bullitt because she allowed him, in those early days, to produce what was probably more live television than occurred anywhere else in the country. As a result, Seattle may well have been a better informed community, better connected to its own local character, its people, customs, and events, than most American cities in the early 1950s.

Live broadcasting took as much chutzpah as creativity. Under Schulman's leadership—which included scathing reprimands and middle-of-the-night phone calls—the KING remote crew was seen all over the city and environs. The doughty little bread truck with the royal symbol on its side was a familiar sight to Seattleites, who crowded around to watch the crew set up equipment for an event. For one early live broadcast, the crew rushed to the Ravenna neighborhood to broadcast the rescue of a man trapped in a construction cave-in. In the darkness, they stumbled over cables to set up lights, while a narrator brought Seattle the rescue as it unfolded. When the Seattle Cedar Mill caught fire, they lurched over to Ballard where, upon realizing there was no audio, a crew member dismantled a pay phone and somehow hooked into sound. They launched forth to the opening of the legislature in Olympia, dragging one camera inside to the main floor while another got stuck in the elevator on the way to the second. They moved out into the business world with a weekly series called "Richfield Success Story," clambering over uneven floors, around machinery, upstairs and downstairs in sawmills, factories, and offices, dragging their cables behind them. When they went to Tacoma to cover crime hearings on prostitution and racketeering—one of the first stations to televise in court—they created a sensation in days when such controversial activities went unmentioned. For the McCarthy hearings in 1952, they had a driver meet the plane carrying kinnies from Washington, D.C., to whisk them to the station in time for late-night telecasts. From a rowboat in choppy waters, a small, seasick team filmed Florence Chadwick's attempted swim across the Strait of Juan de Fuca, then rowed the results to a barge from which it was taken by helicopter to be developed and shown that night. Aboard a troop ship returning from Korea, they "scooped" the usually filmed news by originating live pictures of soldiers returning home.

Dorothy relished the activity and was unafraid of controversy, provided that the program content was solid and constructive. She found the Tacoma hearings "very dramatic . . . I believe showing people how that sort of investigation is done in this country may be one of the greatest arguments against Communism," she noted in her diary. She worried about canceling children's programs in order to air the hearings, but insisted, "We must be fair to those who have been accused, so that they may have a chance to clear themselves before the same audience." She authorized a program on the atomic bomb, which according to her diary, she found "very moving," but also required that it be followed by a panel discussion of civic, religious, and education leaders "to suggest concrete action." When Senator Joseph McCarthy came to town in 1952 to speak for a political candidate, she insisted that Senator Magnuson be present to speak also and was delighted when the station's attorney, Dick Riddell, refused at the last moment to allow McCarthy on the air because his speech was defamatory to an individual. Knowing that this might happen and that the demagogue would raise unshirted hell, she monitored the "non-program" at home and laughed when, instead of McCarthy, a black musician appeared on the screen playing "Nobody Knows the Trouble I've Seen." Although McCarthy threatened to shut the station down, nothing ever came of it—except newspaper stories nationwide profiling the little Northwest station that had stood up to the powerful senator from Wisconsin. Later in the 1950s, when the station produced its first documentaries (among the first television documentaries ever done) on Seattle's port activities and Eastern Washington's migrant workers, she was immensely proud of the results. Her gamble on sending pictures through the air was paying off, winning a reputation for bold, innovative, break-through broadcasting.

Not surprisingly, any program that could have the word "king" in front of it, did. "King's Reign" featured wrestling (which Dorothy detested); "King's Ransom" was a quiz show; and "King's Queen" was a popular cooking show hosted by Bea Donovan, a kindly cuisinière who shared her finished products with the crew. Within two years of its purchase, the station was broadcasting from 8 A.M. to 10 P.M., with six live half-hour programs daily, produced back-to-back.

Everything that could go wrong did. Live television was a comedy of errors, a makeshift, make-do operation with gaffes and goofs of every kind. Tubes, generators, cameras, and cables failed regularly. Time rolled over scheduled limits—what few sponsors there were got good value for their money as commercials extended two or three minutes because products, as if by diabolical design, refused to function. Lawnmowers and sanding machines wouldn't start or wouldn't stop; biscuits exploded, cooking sauces caught fire, and fake snowflakes stuck in singers' throats. On one program, a Chinese cook flavored his culinary masterpiece with "penis oil." On another, a German weightlifter bent over to pick up his bar at the very moment an English bulldog waiting on the sidelines passed wind. There were frequent and long seconds of silence as the crew, convulsed with laughter, tried to regain control and continue.

Everyone—on and off camera—had to be adaptable during those early years. Employees learned to push the grand piano back and forth quickly between the two studios rented shortly after Dorothy's purchase, while the loud thumps from a fishing supply factory overhead kept newsmen shouting and live program schedules shifting to deal with the din. Engineers, in anticipation of on-the-spot repairs, carried tubes, tape, and spare parts in their pockets; floor directors also doubled as performers and swept the floors. Cameramen, rather than bouncing over the cable strewn across the floor, perfected a whiplash technique of cable-flipping that was so fast that viewers barely noticed a split-second blur across the screen every now and then. Most shows were unrehearsed and scripts appeared only seconds before air time. No one seemed to mind the eighteen-hour days. Without complaint, they got up at dawn to televise Easter sunrise services and stayed up until midnight when there was an eclipse of the moon, while Schulman shouted, "Cue the sun" and "Cue the moon."

"Just keep talking," was the performer's watchword. Actress Ruth Prins didn't blink an eye when a robber pursued by police ran onto the set of her popular children's program, "Wunda Wunda," but her voice did go up an octave or so when, on another show, the tame lion sitting beside her began to munch softly on her arm, removing her sleeve in the process. Nor did floor director Jack Fearey complain when he received mind-boggling weekly "menus" for a program called "Community Workshop," hosted by Elizabeth Wright Evans. "Betty Evans would call and say, 'Let's see . . . We're going to have a trained seal and two dogs and an arrow shooting contest and, oh, I forgot, the Seattle Symphony will show up too . . . ' They were wild programs that didn't always make sense, but there wasn't anybody worth mentioning in Seattle who wasn't on the air."

"Improvise" was another watchword. For close-up shots of unobtainable scenes, objects, or people, cameramen focused on magazine photos and performers searched their closets at home for costumes and props. For one scene that required an overhead shot, Schulman brought in his bedroom mirror, hung it over the set, and shot the scene into the mirror from a camera on the floor. When the first Gold Cup hydroplane races ran on Lake Washington, two cameramen, Earl Thoms and Al Smith, invented a 100-inch lens that caught close-ups of the drivers as they sped by. Considered a valuable innovation for its time, the lens was later loaned to the networks for use in similar events. "We had no precedent, no patterns to go by," recalled one of the early staffers. "We were just running from moment to moment, learning as we raced along and all growing together." They were making television history.

Dorothy's favorite among these improvisatory efforts was a program called "March On," a military extravaganza aired every week. "When a colonel came over from Fort Lewis asking to make some short announcements on the air," she remembered, "Lee jumped at the chance to use the musicians and singers in the service. He told the colonel to put up a notice for talent and then produced a full hour-long weekly show with all kinds of different numbers and a cast of about seventy-five people, all in costume. There'd be a snow scene for Christmas with a lieutenant up on a ladder by the lights, shaking cornflakes down on a corporal singing Christmas songs. They wrote their own music and it was tremendously popular."

It didn't keep the coffers filled, however, and the money that fueled all facets of Dorothy's life was fast pouring away. The Coliseum Theater needed remodeling, radio was just barely holding its own, and television was going to require expensive upgrading. A review of her finances sent her home with a headache and a note that said, "Awfully low in my mind." Dorothy attacked the problem head-on in January 1950, a time when she had usually traveled south for the sun in southern California. At her desk in the 1411 Building, she sharpened her pencil and began to cut expenses, arguing with Fred about new equipment and with Henry about unnecessary personnel. Working through a maze of figures that she came to know very well, and worrying until late each night, she saw that the "losses for a while" she had anticipated were amounting to about $20,000 per month for television alone within the first few months and would continue for another year. Her diary reflected a depressed state of mind, with entries like, "Stayed awake all night in a deep pit of fear and discouragement . . . Couldn't sleep—how did I walk deliberately into such a financial mess . . . The picture is awfully black—I mean red." To tide herself over, and using Stimson Realty Company as collateral, she took out a line of credit for $200,000 from her friends at Pacific National Bank. Then she prepared to travel east to firm up contracts for the future.

ON HER FIRST BUSINESS TRIP TO NEW YORK AS A TELEVISION executive, Dorothy was surprised to learn that the FCC freeze was working in her favor. There she and Haley visited the heads of all four networks and came away greatly encouraged. Everyone wanted KING-TV to take their programs— NBC, CBS, ABC, and Dumont. Meanwhile, Henry Owen reported from Seattle that "business was growing fast." As her plane left New York a few days later, she drifted homeward on a high of her own making. She had always believed that AM radio was the backbone of broadcasting, the proven money-maker, and that television would never be so reliable, but now she wasn't so sure. From this vantage point, she wrote, "Think I've been underestimating our advantage in having TV—maybe its relative importance to AM is much greater than I had thought."

The FCC freeze that might have lasted a month lasted forty-five months— during which Dorothy Bullitt had the only show in town. She carried all four networks and, at the same time, managed to honor her commitment to local programming. "It was wonderful! We made hay! We took everybody's money— all of the networks. We sold everything—the station's signature, the time of day, even the test pattern. We had a job to keep them all happy because they fought for every minute of time. We didn't know what programs to put on between the networks; we didn't have much, but we sold it all. Everyone had said there wouldn't be any receiving sets, but people bought sets like crazy—we had surveys to tell how many were sold each week. About halfway into the freeze, the competition began to have fits. They were furious! For almost three years, we blew our horn full tilt. We raked in the money, and that's what saved us." A little over a year later, there were 38,000 sets in Seattle, all tuned to KING-TV, and from then on the numbers increased exponentially.

Dorothy's life had by now become a baroque juggling act, balancing broadcasting with board activities, civic committees, family, and friends. Except for her real estate activities, which she had turned over to her son, she managed to keep her place on six boards and, during the 1950s, added two more—the Seattle Library Board and the University of Washington Board of Regents. Her health suffered with this gruelling schedule. "My head spins and doesn't work," she complained repeatedly about the whirlwind of activity. "I am ill-tempered on general principles." From time to time, she would take to her bed with a headache or a cold, probably more from exhaustion. For social life, she attended dinner parties and plays but preferred a congenial mint julep with Frances and Henry Owen followed by a game of canasta. "I know cards are stupid," she wrote in her diary, "but I enjoy the people I play with and I can't keep my mind on a book, don't want to go out, and can't go to sleep early." For relaxation she spent hours at mindless chores—raking leaves, sanding tables, cleaning out drawers and cupboards, rearranging stationery and the endless supplies of pencils, tape, pens, and labels that she loved to use—as if to put order in her life and quiet the chaos in her head.

At work her mind was in constant motion. Her techniques were subtle, so it took time for her managers to interpret her tactics. She ruled by indirection. Some did not catch on, such as a secretary who approached Harriet Bullitt at KING one day, saying, "Harriet, I think your mother just fired me, but, you know, I'm not sure." After reviewing the conversation, Dorothy's youngest, who was as frank as her mother was indirect, replied, "Yes, she fired you all right." One who caught on fast was Ancil Payne, who became CEO of King Broadcasting during the 1970s and 1980s. "Dorothy Bullitt was a complex person with her own ideas and various indirect ways of expressing them and damn few could read her very well," he observed. "First of all, she didn't share all she knew. She was, well, devious in her approach. In conversation she never got to the subject right away. There was always a certain amount of small talk, and in time I got to know that the third thing she brought up was what she really wanted to discuss." Payne, who was particularly amused by this, was capable of the same tactic. "She also used all of the feminine devices. She could turn on tears, dab her eyes, and be sentimental to get what she wanted. She put a lot of corn out there in the trap, so the chickens would come and fall in," he said. "For instance, I hadn't been with the company very long before I realized that when Mrs. B. said 'yes' she generally meant 'no' and vice-versa. It was a management technique—if you came in with a proposal to her, she not only asked questions, she left you in the position of defending your case, and in the process, you realized that you also carried the obligation for the decision. She'd conclude with, 'If you believe that's what we should do, then we'll do it.' But the real message was, 'Young man, this is *your* decision and it had better turn out well.' It was done with finesse, very skillfully, and with great care, and it was one of many ways in which she got the very best from her employees. Mrs. Bullitt rarely played her hand openly—she had a full deck, you just didn't know where it was!"

She spoke in stories and parables, Payne recalled. In 1959, after she had bought KGW in Portland, she summoned him into her office one day to ask why they were buying a set of chains for the news wagon in Portland. He explained that, although it didn't often snow there, the newsmen did have to go up into the mountains. She replied, "Yes, I'm aware of that, but my concern is that last summer when I was down there I was going through the carpenter's shop and there was a set of chains hanging on the door. Why can't they be used?" "It wasn't so much the chains we were discussing," Payne continued. "Basically, she was saying, 'Keep your eyes open and know what's going on in the company. Be observant, and if there are chains in the back room, you should know about it.' "

Dorothy also knew exactly what she wanted from her board. She conducted each meeting as though she were directing a play, with various vice-presidents as actors in supporting roles. The plot—the action to be taken—was always planned in advance. She did not like surprises. "Mother never called a meeting without having made all of her decisions in advance," daughter Patsy recalled. "She hated new ideas or items sprung on her unexpectedly." When the curtain went up, each actor recited his lines, well aware of who was really in charge behind the scenes. As a performer, Dorothy underplayed her part perfectly, shying away from center stage as expertly as she avoided the spotlight on other occasions. At the head of the big boardroom table, she sat quietly, toying with a pencil, while subtly steering decisions her own way, guiding the discussion through the executives who appeared to be at the controls. Attorney Richard Riddell, the only person who served on King Broadcasting's board throughout the company's history, remembered those meetings well. "One of the things I enjoyed tremendously about her was the way she managed the men who worked for her," he said with a broad smile. "She'd be at a board meeting with an idea about something she wanted done. Either she'd raise a question or somehow the subject would come up for discussion. First, she'd turn to Henry Owen and say, 'What do you think about that, Henry?' Henry would speak his piece, and then she'd turn to Otto Brandt and he'd have his say. Then she'd kind of go around the table and wait quite a little while until someone came up with the essence of her own conclusion. At that point, instead of saying, 'That's what *I* think,' she'd raise her eyebrows and acknowledge that, 'Hmm, that makes some sense . . . ,' as though it were a brand-new concept to her! She was such a smart fox—she was just waiting for some man to make the right pitch and then to very smoothly have it accepted by everybody. Her greatest ability was in managing people—plus an ability to see through a brick wall."

Ego gratification was not her goal at these meetings. She didn't have the tolerance for it; besides, she was in control, so why waste time on such silly behavior? Squabbling, humiliating others, or righteous indignation didn't belong in her boardroom; nor did self-congratulation, conspiratorial winks with favorites, or claiming the superiority of her ideas. "I never saw her dress anybody down, ever," Riddell observed. "I'm sure there were times when she had strong exception to things being done or said, but she didn't criticize anyone in the presence of others." Dorothy Bullitt's goal was larger and really quite simple: to get done what she wanted done in the smoothest possible way. At board meetings, the stage was set, the show went on, and everyone knew his role down to the last nod, smile, and yea vote.

In the office, she didn't just drift through the halls, dispensing charm like Lady Bountiful. She worked as hard, if not harder, than her personnel. During these early years, she managed with a zoom lens, keeping a distant eye on her long-range goals, but focusing close-up on the day-to-day groundwork necessary for success in this new arena. Over the next years, she became intimately familiar with FCC forms and regulations, program and union contracts, audience measurements, studio leases, cash flow sheets, network rate structures, operating breakdowns, tax relief, deferred charges, and, of course, the budgeting process ("am determined to establish tight controls"), for which she sat at her desk, meticulously evaluating expenses one at a time. It was full-time hands-on work. She scrutinized everything from amplifiers to advertising sponsors, approved everything down to the new studio drapes, and drove to the freight yards to witness the arrival of the new antenna. At night from the sunroom at her brick house on Galer Street, she monitored the end product—a practice that continued until the end of her days. With the television set going full tilt, she and Gloria kept one eye on the screen during cocktails and dinner. Mispronunciations and bad grammar were particularly offensive. She noted each one on a slip of paper, including date, time, and program. "12 Noon— announcer said Franch-<u>ote</u> Tone, instead of Franch-<u>o</u>! . . . Jan 29—Community Workshop—introduced by man's voice off-screen, 'Your <u>host</u> Betty Evans'— why not hostess? . . . Weekend digest, Sun eve—the <u>eye</u>talian floods—Francis of Assissy—he admini<u>strates</u> well?? . . . 6:32 TV News—Repungent—what I think he meant was 'repugnant' . . . Tues Theater Revue—Someone said, 'No bars hold' instead of no holds barred! . . . Friday 2:15—State of Wash was formerly land of Al-bye-own—should be Al-bee-on!"

Hundreds of these notes were found among her papers, some more quirky than others. When she noted that a host on a local quiz show had mistakenly credited Victor Hugo with writing the operetta *Naughty Marietta* when it should have been Victor Herbert, Dorothy added indignantly, "Is this the same man who referred to the "planet *Juniper?*" Malapropisms such as "There's a movement underfoot," mispronunciations like "inTEgral" rather than "INtegral," and just plain wrongisms like "spontinuity," "interduce," "heart rendering," or "nucular" were noted just as mercilessly as Mrs. Dow of Dorothy's days at Briarcliff might have done. This habit held throughout Dorothy's life. Years later, when her granddaughter Wenda became interested in broadcasting, Dorothy advised her that the two most important subjects she could study would be Latin and poetry, Latin for learning the derivations of words, and poetry because "that was where you really learned to use language."

Above all, Dorothy kept a keen eye on expenses and what she described as the "bottom right-hand corner." When the budget got out of line or monthly accountings began to look skimpy, she was quick to get out her pencil. She was also quick to confer with her field marshall, Henry Owen, who in turn did the dirty business of disciplining whoever was at fault. "No one was ever mad at Dorothy Bullitt," Ruth Prins remembered. "She always put up a straw man who took the blame." Certain expenses aroused her suspicion. She particularly hated to pay high fees for fancy packaging, salesmen's lunches, or such vague activities as "public relations." James Neidigh, one of the station's first salesmen, remembered a trip he took from New York to Seattle. While waiting for his plane, he noticed that Mrs. Bullitt was also in line as a passenger. Thinking she might sit next to him en route, he chose a double seat in first class and was surprised to see her pass on by into the coach section. He knew he'd hear about it on Monday morning and he did. When she bought the Baron Building—a former furniture store on Aurora Avenue that would serve as King Broadcasting Company headquarters for many years—Dorothy privately estimated the remodeling expenses at about $300,000 and then warned her top people to stay within those limits. "I outlined our policy of preserving cash and told them they could have $250,000 for remodeling and equipment, moving, and installing, including phones and carpets," she noted. "This for their own protection and looking to lean years ahead. Long meeting—long faces—they took it very well." And she took the remodeling plans apart, sending down a long list of questions and comments such as, "Who gave Hunter a sofa? Ask them please not to specify sofas for everybody . . . Pantry—why do we need sink? If it's going to cost a lot, leave it out . . . Why three hot plates for kitchen in board-room? Don't think we need but two . . . Why size of toilets reduced? . . . Vestibule—Why all the fancy around the columns? Storage—don't fir around columns. Leave room unfinished except for vinyl floor covering." This was micromanaging with a vengeance.

Just as at The Highlands, nothing was to be wasted. Stories of her penurious ways became legion. To paint the refurbished office building, she bought surplus paint from the Bremerton shipyard. It was battleship blue-gray, known around the station as "Bullitt blue," Dorothy's favorite color. Another Bullitt-blue item, the Ford she drove well past its prime, was the oldest car in the company parking lot for many years.

She liked to have equipment used and re-used, a generational legacy from her parents and Ohata, the thrifty manager of the Bullitt machines and ménage. "How about a program called, 'Put By' to illustrate and dramatize various kinds and ways to save?" she wrote in her notes. She sat in her office wearing "cuffs" from fruit wrappers to protect her silk blouse; she steamed and re-used uncan-celled stamps off envelopes, and wrote with pencils shaved down to the nubs. She sent word down to the station engineers to replace nothing unless it was unfixable and, when attending the NAB meetings, to avoid the hotel basement lest they be tempted to buy the new equipment exhibited there. When she heard that the bald eagle, America's national symbol, was a scavenger that often ate garbage at dumps in Alaska, she considered this, then cocked an eagle eye of her own and barked, "What's *wrong* with eating garbage? Someone has to do it—it should be used!"

Once Dorothy fixed on a wasteful detail, there was no arguing with her. Flapping her hands in her pockets, she appeared in Ancil Payne's office in the 1970s to ask, "Who takes care of the typewriters?" "It was a rhetorical question," Payne said, "because she already knew who had done that since year one." "Well," she sniffed. "There's a typewriter on the closet floor in the Radio Divi-sion. It may not be any good, but there's no reason to have it there. And there's a radio that could be sold even if we only get ten dollars for it—it should be put to use." On another occasion, examining a bill for leather briefcases, she demanded to know why such a purchase had been authorized. When Henry Owen explained that the salesmen needed them for their presentations, she answered, "Well, the company should never pay for something like this. They should have their own." When Henry said they simply didn't, she replied that, rather than embarrass the men, she would pay for them personally. Even as late as 1980, when decorators were furnishing her new $18 million King Broad-casting corporate offices, she complained that they were making her buy new "fancy" filing cabinets. "What's wrong with my old ones?" she asked indignantly, pointing to two ancient steel strongholds that she had covered years before with fake wood contact paper, now peeling. "Look," she said, pulling out the drawers, "they work perfectly well. I don't *need* anything new."

Although quirky about spending for small items, Dorothy spent freely on things that counted—good managers and good equipment. In the 1950s, as Lee Schulman described it, "Television technology was changing by the square root of the previous day." Since New York was the center of these activities, she brought New York to Seattle by hiring two men who became valuable professional aides—James Middlebrooks, an engineer from ABC who was thoroughly familiar with the technical innovations appearing daily, and Otto Brandt, the capable ABC vice-president who had tried to help her with a radio affiliation in 1949. When Andy Haley asked her why she had hired someone who had refused her an affiliation, she replied, "Yes, he turned me down, but he was very nice about it." Besides, Brandt had not refused her, the president of ABC had; Brandt had been loyal and she was rewarding him.

Once hired, Brandt made the mistake of saying, "Well, now you can stay home and play bridge and not be bothered with this nasty business any further." Whereupon his new boss made it clear in no uncertain terms that she would do nothing of the sort. Dorothy described Otto Brandt as "Prussian," and over the many years that he worked for her they clashed every now and then, particularly when he made decisions without her knowledge or tried to supplant her in any way. Found among her papers was a draft of a memo to him on one such occasion, written in an imperious tone that recalls Dorothy's mother, dressing down her rebellious daughter. Whether she sent it or not, is not known.

Otto:

Your reports to me have been unsatisfactory. Items have been dropped casually—in a corridor, at the coffee counter, at a cocktail party, permitting you to say, "Why, I told you about that."

From now on I should like to have thorough and unbiased reports made in the office during normal office hours. Incomplete disclosure can become an art that is most insidious, and I have sometimes found that I have been told of an incident or a situation, but not *all* of it . . . I also constantly receive the impression that you stand between me and other members of the staff—not as an interpreter of my wishes and standards—but as their protector from me.

Do you want to be the best manager in the country—which you can be—or do you want the staff who work with you to think you're just a "dandy fella?"

Think hard and be honest with yourself and you will recognize that what I am saying is true—and these qualities will stand in your way until you can change your attitude and look at your responsibility to me and to the other stockholders that I represent from a different angle.

She knew he could take it. Dorothy noted more than once in her journal, "Otto's German nature will accept strong talk." As her new broadcasting general manager, he brought some East Coast know-how, status, and sophistication to the new station, along with a certain authoritarian manner which, as long as it wasn't directed against her, suited Dorothy just fine.

With Middlebrooks and Brandt on board, Dorothy's station got the jump on industry changes. When the phone company was preparing to bring in cable—which meant live network hook-up to Seattle—Dorothy, Brandt, and Schulman "marched down there" to convince top phone company officials to bring cable in (via a multi-hop microwave circuit) before the political conventions of 1952. Thanks to Schulman's persistence ("I sat there breathless while he practically gave away the station, engineers and all!"), cable arrived earlier than scheduled, bringing on-the-spot coverage of the convention not only to Seattle viewers, but to Portlanders who, although they had no television station of their own, flocked to the Civic Auditorium to see (via closed circuit relay from Seattle) Eisenhower nominated for the presidency.

Thanks to the savvy and connections of Jim Middlebrooks, Dorothy learned about the intricacies of color technology. In 1954, at Middlebrooks's urging, she and Henry and Frances Owen went to the Kodak Corporation to acquaint themselves with this new development. As they drove through the snow to see the color labs in Syracuse, New York, Dorothy recalled, "I told them that no part of this country was as beautiful as ours and that KING should have the first tube of color to show it." Not many months after that, KING televised the first color program west of the Rocky Mountains.

There were other innovations. In 1956, she and Middlebrooks met at the NAB meeting in Chicago to preview a mind-boggling new invention—videotape. "The night before the convention opened, we were snuck into the Ampex suite in the hotel and we saw videotape," Lee Schulman remembered with awe still in his voice. "None of us believed what we were looking at. We couldn't foresee such a thing existing. It astounded Mrs. Bullitt, who right then and there turned to Otto Brandt and said, 'Buy it.' " KING was the first independent television station to own a videotape machine.

Although all sets in Seattle were now tuned to her station and the money was coming in, Dorothy knew that the station faced financial uncertainty when the FCC freeze was lifted. At that time, she guessed, the networks would probably return to their radio affiliates and she would still be paying on the huge debts incurred from buying new transmitters, towers, and other equipment. This was confirmed when she tested the market. Meanwhile, the bills poured in—for equipment, sales commissions, and promotion costs, for expenses she had never incurred in real estate. "My cash funds are very low," she noted in her diary. She raised some cash by selling two pieces of her mother's jewelry, a pearl-and-diamond collar and a platinum bracelet studded with forty diamonds. She began to think about selling radio, television, or both. She put out the word among broadcasters and went to Emma's brother, Cebert Baillargeon, to see about "possible interest among Catholics for AM purchase." Although there were a number of offers, no one came up with enough. "Don't know what to do," she wrote in her diary. "I can't seem to give it away." Unsure, she waited. In May 1950, attending NAB meetings in Chicago and sales meetings in New York City, she suffered a mild heart attack and was hospitalized for a week. However, this sickness seemed to be only a small annoyance in contrast to her worries over financial health.

Then, within a few months, the situation began to take care of itself. As television set sales increased rapidly, so did advertising. At the end of 1950, television brought in its first profit of $72,000; in 1951 it increased to $419,000 and attracted the investor she was seeking. "A man named Tom Brooks contacted me on behalf of the Hearst Corporation to buy the company," Dorothy recounted. "I had mixed feelings. I didn't want to let it go, but I didn't have any more money and I was getting head over heels in debt. I was having to sell prime real estate to take care of the broadcasting debts, and I had to consider it. I told him I'd think about it. I had known for years that most respected businessmen looked down their noses at the sight of Hearst. He and his people had a reputation for being dirty newspapermen, printing all of the scandals. But when I met with them I liked them. Mr. Brooks, who was head of their broadcasting operations, was very much a gentleman, never fresh. He kept repeating that Mr. Hearst never invested more than 10 percent or else he wanted the whole thing. I said, 'Try 25 percent if you want, otherwise I don't want to sell it at all.' They wanted to put two men on the board and I said, 'Fine. We need their counsel and experience.' Finally I went east to meet the president of the company, who was very pleasant and shrewd. I brought our figures and, in looking them over, they were puzzled by a huge debt of $360,000 owed to one stockholder and asked me who it was. I said, 'Me,' and for some reason they thought that was awfully funny. Then, just as our deal was closing, they asked to come out to see our radio tower because it had been on our books for only $22,000. So Mr. Brooks and an engineer went over to Vashon Island where the tower was and came back laughing, saying, 'We wanted to see it because it was valued so low on your books that we thought you might be using trees!' Then they left with an option to buy, but just before everything was finalized Mr. Brooks dropped dead of heart failure. My heart went into my boots! He was the only friend I had made at Hearst and what would become of me? I wasn't sure, although I had been treated as nothing but the greatest person in the world and they recognized me, I think, as honest but kind of stupid. Anyway, when the president of the company finally called, he said it was up to me if I still wanted to complete the sale, but that if I had any qualms they would tear up the option. I said, 'Let it go through,' and breathed a great sigh of relief." The Hearst Corporation paid $375,000 for 2,500 shares, one-fourth of King Broadcasting Company.

The financial boost from Hearst helped Dorothy prepare for the lifting of the freeze. More important, it gave her support and assurance that she was not taking on the responsibility alone. Anticipating the competition, Dorothy authorized an application to increase the power of the television station to 100 kilowatts.

A network affiliation still remained the major obstacle. She went after one using all of her intuition, female wiles, and ability to judge character in the process. To wrest CBS away from KIRO, she became the confidante of Saul Haas's wife, Dee, and even hired KIRO employees at KING in order to know what was going on at that station—all to no avail: CBS told her they would return to their radio affiliate. NBC, her preference because of its quality programming and powerful position in broadcasting, also seemed disposed to revert to its affiliate, KOMO, especially because of the friendship between KOMO owner O. D. Fisher and RCA board chairman David Sarnoff. As for ABC, Dorothy delayed trying to secure what she described as the "least desirable, not much of a network" affiliation. ABC's merger with Paramount Studios gave its programs a "show biz" quality that Dorothy found offensive.

The FCC's freeze on new television stations was lifted on July 1, 1952. In the network shakedown that resulted, Dorothy learned some lessons. "It was funny, really," she remembered. "The first new station to be built was Channel 11 in Tacoma, owned by Frank Baker. He owned the *Tacoma News Tribune* and one day he called and said, 'What do you know, now I've got a television station. I don't know what to do with it—I'm coming over.' So I got Otto and Henry, and the three of us advised him about where to go for equipment and all sorts of other things. Then he said, 'I suppose the best network to try for would be Dumont because the others are waiting to return to their radio stations,' and we agreed sagely that it would probably be best. So he left and we assumed he was going to apply for Dumont but it wasn't very long before CBS did an about face and announced that they were moving to Channel 11! Can you imagine? We laughed about that for a long time, for having been so helpful to Frank Baker about how to do things and the first thing he did was to steal one of our best networks! We had advised him just a little too well." As for NBC, it went to KOMO, as feared. Dorothy was left with ABC radio and television, the "not much of a network" she had downplayed all along. By that time, she was grateful to have it because King Broadcasting's profits took a plunge. This meant a loss of $500,000 in gross advertiser billings in the first year after the freeze, but the loss was cushioned by the association of the Hearst Corporation, the affiliation of ABC, and several years' worth of contacts in the community and in the industry. Within a short time, she had secured a solid position in broadcasting.

AS TELEVISION GAINED POPULARITY IN THE 1950S, ETHICAL standards in programming and advertising became an issue for broadcasters and producers. Low-cut gowns and high-cut bathing suits, ads for liquor and personal hygiene products, programs sprinkled with "hells and damns" and depicting divorce and violence appeared nightly in American homes, raising cries of concern from parents and other affronted viewers. Some sort of controls were needed to regulate "taste" over the airwaves. Accordingly, in March 1952, the NAB instituted a five-member board to regulate and monitor standards for good television practices. The purpose of the National Association of Broadcasters Code Board was to establish guidelines that member stations could use in determining what was acceptable broadcasting. Stations were not bound to conform, but knew that when they flashed the board's "Seal of Good Practice" on the screen it would inspire viewer confidence. The guidelines set high ideals for programming: the advancement of education and culture, responsibility to children and community, standards for accuracy and fairness in political, religious, and other news events. They also dealt with standards in commercial advertising—its subject matter, methods, and length of presentation.

Dorothy was perfect for the job. She had already been monitoring her own station for a couple of years; now her ideals would reach a wider audience. "We met in D.C., sometimes every month, and were paid only for our travel. We discussed all sorts of things very seriously, from fair practices in elections to accuracy in the news to programs about bumps on the head, you know—phrenology. We were awfully loose, no one with a hammer calling us to order. And there was a lot of talk about policy decisions for advertising—where ads should go, how long they should be. We'd review products and the wording of ads. We were all revolted at hemorrhoid ads, for instance, and it became such a

Dorothy was the only woman member of the National Association of Broadcasters Code Board in the 1950s.

big deal that the president of the advertising company came down to justify why they needed to put them on television, shouting 'It's our *business;* there's nothing wrong with having hemorrhoids!' "

For eight years, between 1952 and 1956, and again between 1959 and 1963, Dorothy and other members of the NAB Code Board met to discuss truth, decency, and reasonableness in television, to balance the creative against the profane, obscene, and vulgar, trying to keep the bathroom—with its laxatives, deodorants, depilatories, and toilet paper—from dominating the American living room and the dinner hour. Dorothy flew home after these meetings with written reminders to put into further practice what she had already been preaching. "Someone with taste, understanding, and good judgment should monitor all KING programs and make full report on violations," her notes proclaimed. She sent out word that all movies should be previewed for appropriate costuming, and KING programmers spent their evenings at home, editing films two at a time, on the lookout for what they labeled "tits and togas." From the command post of her sunroom, Dorothy monitored television every evening, alert to infractions of good taste and ready to pick up the phone when they occurred. She was particularly suspicious of ABC's offerings and either canceled them or kept a running record when the subject matter offended her. One affiliate show called "Nothing but the Best," received the notation, "Low-cut gown—cleavage problem, network says it is lighting—Ha!" In another, she noticed that "the sunburn line stops and shows below the bathing suit mark." To the annoyance of ABC, she had murder mysteries rescheduled for later hours so that children couldn't watch them.

Michael Bader, a young attorney in Andy Haley's law firm during those days, remembered the importance of the code board and Dorothy Bullitt's role on it. "The code board wasn't composed of big-winded businessmen who had sold more television time than anyone else—those people weren't chosen," he said. "It was made up of the most significant figures in the ethics of the business, people with standards. Dorothy Bullitt, as one of them, was largely responsible for the moral upbringing of our world as it was developing under television. She was, even then, regarded as a person of exceedingly high standards, particularly in the areas of children's television, news, and public affairs. She was someone who was doing more than making a ton of money off this newly lucrative medium."

Educational television was also of prime importance to Dorothy Bullitt. In 1951 she initiated the first regular education program in the region. Presented every weekday, "King's Bench" was a cooperative effort between the station and several institutions to produce panel discussions on current problems. She carried her zeal for education to meetings with fellow broadcasters, but the topic usually fell on deaf and more commercially minded ears. At the FCC, she was relieved to meet someone who shared her interest in noncommercial television. "She was a Russian Jewess by the name of Frieda Hennock, a lawyer, who was the only woman among the FCC commissioners. When I heard that during the freeze this woman was fighting to set aside noncommercial channels for education, I went to her and said, 'I think you're in there because there should be a grid of educational stations across the country.' As the allocation of frequencies proceeded, Frieda Hennock began to put 'stars' [to indicate prospective educational channels] at different locations. I stuck right with her and the men hated both of us because they wanted everything commercial. But she held on like a puppy to a root, threatening hell and high water, and I put up what little fight I could, though I didn't have much to spare. I was so green that at one big broadcasters meeting I sat right down in front—here was I, trying to learn— and when the chairman asked how many were in favor of educational stations, I jumped up and looked around and no one else was standing! I was fool enough to do that—it wasn't at all to my advantage. The commercial broadcasters regarded me as a horrible renegade, but I just believed in it. Unknown to me, that incident gave me a sort of prominence among them. From then on, they wanted to know what 'that woman'—me—would stand up for."

Among the 242 channels reserved for education after the freeze, Seattle was assigned Channel 9—a VHF frequency with better coverage characteristics than the UHF channels set aside for many other cities. Dorothy was delighted at the opportunity but disappointed that no application to build a station was forthcoming. In her own determined way, she set about in 1953 to secure an educational channel for the city before it was reassigned by default to a commercial broadcaster (a competitor that she definitely did not want). "When our television station was upgraded in frequency," she recalled, "we were left with this little transmitter and a lot of equipment built for very low power. We could have sold it, heaven knows—no one was manufacturing that sort of equipment so soon after the freeze, and we needed the profit—but, since I had taken a part in promoting educational TV, I thought, 'Now, it's my turn to put my pocketbook where my mouth is.' I wrote the University of Washington, saying I'd like to give them a transmitter and equipment so that they could start a television station. They would have to build their own tower, I told them, but we would give them the other things they would need—and it was worth quite a piece in dollars [$182,000]. Since Channel 9 was just sitting there with no one applying for it, I thought this might get things started."

Dorothy's generosity fell on deaf ears. "I took the proposal to an English professor at the university—why I don't know, except that I had heard him read poetry on radio and I thought he'd be pleased with it. He read it and said he had no authority to accept this and gave it back to me. He did nothing but throw cold water on the idea. Then I tried to get to the president but there was an interim president at the time who wasn't very friendly. I was getting nowhere until I went to Charles Frankland, president of Pacific National Bank where I was on the board, [who] was also vice-president of the Board of Regents at the University. He went with me but we had the devil's own time trying to make them accept it. I was very badly treated. I was asked very coldly, 'What kind of a tax dodge is this?' The professors scorned television as a terrible gadget that wasn't going to last; they didn't believe you could learn by looking at pictures and wouldn't allow sets in their homes. They couldn't have been more snooty about the whole thing. Finally, after going to Governor Langlie, we got it accepted. The people from the School of Engineering knew its worth and value and were very excited. They were great friends. They took it, and now they have a tower and they've always used it and been glad to have it." Thirty-five years later, Dorothy's memories of the whole episode were touched with irony. "How funny that seems now to be told that you couldn't learn by looking at pictures," she said, shaking her head sadly. "Now it's coming to a point where it's the only way people will learn. It was as deflating as anything to be greeted with suspicion like that, but I didn't see how the University of Washington would get started unless we gave them a push of some kind."

Broadcasting was a murderous and bloody business!
I was just leaping over obstacles and running on
instinct as fast as I could.

11 RUNNING WHILE OTHERS SLEEP

1952–1959

NO SOONER HAD DOROTHY STABILIZED HER STATIONS financially, than another opportunity arose. As the freeze was about to be lifted in 1952, Andy Haley suggested that she bid for a television station in Portland. There were two frequencies available and there would be a competitive hearing before the FCC. Dorothy thought it over in characteristic and strategic style, listing her reasons for and against. A Portland project would divert her attention and resources from Seattle at a time when she should be harboring them to meet the competition there, and she knew she had to prepare to finance the technical developments (color television was advancing rapidly) about to appear in the industry. "Industry is new and highly technical," she wrote in her research notes. "Any business whose investment depends on findings of scientists is subject to sudden change at this stage." On the plus side, Portland was close, a natural regional "fit," and she didn't have much to lose; if her bid was successful, she could always take in new stockholders to build a station and even sell it later at a profit. But the most important reason for acquiring another station, she knew, was that it could increase King Broadcasting's stature in her negotiations with the networks for affiliation. She decided to push for Portland.

When Dorothy called Andy Haley, he told her she needed investors from Portland, otherwise her absentee ownership would lessen her chances for a favorable outcome. The Portland investors would have to possess three qualities. "One was money," Dorothy remembered of his list. "Second was an adventurer's spirit—people who thought this was something intriguing and were willing to take the risk, and the third was that they be civic-minded, with a

247

record for having taken part in the community." She located five investors, who took a 40 percent interest: Henry Kuckenberg, Gordon Orput, Paul Murphy, Calder McCall, and Prescott Cookingham, their lawyer. At Ray Wright's law firm, Dorothy and Prescott Cookingham signed papers in separate offices, while the attorneys went back and forth with proposed changes. "As it turned out," Dorothy recalled, "one of the changes they wanted would backfire on those men later. It required that if I, as majority shareholder, ever sold my 60 percent, they would get the *same* price per share that the controlling interest would receive. Now, I knew that the controlling interest often received more per share but I said, 'OK, fine—we aren't buying just to sell out anyway.' But I added, 'If I decide to sell, then they must sell also.' Ray Wright said, 'Oh, they'll never do that.' I said, 'Well, if they don't, all right, but that's the only way I'll do it. I don't want to get myself in a bind. I don't want to get caught losing a possible sale because they wouldn't turn their interest loose.' Well, he came back and said, 'They did it! It's all signed.' That clause was very simple really, but it was to make a great split between us in the future." The group agreed that, if they won the application, they would contribute a total of $700,000 to build a television station, with $200,000 coming from the five Portland investors and $500,000 coming from Dorothy (via a loan from Seattle Trust and Savings Bank). Pioneer Broadcasting Corporation, as they called themselves, filed for Channel 8 two weeks after the freeze was lifted. Three other applicants also filed: a group of absentees who later dropped out; another called Portland Television, Inc. which, because it was local, carried some clout; and, most dreaded of all, the colossus of corporations in those days—Westinghouse. "They were huge," Dorothy said, spreading her arms many years later. "They were powerful and secure—their motto was, 'With Westinghouse you can be sure'—and they thought we were some little West Coast joke out there just waiting to be trounced. We were nothing! But we went ahead anyway, we had nothing to lose." Thus began what Dorothy called "The Battle for Portland," a David-and-Goliath contest of hearings and harangues that she described as "barbaric" because of the ruthless research into the character and background of every applicant and "historic" because it was one of the longest and bloodiest hearings in FCC history.

For the hearing in Washington, D.C., all applicants had to demonstrate that they could serve the public's, and particularly Portland's, needs, as required by the Federal Communications Commission. Upon the recommendation of the hearing examiner, the seven commissioners would then make a final ruling. In starting the application process, Dorothy recalled, she first had to show her intent to serve the community. "You had to show you had 'cased the joint' by questioning people about what they wanted and how a television station could help them. There was a little old woman down there who was a writer, a friend of Gloria's and very active in the Junior League. Her name was Helen Platt and she was a little bit of a thing, as frail as a feather. Gloria said, 'We'll get Helen—her people came to Oregon by wagon train and she knows everything that ever happened in Portland.' So we went down there and Helen put us in contact with all of the agencies in the state. We sent her out into the countryside in a borrowed car—she didn't have one—to talk with little bitty towns, asking what were their problems and what could television do for them. Helen would go into a little town and stop at the drugstore or the courthouse and say, 'Who's the mayor and where is he?' Someone would say, 'Well, his last name is Jones, and he's got an orchard over there.' So she'd plow through rough ground until she found the mayor who might be in the orchard or the pool hall, for that matter, and interview him. She went to every county in the state doing this thoroughly and writing it all down. Meanwhile Gloria and I went to the Children's Hospital, the YMCA, the Association for the Blind, and all of those places, and to the three top religious leaders of the city. The rabbi—I can't remember his name—we had to hunt him down. He wouldn't answer the phone and we couldn't find him at home. Finally we caught him coming down the steps of the synagogue and we jumped out of the car and got our interview. We wrote down each of these interviews and the things that people wanted—a drainage something here and a law keeping the freeway from going there or whatever—all those things that little towns need. It took us several trips to Portland and a few months to prepare."

When the application was finally assembled, it consisted of thirty sets of exhibits, weighing 350 pounds. They took it back to Washington for the hearing. A few weeks after arriving, Dorothy and Gloria sat in the lobby of Washington's Mayflower Hotel, where they beheld the enemy for the first time—a corporate behemoth in wedge-shaped formation—seven lawyers and engineers armed with briefcases and led by their president, all wearing, as Dorothy later exaggerated it, "their swallowtail coats and striped pants." As the Westinghouse warriors crossed the lobby, they noticed the opposition sitting primly on the sidelines—two little ladies in hats, one conservative dark straw and the other bright silk flowers. Without a glance in their direction, the men smiled in corporate unison at the thought of cornering such pitiful prey. As the hearing began, Thomas Kerr, of Portland Television, Inc., had a similar impression when the contingent from Pioneer Broadcasting appeared in court. "In came this big guy by the name of Haley, roaring along at the front of his team, and behind him came two women—one looked to be the president of the U.S.

Junior League and the other had to be the head of the American Garden Club," Kerr later told King Broadcasting CEO Ancil Payne. "I said to the fellow next to me, 'If we can't beat those two old women, we should take the night train out of here so we won't be seen.' " Years later, he remembered, "Before we finished, they had run our heads right through a pencil sharpener. I had never taken such a beating in my life. We actually did leave in the middle of the night."

As the hearing opened, each applicant's exhibits were distributed to all parties, an exercise that only focused further on the seeming superiority of Westinghouse. "Westinghouse had submitted bound books with imitation leather covers that announced their name in gold on the cover. It was a beautiful printing job, very expensive," Dorothy remembered. "Then came ours . . . and it was a disaster. There was something about the print that put everyone in tears, some sort of terrible ammonia thing that made the whole room begin to reek! I was terribly embarrassed and offered to reprint everything but the examiner said, between her tears, 'No, no, it will be all right.' "

Dorothy had done her homework before going to Washington, D.C., but now she was in school. For five months, she and Gloria worked constantly under the tutelage of Andy Haley who, at the end of each day, assigned them research projects to tear holes in Westinghouse's case and reinforce their own. If the women weren't attending the hearing, they were at the Mayflower or at Haley's office surrounded by piles of paper. There was scarcely time to grab a hamburger at the White Tower around the corner. Dorothy would often get up early and work all day, searching renewal applications of all Westinghouse radio and TV stations, comparing and analyzing program schedules nearly until midnight. Meanwhile, Westinghouse's supreme confidence eroded her optimism; she was intimidated and fearful of some setback they had not anticipated.

One day a dolly piled high with files arrived in the hearing room. "Andy took one look at that enormous amount of material and suddenly said, 'It's Hearst! They're going to take Hearst apart like a watch and discredit both of us!' " Dorothy had known that Hearst's reputation was controversial and that it could provide tremendous fodder for Westinghouse against her application. She had a hurried conference and decided to try to buy back Hearst's 25 percent interest. "This was going to be a tremendous gamble because it represented a major change in our corporate structure and you weren't supposed to make such changes in the middle of a trial," Dorothy recollected. "I phoned Mr. Huberth, the chairman of the Hearst board, and told him about the heap of evidence being brought against Hearst and asked if he would like to consider our purchasing back their stock. He said, 'Well, I think we should give it serious thought because we have other cases coming up and the display of all this material might hurt us in the future.' He suggested that I come to New York immediately, so Stim and I flew up then and there. We offered them a profit, but not a big one. They accepted graciously—I think we were in that office only about half an hour—and we were on our way with the stock certificates back to Washington."

At the opening of the next morning's session, when Andy Haley announced that Hearst had sold its shares back to King Broadcasting, the Westinghouse lawyer was furious. He demanded that King be thrown out of court. The hearing examiner told him to sit down and announced that she would make a judgment about the issue in a few days. Her ruling: "I find nothing in this transaction that is an infraction of the rules." It was a narrow escape.

The next major issue arose over the 60–40 percent clause between the Seattle and Portland owners that had been inserted in the contract at the last minute. Dorothy recalled the dreadful moment: "When Paul Murphy, who was a large, rich-looking man and always very cocky, took the stand, the Westinghouse lawyer pointed to him and said, 'Mr. Murphy, how long have you been in business?' 'Oh, all my life,' was the confident reply. 'Since I was growing up, since I left college.' 'Well, then,' said the lawyer, 'You've had a good deal of experience in business.' 'Oh yes, of course.' Then the lawyer said, 'Well, did you agree to a clause in your partnership agreement that held that if Mrs. Bullitt ever sold the station, you would have to sell at her price?' Mr. Murphy said, 'Yes, I did.' 'Well, then,' the lawyer said very smugly, 'I'm sure that with all your experience you realize that she could have sold her interest to her son for $1.00 a share and, according to the clause you agreed to, that's all you would get!' Well, the roof lifted right off! Mr. Murphy was absolutely livid! Here he had posed as such a sharp businessman, and this humiliation nearly killed him. He had been made a fool of publicly, and Andy had all he could do to keep him from going home to Portland that night. We were never friends after that incident. From then on, I had nothing but trouble with those men."

Westinghouse, too, was making errors. "They made a great mistake in selecting their attorney," Dorothy said in appraising the hearing. "A high-priced criminal lawyer named Turner from one of the biggest law factories in New York—ten floors or something—who knew nothing about the FCC. He was a mean man, really. He put the president of Westinghouse on the stand—a man named William Price who had appeared on the cover of *Time* magazine—and asked him why Westinghouse wanted television stations. Mr. Price responded promptly, 'To sell our refrigerators and toasters.' No one had coached the poor man and that was simply *not* something to say before the FCC."

Andy Haley had a great feeling for the audience and a long friendship with the hearing examiner. When it neared time for Dorothy to testify, he instructed her to write out all the questions he should ask her on the stand. After she turned in a lengthy list the next day, he told her next to prepare the answers in detail. Dorothy was the last to testify. By that time, she and Andy had gone over every nuance and she had learned her responses perfectly. Haley instructed her to speak clearly, not to raise her voice, and not to look at the opposition. As Westinghouse's attorney smiled sarcastically and rolled his eyes, Dorothy's answers were clear, concise, perfectly measured, and memorized. In her low voice, she listed the percentages of air time she intended to allot to religious, educational, and community programming, and slowly recited the entire program schedule and the company's balance sheet, item by item.

Throughout Dorothy's cross-examination by Westinghouse, Andrew Haley remained on the sidelines, ready as a cat for the pounce. He watched carefully as his dignified client stood her ground and as the Westinghouse attorney became increasingly frustrated and more flagrantly insulting with his questions. When the innuendos and insults reached a peak, Haley finally rose to defend his quiet-spoken client, this "distinguished woman" who had done nothing but better the community for so many years. With dramatic intensity he repri-manded the opposition in How-Dare-You tones, while Dorothy sat demurely on the stand, her eyes downcast, her gloved hands folded in her lap. Pointing to his client, Haley praised her impeccable character and civic contributions. He reviewed the history of her accomplishments and plans for what could only be Portland's finest television station. He railed against the scurrilous behavior of Westinghouse, whose conduct in this case could only show how poorly that company would serve the public in Portland. In the end, he left little more than shame and regret in his verbal wake and the hearing room was silent. Michael Bader remembered that particular day with smiling admiration. "It was always a grievous error to attack Mrs. Bullitt," he said. "I'd swear Andy Haley maneuvered Westinghouse to a place where they would attack her, and then he'd move in to defend her, always at the right time. I don't know whether they planned it that way, but the two of them worked together very well."

Dorothy would have to wait two years for the FCC's decision. During this time, she and Henry Owen used every contact to try to determine which way the FCC commissioners would vote. FCC Commissioner Frieda Hennock, Dorothy's earlier ally in the fight for educational television channels, came in handy during those days and Dorothy didn't hesitate to court her. "After our fight for educational TV that commissioner was in my pocket," she boasted later. "She did a lot of illegal things—she asked me to her apartment, cooked dinner, discussed my case, which she never should have done. But I wasn't the

In a David-and-Goliath contest, Dorothy won out over the Westinghouse Corporation to establish KGW-TV, the first television station in Portland, Oregon.

one to be in trouble—she was. We sat there having drinks by the hour, while she told me all about the commission."

The saga grew more elaborate when, only a few months before the FCC's decision on Channel 8, a radio station came up for sale in Portland. KGW was a station with a reputation for excellence and Dorothy was immediately tempted to buy it. Buying KGW would demonstrate further interest in the Portland community, impressing the FCC. This time Dorothy proposed that the Portland men own controlling stock. "I knew it would make them feel good and I knew also that the hearing examiner would be aware that, in this instance, Portlanders were in charge, which was not a bad thing. But the most important thing was that I knew that the tail would never wag the dog—radio would never run the company, television would. I was going by instinct, but I thought the clout would be with television and that's where I had the majority interest. They could have 60 percent for the pride in the small thing and we would take a humble 40 percent and still own 60 percent of television. The Portland people never believed we'd get television anyway, so they were happy." In January 1954, she bought radio station KGW.

In October 1955, the day of decision arrived. Dorothy was in Washington, D.C. A young man from Andy's office came down the aisle of a Senate hearing Dorothy was attending, leaned over, and whispered, "You got the Portland decision." She must of yipped or shouted because a man next to her leaned over to say, "Westinghouse is sitting right behind you!" Dorothy ran for a telephone. Westinghouse didn't lose cases like this. One of the major points in King Broadcasting's favor was Gloria's attention to children's programming. The next day Dorothy was delighted to read about her victory in a *Variety* article that mocked Westinghouse's well-known motto with the headline, "Westinghouse Cannot Be Sure."

If the battle for Portland had been won, the war for Portland was just beginning. In 1955, the disagreements between Dorothy and her partners, aggravated by the "insult" to Paul Murphy during the hearing and the different temperaments involved, were snowballing. While television was held in suspension, radio became the battleground and there Dorothy, with only 40 percent interest, lacked the weapons she needed for control. In the complex struggle that ensued, with its varying personalities and methods of doing business, it soon became clear that Dorothy wanted all of Portland—radio and television—which meant that "The Murphia," as she now called the Portland partners, had to go.

The Portland investors enjoyed the prestige of owning KGW. They enjoyed lording their control of radio over Dorothy, who was helpless to influence their management and money decisions. When she received reports in Seattle that they had fired the longtime station manager, she was furious and frustrated. She disliked their editorials, saying she was "thoroughly shocked by the shameless way they treat the air." Worst of all, KGW was losing its financial solidity. It had lost $90,000 in little more than a year since its purchase. Trips to Portland were becoming more and more disagreeable. Board meetings were reduced to name-calling and arguing. At one meeting Kuckenberg shouted that he would sue Dorothy, whereupon he and Andy nearly came to blows. Dorothy remained cool. "They threatened to sue me for perjury," she remembered with a laugh and a shrug. "I never knew what that was all about, but I suppose anyone can sue anyone." At another meeting, the group received a list of expenses to authorize. When the vote came, everyone voted "Aye" except Dorothy, who refused to authorize them because the figures involved were different from those originally proposed. "I didn't like being given figures before the meeting and having them different when we met," she bristled many years later, adding with a sardonic laugh, "That got their attention in a hurry." But her adeptness only added fuel to the animosity accumulating.

As the bitterness escalated, Dorothy strengthened her rationale and resolve. She allied herself with Calder McCall, a Portland stockholder who also had been feuding with his fellow investors. He became her inside man. "He'd call and report that they were hiring relatives and cutting into expenses, reducing things we needed, cutting subscriptions for news." Rapidly Dorothy was accumulating reasons for a split, and there were plenty.

The break came when Dorothy received a call from board president Gordon Orput, requesting another meeting. Orput was a level-headed businessman, the only one Dorothy could relate to. She went to the meeting, saying this would be her last, armed with double-barreled intent. "I went to a lawyer in Portland and asked him to draw up two resolutions for the meeting: one approving the seventeen-page equipment list from RCA for the new television station—a bill of $1.4 million, I think . . . and another calling for their money, the dollars they had originally pledged, to build the building. I brought those two pieces of paper to the stockholders' meeting. It was a full company meeting and Orput said, 'Sit by me, I'm in deep water.' So I gave him the first resolution while Jim Middlebrooks proceeded to explain in a very low-key way about every page of screws, nuts, and bolts of equipment. He made a very attractive story about how it would be state-of-the-art equipment, etc. The total was in large type at the bottom and when he had finished, Orput said, 'That's what it will take to build the station. Will you approve this order?' They all said, 'Yes.' Then I slipped him the next piece of paper calling for their money, and whispered, 'Now put up your dukes.' When he read it, his face blanched. In a moment, he whispered, 'I need to speak to you out in the hall.' There he gasped, 'I can't do this! They'll kill me!' I said, 'What do they expect? How do you think we're going to pay for this thing we just passed? They just voted to spend this money and they have pledged it. We'll put up ours and they put up theirs—it's that simple.' He said, 'But the roof will come right off!' And I said, 'Well, it will have to come off because there's no other course. We have our permit to build and it's time to put a spade in the ground.' " Dorothy held her ground, saying she would stay in Portland until the board acted. She and Orput went back in and told everyone they would adjourn until nine in the morning. "They had just put their heads in a noose," she crowed.

Orput spent the next day smoothing feathers. "When he asked for their money," Dorothy recounted, "they said they wouldn't invest any money with me, or words to that effect. Finally he said, 'Well, maybe you could buy us out.' " Later that night Orput had something on paper. Dorothy agreed to the purchase and flew back to Seattle. That night she confided to her diary: "Can't imagine how men can be so stupid as not to realize that in their bad treatment of us in radio with their 60 percent majority, they were making a pattern for our treatment of them in TV." The Portland investors eventually relinquished to Dorothy their 40 percent interest in television and sold her their 60 percent interest in KGW radio. They had lost interest in both Dorothy Bullitt and television and knew that refusal to submit to her demands would do no good. "By that time I was angry!" she scowled years later. "If they had refused me, it would have gone to court and they would have lost. I didn't get rid of them— they got rid of themselves."

She was relieved to have control once again. As usual, she rewarded those who had helped her and punished those who did not. Calder McCall, her "mole" during the siege, was invited to be on the board of King Broadcasting and he accepted. When construction of the new station was complete, she gave the station's old site, including land, building, and power lines, to Portland Educational Television. The new station, both radio and television, opened to a grand party for all of Portland's most prominent, but the former owners were conspicuously uninvited. Whether or not this annoyed her former business associates was not known, but their bitterness in the aftermath of the dissolution was common knowledge. Ancil Payne, King Broadcasting's general manager in Portland, recalled that at the time the Portland business community feared Dorothy Bullitt. "They thought she was one of the meanest, toughest old ladies they'd ever come across," he said. "The Portland men felt they had been used, that they had been brought in to demonstrate that they were a qualified organization, that they had not been told about how much it was really going to cost and had set aside only so much money. When they couldn't come up with more, she forced them out.

"The opposite view," he added, "is that they got into it with little money and thought they were going to make millions right away. When the venture required more than they were willing to put up, she simply bought out their stock." One thing was for sure, he concluded, "You didn't cross Mrs. Bullitt an awful lot."

THE NEXT ACQUISITION CHALLENGE CAME IN 1957, WHEN Spokane station KREM-AM, FM, and TV came up for sale for $2 million. An ABC affiliate station, KREM had been owned by an early broadcaster, Louis Wasmer, who wished to retire. The chance to buy into Spokane was the realization of a dream Dorothy had long held in the back of her mind. KREM would complete her "empire" and crown King Broadcasting by rounding out her beloved northwest corner of the country. It was such an uncomplicated transaction after the endless troubles in Portland that she felt sure there must be something wrong, something hidden that she didn't see. She pored over the figures, looking for problems, searching for hidden drawbacks. "Why would he sell?" she asked daughter Patsy as she bent over the balance sheets. When

In the 1950s, Dorothy courted broadcasting executives to secure a network affiliation for KING. Here she meets with Senator Warren Magnuson and CBS president Frank Stanton.

Patsy replied that it was probably very simple—the owner just wanted to retire—Dorothy was surprised. "It never occurred to Mother that a man her own age would consider quitting his work. After all, she was sixty-five and she was just getting started." In July 1957, one month after she settled with Portland, Dorothy signed a check for $25,000 as down payment for KREM Spokane. She did so with a sense of completion. She now had a small but very profitable kingdom of stations, another "My Three" to bring her as much pride as her children always had.

One more goal remained for Dorothy in securing her growing business—a network affiliation for Seattle and Portland that would provide income and good programming. She was unhappy with ABC, tired of the lightweight subjects the network provided, and didn't hesitate to reject programs when they didn't meet her standards. "I was never satisfied with ABC," she said. "It had all of the Hollywood tricks of the trade and ways of doing business I didn't like, and anyway they didn't have many affiliates. They lied and pushed and did whatever for an extra dollar—that wasn't the way we were trying to build a station."

The dissatisfaction was mutual. In 1956 an ABC representative made a public statement that KING was the most difficult of all its affiliates. "We have our principles!" Dorothy asserted in a loud deep voice. To which he countered, "You can't afford to have principles—you're the poorest station we have." "She was so damned mad," Ruth Prins recalled, "I'm sure that's when she decided to find another affiliation." Dorothy went to New York to talk to ABC president Robert Kintner. At an uncordial meeting, Kintner declared ABC would not affiliate with King Broadcasting in Portland if the Seattle pattern was to be repeated. "I was *angry* to be sure," Dorothy remembered of that meeting in New York. "They wanted us to put on all kinds of trash and we wouldn't carry it. It wasn't up to our standards and I told him we had quality rather than junk in mind."

She went again to CBS, as she had done before, but her efforts brought on more intrigue than real interest. She really wanted NBC, which then had the best programs, the most clout, the most affiliates, and was, as she pronounced in a long drawn-out voice, "refined."

After rejecting her over five years ago, NBC had returned to its radio affiliate in Seattle, KOMO, when that company built a television station after the freeze. Dorothy knew that, back then, NBC's decision was based in part on board chairman David Sarnoff's loyalty to his old friend O. D. Fisher, who owned KOMO. This time, her quest for affiliation would be different. She knew that her station had performed well for NBC during the freeze, when KOMO was not willing to gamble on television. Now, according to Dorothy, KOMO was "living on the network without giving it the support of local business. KOMO just took and took, used their shows and their network but didn't promote them in any way." This time in her bid for NBC network affiliation, she would "go higher, where the water runs clear." That meant going to Sarnoff herself.

"General" Sarnoff, founder of the Radio Corporation of America (RCA), father of television in the United States, was an imposing presence in physique and reputation. From a youth as a work-driven Jewish immigrant in New York, through years of ambitious striving, first as an engineer and later as an executive, he had achieved the premier position of power in communications as chairman of the board of RCA. Known as "the General," he was shrewd, tough, and demanding of all who worked for him.

Dorothy went after David Sarnoff just as Conrad Westervelt had pursued her during her courting days—mercilessly. Her determination ultimately made Sarnoff himself shake his head in admiration. She tracked him down. She courted him directly and indirectly, using every opportunity and connection she could. She enlisted the influence of anyone with clout. Armed with bottles of Scotch, she met with NBC lobbyists, senators, and their aides, hoping they would carry her wishes to the source. She revisited Harry Bannister, head of NBC's affiliates in New York. She buttonholed NBC executives at every NAB meeting to tell them again of her interest. Saying that she "just happened to be in town" (when she had traveled thousands of miles for that express purpose), she waited patiently in NBC's outer offices for a chance to put in her word and in hotel rooms afterward for an encouraging phone call.

In 1953 she found the chance to meet the General himself. The occasion was a joint RCA-Navy dedication ceremony for a new globe-encircling, million-watt transmitter—the most powerful in existence—located in the Cascade

Range near Arlington, Washington. As luck would have it, the ceremonies were being organized by one of Dorothy's acquaintances, Rear Admiral Allan E. Smith. General Sarnoff would send the first message from a transmitter building to the gigantic antenna network established in the Cascades.

Dorothy at first assumed that Sarnoff would be entertained by his friend O. D. Fisher, but, thinking she had nothing to lose, she talked to Admiral Smith, who used his connections to see if she could entertain the General and his staff for dinner at her home. To her surprise, he accepted, and the evening was a rousing success. Dorothy corralled a congenial mix of family, including Stim and Patsy and spouses, and did not include any executives from King Broadcasting. The maid taking orders for cocktails asked Sarnoff to mix his own martini in the kitchen because she had no luck with such drinks. When Dorothy, embarrassed to find him mixing drinks in the pantry, protested, the General just laughed, put his arm around her and said, "Ah, it feels good to be treated like a human being instead of a dignitary." During dinner, Dorothy leaned forward at the appropriate moment to ask the General to tell the story about the time he received news of the *Titanic* sinking. "He then regaled us with the well-known story about how, as a boy at Wanamaker's department store in New York, he had been in charge of wireless communications. While working in a little corner of the store, he was the first to pick up the message from the *Titanic* that it was in distress and sinking. Sarnoff told the story blow by blow, and there was a great silence when he described how the police had to guard the doors of the store during his seventy-two-hour vigil because relatives of the *Titanic's* passengers crowded to Wanamaker's to find out if that boy could find out who had survived. He loved that story and it lost nothing in the telling. For the opening of the Navy installation that day, he had brought with him the same operator's key to test the strength of the new transmitter."

As part of her campaign to affiliate with NBC, Dorothy had done her research. She kept an index card file on NBC's top executives, noting everything she had gleaned about each one, including preferences in politics, cigarettes, and drink, favorite restaurants and charities. The General himself had retired as chairman of NBC, making his son Bob president. She recorded that Bob "works closely on NBC matters, appreciates and supports Toscanini, and smokes cigars with disposable monogrammed mouthpiece." Mrs. David Sarnoff, the General's wife, was described in detail: "French—speaks with accent. Has worked with and for NY Infirmary for Women for 20-odd years and raised much money for it. Head of Volunteer Service there and very faithful. Very limited social life, as husband's friends are principally business associates. Spends Mon, Wed, and Thurs at her office in hosp. Doesn't like to fly."

This information paid off. A few months later, Dorothy was in Washington, D.C., at the office of Frank Russell, an NBC lobbyist. ("Drinks Scotch on the rocks—is on a diet for his weight. Great friend of Arthur Godfrey.") "Someone came in and said, 'Here's an extra ticket for the dinner tonight,' and Mr. Russell offered it to me. I said, 'What is it for?' It was [the tenth anniversary] celebration of 'Meet the Press'—a banquet at the Mayflower for free. I couldn't turn that down. I put on my best clothes and was there so early that no one else was around. At cocktails beforehand I didn't know anyone, but there were little clumps of people talking and [I] overheard someone say, 'Are the Sarnoffs staying over tomorrow?' The answer was, 'They're going home in the morning.' That's all I knew—except that 'home' was New York. I also knew that Mrs. Sarnoff didn't care for flying. Then I thought they probably wouldn't have to get up early and so would probably be taking a ten or eleven o'clock train. So I got a ticket on the Congressional, the better train, and stationed myself in a parlor car, reasoning that the Sarnoffs would probably have a drawing room but would have to pass through the parlor car section to get to it. Sure enough, as I came in, the door to a drawing room was open and there sat the General, Mrs. Sarnoff, and their son, Bob. I didn't turn my head. I just took one of the swivel seats and never turned around, hoping that sometime somebody was going to have to go to the toilet or the dining room. I didn't read anything that would take my eyes off the aisle. Pretty soon the General went past. I thought, 'He'll have to come back—what'll I do? Stick my foot out and trip him?' As it turned out I looked up just at the right time and he said, 'Well, well, who have we here! Come in and sit with us!' So . . . I sat with them through lunch in the dining car and all the way to New York. I was in heaven! Until the train trip we had never really sat and talked. The General remembered with amusement the party at my house when the maid had not been very good with mixing cocktails and he had mixed his own drink in the pantry. I came right out with the business of affiliation, asked him, and told him we'd do the best job for him. We talked about Channel 5 all the while and he laughed like everything because I was so obvious and pitching so hard." Before they said good-bye, the young Sarnoff smiled and said to Dorothy, "You have nothing to worry about but your patience."

Dorothy's trips were arduous. Although Andy Haley had urged her to "live close to NBC in NYC and we will get the affiliation," the constant effort of making appointments, listening to industry gossip, waiting for phone calls, cajoling, and conspiring was taking its toll. "NBC wanted to talk affiliation, but talk was all they did." At the same time, she also considered going independent, or even selling Portland entirely. With so many scenarios on her mind, her notes became a maze of initials and circuitous plans. One read: "Asked AGH to suggest to RH that RK ask me to meet him." When not at a meeting, she holed up in hotel rooms, awaiting an important phone call while she smoked and worked her jigsaw puzzles. She became so adept at them that she ordered intricate handmade varieties without pictures to work from. "I didn't dare leave the hotel room for fear if I went out I'd come back and find a slip under the door," she recalled with a rueful expression on her face. "I didn't leave the room. I had meals sent up and I sat there and fitted pieces into pieces."

There was just enough encouragement that she held on. At one appointment with Bob Sarnoff she noted, "Sarnoff couldn't have been more cordial—seemed very familiar with entire Port[land] picture. Said it is unanimous wish to affiliate with us but not now." Senator Warren Magnuson reported that the General was definite about NBC's plans to affiliate with her but that it was not yet the right time. Frank Folsom, president of RCA, told her he had heard the same. The only thing left, as Bob Sarnoff had predicted, was to keep her patience. She had done her homework, knocked on the doors, made the alliances, the phone calls, and finished the jigsaw puzzles.

Finally, the phone call came. She rushed to New York, where Bob Sarnoff called her at her hotel and said, "Well, you've got it—you're in—we want both KING and KGW. When will you come over?" Dorothy got Andy Haley up to New York and the next morning they went to the president's office and ironed things out without any great discussion. Harry Bannister, NBC's affiliates man who had dealt with Dorothy for so long, arrived for the champagne and toasts. "Mr. Bannister held up his glass," Dorothy reminisced. "He said, 'I'm not accustomed to saying no to women, but I would like to offer a toast to the most persistent woman I've ever known in my life!' "

KOMO was furious. The station sued KING, charging that King Broadcasting, with two NBC stations, was in violation of the Sherman Anti-Trust Act. The lawsuit was dismissed after King Broadcasting settled with KOMO for $250,000.

In October 1958, NBC formally affiliated with KING-TV in Seattle and KGW-TV in Portland. It was a moment of great triumph for Dorothy. "Nothing could have made me happier," she remembered of those days. "It was what I had worked for for many, many years." KOMO's general manager, Bill Warren, O. D. Fisher's son-in-law, never spoke to her again, and once even stepped out of a receiving line rather than shake her hand. In Dorothy's mind, it was a business decision and in her business world, competition and performance counted. KOMO had not performed well, according to her version of events. "KOMO never did understand what happened, I'm sure," she said of the incident. "They thought it was some magic between me and Magnuson or Congress, but there was no evidence to support it. The real thing was that they had become awfully slack, taking their relationship to NBC for granted. It was their lax management, combined with the fact that we opened a station Portland that gave us that affiliation. We really didn't *win* NBC. KOMO lost it—just like they neglected General Sarnoff when he was in Seattle." As for the network nabbing: "If you can get a network away from someone, you should. And the only way to keep someone from getting my network is to do a better job than ever before. No one has ever done that to me because nobody else does as good a job."

This remarkable decade of achievement was recognized in 1959, when Dorothy was named Seattle's First Citizen by the Seattle Real Estate Board, the first woman ever selected. However, the ceremony was a disaster for her. Planned by real estate executives, the occasion was described to Dorothy as a banquet for eight hundred, to include Senator Warren Magnuson, Governor Al Rosellini, Mayor Gordon Clinton, and a host of prominent citizens at the Olympic Hotel ballroom. They did not tell her about the surprise program, arranged by King Broadcasting people, a Hollywood-like extravaganza that combined closed-circuit television and live participants, all singing the praises of Dorothy Bullitt. Modeled after the popular television program "This Is Your Life," it was introduced (on film) by Steve Allen and Ralph Edwards, who brought up to the stage or onto the huge screen a parade of unexpected people from her past, including ex-Postmaster General James Farley; Joshua Green, owner of the Minor Avenue house of her growing-up years; Herbert Coe, former chief of staff at Children's Orthopedic Hospital; Bob Sarnoff, chairman of NBC; and daughters Patsy and Harriet, who had flown in from California and Florida.

"It was terrible what they did to her, really," Patsy remembered. "Mother had invited a professor from Los Angeles to contribute something elevating for the occasion, but he was pushed aside. Harriet and I were sworn to secrecy not to tell her, but we knew better than to hit Mother with a surprise. She hated to lose control or composure in public. So, on the morning before the banquet, we went over to tell her, and she cried because she was so moved that we'd be there for her. No one seemed to care about how she might feel. The realtors and the King producers had their own agendas; they just wanted a good show and they used her."

Decades later, Dorothy remembered being embarrassed that Ralph Edwards's name was left off the program and that Stim had not been invited on stage along with his sisters. Dressed in blue chiffon with a corsage pinned to the neckline, Dorothy smiled as she received a bronze plaque and graciously thanked one and all on behalf of the constellation of people who had given shape and direction to anything she might have attained. Speaking quickly, "lest others ask for equal time," she finished with a memorable quip: "My husband, Scott Bullitt, once told me 'when you see you've got the jury with you, stop talking—they could change their minds.' " She left to thunderous applause, went home and threw up all night long. Nonetheless, the ceremony confirmed that, just as so many years ago she had known that, "First Hill was mine," now she knew that Seattle was hers.

She had gained riches on many levels and earned them all. The woman who, as a girl, had laughed at her laziness, had used every opportunity to reach her goals. She had risked and won, but between the risking and winning lay the work. Daughter Patsy said of her accomplishments: "The race goes to those who run while others sleep, and that's what Mother did. She worked twenty-four hours a day, she worried, and she waited endlessly in hotel rooms to get what she wanted. While the Westinghouse people slept snug and smug in their beds, Mother was, literally, up all night working. And while KOMO's Bill Warren dined at the Rainier Club, Mother was running after General Sarnoff. Mother ran while others slept."

In 1974, when Dorothy was speaking at a luncheon, she was asked about her career in the 1950s. Laughing huskily, she downplayed her remarkable achievements: "Oh, I never thought of it as a career. I thought of it as a race in which you ran like the very dickens—you just ran as fast as you could."

I resent being classed with the OLDER anything.

12 LETTING GO, HANGING ON

1960-1972

THE FIRST CITIZEN'S CELEBRATION WAS A TURNING POINT OF sorts for Dorothy Bullitt, for it summarized, in however superficial a way, thirty years of her public life. Once the evening was past, she tried to put it out of mind. Donning one of the classic, conservative suits she had worn for decades, she prepared for the next workday, her mind already at the office and her eyes glancing only briefly at the mirror as she applied her lipstick. Were she a more self-absorbed person, she might have paused a moment to appraise her own reflection.

The woman in Dorothy Bullitt's mirror was now a silver-haired patrician. She resembled a wellborn headmistress of some elite girls school—discriminating and composed, agreeable yet firm in expression. In spite of the pleasant smile and the cloak of modesty she wore, her body now spoke a language of its own. Her face and carriage conveyed subtle glints of a breastplated warrior with many battles won, one whose iron will had over the years been forged into steel. Dignity and determination were settled in her steady blue gaze, etched in the firm set of her lips, the sure grip of her hand, and the proud lift of her aristocratic chin. There was now a confidence in her carriage that had not been evident in earlier days. Her squared shoulders and broad chest now spoke more of power, a bearing that said, "Do Not Even Think of Messing With Me."

Yet her essential femininity always held sway. "Dorothy Bullitt was first and foremost a lady," a King vice-president once observed. "She may have pretended not to be, but she was a lady and exercised her power in that fashion." Her charm, instilled by her mother as simple "good manners," was now, after decades of human contact, a shining art form. At age sixty-eight, it was an irresistible blend of empathy and gentle humor that rose from a genuine liking of people. It was so natural, so seamless, that those who looked for flaws in the fabric—those tiny tears that reveal insincerity—rarely found them or even wanted to, since she was such good company. "Mother had no veneer, really at all; she was totally unself-conscious," Dorothy's youngest daughter recalled. "What you saw was what she was. Even though she concealed some of herself sometimes, there was nothing unreal about her. It was all real—what you saw and what you didn't see." A grandson, Bill Collins, was forever fascinated by this aspect of the grandmother he called "Mamie." After years of family gatherings, visits to her office, and numerous tête-à-têtes with her, he could only shake his head with smiling admiration. "She had so many different kinds of manners, so many different methods," he said. "She could remain herself entirely and yet she was so many different people. Most who can do that are real phonies; they change the mask at every moment and they're thinking all the time. But Mamie, whose life was filled with such diffuse groups of people, could remain entirely herself and play to someone right where they were without being phony at all. She entered people's lives without bulldozing or intruding; she came in close but never meddled. Her manner was never studied, as some British aristocrat might be, according to specific social routines; it was very direct, aimed at the person rather than the drawing room."

Her charm had many facets. She could be self-effacing without false modesty, she could knock herself without being demeaning, she could play the fool with utter dignity—either for a laugh or to lull someone into a false sense of security. One never knew exactly what the scene might entail but it would always be vital, personal, and real. As Bill Collins put it, "She had so many methods but no real disguises, so many manners but very few masks. She was always still Mamie."

At the beginning of the 1960s—the decade of the angry feminist—Dorothy Bullitt was a rarity: an autonomous, accomplished, and comfortable female with no man before or behind her. Obstacles lay ahead, however, for the next decade brought on a transition of the most difficult kind. It included loss of friends, goals, power, and—most dreaded of all—control. It was a trying time of letting go, of releasing reins. For someone accustomed to riding four-in-hand over everyone and everything, this presented as much challenge as any Dorothy had surmounted in the past. With King Broadcasting stabilized, and network affiliation secured, her life was less driven, less challenging. She needed to find new avenues of excitement and interest. There was less need for hurried long distance calls, or late-night trips to meet Andy Haley at the airport, no

In 1961, Dorothy and Dee Terry Payson took a 7,000-mile boat trip through the inland waterways of North America.

more furtive negotiations in bathrooms or department stores, no more coded conversations with Henry from some East Coast phone booth. The need for quick thinking—the planning, plotting, strategizing, coordinating, followed by decisive action—would no longer be necessary. Even the broadcasting gossip would cease to resonate with promise of out-doing the competition. For someone still endowed with formidable willpower but now undirected goals, this transition was bound to be difficult.

While Dorothy was "letting go," she was also receiving more rewards for her work. She became a collector of certificates, diplomas, and statues. She received two honorary doctorates, one from Pacific University in 1960 and another from Mills College in 1964. Her first reaction, she recalled later with a shrug and a smile, was, "A Doctor of Humane Letters? I'm not humane and I don't write letters . . . I'm certainly no intellectual, but if they wanted to call me a Doctor of Humane Letters, it was all right with me. Heaven knows, I've been called worse." She did enjoy standing shoulder to shoulder with the scholars, which assuaged her feelings of inferiority about lacking a college education. The National Conference of Christians and Jews presented her with a national citation for her devoted service to all races and creeds. The American Women in Radio and Television honored her with the Robert E. Eastman Award for "conspicuous service to broadcasting." In 1968 she received an Emmy from the National Academy of Television Arts and Sciences for twenty years of television excellence in the United States. Aware that most such awards were aimed at garnering donations from her, she was ever gracious, but seldom obliged with money.

In 1961 Dorothy bought a forty-two-foot yacht, christened it the *Mike*, and with Dee Terry took an extensive four-month boating excursion around American and Canadian inland waters. She flew back to Seattle renewed and refreshed. As her plane descended, she was struck by a series of flashbacks. Below, Seattle stretched and sprawled into suburbs—a far cry from the stump-crowned hills and vast hinterlands of her childhood. In its center sprouted a giant steel sculpture that represented the first stages of the Space Needle under construction for the Century 21 World's Fair. Its sleek shape supplanted the diminished and dowdy Smith Tower that had symbolized the city's stature and prosperity in her girlhood.

The broadcasting company she returned to survived her long absence without crisis. She plunged back into a crowded schedule. She attended NAB meetings and stopped in Washington, D.C., where her visits with Senators Magnuson and Jackson and attorney Andy Haley were now more leisurely. At home in Seattle, Gloria Chandler was her constant companion, having shared in every facet of Dorothy's life for the last ten years. She was a regular dinner guest at Dorothy's house, where they ate in the sunroom, gossiping about the stations and criticizing television programs. Often Gloria stayed overnight, though she owned a small house not far away. They were a "onesome." When Dorothy was invited out, she usually included Gloria. A few wondered if the two inseparable women were lovers, which almost certainly they were not, although they were extremely dependent on each other for emotional support. Over the years, the friendship had become symbiotic. Gloria had provided the professional entrees and Dorothy had supplied the drive. Dorothy depended heavily on her for shared enthusiasm and constant attention—the unfailing applause and approval that Gloria extended. In turn, Dorothy provided a sense of belonging, a sense of home for Gloria, who was an orphaned child at heart. A card that must have accompanied a gift was found among Dorothy's effects after her death. It hinted obliquely at her unexpressed feelings: "Gloria—For you from me, and it is *so* little. I've tried before and I still can't find the right words. I think you know but you don't know how much . . ."

During the 1960s Dorothy's circle of friends continued to widen, extending to anyone of importance in the arts, education, politics, and business throughout the region. At KING, she chatted with well-known figures appearing on television, although she shunned the more glamorous celebrities in favor of prominent commentators and politicians, whom she found more interesting. One of her favorite politicians was Attorney General Robert Kennedy, who visited with her before a television appearance in Seattle in 1961 and who afterwards wrote to say how much he had enjoyed their discussion. She was as comfortable with humbler folks—the women from the coffee shop and the guys who knew how to fix and make things run. She was a pal of Harry Truman, not the president but the crusty old codger who owned a lodge on Spirit Lake at the base of Mount St. Helens. (A Northwest character, Truman refused to leave his rustic digs when the volcano began to erupt; his body was never found.) She much preferred to sit with a group of old salts talking diesels than to stand in a reception line. "She was a vibrant lady," remembered Bob Beebe, one of the skippers who knew her. "She could talk to someone like me as well as any executive she was used to associating with." He remembered one evening when she came to a party of "boat people" who had not expected her to attend such humble festivities. Perched on a stool in the galley, she was as comfortable as the old slacks and jacket she wore, laughing and smoking, asking questions and telling tales.

Although most of Dorothy's meetings outside the boardroom were now conducted as long lunches, she still attended the occasional seminar and symposium, albeit with less intense interest about the content. She recorded her quirky comments on paper wherever she went. At one conference on urban affairs, after a long page of handwritten notes, she added a warning either to herself or someone else, writing in large print, "I'm so sleepy that my head is about ready to fall off. Don't let me fall on the floor!" On a trip to the Aspen Institute for a seminar on the future of broadcasting, she took few notes, except to pencil a critical review of the airlines on the back of her ticket: "Seattle to Denver—Continental Air—pleasant girls, neat uniforms—good meal—Bloody Mary $1.00. United Air—girls with ungroomed hair—homely uniforms, wool jumpers with U all over them—no smiles, heavy make-up—three sandwiches, meat served with *spoon,* too fat to bite—Bloody Mary $1.50." No place, however sacred, was safe from her comments. While listening to Dean Leffler deliver his weekly sermon at St. Mark's Cathedral, she could not help but write down a few questions on the back of a collection envelope: "Great emphasis on forgiveness of sins—is it too much? Should there be more identification of *specific* sins? Recognition and labeling?"

Dorothy's daughters shifted location and lifestyle during these years. In 1956, Joe Collins left his position with the old Stimson Realty Company, which Dorothy had renamed the Bullitt Company, to take a job as a real estate appraiser in San Diego. Patsy and her three young children, Jacques, Charles, and Bill, relocated, much to Dorothy's regret. As Center of the Universe, she blamed herself for their defection. Although claiming she never interfered in the lives of her children, she was surprisingly unaware of the control she exerted over her son-in-law. She had tolerated his management of the 1411 Building as long as he did it her way. When he made the slightest autonomous decision—such as when he replaced hot air machines with paper towels in the ladies' rooms—she restored the original devices.

The loss of Patsy was assuaged somewhat in 1962 when Harriet moved back to Seattle from Gainesville, Florida, with her two children, Scott and Wenda, having divorced her physician husband, Bill Brewster. Dorothy received this news with sympathy and a certain measure of relief. Bill Brewster, the "intense young man" Dorothy met in the 1940s, had, over the years, become alcoholic and hypomanic to such a point that he had lost his position as a clinical and research anesthesiologist at Massachusetts General. The couple moved to Gainesville, Florida, where they worked at the university—Bill as a clinician and researcher and Harriet as a protein chemistry technician. The marriage stabilized for a short while but soon Brewster was again troubled. His bizarre behavior, later diagnosed as psychotic, included feverish spending sprees, chartered airplane trips, paranoia about Nazis and Communists everywhere, and the conviction that he would soon be traveling to outer space. Harriet was forced to commit her husband to a hospital for a time, but treatment was unsuccessful. It was a tragic situation and, as Bill's behavior became more erratic, Dorothy's concern for her daughter's welfare grew. Harriet filed for divorce but when she told her story to a Florida judge, he took out a Bible from his desk drawer and began to read to her from the Book of Job. Mental reasons, he told her while escorting her to the door, were not grounds for divorce. Months later, when Harriet reported that Bill was newly engaged in parachute jumping, the same judge exclaimed, "That does it!" and granted her a decree.

Harriet returned to Seattle with plans to complete her degree at the University of Washington. After a short stay with her mother on Galer Street, she found a house for herself and the children. "It was Mother's household with everything done her way—it wasn't an independent situation." Harriet returned to school and in 1965 received her degree in zoology. To understand herself and her failed marriage, she also embarked on an intense program of psychoanalysis, which led her into the labyrinth of early life at The Highlands, the devastating loss of her father, and the impact of his last words to her. This time of self-discovery and nurturing came as a great relief for Dorothy's youngest child after years of an often abusive marriage. She returned figuratively to the woods of her childhood, to the outdoors where she had spent so much time as a girl. In 1966, she founded a nature journal for the Pacific Northwest, which celebrated the region's natural beauty. Published monthly, first as a small newsletter called *Pacific Search,* it appealed to the many outdoor lovers in the area. Subscribers came first from memberships of the Pacific Science Center, the local Audubon Society, and mycological organizations, then from the Oregon Museum of Science and Industry and regional natural history societies. Within a few years, what had started as a newsletter for about three thousand readers was now familiar as a journal written by volunteer writers and scientists (including the first published cartoon by Gary Larson), many of whom are now well-known in the region. As the subject matter expanded into cities and culture, the publication was further enlarged, reformatted, and renamed *Pacific Northwest Magazine,* eventually reaching 75,000 readers each month. Throughout its evolution, from newsletter to sophisticated color magazine, it provided thousands of readers with a view of life and nature best described as Northwest. Harriet had found her niche.

FOR A COUPLE OF YEARS IN THE EARLY 1960S, DOROTHY KEPT her hand at the company helm. She could see that King Broadcasting Corporation would thrive after paying the debts incurred in its infancy, but that this was no time to take on more challenge. Meanwhile day-to-day operations were becoming too tedious and predictable for her entrepreneurial taste. Pioneering a new small company was exciting, but administering a big company was boring. With Gloria, she made frequent trips to Portland and Spokane, and regularly held board meetings in her large office in Seattle lined with photos of the famous. At home for longer stretches of time than in many years, she had more time to order her life, putter in the basement library, catalogue her extensive record collection, and take inventory of the tremendous accumulation of valuables tucked away in cupboards and closets.

She started to give more things away to her children, who were each to learn that the gift, once given, was still more hers than theirs. They themselves were, after all, extensions of their mother and so their gifts could be redeemed at will. Although she gave Harriet a sapphire bracelet for her graduation from high school, Dorothy wore it herself for the rest of her life. "It was not that Mother wasn't generous—she was enormously generous," Patsy explained. "It was a matter of control. She simply couldn't let go. It took us all years to realize that when she 'gave' us something, it was more a loan than a gift. And if you didn't take proper care of it—insure it, lock it up, or whatever was necessary—she would just as easily take it back—and did. Also, if the gift included a deed, title, or registration of some kind, you got the gift, but not the paper." The two girls saw this happen in the 1940s when their mother gave them wedding gifts: Harriet received land in Leavenworth but without a deed; Patsy received a house, though her mother kept the title and later even sold it to someone else. So, in the 1960s, when Dorothy asked Harriet if she would like to have the piano—the living room grand that had belonged to Fritz Kreisler—her daughter was mildly surprised and accepted happily. She was even more surprised and pleased when her mother gave her some of grandmother Harriet's jewelry—a diamond-and-emerald ring and bracelet. But the greatest surprise came when, after Harriet moved to a "less suitable" house, Dorothy took back the piano and whisked the jewelry away into a safe deposit box when she found it lying in an unlocked drawer of her daughter's dressing table. Dorothy also gave Patsy jewelry that had belonged to Harriet Stimson. If she had planned to take the items back later, she was foiled and frustrated to learn that her older daughter had sold them to pay for her son Charles's schooling. "Mother didn't like that one little bit," Patsy recalled, "mainly because she wasn't in control."

The grandest gift Dorothy gave to her son. In 1961, she asked Stim if he would take over as president of King Broadcasting. She was nearly seventy, she told him, and she had achieved some level of satisfaction in acquiring the stations. Now she wanted more freedom from the day-to-day operations. He was her natural successor—the eldest, the son, and man of the family. If he would assume this responsibility, she would stay on as chairman of the board. What she didn't say was that she had always wanted a prominent position for him, one that placed him in the family forefront. And what she probably didn't realize herself was she was asking her son to take his father's place. For many years, in addition to his law practice and to helping her with King Broadcasting legal matters, Stim had been managing the family real estate holdings as president of the Bullitt Company. This additional role was to put him in charge of most of her business affairs.

Stim also ran the Bullitt Foundation, an organization set up in 1952 at the suggestion of Andrew Haley for sheltering taxable money and for making donations to charitable causes. The foundation, which had no particular funding focus, began with a $100 deposit and over the years received sporadic small deposits from Dorothy and a few contributors. It grew slowly but without steady attention from Dorothy. Patsy explained, "Mother enjoyed making money, like her father, but she didn't quite know how to give it away. She did it in a nonfocused way, usually giving to projects run by people she liked. She never settled on a foundation goal—except that it should serve as a conduit to take care of our favorite gifts." The foundation's main purpose, her children came to realize in time, was to call them all together. Saying, "We must have a meeting, dear," Dorothy would summon Patsy from San Diego and Harriet and Stim from their increasingly busy lives. "Mother's great pleasure was to have meetings, particularly with us," Patsy remembered. "Gradually we began to realize that this was the foundation's real function." Patsy was furious on one occasion when she arrived in Seattle for an "emergency meeting" only to find her siblings off doing other things and her mother waiting to have a chat. "What am I doing here? I have things to do, too!" Patsy shouted at her mother. She stormed out of the house and returned to San Diego.

At the foundation meetings, the family donated small amounts—one or two thousand dollars at first—to "pet projects" all over the country. Harriet tended to choose environmental causes, Stim civic causes, and Patsy social and religious causes. Their mother usually chose hers on the basis of the person in charge of the cause. Over the years, she contributed heavily to St. Mark's Cathedral, not so much out of religious fervor, but because she enjoyed the company of Dean John Leffler, who often stopped by for a drink in the evening. During the 1960s, the foundation still remained unfocused but the grants gradually grew larger—totaling $600,000 for the decade. Although awarded largely to various churches and schools nationwide and civic projects in Seattle and Portland, the grants also reflected the racially turbulent times. Over these years, the Bullitt Foundation contributed to the American Civil Liberties Union, the Lawyers' Committee for Civil Rights, the Center for Study of Democratic Institutions, and the National Committee Against Discrimination in Housing. It also provided tuition for the college education of several black students, including the Columbia Law School education of James Meredith, the civil rights hero shot during a freedom march in Mississippi.

After considering carefully his mother's proposal, Stim accepted the position of president of King Broadcasting. He did so to some degree out of filial duty, but in larger part because the job offered him the opportunity to carry out some ideas he had been mulling over for years. He weighed these against the minus factors of leaving the law, which he enjoyed, and turning to a family enterprise in which his mother might well interfere. Although respectful of the company's profitmaking needs, he saw it also as a vehicle for social betterment. An unabashed idealist, he wanted to use mass communication to lift mass consciousness. He wanted also to make the company a model of social justice, with racial equality in all facets of its operation, and with educational benefits and profit sharing for its personnel. The company could set its course, as he wrote in the first policy manual, toward "sunlit uplands with bountiful and fulfilling lives on a high plane for all."

Stim moved to King Broadcasting in 1962, at the same time keeping his partnership with the law firm of Riddell, Williams, Voorhees, Ivie & Bullitt. He chose a small windowless office, of which his mother disapproved, to avoid "the arrogant trappings of outer authority." His mother continued to occupy the corner office—the grandest quarters in the building—furnished with board-room table, fireplace, and grandfather clock. She vowed firmly not to interfere with the new regime; the day-to-day was now her son's responsibility—a vow more easily taken than kept.

DOROTHY TURNED TO OTHER PURSUITS. IN 1961 GOVERNOR Rosellini appointed her to a commission studying a proposed inland waterway that would connect the south end of Puget Sound to the Columbia River, via Grays Harbor and Willapa Bay. It was an old idea that had always been dis-carded because of the enormous costs involved. Such a waterway appealed to Dorothy's love of the region and its waters, but she saw that it might bring eco-nomic benefits as well. Depending upon the exact route chosen, the canal could save at least 150 miles of navigation in treacherous coastal waters. It would give craft of all sizes, from the smallest cruiser to the largest barge, access to an inland waterway that stretched 1,800 miles from the Inland Passage to Alaska to the inland waters up the Columbia River into Idaho. It would save crossing the dreaded Columbia Bar, known as the "Graveyard of the Pacific," and one of her great nautical fears. She had crossed the Bar only once, and it was the only time she had been seasick.

Dorothy launched into the canal project with the fervor of a zealot on cru-sade. "That's why I appointed her," Al Rosellini remembered, laughing. "Dorothy Bullitt was thorough in everything she did." A tsunami of paper and photos accumulated as she researched comparable canals, calculated nautical miles and vertical drops, compiled lists of coastal shipwrecks, and estimated possible income to be derived along the route. To advance the canal cause, she wrote everyone from congressmen to locktenders. She sent out a questionnaire to two thousand boaters and marina and yacht club managers from Alaska to Oregon, asking if they would support such a project. She spoke on panels and gave slide shows, describing the proposed canal as a major investment ("As great as the washing away of Seattle's Denny Hill or the construction of the locks between Puget Sound and Lake Washington"), but one which would also pro-vide new solutions for flood control and drainage, new avenues for recreation, power, military, and commercial shipping. At meetings of the Inland Empire Waterways Association or the Columbia Basin Inter-Agency Committee, she dramatically sketched a verbal voyage on sheltered waters from Skagway, Alaska, to Lewiston, Idaho, a voyage that would not only provide scenic pleasure but practical benefits of new money, payrolls, and more industrial freshwater sites for related businesses along the way. In her deep voice, she predicted a waterway laden with the fruits of the Northwest—grain, minerals, and forest products— being transported to Seattle and other deepwater Puget Sound ports for further shipment to foreign markets. As for pleasure boating, "It is a very friendly thing to travel an inside passage," she said with smiling assurance. "Such cruising in this corner of the country could not be exceeded by any other." People who heard her could not help but agree. Those who received the questionnaire returned it with 90 percent approval, including their willingness to pay a toll. But in 1965, when the Army Corps of Engineers came up with the actual cost of such a gigantic venture, it was upwards of $500 million, and the benefits did not outweigh the costs. The wave of enthusiasm had swept in . . . and out. Dorothy regretfully put away her files but predicted, "It will come up again."

One curious side effect of the whole canal episode was the friendship Dorothy formed with her assistant, a young diminutive blonde woman from Spokane. Kitty Kelley spent hours with her boss, researching and cataloguing the masses of material. Over many months, she came to admire "Mrs. B," confiding in the older woman her plans for the future. When Kitty decided she wanted to work in Washington, D. C., Dorothy encouraged her, persuading Kitty's parents to give their permission, and contacting Senators Jackson and Magnuson, who each offered her a staff position. Kelley chose instead to work for Senator Eugene McCarthy, leaving the Senate four years later to become a researcher for the editorial page of *The Washington Post*. Eventually Kitty Kelley authored best-selling biographies about four national icons of the 1970s and 1980s—Elizabeth Taylor, Jacqueline Kennedy, Frank Sinatra, and Nancy Reagan. The books, each more provocative than the last, attracted millions of readers and millions of dollars for the author, along with threats and lawsuits that never materialized. "Kitty was such a nice little girl when she worked for me," Dorothy said with mock confusion. "Today she's entirely different—much more glamorous and a lot tougher. But even now when we see each other, she reverts right back to the way she was!" She understood her. Dorothy Bullitt had great ability to see the soul and empathize with experience. "Kitty is a character but she's also very smart," Dorothy said, lifting an index finger to the air. "She has broken a lot of rules, attempted impossible things and done them, and her life has not been easy. I feel it."

When Kelley came to Seattle for talk show appearances at the debut of each book, she knew that at KING she was safe because Dorothy Bullitt was waiting in the wings. "The first time they were prepared to rip me from stem to stern," Kelley remembered with a knowing laugh. "The talk show host was ready, all

Dorothy rescued the Stimson, *a tugboat once owned by her father, and had it lovingly restored.*

puffed up—having read all of *People* magazine. Just before the interview someone came in and said to me, 'Mrs. Bullitt is waiting for you after you are done.' Well, the talk show host just deflated and the interview went beautifully. And I thought, 'That's my Mrs. B.' "

Dorothy's interest in boating continued. By this time she had acquired a forty-five-foot Matthews yacht and a thirty-six-foot Tolleycraft with the idea of starting a small charter business. Her "fleet" was enlarged further when one day she found her flagship by chance. "I was wandering out the St. Vincent de Paul dock on Lake Union to see the historic ship *Wawona*. As I threaded my way between the bathtubs and toilets and things, I saw a little old worn-out tugboat tied up on the dock. Through the peeling paint, I saw the word *Stimson* on the side. It was Father's name! Well! I had never seen the boat before but knew he had had a tug built in the early 1890s to bring booms from the logging camps and deliver lumber to the sailing ships in Shilshole Bay. This boat was so bad and so old that it had to be the same one." She learned that the price was $3,000—"far too much for a boat in that condition." Some time later, when she learned that it had sunk, "the price came down quite a bit!" The *Stimson* was back in the family for $1,000.

Dorothy admired its "low simple design," the lack of chrome, brass, or varnish, the stark integrity of a no-nonsense working boat. In her mind's eye, she could see it back at its old logging pursuits, describing it as a "little old reliable sheepdog of the sea, herding her flock and occasionally rounding up a stray." The *Stimson* had survived a checkered past and was clearly showing its age. In fact, when Dorothy's insurance agent stepped on board and dropped through the deck, the new owner knew she had a job ahead. "The people at the boatyard said, 'Take it out into the Sound and sink it—you'd be money ahead.' They were right, of course, but I felt sentimental about the old boat." The *Stimson* was one of the last watergoing souvenirs of the Northwest timber industry. Above all, it was her father's boat. The restoration required $48,000, plenty of patience, new wood, and old-time skills. At its rechristening, Dean John Leffler prayed for blessings on the craft in memory of the two brothers who had built her— C. D. and Fred Stimson—while Dorothy's youngest grandson, Benjamin Bullitt, cracked a bottle of champagne over the bow. When the *Stimson* appeared on opening day of the Seattle yachting season in 1966, it was the star of the parade. Standing on deck, encased in the sweeping Italian police-man's cape her husband had loved to see her wear, Dorothy relished the ride. Although her foray into charter boating failed to produce phenomenal results, she didn't seem to mind.

One civic project she took quite seriously was serving on the University of Washington Board of Regents from 1958 to 1965. Early on, she acted as liaison to the University of Washington School of Medicine ("It was sort of a god-mothership"), bringing the needs of the faculty and staff to the attention of the board. She also had some contact with the School of Communications, although it was not her focus as a regent. In 1962, she became president of the university's board of regents, a position she assumed in her usual self-effacing way. Thanking the members for their confidence, she said, "I hope you will not regret it. I approach this assignment with considerable trepidation." Then she proceeded to talk boldly about the goals of the university and the destiny of the Pacific Northwest. Dorothy formed a friendship with university president Charles Odegaard, "a truly educated man." She particularly admired the way Odegaard handled the difficult days when students, angry about racial injustice and the Vietnam war, literally climbed the walls to get to the university presi-dent. "I was on the board of regents the day he came in and I always admired him so much. When the students got out of hand during the 1960s, they had to get the police to guard his door. Finally, the students climbed up the side of his building and he let them in the window! They crowded his room to capacity and he listened to them. He couldn't grant them everything, but he listened." Odegaard described Dorothy's role on the board as "very influen-tial." She broadened the scope of the regents, he said. "The 1960s were days of great social change and we needed that broad perspective on the board," he explained. As usual, Dorothy remained silent during the monthly meetings until others had spoken. "Finally when she did speak up," Odegaard recalled like many others, "she invariably made some sensible addition or clarification, and

Who blinked first in this historic encounter in 1962?

often the whole discussion was concluded then and there." Her fellow board members, all males, were fond of calling her "the best man of the board"—and each time she heard it, she pretended it was for the first time. Odegaard relied on her. Once, when Dorothy couldn't attend a board meeting because of a sprained ankle, he sent a state patrolman to carry her out of her house and bring her to the meeting. Odegaard enjoyed lunches with her, when, in quiet conversation, they ironed out the problems of the world. "She had an extraordinary combination of wisdom and practical sense," he said. "What's more, in her own way she was a visionary with an adventurousness about her that few people have." She was capable of great intuitive leaps, he felt, understanding the turbulent times, though she wasn't really of them.

While a regent, Dorothy met John Kennedy, a man she admired without reservation. In 1962, the University of Washington celebrated its centennial with a convocation and an address by the president of the United States. Dorothy chatted with Kennedy before the ceremonies ("We got dressed together in the robing room") and someone snapped a revealing photo of them together—two strong personalities, each eyeing the other in an appraising way. In September 1963, when Kennedy was in town at the Olympic Hotel, he asked to see Dorothy Bullitt again. Kennedy greeted her cordially and the two chatted for an hour with no particular agenda. Dorothy recalled that "the president

Letting Go, Hanging On   277

showed me every courtesy. He was a very bright, level man—very much in *control*"—a quality she admired. John Kennedy was one of three people outside her family—all politicians—whose names and dates of death were recorded by Dorothy among significant Bullitt family events. The others were Franklin Roosevelt and Adlai Stevenson.

One episode at the university put Dorothy in an awkward cross fire of loyalties. In 1961 the Frederick estate at The Highlands came up for sale. Formerly owned by pioneer merchant D. E. Frederick of the Frederick & Nelson department store downtown and the same shy Mr. Frederick of Dorothy's childhood, the estate included twenty-five acres of landscaped grounds and a palatial home, filled with chandeliers, paneled walls and marble floors. In 1930, the fifty-room, three-story mansion had cost $500,000 to build; in 1961 it was worth $2 million. The estate had been offered to other members of The Highlands, but no buyer was forthcoming. The regents saw the estate as a possible faculty retreat—a private place where scholars and professional leaders could meet to exchange ideas and information, a facility to bring prestige to the university and to compare favorably to one owned by Columbia University. The fire-sale price, $175,000, was a bargain, and the money was available from reserves accumulated from self-sustaining educational activities. To wide approval from the public and the media, the university bought the Frederick house.

Almost unanimously The Highlands old guard rebelled against what they considered a threat to their privacy and the refined atmosphere they sought to maintain. Fiercely opposed to the university purchase, residents declared it an invasion, which, if allowed to go forward, would lower property values, increase traffic, bring people of unknown origins through their discriminating gates, and establish a dangerous precedent. Threats ensued. The university considered using the right of eminent domain. The residents replied that they would deny use of the community's roads, water, and other facilities.

Dorothy was in the midst of this melee. She was caught between the belief that the seminar center was a valid acquisition for the university and the reality of accommodating old friends. She tried to persuade the Highlanders that it was a good idea, but her charms and convictions were ineffective. She telephoned each resident. Bill Allen, president of The Boeing Company, replied that he felt obliged to support The Highlands' board; Claude Bekins, owner of both Bekins Van & Storage and her old home, Greenway, refused to be involved, as did Paul Pigott, owner of Pacific Car & Foundry and her parents' home, Norcliffe. She defended the university to Bertha Boeing, a friend of many decades, only to find that their comfortable conversations were replaced by letters from attorneys. She learned that one resident who owned a mansion had called The Highlands chairman to ask haughtily, "What would prevent me from turning my place into a boarding house for colored people?"

"Mother got the blame for the university's action, although she didn't instigate it," daughter Patsy recalled. "They didn't want those bearded professors in their lovely surroundings. It got quite nasty; people, all of whom mother knew, wrote letters to the regents saying, 'How dare you!' They snubbed her at the Sunset Club—or else she imagined that they did. Mother was terribly embarrassed and it affected her beyond all proportion. She took their reaction personally and believed The Highlands had turned against her." Harriet, too, remembered her mother's consternation. "It was such an emotional experience that Mother ground her teeth and broke a crown," the younger daughter remembered, adding, "I doubt if there's been anything in her life to make her so angry." Helpless to justify her position, she became obsessed by what appeared to be a rebuff from lifelong friends (both situations entirely strange to her).

Eventually the university relented and sold the house back to The Highlands, Inc., who in turn sold it to a developer. This turn of events inspired the *Seattle Post-Intelligencer* columnist Emmett Watson to sum up the whole episode: "Mr. McNicol [the developer], exercising his clear right as the owner, is now selling off considerable parts of the interior, including chandeliers, parquet floors and the seemingly priceless wood paneling. All of which, I trust, makes residents of The Highlands breathe easier. After all, you never know who might show up at a scholarly seminar." Dorothy couldn't laugh it off. She never got over this "betrayal" by old friends, and for several years, she was so obsessed with the Frederick matter that it dominated every visit with her children.

The obsession was understandable, for the Frederick house was only a symptom of passage. More than losing friends and losing face, Dorothy Bullitt was losing force. For the first time in her life, her prodigious will was thwarted, and she did not take kindly to being crossed. Although such setbacks might occur with painful regularity in the lives of others, it was devastating to someone so sure of her personal power and so convinced of the importance of her actions over the years. The Center of the Universe, she who had ruled heaven and earth for so long, was beginning to experience a partial eclipse. Ineffectiveness presented a challenge like none she had met before. During her seventies, she began for the first time to experience real limitation—the frustrations of favorite projects unfulfilled, the dismissal of her ideas as unimportant, and the knowledge of decisions made without her consent or control.

Frustration came in steady doses. In 1963, thinking to create a practical tribute to her mother's memory, she donated a Steinway concert grand to the

Seattle Opera House and was thrilled to learn that it would be "christened" by the world-renowned pianist Artur Rubenstein, in concert with the Seattle Symphony. At a dinner party after his performance, Dorothy heard someone ask the maestro how he had found the piano and was appalled when he replied with a shrug, "Oh, it was so-so—not a terribly good piano." Dorothy didn't say a word but she was certainly furious—even more furious a few years later when she learned that the Steinway grand had been left outdoors by mistake and was ruined in the rain.

That same year, she took a trip to the Holy Land on a People to People tour, one in which the travelers met their foreign counterparts in an effort to understand each other's occupation and way of life. Although Dorothy enjoyed the trip, she was disappointed when her own television station was not even interested in acknowledging the uniqueness of the adventure. "I was so annoyed because the station never took it seriously at all," she said with a certain petulance.

DOROTHY'S FRUSTRATION WAS MOST INTENSE AT KING Broadcasting, where Stim was now in charge as president. Like Harriet with the piano and Patsy with the jewelry, Stim seemed unaware that the grand gift he had received was "on approval." Instead, the son had taken his mother at her word and was making decisions and changes to shape the company into what he wanted it to be. Although Dorothy had given him complete authority, the thought that he would act independently came as a great surprise. "Mother never questioned that she wouldn't be involved—that was an axiom of her life," Harriet explained. "She always thought that she was going to run everything. She had never initiated a retirement program because she didn't expect to retire, and she kept her big office because she automatically assumed that, one way or another, she would be running the show." Patsy concurred: "Mother probably assumed she would be running the company through Stim. I don't think it ever occurred to her that he would take independent action without her involvement," she said. "In Mother's mind this made a certain kind of sense because her children were really only extensions of herself. And, after all, Stim was her son, wasn't he?"

Over the decade of the 1960s, Dorothy watched as Stim made changes that at first surprised, then frustrated, and finally alarmed her. Whereas she had run a small seat-of-the-pants operation that succeeded because of her ability to communicate with people, she saw that this was not her son's style. Naturally scholarly and introverted, Stim lacked the "schmoozing" talent that had served his mother so well. Instead, he administered by memo and scheduled meetings with key people. It was not his method to remember birthdays, listen to employees' problems, or wander the halls just saying hello. If he spent time in the coffee shop, it was while reading a book by himself.

He was now running a larger organization of some 450 people that needed to be more systematized in approach. Not long after taking control, he set out to make the internal company structure more efficient, establishing a budget system and modernizing the accounting department with computers to replace the antiquated bookkeeping methods that had cluttered cabinets with columnar pads and filled shoe boxes with canceled checks. He wrote a personnel policy manual, initiated a profit-sharing program, and provided educational benefits for employees, all of which Dorothy never considered necessary. As Patsy put it, "To Mother, employee benefits meant giving the people you liked best a nice present on Christmas." She tolerated her son's interest in hiring minorities— blacks and Chicanos, principally, but also women—though it seemed an awful lot of trouble for so few people.

Stim insisted on hiring college graduates, mostly from Ivy League schools, over local applicants with experience or vocational training. It was a policy that irked his more practical mother. These newcomers, in Dorothy's mind, were uppity foreigners with too much education and too little experience who could never know or appreciate the Pacific Northwest like the hometown boys. Her prejudice was confirmed each time some young disc jockey or tweed-jacketed commentator spoke authoritatively about "*the* Puget Sound," or mispronounced familiar towns such as Puyallup or Skamakowa. She worried too that, with these new college-educated employees and her son's own political inclinations, the company would project too much of a liberal cast. She was very nervous when Stim went before the cameras in 1966 to read a controversial editorial—KING-TV's first—against the Vietnam War. Stim's editorial stance earned him a place on Richard Nixon's "Enemies List" and his mother's eventual admiration.

Dorothy expressed her concern only to her daughters. They were busy with their own lives, Patsy with a young family and a civic life of her own in San Diego, and Harriet with a publishing career and a second marriage to Seattle psychiatrist, Sid Rice. Throughout the 1960s, Dorothy phoned them repeatedly to recount her latest worries. "Can't you do something with your brother?" she asked at first, as she paced the floor at home. "Of course we couldn't change Stim and didn't really want to," Patsy remembered, "but when we suggested that she speak to him herself, Mother always said, 'I would *never* interfere with your brother.' When we asked if she wanted someone else as [company] president, she'd say, 'No, no, but I want him to change.' " At board meetings, she made no scenes or demands, even though these gatherings were less a forum for discussion and were increasingly a rubber stamp for what her son had already decided. When Stim asked his two sisters to join the board, she was pleased but surprised—the idea had never occurred to her. Realizing that Patsy and Harriet could now be involved, she urged them to take more responsibility in the company. Knowing also that they were both living on limited funds, she began concluding her calls with an ominous, "Well, this is your problem, dear. It's your money and you need to watch how it is managed. It's your income and it's your outcome."

In her frustration, Dorothy found ways of letting her presence be known within the company. One was to reach out for her "right-hand man" without regard for where he might be. During a high-level budget session, for instance, a secretary interrupted Stim to tell him that his mother was on the phone. "Thank you, I'll call her back, I'm in a meeting," he replied. A few seconds later, the secretary reappeared to say, "Your mother says she is to speak with you now." Feeling very much like a mama's boy, the company president left, only to find that she was not "hanging on a ledge waiting for rescue but just wondering about something that very well could have waited for some other time."

Dorothy also held court with other executives who sometimes drifted in and out of her office. Often they came to her to appeal or argue some decision that Stim had already made. She listened sympathetically, nodding, "Yes, yes, I understand." And because she seemed to be giving her blessing, some executives left her office feeling encouraged to undermine her son's authority.

One evening when Stim, Patsy, and Harriet were gathered at their mother's house, Stim began to complain about station manager Otto Brandt. (Brandt later left the company, but at that time was doing frequent battle with the "rich kid" in charge.) To her daughters' shock, Dorothy turned to her son and snapped, "Well, he's the one who earns the money. You're the one who spends it." And spend money he did. Stim's innovations with policy and personnel were small when compared to other ventures he initiated. Although lucrative and necessary, game shows and soap operas were lowly fare, so Stim sought to upgrade corporate taste by expanding into other more creative media. He became interested in film, in spite of warnings that a small, independent film company could never compete against the big Hollywood studios. At considerable expense, he financed a feature movie called *The Plot Against Harry* and formed a film company, King Screen Productions, to make an assortment of documentaries that he hoped would be syndicated on television. One production, *The Redwoods,* won an Oscar for best short documentary, but never saw much distribution. King Screen Productions was a costly gamble. Dorothy didn't know what shocked her more, the outflow of dollars or the bearded and bathless bohemians who now began to appear in the coffee shop at King. In her office, she fussed and fumed and flapped. She could tolerate erratic behavior, but these creative types with their long hair and messy clothes were also unmannerly and rude—two of the worst sins in her mind.

In 1964, Stim started *Seattle Magazine,* a sophisticated monthly publication that he hoped would capture the essence of the city. Its content was as controversial as the times, and as Dorothy read each issue, she bristled at the subject matter. Published by the Ivy Leaguers and New Yorkers her son had imported, the magazine turned out articles that she felt were smug, patronizing, and excessively provocative. Mercilessly, the editors and writers took apart every venerable institution in town, from its Boy Scouts to its Grandes Dames. The latter, an article about her old friends, was particularly irritating to her. Nor was she the only estranged reader. Advertisers fell off as the caustic subject matter alienated the business community.

"Mother thought we were getting into enterprises that weren't healthy and she didn't think would work. She didn't like the people being hired and the unequal pay scales," Harriet remembered. "She thought some of Stim's advisers were disloyal and she kept urging [Patsy and me] to get involved. '*Do* something,' she kept saying—she didn't know what we should do—but she wanted us to do something." Dorothy stewed as she saw all of these new ventures being supported by the (thus far) steady revenues from television, a situation that began to demoralize the broadcasting staff. Profit-sharing meant that people in money-losing departments shared profits with those in money-earning departments. "We felt like the drones," said Barbara Stenson, a news reporter. "We slobs in television were the fundraisers for those other, more noble projects—the quality documentaries and feature magazine articles. For us, it was a mess, but broadcasting was a license to steal in those days, so the money rolled in anyway."

But the continuing financial drain for these projects could not go on forever. When it came to the bottom line, Dorothy Bullitt always kept her focus. To the public and to employees, she was never critical of Stim's business decisions. She told Portland station manager Ancil Payne, "I am going to support Stim. I don't care if he loses every dollar in this company. He'll have my total support." But Payne observed that, "Mrs. Bullitt often said the opposite of what she meant." And he never forgot the dictum of his mentor, Henry Owen: "Mrs. Bullitt isn't a social worker—never forget the bottom line. Money is one of the marks of success in life, and she doesn't like to lose, period."

Personnel had always been Dorothy's primary focus, so she naturally worried that some of her favorites might be fired. Logan Bullitt, Dee Terry (Bullitt) Payson's son, did no work but had been receiving a supplemental salary from the company as a sinecure; when Stim discovered this, he had it stopped. He also set the company retirement age at sixty-five years. Of course, this didn't include Dorothy but it meant the loss of her cronies, Henry Owen and Gloria Chandler. As she paced and puffed in her office, she came up with a solution. There was a two-story brick building on the station property into which she would move Henry, Gloria, and herself. It would be their sanctuary—a cozy club, just like old times. Stim agreed to the move. Eventually the trio was joined by a fourth— John Leffler, retired Dean of St. Mark's Cathedral, who had a weekly religious program on KING-TV. Ensconced in the refurbished "brick house," Dorothy, Gloria, and Henry shared a secretary and congenial company from a steady stream of visitors from the "big building." Clara Stenstrom came over from accounting to review figures; and Fred Stimson, night engineer at the transmitter, dropped in to shoot the breeze every day, telling tales and gossip about the latest setbacks and cutbacks. Dorothy's "fan club" from the 1950s—anyone from photographers to cooks and comptrollers—stopped by for a smoke and the latest station gossip. The information most important to Dorothy was gleaned by Henry Owen during his frequent forays into the halls in the King building. There he picked up the crucial company news and brought it back to Dorothy, which in turn usually prompted another phone call to daughter Patsy or Harriet.

Not all of Stim's acquisitions caused Dorothy concern. Many of them proved shrewd and far-seeing. She approved of his establishing a videocable division in 1965, which assembled eight cable systems between Seattle and Los Angeles. She was interested when, a few years later, Stim started what became a fleet of mobile television vans that could be rented and sent anywhere in the world. Known as Northwest Mobile Television, the venture was expensive to start up, but served a definite need and still thrives. And at first sharply disapproving, she later accepted the stylized crown logo that Stim commissioned and that King Broadcasting Company has used ever since.

In 1968, Dorothy's low-level irritation changed to high-level anxiety when Stim told her and his sisters that he planned to merge the Bullitt Company into King Broadcasting. "I wish he wouldn't do that," Dorothy said huskily as she discussed the matter with Patsy in San Diego. "It's not a good idea." Her daughter, weary of being expected to be an intermediary, asked why not. "Because we will lose the name Bullitt," said Dorothy in dire tones. When her daughter countered that the Bullitt name was carried in the foundation,

Dorothy replied enigmatically, "That's different, dear," probably meaning that the foundation didn't have enough stature. Then she added her usual plea, "Can't you talk to your brother?" There was no way Stim's sister would or could dissuade her brother. Nor would it have made sense to interfere. Stim was doing quite well by the Bullitt Company's real estate acquisitions. When he began buying properties along First Avenue, overlooking the Seattle waterfront, Dorothy was enthusiastic. "Father used to always say that if you placed the handle of a fan at the waterfront along First Avenue and then spread it out over the city, that is where the city would build," she was fond of stating. Stim also purchased four small islands in British Columbia's Gulf Islands. Dorothy loved this area and visited the islands frequently over the years when she was boating. They were, as she described them, "inspirational, a good investment, and also accessible if something dreadful ever happened"—the refuge she envisioned in case of war. Only one purchase really displeased her—a plywood manufacturing plant in Okinawa, Japan, because it wasn't a Northwest venture and much too far away to manage properly.

Communication between Stim and Dorothy began to decay the more one took independent action and the other refused to listen. Never one for long meetings, Stim would pop into her office with a question or a comment and get caught up listening to Dorothy ramble on about her friends at The Highlands. Patsy remembered: "Stim only wanted to spend ten minutes with Mother, telling her what he was doing in the company, while her wish was to have him sit down and spend two hours. Fred could sit there for hours, she reasoned, so why couldn't Stim? For years they couldn't synchronize; they never wanted to talk about the same thing. Mother just couldn't quite listen and she certainly couldn't let go of the company. It was as if she had given birth to the baby, turned it over for adoption, and then didn't like the way it was being raised."

This attitude was as understandable as it was tragic. Dorothy Bullitt had fed and nurtured her "fourth child" for many years, had infused it with her life's blood and taken very little in return. True, the company's net worth was still healthy ($25 million), but in 1971 broadcasting was adversely affected by factors beyond its control. That year, the FCC ruled against cigarette advertising on the air. That same year, Boeing's employment dropped to below 40,000 from a high of 95,000 three years before. Seattle was experiencing an economic depression so severe that two members of the nearly defunct real estate profession, in a gesture of macabre humor, leased a billboard near the airport that read, "Will the last person leaving Seattle please turn out the lights." At King Broadcasting's annual meeting, the board of directors and shareholders were distressed to hear that eight of the company's major holdings were operating at a loss.

Stim wasn't all that happy himself. His plans to achieve the "shining uplands" had become tarnished by frustration and discouragement. He found himself miscast, much as his father may once have been. Stim Bullitt was an attorney, comfortable with discussing a wide range of ideas among his peers in a civilized, collegial atmosphere. Philosophical by nature, he was inspired by the possibilities of bettering the human condition. He was not a businessman content to count success by profits alone, nor was he at ease with subordinates or tolerant of their ambitious agendas. He couldn't align his goals with "Let's Make a Deal" or "The Dating Game." He had no interest in glad-handing at NAB conventions or backslapping at NBC affiliate meetings. His sister Harriet described him as "a risk taker with high ideals. Stim liked the intellectual challenge and the influence of broadcasting. He liked the profitability and the plans for diversity, but he hated the whole marketing base of broadcasting. The ham-and-eggs mentality, the meetings about scheduling hockey games or advertising—all of that was boring to him."

Instead of sunlit uplands, Stim found himself a stranger in an arid land of advertisers and affiliators, station managers, producers, and disc jockeys. These show-biz types, sycophants, and snobs scoffed when they saw his small spartan office and kept him waiting when he went to theirs. King Broadcasting was a milieu entirely foreign to his basic nature. He was a mountain climber, happy to scale hazardous peaks alone, not a cheerleader eager to rally employees. Many of the ventures that he had initiated himself—projects staffed with the more creative types that he had brought into the company—were failing fast enough that he knew they could not continue. "I wasn't a very good administrator in many ways," Stim commented many years later. "In hiring, I gave too much weight to brains and education, not enough to experience, and I lacked follow-through. I took the company into some business ventures that failed and there were financial setbacks—although measured from beginning to end, the company made a lot more than it lost."

Depressed, Stim began to keep more to himself and his office. His sister Patsy, sensing his state of mind, flew to Seattle without telling her mother and met Stim at the Olympic Hotel for breakfast. "Patsy, in her customary perceptive way, said to me, 'Stim, you're not having a very good time. Why don't you quit?' " Stim recalled. "I said, 'That's a good suggestion. I think I will. I'm going to try to get a couple of more things done and I'll do it in six months.' " To improve the administrative structure, Stim had asked Ancil Payne, Portland stations manager, to take the position of executive vice president in Seattle. Hired in 1959 as assistant to Henry Owen, Payne took his boss's place as vice president of business in 1963 when Owen retired, then became vice president in charge of the Portland stations in 1965. Tall and slim, with wavy dark hair that turned silver before he retired, Payne was an elegant mixture of sophisticated urbanite and comfortable homebody, who combined worldly wit with enough humorous anecdotes and stories from his native Oregon to make him approachable and real. He was a shrewd social and political creature, naturally adept at handling people of all backgrounds and vintages. His interest in politics had begun as a Young Democrat at the University of Washington, where he first met Stim Bullitt. After graduation he became Northwest regional director for Americans for Democratic Action and later worked as administrative assistant to Congressman Hugh B. Mitchell. He had also run a trucking company in Alaska. Payne's political and business experience, plus his natural ability to communicate and inspire confidence, had made him successful in King Broadcasting's Portland operation. It was hoped that he could bring the same attention to the operations in Seattle where both staff and equipment were suffering from inattention.

Dorothy was delighted with this news. She knew Payne and his potential as an administrator, referring to him often as "the best manager in the business." And by this time Ancil knew her and had a lively appreciation for her uncompromising "athawrity." He remembered an incident when he had first come to King Broadcasting. Dorothy had learned that Monroe Sweetland, a candidate for secretary of state in Oregon, was being attacked by right-wing fundamentalists for being a Communist. "I think it's dreadful about what's going on," she told Payne, remembering how Stim had been maligned during his congressional campaigns. As the conversation continued, she began to consider having an editorial delivered on the Portland stations. It would be a first for Portland—previous stands had been commentaries—and she asked Payne if he agreed. He had barely answered yes when she countered with, "How soon can you leave for Portland?" A few hectic hours later, Mrs. Bullitt and Payne arrived at KGW to discuss the matter with station manager Tom Dargan, Maureen Neuburger (future U.S. senator), and commentator Tom McCall (later governor of Oregon). A few more hours later, the team adjourned for a steak dinner and Ancil Payne wrote the editorial and confirmed it with Stim in Seattle. "When it came to reading the editorial, I knew that Tom McCall was reluctant to do so because he had Republican ambitions of his own and he felt it might alienate some of his possible constituency," Payne remembered with a grin. "In his effort to escape viewers and listeners, McCall tried to bury the editorial on radio at mid-morning and air it on television sometime in the afternoon. Well, he couldn't get that one past Mrs. Bullitt. When he told her his schedule, she smiled benignly, leaned forward, and in a deep velvet voice said, 'Oh now,

Tommy, we didn't come all the way down here to have it run once in the afternoon. I want to see it run several times throughout the day and at the end of the news—that's where it really belongs. And I want to hear it on the radio frequently over the next three days. Please find the schedules and bring them back so I can have them in hand to listen to them and see how they sound.' Well! That was that in short order," Payne said, savoring the memory. "There was no question about who was making the final decisions. Dorothy Bullitt wasn't born in a Mason jar, you know. Whether she understood McCall's reluctance to editorialize in this case or not didn't matter. She just wanted it done. When she made up her mind about something, I tell you, that was it."

However, years later, when it came to her son and his management of King Broadcasting, Dorothy Bullitt had made up her mind not to interfere, at least directly. Then in 1971 a series of incidents combined to bring the issue of Stim's management to a head. The Los Angeles Times-Mirror, which owned the *Los Angeles Times,* made an approach to acquire King Broadcasting through a merger for Times-Mirror stock. Stim, favorably impressed by initial conversations, saw that this form of transaction would give King Broadcasting shareholders Times-Mirror stock that could either be sold on the open market or held without sustaining income tax liability. It would also accomplish his goal of getting out of broadcasting.

The proposal was interesting enough that he told his mother about it. Alarmed, Dorothy passed the word on to her daughters who shared her objections to such a move. "It was the worst time of all to try to sell the company even if we had wanted to," Patsy recalled. "With the station's cash problems and the poor local economy, the Times-Mirror would have had the bargain of the century." After a flurry of family calls, Harriet finally phoned her brother on behalf of the principal owners, telling him to stop further conversations with Times-Mirror representatives.

Not long afterward, Henry Owen reported that the company president and the new executive vice president on whom so much was riding were at loggerheads over who was in authority. When Dorothy passed this news on to Harriet, she got her daughter's full attention. "There was disaster in Mother's voice," Harriet remembered, "and for the first time, I saw that her worries were real. We knew it would be terrible if Ancil left—he was a very good manager who could bring in qualified people and keep them happy. Mother said something must be done, and I agreed." As if on cue, Dorothy's worst fears were soon confirmed when Henry reported that Ancil Payne had written out his resignation. Again the phone calls flew back and forth, followed by a late-night meeting with Payne, a hasty arrival by Patsy, and a reluctant decision by the sisters to confront their brother. During this time, Dorothy was not directly involved, but she was kept informed and made no effort to change the course of events. Remembering those days with regret, Harriet said, "It wasn't until things got so bad—with the company losing money, Ancil threatening to resign, Stim locked up in his office depressed, and Henry urging that Stim had to go—that Mother realized that Stim wouldn't change and that someone else needed to be president. But it was up to us to do it."

As they stood outside Stim's office at King Broadcasting, Harriet turned to her sister and said, "How do we go in, Patsy, without looking like a couple of Sherman tanks?" "What else can we do?" her sister replied. At that meeting they told Stim they wanted changes on the board's executive committee, with Dorothy and Patsy made members and Harriet made chairman of the committee, replacing real estate investor Bagley Wright, a friend of Stim's who would soon resign in anger. Finally Patsy asked her brother to resign as president to become chairman of the board; she also told him that Ancil Payne would become chief executive officer. "That was the worst—it was devastating for all of us," Patsy remembered and her sister agreed. "Stim didn't want to feel like a quitter," Harriet said, "but finally Patsy persuaded him." Her message was simple. "I told Stim that we didn't want him to be our business manager, that we wanted Ancil to handle the broadcasting business," Patsy recalled, not without some lingering pain. "And I told him that we wanted him back as our brother." Reluctantly, Stim complied.

Hurt and humiliated, Stim took his leave of King Broadcasting, as he later described it, "under strained and awkward circumstances." He had once told his children, when they had asked how he would choose to die, that he wanted an old-fashioned hero's death—sword in hand, wounded everywhere but in his back. The day he left King Broadcasting, he no doubt was suffering from wounds on all sides. In his mind, his sisters had booted him out of a job that he had been going to leave anyway. Years later, he described his reaction with a wry smile. "I felt like the man who was run out of town on a rail and when asked how he felt about it, said, 'Except for the honor of the thing, I'd just as soon have walked.' Well, I would just as soon have walked six months later."

Although his sisters insisted that as chairman of the board he was still part of the company, Stim felt that separate ways was the only solution. Within a year, the family, Dorothy included, agreed to a division of property. The separation of shares and subcompanies was no small task, requiring two years' worth of tax clearances, stock exchanges, license changes, and legal work at meetings that were sometimes tense and traumatic. The four family members, attorney Dick Riddell, Ancil Payne, and a small number of key officers and financial advisers met in a private room at the Washington Athletic Club. "It showed the mettle of the Bullitt family," Dick Riddell observed. "They were able to handle a very difficult situation without having anything publicly known, even within the company itself. In closed session, we sat there and hammered out a division of assets, without pounding the table. Strong feelings were sometimes expressed, but never in a nasty way. Sure, there were arguments about the value of certain assets—Stim might take one stand and Patsy, Harriet, and Dorothy would jump on him all at once—but no one had to be quieted down because everyone was so genteel." He added, "The only occasionally disturbing sound was the scrape of steel against steel in their voices."

The split effectively unmerged the Bullitt Company and allocated to Stim the family real estate—the Canadian islands, the 1411 and Logan Buildings downtown, and the large stretch of Seattle property along First Avenue (that would become Harbor Properties many years later). King Broadcasting Company, a clearly separate entity, went to its major shareholders: Dorothy, Patsy, and Harriet. They retained Ancil Payne as president, signing a contract that guaranteed him the autonomy he required. Payne recalled the separation process as a "terribly and genuinely emotional experience for this family. It started out all right, but before it finished there was a lot of tension and we went through agonizing periods when the Bullitts would probably have preferred to handle things themselves." He added, "I do think they came to an understanding of each other that perhaps they had never had." Payne regretted the loss of his long-standing friendship with Stim. Years after his own retirement, Payne mused, "I miss sitting down with him and talking philosophically because there we were very closely aligned."

Dorothy's role in all of this appeared passive, although many—her daughters included—maintained that in her way she had orchestrated the whole thing. One thing is clear: it would never have happened without her consent. Equally clear was the fact that Dorothy was sorry that it had to happen. Her son assigned her no blame. "Mother didn't take an active part in any of it," Stim recalled. "She faulted no one, but I got the impression that she was distressed and saddened by the whole situation." For the rest of her life, Dorothy avoided talk about this difficult passage. She would dismiss it by saying, "Oh, Stim and I had different ideas about our approach to broadcasting. He was awfully good for the company during the ten years that he was president, but he is much more a scholar than a pragmatist—in fact the two don't necessarily jibe. It just wasn't his dish—he's a perfectionist and a noncompromiser."

Dorothy dismissed the subject so thoroughly that, according to her daughters, she forgot her own role in the whole episode. "Mother wanted everything to be perfect," Patsy concluded. "She wanted Stim not to be angry, Ancil to manage the company, and us to get the job done. She had told Harriet and me that it was '*our* problem and *our* business,' yet after it was all over, somehow it became *her* company again. Once she went so far as to say, 'How could you have done that to your brother?'!" With a rueful smile, Patsy explained, "We were still learning that Mother never really gave anything away—instead she delegated it on the unspoken basis that the delegee would do whatever Mother wanted, and if it didn't work out that way, she took it back. With Stim, she gave him the company *directly* thinking he would do everything 'just right.' She didn't count on his being his own special individual—a lawyer and not an administrator—and when she finally realized it wasn't working her way, she took it back *indirectly* through Harriet and me." Ancil Payne had his own way of paraphrasing the whole process after years of schooling in Dorothy Bullitt's taciturn tactics: "She won't say anything, and she won't say anything, and she won't say anything, and then one day she'll come down and cleave you in twain because it is her company and it always will be."

Ironically, most of Stim's innovations proved very wise. He had laid creative foundations for a more modern company, better equipped to deal with the changing ideas and times of the 1970s. The Bullitt sisters are quick to credit their brother for much of King Broadcasting's subsequent success. "Personnel benefits—profit sharing, education, retirement—were due to Stim," Harriet explained. "Stim hired blacks and women before it was popular or there was pressure to do so. By the time he left, the company employed more blacks in responsible positions than in all other Northwest stations combined. This didn't represent a lot of people at first, but he set the policy for the additional hiring that opened up later. He brought in a lot of talented people who, if they didn't all make the company money, earned it a reputation for excellence. Some of them became valuable administrators. In terms of profits, Stim's early investment in videocable eventually became the company's major asset, providing better than half of its cash flow, and the fleet of mobile television vans became the largest such enterprise in the world."

————

ALL THREE OF DOROTHY'S CHILDREN CAME OUT OF THIS decade of transition aware that they were still learning, sometimes by default, about their mother and about each other. Their mother, now nearing her eightieth year, was beginning to turn to them for support and attention after being so consumed with other things for most of her life. This was a mixed blessing, for when Dorothy Bullitt turned and focused it was difficult to hide or say no.

As a result, Her Three were having to fine-tune the art of being loving, respectful, and firm at the same time—a balancing technique that each perfected in his or her own way. More than anything, the Bullitt siblings learned from the ordeal of Stim's departure and the split-off of the company how much they meant to each other. The money and material goods involved in this incident, the issues of loyalty and fairness, were fertile grounds for an irreparable rift in any family. Not so the strong-minded children of Dorothy and Scott Bullitt. Threading their way through rapids, they addressed and overcame the dangers, to find in the end that they were closer together. They realized that no matter what material goods were at stake—the company, the foundation, or their mother's fortune—nothing was worth destroying their love for each other. This realization did not come easily or comfortably. Their father, by his example, had shown them the tolerance and forgiveness to weather any family storm, and their mother had shown them the sheer willpower to ride it through. Without discussion, each made a conscious decision to get along with the other, come what may—to respect, consider, and love, despite varying interests and needs. For each of them, this was an unspoken commitment, an act of will, and the considerable power behind it saw them through. Unknowingly, Dorothy Bullitt had given Her Three two gifts that she couldn't take back nor would she have wanted to. One was a gift of example that she had lived out and patterned for them, a demonstration of endurance and courage after their father's death when, in extreme adversity, she had "set her soul" and exerted her will to go on. The other was the gift of each other. A certain blessed sort of irony had resulted from this family ordeal, which is that if Dorothy Bullitt did indeed orchestrate the split up of the family business and the removal of her son, she also provided the means and grace by which the wounds that resulted were healed.

It's not how many years you've lived as what you've really done with them.

13 A LIVING LEGEND

1972–1980

BY THE 1970S DOROTHY BULLITT WAS AN ICON IN THE PACIFIC Northwest and in the world of broadcasting. As her business empire continued to grow, with stations in San Francisco, Boise, and Honolulu, so did her fortune and the stories about her. Fueled by fragments of fact, along with the opinions of many who thought they knew her well, and the agendas of others who attributed their own ideals to her, the Dorothy Bullitt legend took on a life of its own. She became a symbol of strength and inspiration, part banner and part bowsprit, patron saint for a variety of liberal causes and holy terror if her orders were disobeyed. She became a trophy to be shined up and shown off on special occasions, to draw attention to and raise funds for others' causes. Now in her ninth decade, Dorothy Bullitt had become a living legend. An aura surrounded her that was so ornate and embellished, fabricated by so many with such conviction that many either forgot or failed to see the real person behind it all.

The stories were legion, abundant fodder for distortion because the very private Mrs. Bullitt didn't speak to the press about her personal life. According to various sources, she was born in a logging camp in Granite Falls and had in girlhood attended the Juillard School of Music. During her marriage to Scott Bullitt, she had stood staunchly by his side in politics, eagerly joining his crusades on behalf of the common man. After his death, she had singlehandedly made her way as a penniless widow with three children, rising by sheer bootstrap-power from the bread lines of the Depression to build an empire in business and broadcasting. Another story had the intrepid Mrs. Bullitt crossing Russia in 1936 on the Trans-Siberian Railway.

Most of the myths arose from her years in broadcasting. Few people realized that Dorothy Bullitt had enjoyed at least a couple of lives of some significance for fifty-five years before she entered the world of radio and television. Stories circulated about how she had rowed out into the ocean to a freighter in order to secure the call letters for KING, trading them on the high seas for a case of champagne. Since the earliest days, rumor had it, she had guided the news staff firmly in the fight for aggressive reporting, requiring reporters to take on controversial issues. She was, according to popular belief, a tireless champion of liberal causes—a fighter for women's rights, gay rights, and racial equality—against anything that even hinted of injustice. To achieve her ideals, she had spent millions, but money meant little or nothing to her. Profit was insignificant in light of her lofty goals. She was thought to be a tireless and ageless presence in her office, reigning actively over her business kingdom and ruling with an iron but well-gloved fist until the day she died.

These myths were minor, however, when compared to those that sprouted at King Broadcasting during the last twenty years of her life. Dorothy Bullitt's persona still permeated the halls at King, even though few employees had actual contact with the silver-haired woman who sat at her large desk every working day. She remained accessible to all yet—to her irritation—visited by few. For King employees, she became the embodiment of what they each thought they stood for, and that embodiment took on grand and grander proportions. While she sat unaware in her office, everyone from the coffee shop to the boardroom invoked her name, citing her supposed wishes and dislikes as if quoting chapter and verse from some gospel according to Dorothy. "Mrs. Bullitt says . . . Mrs. Bullitt would want . . . Mrs. Bullitt doesn't like . . ." preceded any idea to be proposed or rejected, any cause to be pursued or avoided, most of them unknown to her. In the name of Mrs. B, engineers fought for new equipment, saying she wanted only the latest and best. Producers justified the special topics they wanted to cover, claiming that creativity and controversy were high on her list. In the name of Our Lady of King, popular syndicated talk show host Rush Limbaugh was taken off the air because it was claimed his conservative opinions were not to Mrs. B's liking. One overly zealous reporter who allegedly interfered with a police action in progress justified it by saying that this was the sort of thing Mrs. B wanted "her" news staff to do. "Mother didn't even know about most of these decisions," Patsy reflected. "She didn't really like the freedom the news people had—it usually shocked her and she thought they sometimes abused it. Aggressive reporting was much too conspicuous for Mother."

Nor was it true that Dorothy Bullitt cared enormously about certain causes and cared not a whit about money. "People attributed causes to Mother that she really didn't get caught up in and endowed her with a philosophy that wasn't true," said her son, Stim. "In reality, she didn't have any particular philosophy and never concerned herself much with abstract thinking. Instead she had strong moral principles and a great interest in human relations." Patsy concurred: "Mother espoused people and principles, not causes. Certain manners and standards of behavior guided her life—courtesy, honesty, civility, quality, loyalty, propriety, and excellence. She was not so much interested in preserving old-growth forests as she was in preserving old-fashioned dictums like: keep your word, tell the truth, stand up straight, speak clearly and correctly, and be the best at what you're doing. She believed more in the standards of accurate reporting than in the causes for advocacy reporting. She was quite capable of having someone fired for mistreating an employee or a viewer, but she wasn't really much interested in civil rights, in feminism, or in the rights of homosexuals." These latter causes were actually a legacy from Stim's tenure as president of King Broadcasting, but they were misattributed to her as her legend grew.

In terms of "rights"—whether of race, gender, or sexual preference—the Dorothy Bullitt behind the legend was a creature of her social upbringing and her times, holding to a particular set of stereotypes and attitudes toward others— foreigners and people of other races. She was by training and by nature always polite to everyone, regardless of race, color, creed, or cause. At the same time, however, she was privileged and aristocratic to the core. "On one level, Mother regarded almost any foreigner as servant quality—except maybe the English, who were always perfect in her mind," Harriet recalled with a wry smile. Chinese, Japanese, Irish, and Scandinavian were all classed as they might have been early in the century—as good workers, good cooks, clean, helpful, reliable, and loyal. Blacks had played no part in her life until her marriage and then they were either musicians or servants toward whom she was as always courteous. Northwest Indians were considered "a very low type," though the Plains Indians were seen as "noble savages" who rode horses into battle with honor.

"On the other hand, when it came to individuals," daughter Harriet continued, "she had many cherished friends from all races, countries, and classes. If Mother liked someone, none of the stereotypes were important." Fred Ohata, for example, received her highest praise. Without qualification, he was held up to her family as an example of the ultimate among civilized men. She trusted her black chauffeur, James Nesbitt, and flew to his defense if he was attacked in any way. Many friends were Jewish—Benny Priteca, designer of the Coliseum Theater, and Frank Newman, who leased it from her, were her good friends. As for homosexuals, Dorothy was tolerant and curious. Later in life, she accepted her hairdresser's invitation to attend a banquet at Seattle Center for the crowning of the queen of the gay community. Sipping champagne at a table next to the runway, Dorothy and her housekeeper, Sallie Baldus, watched the contestants parade by. They chatted with their six male tablemates, most of them dressed in female garb. Dorothy marveled at the candidates' beauty. Leaning forward, she asked, "How can you tell that they are men?"

About the rights of women, Dorothy was strangely anachronistic. She complained that her nonbusiness female friends were boring. "All they talk about are recipes and what they are going to wear to Maui!" She never sought to bring stronger women friends into her life. When asked to speak to a women's group, she confided to her grandson Bill Collins, "I'd like to, but they might not like to hear what I would say. I'd have to tell them right off I couldn't have been in business without the help of men who told me what to do next. Those men would never have helped a male competitor in the same way, and they kept me in business." She believed that there were certain jobs that only men should hold, for example, a legal negotiator such as Andrew Haley. She would not hire women for high positions in her company. To run a company, according to the gospel of Dorothy, one had to be a man, even as she had needed Henry Owen. She did not expect women, her daughters and granddaughters included, to take on administrative responsibilities. In her opinion, the highest King Broadcasting position a woman could aspire to was news anchor or reporter, and she was uneasy even in the 1980s when a woman was hired as corporate attorney.

That Dorothy Bullitt cared nothing about money was probably the biggest misconception of all. "She loved money and finances," Ancil Payne said of his boss. "She relished looking over financial sheets, all the while complaining, 'I don't understand these figures, there are just too many "Ga-naughts" behind the main number,' and all the while she'd be multiplying it by 6¼ percent interest, computing and compounding it for the first two years before anyone else knew what was happening! She used money very well and always wanted to make a profit. Dorothy Bullitt did not like to lose. You could cross her in any number of ways but you'd better not do it with her pocketbook."

As a result of the Depression, Dorothy had a deep distrust for speculation and never invested in stocks or bonds. "I don't like Wall Street or anything connected with it," she barked in her deep voice that became more raspy with each year. "There are too many kinks in it." She was an entrepreneur who preferred to invest in something over which she would have some measure of control, rather than in others' ventures. Many times in her life, she turned down chances for profit because the goals involved were inconsistent with her objectives. In her personal life, her spending was careful. Any supposed luxury had to have a business purpose—her yacht was purchased in the name of the

During the 1960s, Dorothy had to reassess her role at KING when her son, Stim, became president of the company. (Photo: *Seattle Post-Intelligencer*)

company and her old tug was restored so that it could get back to work again. As Patsy put it, "It was Mother's mission to manage money sharply and she enjoyed every minute of it. Even in her nineties when she peeled an uncanceled stamp from an envelope, a look of triumph would light up her face. Winning at the game of money gave her a rush whether it amounted to 15 cents or $15 million."

IF THE MYTH HAD A LIFE OF ITS OWN, THE REAL DOROTHY Bullitt did also. At age eighty, she was less duty-bound and driven. In the brick building, she was still Queen of King but the business of work was often play. Daily the gang of four—Dorothy, Gloria, Henry, and John Leffler—drifted in and out of each other's offices, broke for a two-hour lunch, and spent the afternoon kibitzing with Fred Stimson when he took his leave from the transmitter or entertaining a small stream of regular visitors from the main building. "It was a little club," Steve Wilson, a KING-TV producer, remembered. "Over there they did anything they wanted. It was a nonsmoking building [with Harriet's environmental magazine, *Pacific Search*, upstairs], but downstairs they smoked, sipped coffee spiked with Bailey's Irish Creme, or swigged a little Scotch now and again. At the end of an hour's visit, we'd all be just hooting with laughter. At Christmas they gave eggnog parties, and if you could drink one and get home, you had accomplished something."

She still attended King Broadcasting board meetings, sitting quietly, digesting the information as it went around the table, feeling her way through the conversation for signs of something not quite right. She remained keenly interested and inquisitive if the situation warranted. During the 1980s, when discussion was underway about the acquisition of a television station in Honolulu, she listened as management extolled the advantages of such a buy. "Does it have a problem with the tower?" she finally asked in that gravelly voice. There was total silence; she had picked the one major drawback to the purchase.

Sometime in her eighties, Dorothy Bullitt finally settled into a comfortable part of her true self. She shrugged off the last traces of rigidity that had inhibited much of her life. Rather than trying to shape her world, she began to roll with it. As she did so, her true sense of humor shone through in the form of wacky one-liners that she zinged off the top of her head like so many sparklers, firing right to the point as if she were reading copy from some unedited tape running across her agile mind. She popped out quips and fizzy comments that flavored any dialogue like some evanescent seasoning that was as pleasing as it was hard to capture. The Bullitt brand of humor was full of ambiguity and absurdity; it was droll, casual, and an utterly natural extension of herself. It didn't stand by itself; it was always attached to the subject at hand. It was a gestalt of words and varied facial expressions—the roll of the eyes, the sly lowering of the lids, the twist of the lips, and a voice with dramatic tone and inflection. It went right to the point—although the point might be a bit off center. Often it was directed toward herself. It was so charming that those hearing it left smiling but unable to pinpoint exactly why. Asked once if she liked popcorn, she replied offhandedly, "Umm, having to clean your teeth afterwards is worth it." Why did she have a dog instead of a cat? With a thoughtful look, hands steepled and eyes on her little poodle Lily, she pronounced slowly, "I love cats, but they don't make enough *noise*." Once a visitor was surprised to find her attired in a blue silk print dress rather than her customary tailored suit. When complimented on the dress, Dorothy looked down at it, brushing imaginary crumbs from her bodice, and exclaimed with a touch of mock smugness, "Oh, do you like it? I do too. It was delivered today from the cleaners by mistake. Heaven only knows what happened to *my* clothes, but this *is* my favorite color." On Election Day 1988, she phoned a friend. "Well, are you all booted and spurred for the election?" she barked brusquely, without announcing who she was (certainly there was no need to) and without awaiting an answer, added, "I'm prepared to take my gun if not to shoot somebody, then to shoot myself—depending upon how it turns out." Dorothy was usually silent at King board meetings, though she found occasion for a zinger now and then. During one King meeting in the middle of a discussion about an unrelated subject, she locked a laser gaze on Ancil Payne and said, "And can you tell me why we have to have 'The Newlywed Game' on the air?" Payne, knowing that the best way to convince Dorothy Bullitt of anything was by appealing to her pocketbook, replied quickly, "Would it make you feel any better about it if I told you how much money it made?" "No," she countered with a twinkle. "But it will shut me up."

DEATH WASHED OVER DOROTHY IN WAVES DURING THE 1970S. Dorothy Terry Bullitt Payson, her first friend, died unexpectedly in November 1970. Without realizing it was their last conversation, the two women said good-bye over the telephone, just as they had said hello over a tin-can telephone nearly seventy years before. Their comfortable chat bade farewell to a lifetime of shared memories. The next death, however, was a greater blow. In 1974, while on a trip aboard the *Stimson,* Dorothy received the unexpected news of Gloria Chandler's death from a coronary embolism. Gloria had been recovering satisfactorily from a recent surgery and when Dorothy called from Roche Harbor in the San Juans to check on her friend, she learned that Gloria had died the previous night. "I was with Mrs. Bullitt when she phoned," skipper Ron Saling remembered. "Suddenly she turned ashen and I caught her, thinking she was going to collapse." When Dorothy arrived in Seattle a few hours later, Harriet and Patsy met her on the airport runway. "Mother was sobbing uncontrollably," Patsy recalled. "We virtually carried her to the car and she kept repeating, 'She wasn't going to die—the doctor said she was recovering—I wouldn't have gone away.' " It was a reaction completely unlike Dorothy's response to other deaths in recent decades. Gloria, her companion and consultant, had filled every void in Dorothy's life and her absence was inconceivable for a time. "It came as a terrible shock to me," Dorothy wrote to a friend. "We planned it all in reverse—I would die first, of course, and all arrangements were made accordingly—for her care after my death." Fifteen years later, Dorothy shook her head, saying, "Gloria had nobody else . . . and I was away on a boat when she died."

Not many months after Gloria's death, Henry Owen crashed his big Lincoln Continental on the way home one wintry night, probably having had a stroke at the wheel. Unable to eat or speak, he lay in hospital for seven months before he died. Henry's passing was the end of an era for Dorothy Bullitt. Gloria and Henry represented the last of King's golden days in her mind; now they were truly gone. As a team, they had planned, plotted, and propelled the company over all of the early hurdles and lived to see it prosper. The trio had shared their retirement with humor and grace, joking that they were the Three Musketeers and the Three Stooges. Now she was left to play her part alone, the last of the old guard. Only Fred was left from the original crew.

———————

DOROTHY WOULD ALSO SAY GOOD-BYE TO A BIT OF HER independence. Concerned about their mother's driving ability at age eighty-four, and taking advantage of the psychological impact of Henry's fatal accident, the Bullitt daughters conspired to keep her from taking the wheel. Pushing each other, one in front of the other, they approached their mother on Valentine's Day to announce warily that they had a present for her. "Oh?" she inquired. Patsy said, "That's right, Mother, you don't have to drive anymore. You don't have to do errands or park the car—we've hired a driver for you, and King will pay the bill." She accepted this gift but still made an occasional bid for freedom, using the extra set of car keys she had stashed away. One foray occurred when she drove herself to work while the rest of the city was paralyzed in a blinding snow and ice storm. When asked why on earth she had ventured out in such conditions alone, she replied confidently, "Because I knew no one would be on the roads and *I* know how to drive in the snow."

In 1979 while the new $18 million King Broadcasting Company corporate headquarters were under construction, Dorothy decided to drive herself downtown to paint her temporary office. Painting gave her immense satisfaction. Equipped with brushes, paint cans, and an old black lunchbox and dressed in one of her French smocks (with pockets for hand-flapping), she arrived on a Sunday morning to take on the kitchen. "After I had finished I was smeared all over with paint," she remembered with a certain amount of glee. "I sat down to make a list of what to do next when somehow the burglar alarm went off. Well, I ran around and tried to turn it off and couldn't, so I grabbed my pocketbook and tried to get out of there but the door was stuck. There I was—dirty as anything, my hair on end and certainly not at my best—when three police cars arrived. Well, the police wanted to know who I was and what I was doing. 'Who do you work for?' 'Well . . . King Broadcasting . . . I was just doing a little painting.' Finally they got the alarm turned off and told me I could leave. I heard one explain to another that I was the *cleaning* woman as I got into my Mercedes and drove off."

After Gloria's death, Dorothy turned to two old friends she had left. John Leffler, retired Dean of St. Mark's, had been a friend for many years. Since his arrival in Seattle in 1951, and for twenty years thereafter, he had instilled new vitality into his parish, transforming the cathedral into a modern religious center filled with ritual, celebration, controversy, and music that ranged from Gregorian chant to rock. Leffler was a popular preacher who spoke to full congregations on liberal politics, the ordination of women, abortion, and war resistance. He had met Dorothy Bullitt at Sunday services, convinced her to televise Christmas Eve services at St. Mark's and became a local celebrity at KING-TV with his weekly chats. Eventually he became part of her "brick building" coterie of intimates, and after his wife, Faith, was confined to a nursing home, he and Dorothy spent many hours discussing current events and their status as elderly fixtures in Seattle society. They shared a certain passion for cigarettes and martinis, and an avid interest in politics, history, and music. Although he cultivated many prominent Seattle matrons, John Leffler was particularly fond of Dorothy Bullitt, whom he praised as "one of the most remarkable people I've known." When he dedicated the new King Broadcasting building, he could not refrain from praising her and concluded his prayer with, "You know, God, that she does not like such things to be said of her, because success has never changed her basic humility. But we know this is true, and you, O Lord, know it's true. So we say thank you most of all for her."

Dorothy thoroughly enjoyed Leffler's companionship. "He was a darling—always jolly," she remembered with warmth. "We were very congenial. He knew I was a heathen and tolerated that. We could laugh and talk about anything." On Sunday mornings, he timed his sermons for the eight o'clock service and Dorothy trotted half a block to the church and stood in the back while he spoke, making sure that he returned to her house for breakfast and Bloody Marys. She looked forward to his frequent visits, dressing up for the occasion and instructing her housekeeper, Sallie, to prepare the silver shaker for martinis, the Dean's favorite libation. On these occasions, Sallie served sandwiches on the patio or dinner in the sunroom. With an affectionate laugh, she remembered, "Mrs. Bullitt would get starry-eyed on those martinis. They would talk and laugh and hold hands, kid about old age—it was a special relationship for them both."

Another friend was Eleanor Clark, some years Dorothy's junior, who had known her since World War I when both girls had been tent neighbors at Red Cross camp and Dorothy had scolded her for wearing her skirts too short. Eleanor was a little bee of a woman, a diminutive dynamo with such a sting to her words that even the most insensitive knew to be wary. Eleanor had been married five times to men who ranged from her hotel manager (she owned Seattle's Richmond Hotel) to a Russian count named Tolstoy, great-nephew of the novelist, with whom she had run a riding stable in Vienna. For years in Europe she had hobnobbed with cultured expatriates (among them the man who killed Rasputin), before divorcing her great love, the count, because of his jealousy. Dorothy was fascinated by her friend's sophistication and quick intelligence, but wary of her moods. One day Eleanor could be chummy and down-to-earth, the next she was imperious and, as Dorothy described it, "playing the countess." It was an odd friendship—Eleanor was conservative, often rude and jealous, while the more tolerant Dorothy sought a balance between having her say and, if the going got too rough, keeping quiet. They disagreed often, sometimes loudly. "We'd banter and bicker," Dorothy said of the friendship. "You would have thought we hated each other." Between skirmishes they liked to go to an expensive restaurant and catch a movie now and then. One night they attended *The Best Little Whorehouse in Texas* wearing huge floppy hats so that no one would recognize them and laughing at how conspicuous they actually were. On another summer evening they viewed *The Towering Inferno,* and they left the movie exhausted. "We felt as if we'd burned up all evening," Dorothy recalled, fanning herself at the thought. "In front of the People's Bank building there was a pool, so we sat on the edge to cool off, took off our shoes, soaked our feet. After a minute we lit up cigarettes, and Eleanor took a long drag and said, 'Well Dorothy, I guess the passers-by think we're a couple of geriatric street walkers whose legs have finally given out on them.' We giggled over that." After another film, the pair wandered into a singles restaurant, where Dorothy ended up inviting the whole crowd to King Broadcasting.

Her children remained a primary focus. In the 1970s each of them went through divorce, which caused Dorothy, as Center of the Universe, to blame herself somehow for their failed marriages. She was more relieved than regretful when Harriet divorced psychiatrist Sid Rice in 1976, for Dorothy had never warmed to him. He wore a cowboy hat, was too interested in the price of things, and generally lacked the finesse and charm she admired in men. In 1974, Patsy moved back to Seattle from San Diego, her children grown and her marriage to Joe Collins worn down. Dorothy received news of the separation with a sympathetic nod, based on her long association with the Josiah Collins family during the early days on First Hill. Although she always had affection for Joe, she never understood his lack of drive; in her mind, he played at his work and worked at his play, dabbling at a career while spending long hours calling on friends, perfecting his game of tennis, or tending his garden. More important to Dorothy was the fact that Patsy, her indispensable middle child, was once again in the fold.

Her fold. Whether Dorothy was conscious of it or not, a familiar dynamic was about to recur, one reminiscent of the early days of Patsy's marriage when her mother had tried to manage the Collins household. It began again when she assumed that Patsy would live with her and was indignant to learn that her daughter had rented an apartment on Capitol Hill. "But your place is here!" Dorothy protested to her fifty-four-year old daughter. She offered Patsy the loan of her car but the daughter soon realized that Mother and her errands came along with it, so she bought one of her own. This mother-daughter struggle was to continue throughout the 1970s. When Patsy built a home in 1978 on property in Woodway bought by Stimson Realty in the 1940s and later sold to Patsy by Stim's Harbor Properties, her mother again disapproved. Upon her inspection of the small A-frame and teahouse overlooking the Sound, Dorothy merely shrugged. "It was a house that Mother hadn't planned," Patsy explained with a rueful smile. "She had made no templates for it; she hadn't chosen the architect. I was using my own furniture, not hers, and the teahouse was not suitable for entertaining her friends.

"Mother was running out of people and I was to become, literally, her Patsy," the middle child remembered of those demanding years. "She had tried getting Stim to do her bidding and that didn't work and she had long since given up trying to control Harriet. She had lost Gloria and Henry, so when all else failed she tried her ever-obedient Patsy." In 1975 the struggle found a new arena when Dorothy asked her daughter to become chairman of the board of King Broadcasting and Patsy accepted, a situation that, although well intentioned, provided fodder for more power plays. Patsy's position as chair brought with it additional roles that she had not expected. It wasn't long before she realized that her mother expected her to fill the voids left by Henry and Gloria. "I found myself cast and began to realize what Mother needed of me," Patsy explained. "She wanted me to sit and watch television with her every night like Gloria and she also wanted me to do her dirty work for her, as Henry had done."

Patsy's first performance as Henry Owen, an unwitting one, occurred not long after she came to King. Her mother was unhappy with her secretary named Dorothy and had already selected a replacement by the name of Doris. "Dorothy was going on vacation and when Mother told me she didn't want her anymore, I said, 'You need to tell her before she goes on vacation so that she understands that she's not coming back.' Mother leaned back in her chair and said, absently, 'Oh, I said something about it . . .' There was something about the way her voice trailed off and suddenly I knew that Dorothy didn't know a thing. Again I said, 'Mother you have to tell her, you *have* to tell her.' And she said, 'I'll tell her! Don't take that tone of voice with me, young lady.' Then, on the appointed Monday morning of secretarial shuffling, Mother called from home and said, 'I'm not going to come down today, dear, and I want you to take care of things for me.' That was when I knew I was to be her Henry." Fortunately for Patsy, the two secretaries didn't arrive at the same moment. First she rushed Dorothy down to the coffee shop, told her that "Mother really needs someone with more accounting experience," and that she was fired. Then she ran back to the office where Doris was waiting to be shown to her desk.

The Henry role extended beyond firing to funding. Dorothy was by now the benevolent target of many people who claimed to be seeking her "advice," but really only wanted money for various causes and pet projects. ("If they send me brochures in color, they're already spending too much money.") Because she enjoyed the human contact and it gave her some sense of power to be so sought after, she accepted their invitations for leisurely lunches. ("I like going to lunch," she said when daughter Patsy asked why she accepted these invitations.) Although she never deluded herself into thinking that people actually wanted her advice, she sometimes gave it anyway. When delegates from the Seattle Symphony came to her office, she told them the last thing they wanted to hear—to get together with Tacoma for funding because she knew a regional symphony would be "much better and more economical." She typically made no commitments. She only smiled, listened attentively and interjected an occasional, "Isn't this exciting! I'm so enthusiastic." The supplicants left presuming that she approved their project (which she usually did) and would give them money (which she usually did not). "Mrs. Bullitt particularly hated receiving letters that said, 'Last year you gave X, and this year you've given nothing,' " her housekeeper Sallie remembered. "To these she'd either cut people off completely or invite them over to her house. After a chat, they'd leave, egos lifted, and wearing broad smiles. She'd charm them so completely about the wonderful job they were doing that they'd leave somehow thinking they had money. Then I'd watch from the window and about the time they got to the curb a puzzled look would cross their faces when they realized that they were coming away without a penny."

Dorothy left the business of directly saying no to Patsy. When a woman from the symphony phoned about initiating a Fourth of July barge concert on Lake Union, Dorothy approved heartily, regaled her with memories of the concert in Venice she had heard with her daughters in 1937, and then called the mayor to tell him what a fine idea it was. Her encouragement naturally prompted a flurry of follow-up phone calls fielded by Patsy in which the confused petitioner said, "But your mother wants to do this . . . ," and the daughter had to reply, "No, she wants it done." It turned out that Dorothy wanted the city to pay for the barge concert.

While Patsy was in mid-melee with her mother, Stim had escaped the battlefield and was leading a calmer life practicing appellate law. During the 1970s, Stim and Kay Bullitt separated and, after three years, divorced. Knowing his mother's great love for Kay—the only in-law that Dorothy had heartily endorsed—Stim delayed the news for a while. When he did tell his mother about the divorce, Dorothy was deeply saddened. In her mind, Kay Bullitt was the finest woman her son could ever find, one whom she herself would have chosen for him. Dorothy never relinquished her devotion to Kay Bullitt, continuing to trust her in private matters, and to rely on her gentility and easy companionship. One lonely Christmas Day when she was ninety-five, Dorothy said, "Kay spent the afternoon—she is such good company. You know, really, I think she is my best friend."

In middle age, Stim took up mountain climbing. A self-described risk taker—physically, socially, and financially—he enjoyed pitting his strength and judgment against unpredictable and unforgiving forces. Mountain climbing appealed to his sense of competition and achievement and the outdoors provided a combination of peace and exhilaration, a sense of freedom found nowhere else. He had climbed about fifty summits on solo expeditions and climbed with others for more difficult assaults, such as Mount Rainier and Mount McKinley. Dorothy was not terribly interested in Stim's passion. When he struggled for a month on stormy Mount McKinley, she didn't pace the floor; he had made two previous attempts, knew the conditions, and had plenty of supplies. Nor did his ascents on Mount Rainier cause alarm—until one attempt via Liberty Ridge in 1979 when she learned that Stim, his son Ben, and two others were missing in a storm. While she worried and waited for news, the climbers clung to life in an ice cave they had hacked out of the ridge when the storm paralyzed them at 12,900 feet.

The storm lasted sixty-two hours and dumped six feet of heavy wet snow on the mountain. Afterward the climbers looked for rescue, but none came, and they began to believe themselves forsaken. To save themselves, the three younger members of the party set out for help down along the steep ridge that they had climbed, while Stim stayed behind to await rescue. He ate his last piece of food, washed it down with the last swallow of water, and waited. Aware that his companions might have been killed in an avalanche and that he too might die, he wrote two notes of instruction to Patsy on yellow paper that had wrapped the last candy bar. One note dealt with practical matters—the location of his wallet, his car, unfinished business at the law office—the other was a message of farewell to be sent to certain people. One whole day passed and most of the next. Alone, Stim began to believe that death was inevitable. Late in the afternoon his musings were interrupted by a search plane and later an Army helicopter that dropped a survival package. As it dipped low, the helicopter's blast picked up Stim's sleeping bag, which had been spread outside, whirled it out over the cliff and into the abyss below. "The rescue package contained a radio, which I pounced upon because I wanted to know what to do," he remembered with some humor years later. "The only thing to be read was a warning that any unauthorized use of it constituted a violation of the Communications Act of 1934. Then I pushed a button and heard a voice from the helicopter saying, 'Holy smoke, George, we've just blown one of those guys off over the Willis Wall! We've got to be more careful!' "

Minutes later, Stim, straddling a seat lowered by cable, was plucked off the ledge. Spinning wildly over an abyss, the survivor was cranked into the helicopter hatch to safety. He learned to his great relief that his companions were alive and safe, though Ben Bullitt and climb leader Eric Sanford suffered frostbitten toes. The day after his rescue, Stim took his mother and sisters to lunch. Handing Patsy a crumpled piece of paper—his last instructions written on Mount Rainier—he told her was very glad to give it to her personally rather than have someone find it in his coat pocket next spring. Patsy replied, teasingly, "I'll keep it, just in case there's a next time," to which her logical brother rejoined, "Well, that would be nice, except I would probably have left the car keys in a different place."

Dorothy had her own grand adventure rafting down the Colorado River in 1977 with her daughter Harriet, and friend Eleanor Clark. The thought that she was eighty-five years old did cross her mind, but it soon swirled away in the excitement of a week-long excursion with her youngest child. "Mother was the oldest person to have rafted the Colorado at that time," Harriet remembered. "We rigged up a seat for her near the back of the raft where she could be relatively dry—but no way would she do that. She sat in the most forward seat and every time we hit a rapid, she was absolutely sluiced with water. Sometimes she was on her knees right up in the forepeak as we headed straight into a huge wall of water, shouting, 'This is just like riding a horse!' She was completely at home with the balance and the motion." From the comfort of her couch a few years later, Dorothy painted a verbal picture of the canyon walls. With one arm raised, she swashed the colors back and forth. "There was a rust color from some certain period of time, then rose from another, an earthquake layer here, and then something green, layer upon layer," she said. "A geologist would lose his mind down there, but just the colors themselves were enough for me."

Another focus of Dorothy's final years was the Bullitt Foundation. Its main emphasis was on preserving the Northwest environment, and, to a lesser degree, education, foreign affairs, race relations, and child welfare. Dorothy read some of the requests as they came in, but she enjoyed making money more than giving it away. She had only the mildest interest in saving wilderness or wildlife. "Do we always have to save the whales?" she asked impatiently.

Uninterested in causes, she preferred to give to the people behind the causes. She gave to St. Mark's because she liked John Leffler; she gave to the Oregon Shakespearean Theater in Ashland because she admired its founder, Angus Bowmer, and because of Gloria Chandler's interest in theater. She gave to Seattle's A Contemporary Theater (ACT) because she liked its director, Greg Falls, who had the good taste to buy her old Highlands home, Greenway. When she learned that Falls had started ACT on his own by drafting local talent and without asking for any funding, she thought that was "pretty decent." "I wrote him a check and sent it," Dorothy recalled with pleasure, "and when it arrived, unsolicited, it just happened that he was sitting at his desk facing closing. He has never forgotten it." It was when she was directly solicited for foundation funding, however, that the awkward moments occurred, such as the time when the dean and president of Pacific University, after solicitous courting of Dorothy, arrived from Oregon to collect their promised money. "They had given her an honorary doctorate," Patsy explained, "which Mother knew full well was not really for what she had done but for what she was going to do by way of donations. Mother had led them to believe a major donation was in the works, enough so that they had already budgeted for it and printed a brochure about it." On the day they drove to Seattle, Dorothy phoned her daughter saying she wouldn't be coming in but that those "Oregon people" were en route and a disgruntled Patsy had to tell an even more disgruntled dean that funding was not available.

In 1979 Dorothy began talking with her children about making a substantial donation to some worthy institution in the form of $1 million of her King Broadcasting preferred stock. Over many months, Stim, Patsy, and Harriet suggested various candidates whenever she called a "meeting" in the sunroom of her home—all to no avail. Patsy remembered their futile proposals: "We knew she liked English, books, and literacy—how about the Seattle Public Library? No. Music—how about the Seattle Symphony? After what they did to my piano? No! The Cornish School? Children's Orthopedic Hospital? No. No. It got to be ridiculous! We began to think it was all a hoax to get us together or that we were playing a game of guess who gets the money! Finally, it was Stim who came up with the right answer. He told Mother, 'If Father were here, he would want to give it to the university for the teaching of American history.' That was it— Harriet called me and said, 'Stim guessed right—he hit the bull's eye!' " In 1980 Dorothy endowed the Bullitt Chair in American History, specifying an

In 1980, KING celebrated the opening of new offices. Network news anchor John Chancellor attended the festivities.

emphasis on teaching undergraduate students rather than research. The first classes were conducted in 1981 by Henry Steele Commager, an eminent historian who was to become an unabashed admirer of the donor. Dorothy was immensely pleased with her son's suggestion. That such a gesture would have meant much to Scott was the finest motive she could envision, and her children agreed. Others, however, attributed the substantial endowment to the myth of Dorothy Bullitt's bold and liberal attitude. "It was something much more touching than that," Patsy explained. "A lot of people are bold and liberal but very few people, nearly fifty years after their husband's death, and without ever saying anything about it, would make such a gesture on that level. She did it for Father and that's really more revealing about her than the notion that she was supposedly a smart, fiery liberal."

Dorothy sought out other family members during her last two decades. She had given her grandchildren the requisite Christmas presents, a mild amount of attention at family functions, and provided for them through family trusts, but she had neglected them on a truly personal basis. She had never been a typical grandmother, clucking over homemade soups or homebaked cookies. (Two of her servants, Jean and Lena, had banned her from the kitchen entirely.) She served better as family matriarch. For their part, the grandchildren, in their early years, knew her legend better than they really knew the person. Those grandchildren living in Seattle found "Mamie" a pleasant but remote presence, presiding at the head of the breakfast table each Sunday while Jean and Lena came and went, serving tumblers of juice, scrambled eggs with bacon and sausage, waffles with hot maple syrup and butter, and thinly wrapped cinnamon rolls—a specialty of Frederick & Nelson. While the grown-ups discussed matters of importance, the children were expected to sit quietly until they were released to read the funny papers in the sunroom. There were eleven in all—Stim's six, Patsy's three, and Harriet's two. Growing up in the 1960s, each was affected to varying degree by that tumultuous decade, which brought with it the problems of drugs, alcohol, and depression, cults and collectives, free love, and the questioning of authority. For the Bullitt grandchildren, the turbulent times were compounded by a sense of familial prosperity that, for some of them, diminished the need for higher education or ambitious accomplishments in their lives.

Five of the eleven grandchildren held temporary positions at King Broadcasting over the years, but none found a career there. If Dorothy had hopes for a corporate "heir" among them, those plans were set aside as the company expanded and became more complex. "My grandchildren would have to know the company from the bottom up and none of them have been willing to do this for very long," she explained, with her customary detachment. "Experience is really the only teacher, and unfortunately they all want to be chairman of the board." She didn't agonize about the lack of a family member at the helm; practicality prevailed, as did the requirements of her company, and it was in competent hands. She loved her grandchildren in her way, but her years of experience with people had taught her that she couldn't direct their lives.

People were really what Dorothy Bullitt was all about. Her long life, when reduced to one motivating interest, had amounted to a vast parade of people of all types. People, more than personal challenge, the innovations of technology, or even the inveiglements of power, had been the one force that had truly fueled her days. Listening to their stories, she lived vicariously. The pageant of personalities with whom she shared talk and time opened, enriched, and deepened her view of life. They released her from the strictures of her own more constrained personality and background; their experiences broadened her, bringing her glimmers of something grander, of the souls beyond each personality who were relishing and wrestling with their time on earth. Her interest in people explains why she preferred the performing arts to the conceptual arts—because human beings were far more interesting than landscapes and a real life preferable to a still life. She could never see enough Shakespeare or opera, because these forms of artistic expression brought her the archetypal dramas of the human spirit as it struggles and stretches in the world. By her later years, Dorothy Bullitt understood human nature so thoroughly that she could judge character immediately with an accuracy that far surpassed the decades she had already lived.

Yet, for Dorothy, closeness to people was never a two-way street. As much as she extended herself to people, she was unable to share herself on deep emotional levels, except only rarely with family and a handful of friends. It was nothing deliberate; a certain remoteness was simply in her nature, and not necessarily something to her liking. It was as if a crucial part of herself, one more spontaneous, trusting, and engaged, had been walled off early on, perhaps as a result of having her emotions controlled as a child. Wenda Brewster O'Reilly, Dorothy's granddaughter and a psychologist, theorized that this "separateness" may have accounted for her grandmother's interest in broadcasting. "There was a level at which Mamie wasn't with anybody, in spite of her warmth and realness," Wenda observed. "She compensated for it by being a broadcaster, a communicator, a person who was webbed into the world socially, intellectually, and politically; but if you asked for straightforward emotion, it came very indirectly. We all knew that she loved us, but it wasn't because she was demonstrative with her feelings."

I don't collect antiques—I AM one.

14 THE IMMIGRANT
1981–1988

APPROACHING HER NINETIETH YEAR, DOROTHY BULLITT WAS familiar with death and loss. "I've never known anyone more thoroughly familiar with mortality," her grandson Bill Collins observed.

In 1981, death struck the Bullitt family a brutal blow. On the night before Thanksgiving, Dorothy's grandson Ben Bullitt disappeared into Lake Washington fully clothed, during a party aboard his sixty-seven-foot yacht *Pegasus*, which he'd bought on credit the week before. High on drink and drugs, for a short while he joked about drowning. Then he shouted from the chilly water to his girlfriend, who became alarmed enough to jump in and try to pull him to the boat. As she brought him partially up to the platform on the boat's stern, Ben slipped back into the water and vanished.

Dorothy's grandson Ben had been living with a recklessness that far surpassed the life of an average twenty-four-year old. With curly dark hair and Byronic good looks, Ben had what his father Stim described as a radiant vitality that seemed to make him feel immortal, as if life would never catch up to the breakneck speed at which he lived. Self-indulgent and irresponsible, Ben broke the law with no thought of the consequences, cheated on his taxes, drove his car at terrifying speed until his license was revoked, was forced to close the small antique shop he had been running downtown at First and Madison because of nonpayment of rent. By the time of his disappearance, he had managed to borrow $600,000 from five banks in the Seattle area. Living on the edge, he was a prominent member of a fast-moving, money-flashing crowd that sold and profited from drugs in the city. Among his friends was a self-styled "financial consultant," Bob King, an Alabaman with a murky past who seemed to have a Svengali-like hold over Ben. When Ben purchased the *Pegasus*

311

for $360,000, Bob King took a $50,000 commission from the loan proceeds for negotiating the deal. He also encouraged Ben to form a corporation to deal in the purchase and management of real estate. The two were often seen around town together in a chauffeured limousine. Sometimes they stopped at King Broadcasting where, unknown to Dorothy, they made phone calls, invoking her name during conversations to impress whomever they were calling.

Dorothy had been aware of Ben's activities, mostly from second-hand accounts. She witnessed the agony his parents experienced as they helplessly watched their adored son throw his life away. She stood by in sympathy as Kay repeatedly tried to believe in and help her son and as Stim moved from deep distress to sad resignation when Ben's course became fixed. Although Dorothy was never taken in by Ben's charm, she did not refuse to see him. When he opened the antique shop, she lent him furniture, including her grandfather's pool table from the T. D. Stimson home in California. When he asked to borrow money, she refused, saying only, "Ben, I just can't do it." With a certain fatalistic set of mind, she knew that it would do no good to lecture or intervene.

When Patsy arrived at her mother's house the morning after Ben's disappearance, she found Dorothy sitting alone quietly in the sunroom. "Mother wasn't weeping, but she was almost speechless with sorrow for Stim and Kay," Patsy remembered. "All she could say was 'my heart just breaks for them.'" Suddenly, the quiet grief was shattered when Bob King, having pushed past Sallie at the front door, burst into the room. As he stood before them, wearing a trench coat and keeping one hand in his pocket, the two women were struck with an unspoken fear, which both quietly camouflaged with Bullitt composure. When he went over to Dorothy and kissed her, saying how sorry he was, she said nothing, only nodded her head while he talked on about how he had loved Ben and how much he wanted to help. Moments later, with the same firm composure, Patsy escorted him to the door and saw him out.

Divers searched the lake for a month, but Ben's body was never found. Some friends and family believed he had been murdered, but in the absence of a body, there was no real evidence that this occurred. (Subsequently, King was sent to prison to serve three separate life sentences for brokering a contract murder, conspiring to commit murder, and committing armed robbery.)

Remembering Patsy's anguish over the disappearance of her fiancé, Larry Norman, Dorothy knew how important it was for Stim and Kay to find Ben's body and determine the cause of his apparent death to bring the ordeal to a close. "I told Mother that Ben had died because of the way he had been living," said Patsy. "Whether it was murder or an accident, the real cause of Ben's death was the sad and predictable result of living too close to the edge." Years later, Dorothy described her youngest grandson in a quiet low voice, saying, "He was a good piece of work gone bad." Ben's death was a great loss for the family and Dorothy grieved along with his parents and siblings. When others worried to see her so distressed, her son did not. "I felt that this was good news about Mother," Stim remembered, "because it showed her continued capacity for deep feeling at age eighty-nine. Most people that age are either emotionally numb or cynically resigned, and either way they don't have strong feelings. If she could have strong feelings of distress, it also showed that she was capable of joy. It was a reminder that she was still very much alive."

———

IN 1982, DOROTHY TURNED NINETY YEARS OLD, AN OCCASION that she chose to ignore completely. "I have these genes in me that keep on rolling," she said wryly about the decade she was entering, "but I'm running against the speed limit." If mortality was at her heels, she seemed determined to give it merry chase. She bought herself some wide-based tennis shoes to secure good footing, even though her balance and reflexes were still good. Thus equipped and still outfitted in the same conservative suits she had worn since the 1940s, she bade her driver good-bye each morning, entered the new King Broadcasting building, and pressed a gloved knuckle to the elevator button. Once on the fifth floor, she trundled along the halls to the executive offices, dispensing greetings and comments along the way.

Inside the office suite that she shared with daughter Patsy, secretary Jinny Kyreacos, financial assistant Clara Stenstrom, and friend John Leffler, the camaraderie was tempered by competition between mother and daughter. Although Dorothy clearly had wanted her daughter to take the position as chairman of the board, she couldn't help but bristle when CEO Ancil Payne and others bypassed her office to confer with Patsy. The attention that had been liberally lavished on her for so many years was now being siphoned off. As Patsy assumed leadership, her mother felt discarded. She missed people conferring with her and bustling about her. "I want this office 'stahffed,'" she would announce imperiously, irritated that answering machines now took the phone calls. Her mail dwindled to catalogues and requests for money, and she began to suspect that it was being withheld from her.

Irritated, she began to call her daughter "Chairman." "Where's Chairman?" she would ask gruffly, exiting from her office, hands flapping in the pockets. "Tell her I want to see her." Upon Patsy's appearance, Dorothy would launch into one of her chats about whatever current company situation was annoying her. For an hour or more, Patsy would listen to her mother's complaints about the newsroom's mistakes or certain personnel she wanted fired, and when finally she would interrupt to say that these things had to be taken up through the regular chain of command, her mother would grow sullen, saying, "I don't always trust those boys."

"Generally Mother was right in her complaints," Patsy recalled, "but I wasn't the CEO, and when Ancil conferred with her—which he did regularly—she would never bring up her complaints." As in the 1960s, it was a case of not being able to let go—although in the 1970s and 1980s perhaps it was more accurately a case of still wanting to belong.

"Dorothy never really felt as left out as she made out to be," Ancil Payne stated years later. "She always made the final decisions." Payne knew her interests and was in the habit of discussing new acquisitions or the hiring of new managers long before such issues reached the boardroom. "Even late in her life, when I went to her office to discuss buying a cable system in California, she got right to the point," he remembered. "After I had finished describing it to her, she said, 'Well, it's an interesting purchase, but, you know, it's right on the San Andreas Fault.' She'd done her research and was very much in charge." Payne insisted that his boss was accurate in her opinion about all of the company's big moves; if she lacked judgment, in his opinion, it was only in being too conservative in investing the cash reserves.

With her advancing age, some degree of infirmity was inevitable. She took it with typical stoicism and unusual grace. She didn't complain when her breath was short and no one knew when she suffered pain; she never indulged in self-pity or bitterness. Sometimes, out of sheer fatigue or lack of something tangible to do, she fell asleep at her desk. To others in the company, she was humorous and always interested, making it difficult to believe her age. Greg Palmer, a KING-TV movie critic, remembered one lunchroom group discussion about the effect of television on presidential candidates. "I remarked that I had read that if there had been television during Teddy Roosevelt's time, he probably wouldn't have been elected because he had a very high-pitched voice," he recalled. "Suddenly Mrs. Bullitt, who had hardly spoken during the discussion, said, 'I don't remember his voice as being high and thin. Father took me to hear Teddy Roosevelt when he came through campaigning for re-election.' Suddenly I realized, 'My God, she really is that old!' "

———

FOR MOST OF HER LIFE—UP UNTIL THE 1950S, WHEN SHE WAS in her sixties—Dorothy Bullitt inhabited a familiar world; her place in Seattle's historical, social, and economic setting was assured. Everybody knew her name. When she drove downtown, she always saw people she knew, exchanged greetings with them on the street, in the stores, offices, and restaurants. It was a predictable place peopled with elevator operators and gasoline station attendants, with policemen and paper boys on street corners. There were no parking meters, no freeways or one-way streets. When she parked in the Metropolitan Garage, the attendant, Frank Marino, knew her as well as the blue "Mehcury" or Ford she drove over the years. She greeted him personally, passed the time of day, and never had to describe her car or hand in a ticket when she returned. At Frederick & Nelson or I. Magnin, the middle-aged saleswomen who waited on her knew not only her name but her size and preferences; she charged things simply by giving her name. In the stores and restaurants, women wore hats and gloves, real jewels and real furs; their suits were tailored in classic wool or gabardine, matching purses and shoes were leather, and there was no such thing as pantyhose.

For most of her life, things were built to last and the people who used them were meant to endure also. Family, friends, and employees stayed for the duration. Dorothy always had live-in help—she never knew a babysitter or a cleaning lady—and the cook stayed for decades, if not life, in a house that was also built to last a lifetime. People had one watch and one family car, which was good for twenty or more years if you took care of it as Ohata did. Clothes were made of natural fabrics, often by a dressmaker, and passed on to others when outgrown. Children had one coat and one bathing suit, and they knew not to lose or misplace their belongings. Fresh food was served to the family on china plates, and glass milk bottles were delivered by a milkman. The doctor was a family friend who made house calls. Physical health was largely a matter of rest, sunshine, and fresh air. Unknown until Dorothy was in her fifties were antibiotics, plastics, synthetics, frozen foods, and supermarkets. There was no birth control until she was long past child-bearing age; there were no psychotherapists or support groups until long past her middle age—not that she would have taken advantage of them if there had been.

By the time Dorothy was in her seventies, the United States was beginning to shift dramatically with technological and social change. During the 1960s, she adjusted to a pace quickened by jet travel, freeways, and superferries; to new faces appearing daily as commuters came and went from the burgeoning Seattle suburbs; to a downtown of rising spires, towers, needles, and domes; to yet another war; to heroes assassinated; and to the shifts in consciousness brought about by a generation that questioned the values she had been accustomed to hold dear and even permanent.

She adapted remarkably to these profound social changes, to the proliferation of ideas and questions raised during the 1960s. Always ahead of her times conceptually, she understood the issues of women's rights and civil unrest, abortion and birth control, and she might even have secretly sympathized to some degree with the rampant rebellion of the young as they refused to go to war or trust anyone over thirty. She enjoyed the time saved by air travel, but sometimes missed the leisurely hours she had passed on a train. She missed personal service in stores, hated check-out lines and packaging that caused her to fumble with things like the plastic wrapping on silverware and sugar on airplanes. ("Sugar belongs in the bowl with a spoon, not in a bag that you have to tear apart.") She enjoyed wearing informal clothes, relaxing in an old pair of slacks, but she could never dress up without wearing a corset—not a girdle—similar to one she had worn in the 1920s.

The shifts and shrugs of the 1960s were the beginning of changes that increased exponentially during the next two decades. As computers and consumerism burst into American life in the 1970s and 1980s, a flood of technological advances and a new breed of Northwesterner dissolved the world that had once seemed so stable to Dorothy Bullitt. King Broadcasting, the venture she had started with a handful of employees and two chairs and a camera in a ten-by-twelve-foot room, was now a major competitor in the vast field of communications. The company premises were now full of cutting-edge technology that its elderly founder could scarcely envision, much less operate. Computers, copy machines, calculators, and conference rooms were manned by a quick-witted, strategy-minded staff of affluent young newcomers who wore digitalized watches and designer clothes, lived in condos or expensive suburban homes, and drove fuel-injected cars equipped with compact discs and radar detectors. As they hurried through the halls, many of them didn't recognize the small, silver-haired woman who still trudged to her fifth floor office each day, in spite of the fact that her full-length portrait was displayed in the large lobby downstairs. They didn't realize the real distance she had covered—from high-buttoned shoes to high rises, from wooden sidewalks to satellites. It had been a long, long road.

Dorothy entered into this new dimension like an immigrant coming to a foreign land. Patsy remembered a passage from *Culture and Commitment* in which Margaret Mead stated that those who had grown up during the 1930s and the 1940s had seen more change in their lives than any generation preceding them in the history of the world. "Mother had already seen a lot of change *before* the 1930s," Patsy observed. "When she took her first plane ride—from Montana to Seattle in 1936—imagine how strange she must have felt

At age 96, on a cruise through the San Juan Islands.

after forty-four years of traveling by train. Or imagine how weird it must have been to step into an automated elevator for the first time when she was nearly sixty. She was an excellent 'immigrant.' People who were that old and yet still adapted should be admired for bearing it all. Nobody had ever seen so much change before."

The 1980s, however, were infinitely more confusing and frustrating for Dorothy Bullitt than the two preceding decades. She sometimes found herself a stranger in a strange land. "I don't know anyone here," she said wistfully to Patsy one evening during intermission at the symphony. She, whose mother had founded the Seattle Symphony, who was accustomed to recognition all of her life, was lost in the crowd of unknown people. An elderly foreigner, she didn't know their language; she didn't understand many of their customs; and she didn't always know her way around. But she covered her resistance to these changes with extraordinary social skills. During board meetings, she followed the discussions with interest and offered an occasional piercing question, but when others took out their calculators to work a budget problem, no one noticed that she was doing it the old way—with a pencil. When she received gifts of CDs and videotapes, she thanked the donors graciously, giving the impression that she knew how to use them when she hadn't the slightest idea of what to do. In her home, she refused to install an answering machine ("they are rude"). She never worked a computer or a copy machine; and she continued to wind her watch and clock. Others operated the CD, the VCR, and the tape recorder, or negotiated the freeways and traffic. She got by. She pretended she knew the language, pretended she knew where to go, and pretended she was fit enough to get there. At home she kept herself in familiar surroundings, with souvenirs of the "old country"—the books, antiques, silver, and linen—and out into the new world she took her most prized personal possessions—her principles and her native charm.

Dorothy's ninety-year-old body became an object of detached scrutiny as slowly it began to fall apart. She talked about it in a droll way, looking down at herself as if on foreign territory and with a certain bemused perplexity that brought smiles to the most seriously sympathetic. She was fond of taking inventory with a series of quips, as though she was operating a machine in the process of running down. "My feet crack and make strange noises," she muttered one day while walking along a dock. "I don't always know where my toes are—they're off somewhere on their own. My teeth move around too. Sometimes they hit, sometimes not, but so long as they stay in, I'm OK." In her mid-nineties she fell and hit her head against a large clay pot, breaking it, causing her to remark, "I'm glad to know what my head is made for—I never before knew its purpose." Once when a friend called to say hello, Dorothy seemed hesitant. "Are you trying to figure out who I am?" the caller inquired teasingly. "No," was the husky reply, "I'm trying to figure out who *I* am."

At age ninety-five, she tripped climbing the basement library steps, falling backwards and crushing some small bones in her foot. After much coaxing from her housekeeper, Sallie, Dorothy reluctantly agreed to go to the hospital where the nurse in charge met with Bullitt obstinacy at every turn. "The nurse asked my name and address—that was all right," Dorothy remembered. "Then she asked, 'Sex?' and I said, 'Oh, who cares.' Next she asked my date of birth and when I said February 5, '92, she didn't understand—I was in the wrong century! She asked twice and finally I shouted the date at her—the shouting seemed to help so I was registered." In her hospital room, Dorothy refused to lie in bed but perched atop it like an angry little buddha. When the nurse solicitously pointed to a glass of water and said, "You can put your teeth in there," that was the final straw. "My teeth are *attached*," Dorothy shouted. "You leave them alone! They are my most precious possession."

"Now that everyone knows my age, I've decided to use it," she announced triumphantly at age ninety-five. "Some man I met in a drugstore told me, 'I'm so old I can't do anything—after all, I'm eighty-five,' " she said, laughing. "So now, when someone calls with an invitation, I say, 'I'm sorry, I'm too old, I can't attend. Things are getting a bit too much for me . . .' " These words she uttered in a pitifully creaky voice, followed by a throaty guffaw that indicated just the opposite. However, sometimes she did get caught in deception. When a priest called from St. Mark's to ask if he could come by to give her communion, he learned that Mrs. Bullitt was down at the office. "What! She's ambulatory?" he exclaimed. "Well, I guess she doesn't need me." "No," stated Sallie matter of factly. "She can walk over if she does."

Dorothy Bullitt was still learning lessons as her years rolled along. Although she continued to receive awards and invitations to attend every reception and ceremony in town, she understood the motives behind these showerings of praise. Now the invitations were based not so much on what she had done as on what she might do (make a large donation to whatever the cause), and directed not so much to her personally but to what she symbolized (by attending certain functions she implicitly endorsed them). Generally she avoided these public fetes, not because she didn't enjoy the attention but because of her increasing fragility. One honor that brought her great satisfaction was the Peabody Award that she received in 1986. (It was one of four received by KING-TV over the years, recipient of more Peabodys than any other independent station in the United States). The highest and most coveted recognition in the field of broadcasting, the Peabody usually recognized the work of entire stations or single programs; this was the first time the award was bestowed on an individual. In recognizing Dorothy Bullitt's contributions to the broadcasting industry, the Peabody Board noted her commitment to the highest ideals of local programming.

In her last years, Dorothy Bullitt's eccentricities became magnified as she had less occasion to apply them to practical ends. She still kept records of anniversaries, birthdays, and gifts received, although she gave none herself. As her mother had done, she inventoried her possessions. In dividing up her worldly goods, she seemed to want to stir up some attention and controversy, as if disposing of her last possessions might bind the children more closely to her, or reassert the last vestiges of her parental power. Or perhaps it was as Harriet explained to her sister, "Mother is kind of bored. She'd do anything to have us over to the house."

As her father had done with his real estate, Dorothy gave her children an inventory of all the furnishings and told them to select items they wanted; in case of duplication, she said, they could bid for them, "auction-style." Knowing this was fertile ground for sibling quarrels, they conferred with one another privately and divided up the list without interfering with one another. Upon seeing that there was no duplication, Dorothy insisted that they make their selections again, this time without communicating, and come prepared to trade. "We called each other again and agreed on the outcome," Patsy recalled with a grin. "Mother had finally met her match—she had wanted a bit of bargaining and blood sport but when we wouldn't play the game, she got bored with it herself and dropped the whole thing."

At home Dorothy lived modestly as her house (which she had already deeded to the Junior League) fell into disrepair. She spent money only for housekeepers who shopped, cleaned, and cooked or set out cocktails and crackers when someone dropped by. As for clothing, except for an occasional shopping spree led by Harriet, her suits and shoes were now at least forty years old and she was still loathe to part with them. She decided to give away an old pair of plain pre-World War II shoes, but was ashamed to give them to a thrift shop looking "so terribly shabby." She had her driver take her to buy polish, then painted and shined them until they looked "so very good" that she decided to keep them. She still sought full value for her money. When she needed a license for her little poodle Lily, it required two hours of Patsy's time to drive her downtown, circle the block, park, and wait so that Dorothy could secure the license at a senior citizen's fifty-cent discount. Her friends were either failing or falling by the wayside. Warren Magnuson, the old warrior from the U.S. Senate she had known since his law school days, had by now retired into seclusion. Their friendship endured without much contact. At a Rainier Club dinner hosted by Ancil Payne, they sat together to watch a television documentary of Magnuson's public life—he with part of one leg lost to a diabetic condition, and she, thirteen years older, dressed up in her best blue suit and her hair set in waves. Later, as the orchestra played, she leaned forward and said in her deep voice, "Oh Maggie, so much time has gone by. I wish we were young enough to dance

Old friends Warren Magnuson and Dorothy Bullitt visit for the last time. "Dorothy," Maggie said, "if I could dance with you, I would right now."

again." "Dorothy," he replied in an equally gravelly voice, reaching out to pat her hand, "if I could dance with you, I would right now."

In April 1987, when Dorothy was ninety-five, her friend John Leffler died. He had been a good and humorous companion. Months before his death, he had visited with her at King Broadcasting. From behind the closed doors of Dorothy's office, Patsy and Jinny Kyreacos heard animated conversation interrupted occasionally by peals of laughter. When asked later what she and the Dean had found so hilarious, Dorothy replied, "Oh, we were just planning our funerals." Dean Leffler's death was soon followed by Eleanor Clark's passing. In her last years, Eleanor had intensified in temperament from bee to wasp to hornet—at least insofar as Dorothy was concerned. Although both women had long ago accepted that conflict was part of their relationship, their visits were increasingly volatile. They continued to take summer excursions into Northwest waters refereed by skipper Ron Saling, who once declared to Canadian Customs that he had "two of the meanest women in all of British Columbia on board." Somehow the friendship endured, mainly because (somehow) Dorothy exercised forbearance. After Eleanor's death in 1988, Dorothy received a diamond and sapphire heirloom ring from her, along with a note, "Dorothy, you always understood," and a quotation from Voltaire: *"Tout comprendre, C'est tout pardonner."*

The Bullitt children had to walk the fine line between sympathy and detachment as they witnessed their mother's gradual decline. Each found a solution of sorts to maintaining an independent life and yet giving her the loving attention she needed, and each did it in his or her particular style. Stim saw his mother regularly during her last years. Freed from the conflicts that had occurred during his years at King Broadcasting, the son made an effort to be less distant from his mother. To her delight, he took her to lunch every week and intermittently dropped in for brief visits at her home. He recalled with affection one summer evening when he stopped by after playing baseball in the arboretum. "I was wearing shorts and had fallen and skinned my knee," he remembered. "Mother saw it bleeding, so she took me upstairs to her bathroom, climbed up on the toilet to reach into a cupboard for some fixings, and put a bandage on my knee, murmuring how that reminded her so much of past times. It struck me how child-parent relations can go on for so long. I was delighted at that reminder of continuity." She in turn was delighted when he offered to escort her to the Christmas Debutante's Ball held at the Four Seasons Olympic Hotel. Pleased by his gallant gesture, she bought a long pleated lavender dress for the occasion with as much joy as she might have done seventy-five years earlier and arrived on her son's arm beaming with pride.

Harriet also checked in on her mother regularly while maintaining a cheerful but firm grip on her own schedule. One such occasion was a small party held for Harriet's third husband, Mehmet Sherif, whom Dorothy affectionately called "that Mohammedan." A professor of engineering at the University of Washington and a renowned expert on earthquakes, Sherif was a colorful figure. He was a Turk by birth and claimed to be the last survivor of the Ottoman Empire. His mother, an Ottoman, had survived as a young girl the bloody revolution that swept through Turkey in the 1920s. After finding refuge in northern Syria, she married and gave birth to Mehmet, her only child. When another coup occurred years later in Syria, Mehmet made his way to the United States, where he studied engineering at the University of Arizona and at Princeton, where he received his doctorate. Exotically handsome, Sherif had a taste and appreciation for fine workmanship and art. He also had an appetite for luxury—lavish surroundings filled with antiques, paintings, and many rugs and pillows.

Dorothy enjoyed Mehmet because of his education and his Old World charm. When Harriet proposed a special excursion to celebrate his fiftieth birthday, she readily accepted. It was to be held at Duncan's Saddlery Store, Harriet explained to her mother, because Mehmet's favorite sensations were the scent of leather, the taste of coffee, and the smell of good tobacco. Duncan's, an old Seattle institution filled to the rafters with boots, blankets, and all manner of riding gear, gave permission for the small celebration. "The three of us went down there," Harriet said, smiling at the memory. "Mehmet, Mother, and I wore Syrian robes and we carried along some carpets and pillows, a Turkish coffee maker with special coffee, and a hot plate." As cautious customers eyed the unfolding tableau, the trio pitched a small Bedouin camp in mid-store, propping pillows against saddles and draping carpets over trunks and on the floor. Then Dorothy watched with amusement as Harriet ground the coffee beans and Mehmet leaned back on the pillows, lit a cigarette, inhaled the fumes of leather and tobacco, and all three enjoyed a birthday cup of strong Turkish coffee.

Patsy was her mother's protector and cautious caretaker. Because she spent the bulk of her time with Dorothy at the office, the middle child otherwise set limits on time with her mother. She didn't take her on trips or stay overnight at her house. When it came to invitations, Patsy was often caught in a double bind. Dorothy, now well into her nineties, could no longer cope the way she liked to think she could. At the same time, her children knew it was important to preserve her pride and sense of independence. As Dorothy's sight and stamina began to fail, especially in her last two years, long-distance journeys became acts of bravery in which she had to contend with heavy doors, long walks (she refused wheelchairs), escalators, ramps, seat numbers, and stairs. At age ninety-five, on a trip to visit KHNL-TV in Honolulu, she was met, after a six-hour flight, by the station manager, whisked away on a tour through the offices, and then feted at a large luncheon before taking a plane to Maui—where it took her five days to recover.

Although Dorothy was physically frail, her spirit remained unassailable. She refused to adhere to any set schedule, insisting that her driver wait for her call— just as Ohata had in the old days. She went about her business, keeping it to herself, and ricocheted around town as if she were decades younger. Patsy, realizing that she couldn't control her mother, organized a "surveillance" team of five—Sallie Baldus at Dorothy's home, Jinny Kyreacos in the office, Hazel Leland in the King mailroom, Patrick Wright, Dorothy's driver, and Ruth Wolfe, a secretary situated near the elevators on the fifth floor. Daily these people handed their "subject" off to each other by telephone, tracking her from home to office, on errands, to meetings—all without letting her know she was being observed.

Sometimes Dorothy shot out of her office like a loose cannon, rolling in one door of Frederick & Nelson downtown, out another, and into a cab while her surveillance team stumbled over their phone lines. Once, while five people searched the city for her, she walked home from Swedish Hospital at dusk, trudging along in her tennis shoes past street people and punks, gays, and straights, the drugged, the drunk, and the sober. On another day, Dorothy phoned Hazel, asking to be picked up on Madison Street. "Of course, Mrs. Bullitt," Hazel replied. "Where are you on Madison Street?" "That's none of your business," was Dorothy's reply as she hung up the phone. Patsy was called in to second-guess the location. "Mother never wanted anyone to know when she went to the doctor—that would sound like she was old," she explained, smiling. "So I guessed that she was probably outside the doctor's office and sure enough she was there."

Her children worried that she might be kidnapped, for by this time Dorothy was an enormously wealthy woman. King Broadcasting Company had thrived under the leadership of Ancil Payne with an increase in value of 15 to 20 percent during every year he was president. Dorothy, its elderly figurehead, chafed in private from time to time about Payne's independent actions. "Ancil has always been high-handed," she said once with a helpless shrug and a laugh. "He does what he wants to do and we keep quiet because he is very good. We know we are being run over, but we are being run over very nicely and the company is doing so well that we keep quiet and go along." When it was sold in February of 1992, King Broadcasting owned six television stations, three AM and three FM stations, and thirteen cable systems, along with the nation's largest mobile production company, for a total estimated value in excess of $600 million.

Dorothy thoroughly enjoyed the burgeoning profits of broadcasting, but she always assumed a perplexed attitude about it all. "I never *planned* on making all of this money. Where did it all come from?" When *Forbes Magazine* cited her as one of the four hundred richest people in America, she was critical of the distortions that had earned her this supposed place of honor. Aggregating the whole family's net worth, the magazine claimed that Dorothy Bullitt personally owned all of King Broadcasting stock (much of which she had long since given or sold to her children or which had been distributed to employees under the company stock plan), extensive "downtown real estate" (belonging to the Stimson family, and subsequently acquired properties now belonging to Stim), and *Pacific Search Magazine* (belonging to Harriet). Much to the family's concern, the listing continued for a couple of years, citing Dorothy's net worth at $250 million in 1984 and $275 million in 1985. Patsy called *Forbes* to complain loudly. "Patsy gave them an earful," her mother said with pride. "You could hear her down the hall—'You have done great damage to a very old woman because she could be robbed, kidnapped, stolen, murdered, and it would be your fault and we're holding you responsible. You have put things in your magazine that are not true.' " (At her death in 1989, Dorothy's personal estate was valued at about $40 million.) Finally, after a letter from a family attorney, the magazine changed Dorothy's listing to the Bullitt Family (at $300 million) in 1987 and listed it on a back page.

Dorothy Bullitt's last years were not all filled with conviviality. She spent many evenings alone and alienated, watching television without the interest or energy to initiate social contact. Usually she sat before the fire in her sunroom. Stirring the embers of her life, she ruminated over regrets with litanies of neglect of her loved ones. When she discussed these with a close friend or relative, it was without justification, said more to herself than to anyone present. "There is no relationship that I have had with anybody in my life that is not full of regret," she said one night in a low monotone. "With Father I took so much for granted . . . with Mother I didn't have the appreciation I should have . . . My children I didn't bring up very well—I didn't have to go quite so far afield. Patsy, especially, never understood and she deserved better. If I could do it over again, it would be very different. I'd have been more aware of what they were going through." Expressing some regret about the distance that existed between her children and her, she noted, "Scott used to say something I've always remembered. He told me that 'affection descends,' " she said with a smile and a cascading motion of one hand. "It descends. You can never expect to receive back from your children what you have given them. You can only hope that they will pass it on to their own."

AT KING BROADCASTING, DOROTHY'S IMMIGRATION INTO THE new world of the 1980s was often fraught with frustration and bewilderment. After the retirement of Ancil Payne in 1987, the company's focus shifted from growth, people, politics, and news to an emphasis on efficiency and profit. Under the leadership of CEO Steve Clifford, the company thrived further as cash flow and value grew more than ever before, and managers researched new opportunities for investment. Staggered by the magnitude of the operation and the possibility that it would grow even larger, she chanted her old refrain from the Ancil Payne years, complaining to her daughters, "Why do they always want to be bigger? Why can't they want to be better?" Increasingly, she felt disconnected and disregarded in policy decisions but without the energy or the authority to fire those who were making them. Unbeknownst to her, employees and programs of long standing were dismissed. Letters arrived from people who had been fired without the chance to say good-bye, a policy she knew would never have happened years ago when the company was small. These situations alarmed her. "Personnel is all we have," she exclaimed in frustration. "If we don't have them, we don't have a company—and that starts with the girl at the reception desk. I have friends down there," she added, uneasily, reaching into her pocket to flap her hand. "If somebody fired them I'd be sick . . . Like the head of the engineering department [Ken Hermanson] who has been there since the early days of television. He is very quiet, very silent, but what he knows we cannot duplicate. Someone could well say, 'I don't know him very well—he doesn't talk,' and he might be fired! Or like the little man with the bald head who trots back and forth through the corridors—I think he works in the program department [Del Loder in the traffic department]. Somebody could very easily say, 'Fire him.' Well, he was the elevator boy in the Smith Tower when we bought the radio station and he used to sing the call letters. Someone could say 'What does he do?' and if someone else doesn't know, they might fire him." (Loder retired a year after her death, Hermanson two years later.)

Dorothy was baffled by the new breed of personnel and the lack of quality in programming and performance they engendered. "They are all very smart, very sharp, but they have no public feeling at all. Everyone is concerned with the ratings. They've got to get over the idea that it's only the 'bottom line' of money that counts—that's all wrong," she said, shuddering at the thought. Then raising a couple of fingers, she said, "There are two—one is financial and the other is quality, and it is not necessary to sacrifice one for the other." For the first time, she began to speak out against money, against profit for its own sake in this new affluent world. "With all of the beauty and humanity around us, money is all we seem to be concerned about," she said sadly.

She was equally disappointed by what she considered to be a drastic decline in employees' education. "They don't know English or how to write," she protested. "No one has studied Latin; no one knows a word's derivation. I wonder if ten out of our two hundred employees even know what Aesop's Fables are." It was even more unconscionable that they seemed to have poor taste and an even poorer sense of history, and she had accumulated an arsenal of examples to substantiate her claim. "Do you know," she said once, raising her voice with each word, spacing them slowly for emphasis, "that one employee—and we think we get the best—did not know that we had had a war with Japan? And," she added, while increasing the volume and flapping a hand in one pocket, "he wanted to know if we had *won!*" When the station preempted the president's farewell speech to the United Nations to air a Ping-Pong championship, there was so much flapping that she was nearly airborne with fury, claiming she had to calm down before speaking her mind to Steve Clifford, but when she did he would hear her loud and clear. "In fact," she added crisply, "he might need an earpiece to survive it!" Such cavalier treatment of what she considered an important news event was incomprehensible to her, as was the excessive popularity of some programs that claimed high ratings. One such was "Almost Live," a KING-TV comedy program, now syndicated, which on April Fool's Day, portrayed as a joke such a realistic rendition of the Space Needle's collapse that viewers called the station in alarm. Dorothy's only reaction was, "They have no taste and no one's directing their taste. If we're not going to be rich at least let's get respect and not put fool things on like that. 'Almost Live,' " she added with a majestic and dismissive wave of the hand, "is a nothing."

When Dorothy was ninety-six, she became so disappointed in the lack of standards and the deviation from the original course she had set that she decided to resign from the board. She telephoned Ancil Payne, now retired as CEO but still on the board, to tell him. He persuaded her to do no such thing—as no doubt she had hoped he would. "People don't have any faith in me," she said later by way of explanation. "They want me to be as quiet as a clam. They think I'm so old that I don't know what the 'young' want and everything's changed since I had anything to do with broadcasting." Then she smiled with a sort of shy yet thoroughgoing confidence. "I really *do* know the business pretty well," she said in a low voice. "I know, like everybody else, that society's tolerances have changed, but quality still holds and maybe we'll just have to work harder to make money in the future. I don't think we have to go along with everything so blindly."

She never went along with it all blindly, but she forgot that long ago she had given away that authority. Although she protested, Dorothy Bullitt was well past pulling in the reins on the venture she had unleashed forty years before, nor would she have wanted to if she could. Now she lacked the vitality to push, pull, incite, and inspire. Much had happened since she had first cracked her whip in those early days. So many people and ideas, so much change and challenge had flowed through her life. But now she had reached the limits of her physical endurance and her enormous capacity for tolerance and interest. Now life was more than a little too familiar, too full of lessons already learned. She expressed it to Ancil Payne when he brought a lunch of her favorite cold "saumon" to her house not long after she turned ninety-seven. "You know what's wrong with the company these days?" she said, speaking more about herself than about its employees. She answered her own question quietly, "Not enough people are having enough fun." The grand escapade was over.

I'll know when it's Time's Up. I was not invited
to stay on forever, you know.

15 BOOTS ON

1989

DOROTHY BULLITT DIED AS SHE HAD LIVED—WITH COURAGE and without a backward glance. When the time came, she stared Death in the face and, for a few weeks at least, Death blinked. As she entered her ninety-eighth year, her world and her body were closing down. "I shouldn't still be here," she confided to friends matter of factly. "I'm long overdue—I should be gone by now." Not without humor, she anticipated that one day everything would fail like Oliver Wendell Holmes's "Wonderful One-Hoss Shay," a magical vehicle that finally collapsed "all at once, and nothing first, Just as bubbles do when they burst."

On February 5, 1989, Dorothy attended a luncheon for her ninety-seventh birthday, hosted by Patsy at the old Stimson-Green mansion. It was a small festive gathering of her children, a few grandchildren, and friends. She arrived in fine form, properly besuited and bejewelled, her hair coiffed, and her fragile frame engulfed in her long, old, elegant mink coat. Entering the foyer of her childhood home, she was flooded by memories that poured from the crannies she knew so well—the polished paneling that had absorbed her small imprints, the huge fireplace that had been a small playground for her errant pet bears, the stairs her "fat little legs" had climbed, the hiding places, the bedroom that had harbored her treasures, dreams, and secrets. Now, nine decades later, at the long dining room table agleam with the familiar china and silver, she was surrounded by faces of those she loved. Her eyes sparkled when glasses were raised to toast her health and long life. She seemed to relax and relish the occasion. On the way home, she expressed her pleasure at being among those who made her feel so at ease.

Dorothy's health diminished rapidly over the next three months. There was no single cause, only the relentless process of disintegration, accompanied by ongoing pain from compressed bones and a heart working overtime. "There's nothing we can do," her doctor, Bill Watts, told her sadly during one visit. "We can't make you young again." Other systems were also failing, including her digestion and her unswerving sense of balance. She took to staying at home, limited by failing eyesight that prevented her from reading or viewing television. Her still-agile mind longed for stimulation, but her now-faltering machinery could neither seek nor sustain it. She welcomed those few who visited, taking in their company like parched ground under rain, but was exhausted when they left. Many who wanted to did not visit her for fear of intruding or from worry that her mental powers had failed. Her attorney, Douglass Raff, stopped in regularly to discuss finances and was struck, as always, by her strategic thinking. "I found her clear right to the end," he recalled of their business discussions. "When I saw her last, she expressed concern about the amount of money King Broadcasting had invested in cable television and worried about it because, as she said, 'It seems to me that technology will change and soon satellite communications will make us obsolete.' She had that kind of vision right until the end."

During these last months of her life, Dorothy was at her most shining. The exigencies of life, the egoistic worries and ambitions, even the cool remoteness, seemed to fall away from her face, to be replaced by an uncontrived openness and sweetness that lit up her eyes and softened her mouth. What shone from her was a kind of clarity that is kindled by love, and those few who basked in it were deeply touched. It was pitiable too, for there was something sad about seeing someone so powerful now so diminished, but its effect was so transcendent that one could not dwell in pity too long.

If Dorothy reflected about death during these months, she didn't talk about it to anyone else. Nor, even at this advanced age, did she seem to dwell on thoughts of God or an afterlife. The Bullitt brand of spirituality had always been focused on the "doing" of life, not the contemplation of any deity or the hereafter. Her religious beliefs, a legacy from her parents, were based more on society—morality, honor, propriety, tradition, good music, the King James Bible, and support of the Episcopal church as a bulwark of that society—than on any philosophical or theological interests. She didn't talk to God and wasn't moved by adoration of God or any sense that the deity would take care of her. She had never wrestled with dark angels or demons, nor did she have any philosophical interest in the ultimate meaning of life. As her grandson Bill Collins put it, "If Kierkegaard and Nietzsche were arguing with each other in Mamie's sunroom, she wouldn't have taken sides; she'd probably have turned on the television—and then turned up the volume a bit if their voices got too loud." Hers was an earth-based, here-and-now religion, practical and pragmatic, based on service in the world of every day.

Like an animal sensing impending death, she holed up in her house, trying to keep her comfort and stability in a small familiar world. Even there, a walk to the sunroom or a climb upstairs was arduous because of her constant pain. Only the visits of her children, a few other relatives, and friends enlivened the days and made her ignore the fact that death was descending. During the spring months, she reached out to the grandchildren who were either visiting or living nearby. Whether they knew it or not, she was saying good-bye, and she made the extra effort so that she would be remembered at her best. Bill Collins remembered that she called to ask him to dinner one evening. Expecting to dine at her home, he was surprised to find his grandmother dressed with driver waiting to take them to a restaurant overlooking Elliott Bay. "The restaurant was quiet and almost empty, but Mamie was very animated," he recalled of the evening. "During dinner I spent a lot of time telling her about a project I was working on and acted some of it out for her. She laughed and was excited, asking questions, and suddenly I sensed that this was her final presentation—it was Mamie at her best. When I saw her to the door, instead of her usual wave good-bye, she gave me a hug. Standing on the steps as she closed the door, I knew that it was the last time I would see her."

By May, Dorothy's health had worsened. X-rays showed that her osteoporosis had caused such spinal curvature that it was causing her rib cage to cave in, producing stress on her already failing heart and lungs. Every breath brought pain and nausea, and Dorothy began to use the medication that Bill Watts had prescribed. Deeply depressed, she sent out word that she didn't want to see anyone; her body was too tired and her spirits too low to make the effort any longer. Now only Her Three and daughter-in-law Kay came. Monitoring their mother discreetly, they spaced their visits and conferred with each other about her condition. The sisters, in particular, worried that some unexpected occasion, some act of noblesse oblige, might actually take her life. When, on May 25, Dorothy left the house to attend the funeral of Warren Magnuson, they were alarmed.

The death of Warren Magnuson on May 20, 1989, was a last blow of sorts for Dorothy—the end of a long succession of losses. Yet granddaughter Dorothy, who took her to the elaborate funeral service at St. Mark's, was surprised to see that her grandmother was not stricken with grief. Instead it was a strangely happy occasion. In the sunshine on the front steps, both Dorothys signed the attendance register and then took seats reserved for them on the aisle in the back as a parade of senators, congressmen, and other dignitaries filed into the church. "Mamie was very, very frail but she enjoyed the service with all of the eulogies and music immensely," young Dorothy remembered. "When the congregation sang a hymn familiar from her girlhood at Briarcliff School, 'Eternal Father Strong to Save'—a Navy hymn 'for those in peril on the sea'— she leaned over and whispered, 'Oh, this is what I want for my service.' " Young Dorothy saw no sadness on her grandmother's face. "Mamie was experiencing no loss for Magnuson as she had with other friends," she said. "It was clear that she wanted to be with him—as if this time she was more identified with the dead and absolutely ready to be away from the earth." It was the last outing of her life.

By the time Dorothy reached home after the Magnuson funeral, she was near collapse from the pain in her back. Her condition worsened rapidly over the next days. She dreaded awaking each new day to find her speech garbled, her mind scrambled between dreams and reality. For someone so articulate and protective of her dignity as Dorothy Bullitt, this was unbearable. "I just want to go," she told Sallie in utter frustration one night, confiding that she would like to take all of her pain medication at once. "Mrs. Bullitt, with your luck, you'd just get a tummy ache," Sallie replied, trying to lighten her boss's depressed state. "I'm serious," Dorothy pressed on, "I want to *go*. Maybe I could walk across the street and get hit by a car." To this Sallie, by now close to tears, countered with the worst of all threats: "Come on, Mrs. Bullitt, all you'd do is break another leg and then have to go to the hospital." The conversation escalated as Dorothy asked for her housekeeper's help and Sallie asked in return what her boss would do if the situation were reversed and Dorothy replied she didn't know. It ended abruptly when a tearful Sallie said, "Mrs. Bullitt, if you want to go that bad, ask God and He'll take you." "With that," Sallie remembered, "she gave me one of those looks that said, 'You are no longer wanted in this room.' "

Desperate with pain and weakness, Dorothy spoke to her children the next day. "It's time for me to go and I just want out," she insisted, as they stood around her bedside. "My life is *over*," she told them forcefully, reaching for a cane that Harriet had brought her from New Zealand. "I have nothing more to do and I don't want to be a burden." Taking her mother's hand, Harriet said, gently, "Mother, you're not exactly an Eskimo we're going to put out in the snow, you know. We like having you around." "But I want *out*," Dorothy repeated irritably. "Isn't there a pill I can take? What ways are there? I have had enough." Her daughter replied in a gently teasing tone, "Mother, you've controlled everything in your life so far—do you want to control your exit also?"

"Yes," said Dorothy emphatically. When Harriet reminded her that she had had a good strong body throughout her life, the response was a loud, "Yes, and it's *all used up!*" accompanied by an emphatic thumping of the cane on her bed. She would not be dissuaded. That night Harriet called a physician who had already seen Dorothy a few times. He agreed to come the next morning. Dorothy, however, was still not placated; upon hearing the word "tomorrow," she whacked the bed with her cane and said, "I don't want to die tomorrow morning. I want to die *tonight!*"

When physician Peter Wright arrived the following day, he met with an obstinate patient. As he examined her, Dorothy got right to her point. "I want out and I want it right now. I would like to have a shot to end my life," she stated forthrightly, her voice strong with determination. When the doctor said that was impossible, she interrupted his explanation with a series of comments that began imperiously, "Well, we're very good to our animals," then wavered, and ended with a plaintive "couldn't I get a shot like that? I am in such terrible pain." Again he explained that a mercy killing was inconceivable but he did add that he would step up her medication to assure that she would be free from pain. Downstairs he confirmed to the three Bullitt children gathered solemnly in the living room that their mother was near death. "Your mother is suffering from congestive heart failure. She knows that her spine won't straighten out and her heart won't improve," Wright told them, "but her pain will go away under increased medication." He predicted that she would probably live only a few weeks and recommended round-the-clock nursing care. Patsy picked up his prescription for morphine at the pharmacy. There was nothing else the doctor could do.

The Bullitt children sat and planned their mother's funeral. Aware that it could become a media event, they determined to have the kind of service their mother wanted, the simple and dignified prayer book service read for the funerals of her parents and her husband. "We agreed that Mother would not want a showy service with fanfare, in contrast to the media company she had founded," Patsy stated. "We knew she wanted a dignified funeral, without photos or eulogies by public officials. It said something about her respect for tradition." The Bullitt children planned a private burial of their mother's ashes in the plot alongside Scott, C. D., and Harriet Stimson, to be followed by a traditional Episcopal service at St. Mark's Cathedral. They chose a few of their mother's favorite hymns, among them "The Battle Hymn of the Republic," the traditional Navy hymn, "Eternal Father Strong To Save" and, at the conclusion, "Ye Watchers and Ye Holy Men," a joyful hymn that ends with a resounding chorus of alleluias.

Dorothy spoke with each of her children privately that day, bidding them official and intimate farewell. Typically, she tailored her conversation with each one, saying the enduring words of affection and hearing their reassurance. She was particularly concerned about Patsy, hoping to put an end to any unresolved conflicts that she feared might still be in the air. "There's a refrigerator between us somewhere," she confided in her inimitable quirky way, "and now and again it thaws. I love her very much and want her to do well at whatever she does. She has tried to get out of my shadow and I haven't intended to cast one." Propped up in her bed she reflected, in a voice touched with clear humility, "I have such deep feelings of hope that I will be forgiven." When Patsy arrived at her bedside, Dorothy looked lovingly at her middle child, her Peach—the one who had arrived frail so many years ago and the only one whose independence she had never been able to accept. "I'm so close to the edge that I'm going," she said to her daughter. "I love you so much and hope you'll forgive me. Whatever I did, it was not that I didn't love you." "Oh, I know, Mother, I know," the daughter replied reassuringly. "It's all right. Of course, we have to forgive—we love each other." The Bullitt children had forgiven their mother long ago.

Dorothy had always told Her Three that it was important for them to stick together. It was a refrain they had heard repeatedly over the years, and she set it forth in a letter probably written some time before her death but found soon after her passing. It was also an eloquent farewell because it went to the heart of what she wanted to say and what she knew they needed to know:

My dearest Three in all the World,

So many things are crowding to be said, but I would never know how to say them—most of them have been said over and over. You will sometime know through your own children, something of how much I have loved you. But you may never realize that since the day you were born you have brought me the greatest happiness I have ever had. You are each different in temperament from the other and I am bursting with pride for all three.

I have felt your love come back to me—never doubt that—and I have been conscious of this through all your moods, and at times when you yourselves weren't aware of it. I have the firmest faith in each of you and in your desire to give expression to the best that is in you, and in your capacity and strength to carry it through. I have never questioned your ability to face and meet whatever life holds for you.

I hope and pray that you will stand by each other whatever comes, and keep close in your understanding of one another. Diversity of interest may lead to gaps in contact which could grow unnoticeably, and as each of you becomes more deeply involved with family and cares, it will need constant watching to keep an understanding heart and an intimate knowledge of the other one's feelings and problems.

Be sure that my last thoughts reached out to you in perfect confidence and thanksgiving—

God bless you my Darlings,

Mother

Dorothy Bullitt, as might be expected, did not go gently. After a few days, her body, under the controlled dosage of morphine, relaxed into unlabored breathing and her mind drifted off into uncharted realms. All of her inhibitions also floated away, and both extremes of her character asserted themselves, alternating between thunderous impositions of will and shining moments of pure love. Although refusing all food, she clung to life with an energy that no one had seen for many months. For two weeks, she took those who attended her—her children, Kay, and her nurses—on a trip they would never forget. Lovingly, they went along with every fantastic scenario she created. To their alternating delight and consternation, they found themselves outward bound, voyaging to destinations unknown with a captain of no small degree. Without compass, they accompanied her as she commanded, commended, and scolded the crew, threw some overboard, changed courses, and pointed to horizons they could not see. It was not so much a sail on dreamlike seas as a roller-coaster ride through the twists and turns of her subconscious. As always the trip was rich and varied as only Dorothy Bullitt might have made it.

The family fell right in with whatever script Dorothy offered. For a few days, she worried about reality-oriented loose ends—things she still needed to do. She fretted about disposing of her last personal goods, asking for her jewelry (some of it found in small boxes marked "paper clips" or "staples") and calling Patsy, Harriet, and Kay to her side. As she sorted various brooches, rings, and necklaces, moving them about aimlessly and unable to concentrate on her objective, Harriet said loudly, "Mother, I don't care about your jewelry. You don't have to worry about these things." One evening as the nurse followed her around, Dorothy literally put her house in order, wandering from chest to closet, folding and arranging the contents. The nurse present on this foray was amused to find a small pearl-handled revolver among the papers and pills in the bedside table and a shotgun belonging to her father standing in the closet among a row of lace dressing gowns. It was a circus of surprises and no one knew where the ringleader would appear next.

To prevent her falling, the family blocked the stairway with a couch and chairs. Here Dorothy held "meetings" (always one of her favorite activities) at any hour, day or night. The topics to be discussed made no sense, but no one was requiring sense at this stage. At one small assembly attended by Patsy and a nurse, Dorothy insisted that everyone hold hands and then she leaned into the circle, whispering with a gleeful smile, "Isn't this a power trip?!" She sent for the items that had consumed so much of her time at the office—checks and paper, her favorite pens and pencils to write imaginary directives. Without batting an eye, Jinny arrived from the office with a full supply and spent the afternoon taking dictation and paying nonexistent bills while Dorothy adjusted figures and signed checks, one of them, for some unknown reason, to Gene Autry, who had once refused to sell her one of his stations. "Take a message, take a message," she shouted to Harriet at one of her "meetings." With great display, Harriet procured pad and pencil, replying, "I'm ready, Mother, ready for the message." "Here's the message," Dorothy replied and she opened her arms to embrace her daughter. "Kiss me," she said, her face beaming with love, and Harriet, folding her mother in her arms, fondly did as she was told.

As Dorothy's mind wandered through worlds of her own knowing, the roller-coaster ride took some bizarre dips and turns of truth. She whistled and waved to invisible friends, braided strands of air, and washed imaginary pepper off the walls. Hallucinating, she watched television on her bedroom wall and chuckled that some of the comedies were themselves "off the wall." One day, as Patsy "watched" with her, Dorothy suddenly sat bolt upright and gripped the arms of her chair. "*Peach!*" she shouted in apparent horror, pointing at the imaginary screen, "*What* are they doing? We *must* stop this bad taste right away!" Patsy, unable to figure out exactly what kind of lurid conduct was in process, pretended not to have caught onto whatever it was, but her mother continued, pointing indignantly. "Look at what they're doing! I am *appalled!*" she said in great agitation, "Peach, we must stop this—call the station right now," she banged a fist on her armrest, "*Heads are going to roll!*" Without missing a beat, her daughter got up from her chair and crossed to scrutinize the mythical television set and its dials. "No, Mother," she said, firmly resolving the problem. "See, we've been watching Channel 7, not Channel 5. It's KIRO, not KING." "Whew!" her mother whistled with relief, leaning back in her chair again. "I don't like this bad taste in television—I'm serious."

On another occasion, as she was resting quietly and Harriet was reading at her bedside late at night, Dorothy suddenly sat bolt upright. "We have tickets to the opera. Hurry! I must get dressed!" Looking up from her book, Harriet said calmly, "You are already dressed, Mother, and we're already seated for the performance." Whereupon she got up and put on a tape of Caruso singing

"Celeste Aida" (knowing her mother's love for his voice). Dorothy settled back into her pillows, smiling.

On another afternoon, as the family was seated in the sunroom downstairs, they were surprised to hear Dorothy's unmistakable voice at the front door. "Thank you very much," she was saying to the nurse who had just guided her downstairs. "We won't be needing you any longer." "But, but . . ." protested the nurse. "Yes, yes, thank you. You may go now," said Dorothy, slamming the door in her face. The nurses learned not to protest this treatment and simply went around to the back door to let themselves inside again. One evening, after one of these "revolving door" incidents, Dorothy made her way into the sunroom and declared that she wanted a cocktail—one of those stingers that Andy Haley had introduced her to a long time ago. Trusting no one to mix the ingredients, she instructed Patsy to collect various bottles from the kitchen, but in the kitchen the nurse, who had just entered via the back door after her most recent firing, objected strongly when she heard that her patient was going to have a drink. "But she can't have alcohol," the young woman declared firmly. "She hasn't eaten in ten days and she's on pain medication—you can't do that." "Watch me," said Patsy. Back in the sunroom Dorothy mixed a potent cocktail. As she poured hefty doses of crème de menthe and cognac into a glass, her hand shook so badly that Patsy reached out to steady her. Once the proportions had achieved the kind of "authority" she might have required in earlier days, Dorothy raised her glass in a toast, took one swallow and said, "Aahhhh . . ." One walloping taste was all she needed; she handed the rest to Patsy and said, "Here, you drink it." Perhaps it was the drink, but suddenly she appeared extremely tired and pale. Noticing this, someone in the room leaned forward to ask if she wanted to go upstairs, but Dorothy dismissed the inquiry grandly with, "No, but you may go if you want to."

The family had to be alert for a couple of more days as Dorothy appeared downstairs unexpectedly. One afternoon she moved chairs around in the dining room with a purposefulness no one could understand—until it became clear that she was arranging them for a funeral that was soon to take place. Finally, after instructing her daughters that the chairs should be properly arranged, she gave up on the project with an imperial wave of the hand. "If there aren't enough chairs," she said as she headed for the stairs, "some people will just have to stand."

After two weeks without food, Dorothy became too weak to wander. Gaunt in appearance, her features were as sharpened as the very granite of her New England ancestry. She began to speak in metaphors that held hints of impending death. "I'll never live this one down," she stated, or "I won't get out of this one alive." Sometimes she rose from her bed with a worried expression. "It's time . . . time to go—get my keys," she'd shout. "Time to go home." In those last days, her little dog Lily became as confused as her mistress. Snuggled tightly against Dorothy's side, the dog's forlorn face reflected the sadness of this long good-bye. She was at her side one evening when Dorothy began a long dialogue with Patsy and Harriet in which she told them she was preparing to cross a gigantic gorge filled with dark waters. There were people on the other side, although she couldn't make out who they were, and she wasn't at all sure she could make this crossing because she was so afraid. When her daughters tried to comfort her, Dorothy said, "Everyone is a coward to begin with—even the dog is a coward." She didn't know whether she could do it, she said again and again. "Mother," said Harriet, "I love you so much. Won't you let my love for you carry you over the gorge?" Dorothy's face shone as she said, "It will." "You'll be on your own," she told her daughters and they countered that she too would be on her own. "I'm on my own, I'm on my own," she chanted several times and then added, "but with you two behind me I can do anything."

Soon Dorothy no longer moved from the bed. On one of the last occasions when she did, Patsy helped her into bed and the two played a game they had been enacting off and on. As Patsy reached out to take her mother's bathrobe, Dorothy said, "Don't take off my bathrobe." Knowing her mother very well, the daughter corrected herself. "Mother, would it be all right if you *told* me to take off your bathrobe?" "Yes," Dorothy said, "take off my bathrobe." They played the same game with her slippers until one day, in response to Patsy's request to remove them, her mother replied, "No. Boots on."

On the afternoon of June 29, 1989, Dorothy was wasted away. Her eyes were closed and her body—that vehicle that she had run, ridden, and ruled for so many years—was pale and emaciated. She had extracted full value from it, as with everything else in her life, and it had served her uncommonly well. Now, unable to speak, she held Patsy's hand and tried in vain to move her mouth. "I know you love me, Mother," Patsy said, trying to translate the message, and Dorothy pursed her lips in a farewell kiss. Toward the end of the day, Stim arrived and sat with her a while, as he had every day throughout her last illness. It was plain that she had waited for her son and to hear his voice. Soon after he joined the others downstairs, the life—that extraordinary combination of wisdom, grace, and personal power that was peculiarly Dorothy Bullitt—finally flowed from her. To Her Three sitting silently below, affection descended, pouring from them to theirs and out into the region for which she had such love.

On her deathbed, Dorothy Bullitt lay like an old abandoned clipper ship—one of those swift and gallant craft that had once run with the wind and coasted full-blown around the capes of the world. As her children gathered around her hand-in-hand, they beheld their mother in final rest, the wind gone from her sails. At last, weathered by storms and with riggings worn, she had reached her journey's end. It had been a long voyage, to be sure, harking back to those early images her father had painted nine decades before of Captain Vancouver's magic vessels as they entered her beloved Puget Sound. Along the way, the good ship Dorothy had leaned joyfully into fair winds, danced on sunlit waters, ploughed high and storm-tossed waves, and sometimes waited in frustration as her sails luffed in windless seas. Supported by a large and dedicated crew, she had enriched her cargo, maneuvered the straits, avoided reefs and shoals, tacked, trimmed, and reefed her sails. She had steered by her stars and moved with life's tides, and, through it all, her inner compass had held steady to its charted course. For Dorothy Stimson Bullitt, it had truly been a grand Voyage of Discovery.

INDEX